ANDREW ROSSOS is a member of the Department of History at the University of Toronto.

Russia had traditionally been attracted to the Balkan region for strategic, ideological, and economic reasons. This volume presents an objective diplomatic history focused on five crucial years in the relations between Russia and the Balkan states from the Annexation Crisis of 1908–9 to the outbreak of the First World War.

Internal instability, political and military weakness, and the strong opposition of the other great powers, particularly after the Crimean War, forced Russia to co-ordinate her policy with the wishes of the Concert of Europe. She was compelled to collaborate with Austria-Hungary, her chief antagonist in the Balkans, in preserving the status quo, while she awaited a more opportune moment for an independent policy.

Professor Rossos centres his study on the attempts of the Balkan states to combine and administer the *coup de grâce* to Turkey and block Austro-Hungarian encroachments to the south. The jockeying for position of the great powers of the Triple Alliance and the Triple Entente, which formed the nucleus of the alliances of the First World War, is an underlying theme.

Vacillating Russian policy was torn over irreconcilable issues that divided the Balkan states. The Balkan nations created a system of alliances aimed at ending Ottoman rule in the region. However, their conflicting claims for domination of Macedonia undermined their short-lived unity and destroyed the Balkan system of alliances which Russia expected to serve as an instrument of her supremacy in southeast Europe.

The author's familiarity with Slavic languages, Greek, and Western languages enables him to provide complete accounts of the activities of the period, including much new detail. The resulting work brings fresh insights into Balkan rivalries and Russian involvement in the peninsula.

ANDREW ROSSOS

Russia and the Balkans: Inter-Balkan rivalries and Russian foreign policy 1908–1914

UNIVERSITY OF TORONTO PRESS

Toronto Buffalo London

© University of Toronto Press 1981
Toronto Buffalo London
Printed in Canada

ISBN 0-8020-5516-8

Canadian Cataloguing in Publication Data

Rossos, Andrew, 1941–
Russia and the Balkans

Bibliography: p.
Includes index.
ISBN 0-8020-5516-8

1. Russia – Foreign relations – Balkan Peninsula.
2. Balkan Peninsula – Foreign relations – Russia.
3. Eastern question (Balkan) 4. Balkan Peninsula –
Politics and government. I. Title.

DR38.3.R8R68   327.470496   c80-094856-4

For Cecilia

and

Monica and Veronica

Contents

List of maps

Preface

This study attempts to present a history of Russian diplomacy in the Balkan Peninsula and to review the impact of relations among the Balkan states upon Russian diplomacy during the critical years between the Annexation Crisis of 1908–09 and the end of the Inter-Allied War of 1913. In order to achieve major foreign policy aims, Russia needed the Balkan governments as much as they required the support of St Petersburg and of each other. Collaboration among them proved short-lived, for a variety of reasons, most significantly the tendency of the governing élites in Russia and the Balkan states to place primacy on short-range goals over long-range national aims. The present work is, in this respect, a study of the failure of the diplomacy of mutual dependence.

The central issue dividing the Balkan nations was the thorny Macedonian Question, which defied resolution. It could have been settled in the same manner as the Greek, Serbian, Rumanian, Bulgarian, and Albanian problems: by granting Macedonia autonomy and eventually independence. Such a settlement, which would have served the interests of the Macedonian people,* would, however, have negated the expansionist ambitions of the neighbouring Balkan states, and was therefore not acceptable to them. Russia was interested in the Macedonian problem only in so far as it affected her relations with the established Balkan states and thus her power position in the peninsula. The Macedonian Question was to dominate Balkan politics and consume the energies of the Balkan nations until the Second World War – and even to the present day.

The Macedonian Question aroused strong national passions and antagonisms in the peninsula which have been reflected in the writings of both publicists and

* My book does not deal with the Macedonian national and revolutionary movements, or attempt an examination of their aims. I am, however, preparing another work, to be devoted to the rise and development of Macedonian nationalism, which will analyse the internal aspects of the Macedonian Question.

historians especially in Bulgaria, Greece, and Serbia (Yugoslavia). With few exceptions, even post-Second World War Marxist scholars have not been able to shake off these national influences.

In the West, the study of Balkan history has been largely neglected. Those scholars who have worked on the period 1909 to 1914 have considered problems connected with the Eastern Question from the perspective of European diplomatic history rather than treating them in the context of the Russian and Balkan situation, as the present study tries to do. This is true, for instance, of E.C. Helmreich's *The Diplomacy of the Balkan Wars 1912–1913* (Cambridge, Mass. 1938) which remains the standard work on the topic. The only other study in the English language, E.C. Thaden's *Russia and the Balkan Alliances of 1912* (University Park, Penn. 1965) is a short collection of articles concerned, as the title suggests, with a limited topic, to which my study devotes less than a chapter.

Whenever possible my study analyses the various factors which influenced the foreign policies of Russia and the Balkan states. However, one must be careful not to exaggerate the importance of certain factors. In all these states the majority of people were politically unaware or uninvolved and, in any case, governments possessed effective means to influence the public and indeed even to isolate or silence opposition. Furthermore, the sphere of foreign policy was in the main the prerogative of one individual, tsar or king, who was free to seek advice wherever he wished. As a result, it is often difficult to determine, on the basis of available evidence, how policies were decided and what influences played a part in the actual decision-making process.

This study was begun as a doctoral dissertation for the Department of History at Stanford University. The research was undertaken in the Hoover Institution on War, Revolution and Peace at Stanford, California; the New York Public Library; the Haus-, Hof-, und Staatsarchiv, and the National Bibliothek, Vienna; Universitní Knihovna, and Slovanská Knihovna, Prague; Narodna Biblioteka, and Univerzitetska Biblioteka 'Svetozar Marković,' Belgrade; Gosudarstvennaia Biblioteka SSSR imeni V.I. Lenina, and Fundmental'naia Biblioteka Obshchestvennykh Nauk, Akademii Nauk SSSR, Moscow; Narodna Biblioteka, Sofia; and Ethniki Vivliotheki, Athens. I am grateful to the staff of these institutions for their generous assistance.

I would like to thank the Foreign Area Fellowship Program of the American Council of Learned Societies and the Social Science Research Council for a fellowship which enabled me to carry out the original research for the doctoral dissertation; and the Canada Council and the Centre for Russian and East European Studies at the University of Toronto and its former director, Professor H. Gordon Skilling,for research grants which made possible return visits to Eastern Europe.

This book has been published with the help of a grant from the Social Science Federation of Canada, using funds provided by the Social Sciences and Humanities Research Council of Canada, and a grant from the Andrew W. Mellon Foundation to University of Toronto Press. I would like to thank these organizations for their generosity.

I wish to express my appreciation to M. Jean Houston, Executive Editor of University of Toronto Press, and John Parry, my editor, for their valuable assistance. Finally, I would like to record in particular my gratitude to Professor W.S. Vucinich, my principal adviser at Stanford University, for his aid and encouragement; to Professor I.J. Lederer, formerly of Stanford University; and to Professor Peter Brock of the University of Toronto, who read and commented on the manuscript, for his generous advice and sincere interest in my work.

RUSSIA AND THE BALKANS

Introduction

I

Until the Congress of Berlin in 1878 the focal point of Russia's foreign relations was the Ottoman Empire. The Eastern Question, which revolved around the domination of Constantinople and the Straits, was of paramount importance to her and, since the time of Peter the Great, had occupied a permanent place on Russia's diplomatic agenda.[1] Russian rulers and statesmen strove single-mindedly to resolve it in a manner most propitious to their national interests, but to no avail. The wars waged against the Porte and the diplomatic combinations effected since the reign of Catherine the Great did not bring Russia the sought-for-results. Russia did not gain anything more than what she had won in 1774 by the Peace of Kuchuk Kainarji. The wars of 1774, 1829, and 1878 brought Russia closer and closer to the desired goal, but each time something happened to compromise her plan when success appeared within her grasp.[2]

At the outset the Turks were sufficiently powerful to meet the challenge. The Russians nevertheless believed that with the continuing decline of Turkey and strengthening of Russia, the 'Sick Man of Europe' would eventually succumb. But whenever Turkey came close to collapsing the 'European Concert' appeared on the scene as its protector to forestall the execution of Russia's designs. The Russo-Turkish War of 1877–78 represented Russia's last attempt to impose on the Sultan a unilateral settlement.

At the Congress of Berlin, Russia was effectively isolated and opposed by the rest of Europe. The Berlin settlement also alienated Russia's traditional protégés, the small Balkan nations, whose hopes and expectations were sacrificed on the altar of great power diplomacy. With the exception of Bulgaria, on whose behalf Russia claimed to have fought the war and concluded the short-lived Treaty of San Stefano, they blamed Russia for their misfortunes and decided to part company with her and go their own ways.[3] Serbia concluded a secret alliance with Austria-Hungary on 28 June 1881,[4] followed by Rumania on 30 October 1883.[5] The Dual Monarchy also enjoyed the confidence of the Greek monarchy and close relations with Montenegro. Finally, during the crisis of 1885–86, even Bulgaria split with Russia and joined the ranks of her neighbours.[6]

After 1878 the Russian government's outlook and policy went through a marked transformation. Official circles in St Petersburg at last acknowledged that Russia could not alone decide the settlement of the Eastern Question. Her opponent had not been and was not to be merely the declining empire of the sultans, but the whole of Europe. For, whenever the Near East came into question, Russia had no friends in the West. There were only enemies, who followed suspiciously, and were ready to resist, every Russian gesture toward the Balkans or Constantinople. It became clear in St Petersburg that Russia's diplomatic course in regard to the Eastern Question would, of necessity, have to be modified.[7]

From then until the Annexation Crisis of 1908 Russia sought to impose her aims and policy upon the Balkan states in harmony with the Concert of Europe and particularly in agreement with Austria-Hungary, her chief antagonist in the Near East. The *Dreikaiserbund* (Three Emperor's League), which was resurrected on 18 June 1881, bound these two powers to the territorial status quo established by the Treaty of Berlin, unless and until they decided to modify it by mutual consent and agreement.[8]

The Bulgarian crisis of 1885–86 disrupted the *Dreikaiserbund*. But neither its collapse, nor Germany's refusal to renew the Reinsurance Treaty with Russia in 1890, and the subsequent Franco-Russian Alliance of 1894, prompted any changes in the Near Eastern policies of Russia or Austria-Hungary. Indeed, the Goluchowski-Muraviev Agreement of 8 May 1897 reaffirmed the purpose of the *Dreikaiserbund*. It provided for the maintenance of the status quo in the Balkans for as long as possible. In the event that it could no longer be upheld the two signatories would co-operate to prevent another power from acquiring territory in the peninsula.[9] In this way they joined forces 'to keep the Balkans on ice,' or, as Count M. Muraviev's successor, Prince A. Lobanov-Rostovskii, put it: 'It was necessary for us to put the Balkans under a bell-glass while we concerned ourselves with more pressing affairs.'[10]

Vienna was preoccupied with the national and constitutional problems of its own empire. At the same time, the Russian government had turned its attention eastward, to Central Asia and particularly the Far East, where it expected to encounter less resistance to its unilateral diplomacy. As long as this state of affairs prevailed Austria and Russia did not wish to be drawn into the Balkan quarrels over Macedonia or the recurring crisis between Greece and Turkey over the island of Crete.

As a result of the involvement in the Far East, Russia remained passive and faithful to the entente with Austria-Hungary even when her diplomatic fortunes in the Balkans improved considerably. In 1894, Prince Ferdinand of Bulgaria dismissed S. Stambolov, his pro-Austrian strongman; in 1896 Russia effected a complete reconciliation with Bulgaria, and by May 1902 they had concluded a Military Convention directed against both Austria-Hungary and Rumania.[11] More important still, in June 1903, a bloody revolt in Serbia overthrew the pro-Austrian Obrenović dynasty and replaced it with the Russophile Karađorđević dynasty.[12]

Only after the disastrous fiasco of 1904–05 in the Far East did Russia again direct her full attention to the Near East. Count V.N. Lamsdorf, head of Pevchevskii Most[13] during the Far Eastern entanglement, died in 1906 and was succeeded by A.P. Izvol'skii. Capable, intelligent, and extremely ambitious, the new foreign minister endeavoured to boost his country's as well as his own personal reputation by some dazzling diplomatic success. Since Russia, exhausted as a result of the recent defeat, was not militarily, politically, or economically prepared for risky foreign policy adventures, he hoped to achieve success in co-operation with Austria-Hungary. With this in mind he inaugurated in 1907 highly secret talks which culminated in his meeting with the Austrian foreign minister, Count Alois von Aehrenthal, at the Castle of Buchlau in Moravia on 15–16 September of the following year. There, behind the backs of Serbia and Montenegro, Izvol'skii bargained the South-Slav province of Bosnia-Herzegovina in exchange for a vague promise that Vienna would not oppose the opening of the Straits to Russian war-ships.

On 6 October 1908, Aehrenthal announced the annexation of Bosnia-Herzegovina, and provoked a crisis which threatened a European war. Both Turkey and Serbia protested vehemently. Izvol'skii demanded the promised concessions, but since neither Europe nor Turkey wished to sanction a change in the status of the Straits, he was left empty-handed. To save his own and Russia's prestige he assumed the leadership of the movement of protest against Austria-Hungary. He proposed a European conference to deal with the annexation, and pushed Serbia's claim to a portion of the annexed territory as compensation. The government in Vienna rejected these demands and brushed aside all other threats. In the end, confronted with a blunt and threatening démarche from Berlin, St Petersburg capitulated and approved the annexation in March 1909. Left alone, Russia's protégé Serbia had no alternative but to follow suit and accept the inevitable.[14]

The crux of the matter was this: while Austria-Hungary enjoyed throughout the crisis the unconditional backing of Germany, Russia found herself isolated again as in the past. Her diplomatic position seemed to have improved with the conclusion of the alliance with France and the entente with Great Britain. But as the Annexation Crisis showed this improvement was more apparent than real. Neither France nor Great Britain wished to risk a war in Russia's traditional sphere of interest.[15]

II

The Annexation Crisis resulted in the total humiliation of Russia. It amounted to a diplomatic equivalent of the naval disaster of 1905 in the Straits of Tsushima.[16] Russia's prestige as a great power suffered a grave set-back, and her reputation in the Balkan peninsula reached its lowest ebb since the Congress of Berlin.[17] The collaboration with Austria-Hungary – the basis of her Near Eastern policy for the preceding thirty years – misfired. Russia did not profit in any way; Austria-Hungary scored impressive political, economic, and territorial gains largely at Russia's expense. These gains assured Vienna, at least for a time, of a dominant position in the life of the peninsula. Further spread of the influence of Austria-Hungary to the south would have endangered Russia's traditional historic aims in the area.[18] To check this the Russian government had nowhere to turn except to the Balkan powers.

Count Aehrenthal's policy and victory challenged the national aspirations and interests of the Balkan states as well. The Serbs claimed the annexed province as rightfully belonging to them because it was largely populated by their co-nationals. Moreover, the advance of Austria-Hungary into the peninsula threatened the independent existence of Serbia and Montenegro and, to a lesser degree, of Bulgaria and Greece. Vienna's ambitious designs for Albania and widespread commercial interests in Macedonia clashed with the territorial pretensions of all the Balkan states with the possible exception of her ally Rumania.

The Annexation Crisis and the intensified conflicts of interest between the Austrian and Balkan governments had far-reaching repercussions for the future. The Balkan leaders viewed the 'Buchlau bargain' as an attempt at a partial, if not final, solution to the Eastern Question. For them it was also a timely reminder and a clear warning that their time was running out. Either they closed ranks and agreed to tackle the problem of Turkey in Europe to their own benefit; or the two great powers, Austria-Hungary or Russia or both, would settle the problem in a manner adversely affecting their interests.

During the course of the crisis Belgrade, Sofia, and Cetinje raised seriously the question of a coalition in the future. This was not an altogether new idea – the movement for Balkan unity had a long history.[19] The problems that had earlier divided them still remained unresolved, but the outcome of the crisis altered the situation and introduced an additional strong impetus for unity.

As long as Russia and Austria-Hungary collaborated in keeping the 'Balkans on ice' even a united block of Balkan states would not have been permitted to challenge the status quo. Had the 'Buchlau bargain' been executed in its entirety, to the complete mutual satisfaction of both St Petersburg and Vienna, the 'Balkans on ice' policy would undoubtedly have survived. The fact that it resulted in the overwhelming triumph of one and the total humiliation of the other destroyed the Russian–Austro-Hungarian entente. It plunged the two powers into a mortal duel for influence in the peninsula.[20] Strange as it might appear, this created for the first time suitable conditions for an independent policy on the part of the Balkan states.

From the very outset, however, the Balkan statesmen were well aware of their own limitations and grasped the helping hand of Russia. In order to realize their national aspirations they depended on the protection of Russia as much as Russia needed their support against Austria-Hungary. In the event of a victorious war against Turkey, they counted upon Russia, together with France and Great Britain, to neutralize the certain opposition of Austria-Hungary and possibly Germany. In the event of a defeat they expected Russia to bail them out without territorial losses and to help restore the status quo ante bellum.

The tactics and triumph of Austria-Hungary in the Annexation Crisis had therefore initiated a chain of developments. Russia was forced to seek the assistance of the powers of the Near East to check the further spread of Austrian influence to the south. The collapse of the Russian–Austro-Hungarian entente emboldened the Balkan states to contemplate taking the Eastern Question into their own hands. Finally, the threat from Austria-Hungary and the prospects of dazzling gains from a war against Turkey were strong inducements for Balkan unity. Even Aehrenthal's successor, Count Leopold Berchtold, acknowledged in 1912 that Austria's procedure in 'annexing Bosnia and Herzegovina gave the first impetus to the Balkan League.'[21]

The Annexation Crisis, however, had only established a basis for collaboration. In 1909 it was still too early to tell whether co-operation would grow and develop; and if so, in what form and in what direction. The plans and aims of Russia on the one hand and the Balkan states on the other were far from identical. The Balkan nations, particularly the Serbs and Bulgarians, remained very much divided. It was still unclear whether they would surmount their differences and agree on the final aims or on the methods by which they were to be achieved. It took three years of difficult negotiations before the Balkan system of alliances finally emerged in 1912.

1

Toward a Balkan system
of alliances

I

The humiliating capitulation of the St Petersburg government during the Annexation Crisis provoked in Russia an almost unprecedented public debate. Russia's
foreign policy orientation in general, and its policy toward the Balkans and the
Near East in particular, were exposed to an unavoidable critical reexamination.[1]

Official and unofficial circles of all political shades attacked the nation's
diplomacy. They agreed that it had met an unmitigated defeat and threw the major
blame for it on the contradictory alliances, alignments, and agreements concluded
by Pevchevskii Most since the collapse of the Reinsurance Treaty with Germany.
They could point to the fact that in a Europe divided into two power blocs – the
Triple Alliance and the Triple Entente – Russia enjoyed the full confidence of
neither. To be sure Russia belonged to the Triple Entente. She had been allied to
France since 1894 and aligned with Great Britain since 1907, but in the actual
running of her foreign policy Russia vacillated between her allies and the members
of the opposing power grouping. Indeed, the most significant component of
Russia's diplomacy, her Balkan and Near Eastern policy, was dictated by the terms
of the close entente with her chief antagonist, Austria-Hungary. This vacillation
damaged Russia's credibility as a trusted ally and brought upon her the suspicion of
both her partners in the Entente and her 'enemies' in the Triple Alliance. Consequently, in the Annexation Crisis the Russian government, deserted and isolated,
was forced to capitulate.[2]

The critics, who embraced almost all those in and outside the government
concerned with Russia's foreign relations, condemned the conduct and course of
the nation's foreign policy which produced this humiliation. St Petersburg's dual
policy of depending on the support of its formal allies and at the same time
co-operating with the opponents in the Triple Alliance had failed. As far as they
were concerned Russia could no longer manage to have one foot in each camp. The
two power blocs were assuming unyielding attitudes and a policy of continued

straddling between the two could have led only to repeated set-backs. To improve its badly shaken position and maintain a semblance of influence as a great power in the future it became unavoidable for Russia to associate fully with either the Triple Entente or the Triple Alliance. Russia had to choose between England and Germany. It could no longer afford to flirt with both.[3]

At these alternatives the unity, indeed, unanimity which characterized the debate on Russia's diplomatic set-backs broke down. The old divisions surrounding the orientation of the country's foreign policy, which had started with the conclusion of the alliance with France or even further back with the aftermath of the Congress of Berlin, were reactivated. 'In the higher ruling circles,' commented the liberal *Russkaia Mysl'*, 'the gradual emergence of two parties – the English and the German – is becoming more and more apparent. What are their aims: an alliance with England or an alliance with Germany with the perspective of a Three Emperors League in the future?'[4]

The large landowners grouped around the Council of the United Nobility represented the extreme right in the Russian political spectrum. Traditionally they were anti-British, and consideredd Germany Russia's only legitimate and trusted ally. They did not see any harm to Russia's national interests in the annexation of Bosnia-Herzegovina by Austria-Hungary. Indeed, they believed that Russia should adhere to a policy of complete non-interference in Balkan affairs and in this manner avoid possible conflicts with Germany. There was no reason for feuding between the two northern empires.[5] The recent differences and controversies were wholly unnecessary. They were consciously inspired by London and served British interests only. During a foreign policy discussion in the Duma, V.M. Purishkevich, one of the leading spokesmen for the extreme right, warned that Great Britain was striving to push Russia into a war with Germany. England and Germany, he argued, were engaged in a struggle for world markets and were heading toward a violent confrontation; however, since the British were not eager to get entangled in a conflict with Germany, they strove to trick their recently won 'friend,' Russia, into undertaking the fighting for them.[6] At the end of March 1909, Purishkevich assured a German news correspondent that he and his party would 'devote all their efforts to bring about a break with England and strengthen the sacred Russo-German friendship.'[7]

To the pro-British and pro-French liberals, led by the Constitutional Democratic (Cadet) Party, Russia's collapse during the Annexation Crisis provided a proof, indeed, a justification for the closest possible ties with London and Paris.[8] They saw only two alternatives open for Russia's foreign policy. Russia could either depend on Britain and France and in turn expect support from them, or face the loss of influence in the Near East and unavoidably her decline as a great power of any consequence.[9] In the wake of the crisis they intensified their campaign for the solidification of Russia's position in the Triple Entente. V.A. Maklakov voiced the views of all the liberals when he told a group of French journalists visiting St Petersburg that he only wished 'to see the Triple Entente transformed into a Triple Alliance.'[10]

The Octobrists and the moderate right assembled around the government of P.A. Stolypin were strongly nationalistic and Slavophile, but at the same time showed great admiration for the Germans. 'The German Empire,' wrote A.V. Nekliudov, 'attracted him [Stolypin] by the order which reigned there, by the national patriotism which seemed to animate all classes of population, all political parties.'[11] Even in these circles, however, anti-German feelings rose sharply as a result of the Annexation Crisis. Russia's defeat and the weakening of her position in international relations offended their nationalist pride. They now joined the liberals in the agitation for a change in Russia's foreign policy orientation in favour of a solidified and strengthened anti-German coalition of Russia, France, and Great Britain.[12]

Similar divisions appeared in the debate concerning Russia's future Near Eastern policy. The pro-German right opposed an active policy in this area and continued to view favourably the policy aiming at keeping the Balkans 'under the bell-glass.' It advocated the maintenance of the entente with the Dual Monarchy on condition that Germany would not permit Austria-Hungary, its principal ally, to disrupt it again in the future.[13]

The moderate right elements opposed resolutely any agreement with Germany and expounded a policy of active resistance to Austro-Hungarian expansion or to the further spread of her influence in the Balkans and the Near East. They were deeply concerned with the future of the Straits and the various other issues that promised to arise when the long delayed and awaited collapse of the Ottoman Empire took place.[14] Russia had to prepare for this eventuality. The new course of Russia's Balkan policy was to be based on the support and assistance of Great Britain and France and, more significantly, on the co-operation of the states of the Near East. It required the betterment of Russia's relations with Turkey, Rumania, and Greece, and the improvement of relations between the states of the Balkans. In this manner the moderate right sought to bring into being an atmosphere conducive to the formation of a pro-Russian Balkan confederation aimed against Austria-Hungary. The advocates of this course presupposed that the only rational policy the Ottoman Empire could pursue would be to seek to develop and improve its relations with the Russian Empire and at the same time strive for close and friendly ties with the neighbouring Balkan nations.[15] In the government, besides P.A. Stolypin, this course was also supported by S.D. Sazonov and N.V. Charykov.[16]

The liberals considered the envisaged Balkan confederation as entirely illusory. They were firmly convinced that it would prove impossible to reconcile the interests of Turkey and her neighbours. Instead, they suggested an alliance of the Balkan Slavic states, Bulgaria, Serbia, and Montenegro, as far more realistic and in the last resort more reliable and effective.[17] After the Annexation Crisis, A.P. Izvol'skii became perhaps the chief protagonist of this policy within the Russian government.[18]

In the months immediately following the Annexation Crisis the struggle between these combinations revolved around the expected shake up within the Foreign Ministry and the diplomatic corps. The most important and most sought-after posts were the leadership of the Ministry of Foreign Affairs and the embassy in Constantinople.[19] The new appointments were reliable indicators of Russia's future foreign policy orientation in the Balkans and the Near East.

The crisis and Russia's defeat undermined Izvol'skii's position. Ambitous and arrogant, Izvol'skii tended to be overly independent. In diplomatic negotiations, particularly in his talks with Count Alois von Aehrenthal which preceded the crisis, he relied solely on the support of the tsar. He disregarded his colleagues in the cabinet, including P.A. Stolypin, chairman of the Council of Ministers. When the crisis erupted he had no defenders in the government, and after Russia's forced capitulation his position became untenable.[20] As early as 4 April 1909, N.V. Charykov, deputy foreign minister, was able to inform Count Berchtold confidentially that Izvol'skii would definitely be replaced as soon as a suitable diplomatic post became available. There were three aspirants fot his post: Prince Engalichev, military attaché in Berlin; Count Kassini, ambassador to Madrid; and N.G. Hartwig, Russia's envoy in Persia. In addition to these three, there were, according to Charykov, two 'more solid' candidates: S.D. Sazonov, Stolypin's son-in-law and Russia's representative at the Vatican, and Charykov himself.[21]

P.A. Stolypin displayed a much greater interest in the sphere of foreign relations than is generally supposed.[22] He was determined not to allow again into his cabinet, and especially in the potentially influential post of foreign minister, an individual opposing his ideas. He looked for someone who was more obedient, less ambitious and less arrogant, than Izvol'skii.[23] His son-in-law, Sazonov, appeared the ideal cnadidate. He was a modest man without a trace of personal vanity. His sincerity, honesty, and diligence were surpassed only by what D. Popović, Serbia's minister at St Petersburg, singled out as his greatest shortcomings: impatience, garrulity, and nervousness, which were sharply augmented by the whirlpool of the Balkan wars.[24] More significantly, however, the chances that he might imitate Izvol'skii and strive for greater independence was totally non-existent. He enjoyed scarcely any meaningful influence in the higher circles inside and outside the government, and his experience in high-level diplomacy was highly superficial, indeed, inadequate.[25]

Sazonov's candidacy was resisted by members of the court camarilla and the State Council. Using threats of resignation, however, Stolypin was able to surmount the opposition.[26] In May 1909, Sazonov was appointed deputy foreign minister and for all practical purposes took over the direction of Pevchevskii Most, even though Izvol'skii remained its nominal head for another year and a half.[27] In the autumn of the following year, A.I. Nelidov, Russian ambassador in Paris, was taken seriously ill and died some weeks later. His death afforded Izvol'skii an opportunity to make a graceful exit from the Ministry of Foreign Affairs and to take up the post of ambassador to Russia's ally, France.[28] Sazonov became officially Russia's foreign minister, and remained in that position throughout the Balkan Wars and the first two years of the Great War until he was forced to resign in July 1916.

As long as he remained alive, Stolypin exercised, directly or through the Council of Ministers, a dominant sway in the determination of the foreign policy of the empire.[29] After his assassination in Kiev, on 14 September 1911, both the cabinet and the Foreign Office lost influnece. Court and high military circles and individual Russian envoys in the Balkans, such as N.G. Hartwig at Belgrade, E.P. Demidov at Athens, and M.N. Shebeko at Bucharest, who enjoyed influential connections in the capital, began to encroach on the authority of Pevchevskii Most and played an increasingly prominent role in foreign policy decision-making. Consequently, throughout his tenure as foreign minister, Sazonov remained, in the words of Sir Arthur Nicolson, 'a weak and uninfluential man in his own country.'[30]

The post in Constantinople was one of the most prominent in the Russian diplomatic service and certainly the most crucial in the Near East. In the past strong, aggressive, and imaginative diplomats, such as Count N.P. Ignatiev during the 1870s, were able to influence, if not determine, Russia's Near Eastern policy from the Ottoman capital by the successful manipulation of public opinion at home. I.A. Zinoviev, who had held the post since 1897, was associated with the policy of 'keeping the Balkans on ice' and the entente with Austria-Hungary. In 1908–09 he came under attack from both the moderate right and liberal circles. He was criticized not only for scorning and disregarding public opinion at home, but also for being out of touch with the actual situation in the Ottoman Empire. He had completely overlooked the ripening revolution in Turkey and contributed to the decline of Russia's prestige at the Porte by his openly hostile stand toward the victorious Young Turks. His continued presence in Constantinople was viewed as no longer useful or desirable.[31]

The contention for his post involved three serious candidates. P.S. Botkin, Russia's representative in Tangiers, received the support of the proponents of Russo-German co-operation led by the conservative members of the court camarilla. D.K. Sementovskii-Kurillo, Russia's minister in Sofia, represented the advocates of a Balkan Slavic alliance – Izvol'skii supported his candidacy. The Octobrists and moderate right, including most of the cabinet ministers headed by Stolypin and Sazonov, supported N.V. Charykov, chief spokesman for the policy of rapprochement with Turkey and the Balkan confederation headed by Turkey. After prolonged wrangles and intrigues Stolypin was again able to overcome the opposition, and, in May 1909, Charykov was chosen to replace Zinoviev as Russia's ambassador at the Porte.[32]

II

Backed by Stolypin and the Council of Ministers, N.V. Charykov, who arrived in the Ottoman capital in July 1909, began to work energetically for a Russo-Turkish rapprochement which was expected to pave the way for the Balkan confederation.[33] In his talks with the representatives of the Balkan states at Constantinople he left no doubt as to the real intentions of his government. He emphasized Russia's determined opposition to any alliance of the Balkan nations directed against Turkey.[34] For, as he wrote to Sazonov, the sole purpose of all his efforts was to achieve Russia's most pressing objective, which was to rescue Turkey from a premature and, from Russia's point of view, untimely disintegration.[35]

The Young Turks who had returned to power only a few months earlier, in April 1909, appeared to respond favourable to Charykov's overtures. In the summer of 1909 they needed a period of peace to consolidate their power at home. They feared an antagonistic coalition of the Balkan states, and Russia's policy, as set forth by Charykov, safeguarded Turkey from that danger.

The turning point in the negotiations for a Russo-Turkish rapprochement was reached in early August 1909 when the Russian ambassador commenced preparatory talks for a planned personal meeting between the tsar and the sultan. The two rulers were to discuss and secure a basis for a wide-ranging agreement between their two empires.[36]

This ambitious project, however, did not materialize.[37] Although Charykov remained loyal to the cause and continued his efforts through 1911, he was becoming an isolated figure at home and in the Turkish capital. Once the tensions of the Annexation Crisis began to dissipate, his scheme appeared more and more unrealistic and very few people continued to regard it seriously.[38]

The Balkan confederation, as envisaged by Charykov, would have served as a defensive barrier against the Central Powers, but as early as the summer of 1909 the Turks were already moving toward Germany and Austria-Hungary.[39] In November 1909 the Turkish government sought a military alliance with Vienna.[40]

The Balkan peninsula before the wars of 1912–13

A few weeks later Osman Nizami Pasha, Turkey's ambassador at Berlin, went even farther. He suggested to Count Aehrenthal the conclusion of a full-scale entente between Austria-Hungary, Turkey, and Rumania.[41]

Turkey's turn toward the Dual Monarchy was not surprising. The government in Vienna was the most consistent and adamant opponent of the idea of a Balkan alliance and consequently Turkey's best protector against the Balkan nations whose well-known territorial ambitions threatened the integrity of the Ottoman Empire in Europe.[42]

Charykov's negotiations were further hampered by the intransigent policies of the Committee of Union and Progress toward the Christian population of the empire. The Russian government could not afford to give the impression of indifference to the growing plight of these peoples, whose protection Russia had assumed at the time of Peter the Great or even earlier. The measures employed by the Young Turks to bring about the Ottomanization and rejuvenation of the disintegrating empire were too harsh and only served to further alienate and antagonize their non-Moslem subjects.[43] What they meant by 'no distinction of race and creed' became manifest on 16 August 1909, with the promulgation of the new Law of Association. It prohibited the formation of political associations based on or bearing the name of ethnic or national groups. Shortly after its passage all the Greek, Bulgarian, and other minority clubs and societies in Rumelia were closed.[44] Sir G.A. Lowther, British ambassador at Constantinople, gave an accurate analysis of Young Turk methods when he wrote to Sir Edward Grey: 'That the Committee has given up any idea of Ottomanizing all non-Turkish elements by sympathetic and constitutional ways has long been manifest. To them "Ottoman" evidently means "Turk" and their present policy of "Ottomanization" is one of pounding the non-Turkish elements in a Turkish mortar.'[45]

The eventual success of any Russian scheme in the Near East directed at Austria-Hungary depended on the response of the Balkan states and especially Serbia and Bulgaria.[46] These small nations had foreign policy aims that not only differed from, but ran contrary to, those of St Petersburg. Those countries did not view their ancient adversary seriously as a possible ally. They were not interested in preserving the Ottoman Empire or prolonging its existence. On the contrary, they sought to destroy it, drive the Turks across the Straits into Asia Minor, and attain their expansionist ambitions in the remaining Turkish possessions in Europe: in Albania, Epirus, Old Serbia, Macedonia, and Thrace.

Serbia alone, because of her peculiar position vis-à-vis the Dual Monarchy, found it essential to cultivate friendly relations with Turkey and toyed with Charykov's plan at least for a while. The Austrian annexation of Bosnia-Herzegovina represented a diplomatic setback to both Serbia and Turkey. It was a blow to the national aspirations of Serbia to the north and to the territorial integrity of the Ottoman Empire. Isolated in the peninsula and threatened by Vienna, Belgrade regarded Turkey, the power most concerned with the preservation of the status quo in the Balkans, as her only friend during the crisis. Moreover, Serbia depended on Turkey for commercial and economic reasons. Since the Customs War with Austria, a large part of Serbia's exports were shipped through the port of Salonica. During the crisis of 1908–09 the Serbs were forbidden to import war supplies through Austrian territory and had to rely on the good will of the Turkish government. At the same time Belgrade sought approval of the Porte for a Serbian railway to the Adriatic Sea which would have provided Serbia with a direct access to the sea.[47] For these very reasons N. Pašić, the Serbian premier, implored Izvol'skii, in late October 1908, to use Russia's influence and persuade Turkey to conclude an understanding with Serbia.[48]

On 26 February 1909, the Turkish government acquiesced in the Austrian offer of financial indemnity 'for the loss of crown property.'[49] Turkey's acceptance of Aehrenthal's fait accompli, combined with her shift into the orbit of the Germanic powers in the late summer and autumn of the same year, undermined her worth as an ally for Serbia, and in effect buried Charykov's plan for a Balkan confederation. The Serbian leaders became convinced they could no longer rely on the good will of Constantinople. They had to discover or create other means for the satisfactory solution of the nation's urgent problems.

To Serbia, the annexation of Bosnia-Herzegovina represented much more than just the loss of a Serbian-populated area to which she aspired. It posed a direct threat to the very existence of Serbia as an independent political and economic entity. With the Habsburg monarchy entrenched in Bosnia-Herzegovina, allied to Rumania, and enjoying predominant influence in Constantinople and Sofia, Serbia was isolated and encircled. Politically and economically the Serbs were at the mercy of Austria-Hungary. They had to break out of this encirclement or face the fate of Bosnia-Herzegovina at some future date.[50]

Serbia remained the only Balkan nation without direct access to a free sea. The attempt to acquire an exit to the Adriatic during the Annexation Crisis was thwarted by Austria-Hungary. Needless to say, however, the winning of the exit to the sea over territory under her sovereignty remained an absolute necessity for Serbia and became the most significant objective in the policy of the Belgrade government.[51]

Theoretically, Serbia could have sought access to the Black, Aegean, and Adriatic seas. The Black Sea was out of consideration, since the Danubian route was controlled by two Balkan states, Rumania and Bulgaria; and a move towards Salonica would have brought Serbia into a direct confrontation, not only with Turkey and Austria-Hungary, but also with Bulgaria and Greece, both of which claimed that part of Macedonia. The Adriatic coast, however, was not contested by any other Balkan nation. Since the days of the medieval Serbian state the Serbs had considered the Adriatic as their own sea. Economically it was most desirable because of its nearness and accessibility to western markets and sources of supply. Most significantly, however, a Serbian territorial exit to the southwest, through Kosovo north of the Šar Mountains and northern Albania, would have created an insurmountable obstacle to the further penetration of Austria-Hungary in the Near East.[52]

Serbia's ambitions on the Adriatic could have been realized – after Austria's opposition had been effectively neutralized – only through a victorious struggle against the Ottoman Empire. Russia and the other powers of the Triple Entente sufficed to defend Serbia's territorial integrity. They could not, however, free the country from its encirclement and isolation. To secure and extend her political and economic independence Serbia required the co-operation of the neighbouring Balkan nations and primarily a close alliance with Bulgaria.[53]

This was basically the political program thought out during the Annexation Crisis by Dr M. Milovanović, Serbia's very able minister of foreign affairs. It contained two major planks, one negative and the other positive. The former stressed Serbia's dependence on and need for support from the powers of the Triple Entente to safeguard the territory of the state. The latter called for the realization of Serbia's foreign policy aims through co-operation with the other Balkan nations, which in effect suggested that the Balkan states themselves would decide the future of the Ottoman Empire in Europe.[54]

If this program failed, Serbia would, out of necessity, have to submit to Austria-Hungary. But the forfeiture of real independence would be set off by territorial expansion to the south and southwest, into Macedonia, Old Serbia, and Albania.[55]

The question of Serbia's independence, as Milovanović stated, was contigent on the future conduct of the Bulgarian government. The relations between Vienna and Sofia held the key to whether the Eastern Question was to be resolved by the Balkan nations or by the great powers, guided by the Dual Monarchy. The first solution would have been feasible through a Serbo-Bulgarian alliance. The second would have become inevitable if the Serbo-Bulgarian alliance failed to material-ize. For Milovanović and for Serbia, as D. Đorđević put it, there were only these two alternatives: 'Either with Bulgaria in Skopje or with Austria-Hungary in Salonica.'[56]

Milovanović was fully conscious of the difficulties ahead in reaching an understanding with Bulgaria. He would need the support of the Russian govern-ment, and, to win them to his point of view, he sought to identify the aims of his nation as well as those of the future Balkan alliance as closely as possible with the national interests of Russia. He argued that a united block formed by the independent Balkan nations would not only serve as a barrier between the two Germanic powers and the Ottoman Empire, but would, in addition, facilitate the attainment of Russia's historic ambitions in Constantinople and the straits of Bosphorus and the Dardanelles.[57]

He harboured most of these ideas even before 1908. Thereafter, however, they dominated his thinking completely. For the treatment accorded his nation during the Annexation Crisis obliterated whatever faith he might have placed in the possibility of friendly, indeed, correct, relations between Serbia and Austria-Hungary. The Serbo-Bulgarian alliance, according to A. Toshev, Bulgarian minister at Belgrade, became an idée fixe for Milovanović.[58] Only armed with such an agreement with Bulgaria could Serbia expand into Old Serbia and Macedonia. Only with the consent and co-operation of Bulgaria and the backing of the Triple Entente could Serbia win an exit to the Adriatic Sea and secure its precarious independence. He embraced and drove the idea of a Serbo-Bulgarian alliance with such great dedication and determination that it came to overshadow all other issues on the political scene of Serbia after the annexation of Bosnia-Herzegovina.[59]

Compared to Serbia, Bulgaria enjoyed a rather favourable international position. Without major conflicts with either of the two powers most interested in the Balkans, Bulgaria enjoyed great security. Indeed, for both Russia and Austria-Hungary friendly relations with Bulgaria were desirable and essential. Russia appreciated her strategic location vis-à-vis the Straits and Constantinople. Austria-Hungary required Bulgaria as a check against Serbia and as an outpost for the spread of her interests in the Near East.[60] The Bulgarian government, therefore, possessed a great degree of freedom for diplomatic manœuvring.

Prince Ferdinand was fully aware of his principality's advantageous position. Since 1887, when he ascended the throne, he shifted Bulgaria's allegiance unscrupulously from one power to the other.[61] 'In foreign policy' wrote G.W. Buchanan, 'he [Ferdinand] always made it a rule not to commit himself to any definite line of action. An opportunist inspired solely by regard for his own personal interests, he preferred to pursue a *politique de bascule* and to coquet first with one and then with another of the Powers as he deemed best for the advancement of those interests.'[62]

It was mainly due to this enviable status that Bulgaria, besides the Dual Monarchy, emerged as the only victor from the Annexation Crisis. On 5 October 1908 Sofia threw aside the articles of the Treaty of Berlin which had made Bulgaria an autonomous principality tributary to Constantinople. In an impressive ceremony held symbolically in Tūrnovo, the ancient capital of Great Bulgaria, Prince Ferdinand proclaimed the independence of Bulgaria and accepted the title 'Tsar of the Bulgars.' The following day, in Vienna, the annexation of Bosnia-Herzegovina was announced.[63]

The proximity of these two breaches of the Treaty of Berlin was not accidental. The two actions were obviously co-ordinated. To the great annoyance of official circles in St Petersburg, Sofia had connived with Vienna and in so doing forced the Russian government, which did not oppose Bulgarian independence in principle, into a very difficult predicament. Pevchevskii Most protested the treaty violations, but at the same time had to make sure that these very protests did not endanger the Bulgarian cause.[64] On 12 October 1908 Izvol'skii complained to S. Gruić, Serbian chargé d'affaires in London, of Bulgaria's disloyal conduct. Since Bulgaria's liberation in 1878, Russia had felt obligated to support her because this new nation was really her creation. However, as a result of this present action, Izvol'skii continued, Sofia will experience the consequences of Russia's changed disposition.[65]

Russia, like the other great powers, declined to recognize Bulgaria's independence and Sofia approached Constantinople for a direct settlement. Turkey demanded an extremely high financial indemnity and the negotiations broke down before they had commenced. The tense relations between them deteriorated dangerously at the beginning of 1909, when Turkey, emboldened by the recently concluded settlement with Austria-Hungary, began concentrating troops on the Bulgarian frontier.[66] Motivated by the desire to avoid additional complications in the Balkans, but primarily endeavouring to draw Bulgaria away from the Habsburg and into her own sphere of influence, Russia intervened at this point and bailed Bulgaria out of her difficulties. On the basis of the Russian plan for the financial settlement an agreement acceptable to both Turkey and Bulgaria was signed in St Petersburg on 29 March 1909 by A.P. Izvol'skii and Rifat Pasha, the Turkish ambassador. Three weeks later, on 21 April 1909, Russia led the other great powers in extending official recognition to the Kingdom of Bulgaria.[67]

Russia's mediation bore its fruits. It prevented a possible war in the Balkans, and more importantly, 'from this point to the disastrous inter-allied war of 1913 the Bulgarian Government swam exclusively in the waters of the Entente Powers and passed as their loyal sentinel in the Balkans.'[68] This shift in the orientation of Bulgaria was not solely due to Russia's benevolence. It was dictated by the requirements of Bulgaria's foreign policy aims in a Balkan situation radically transformed by the Annexation Crisis.

After its creation in 1878, the politics of the autonomous Bulgarian principality revolved around the problem of independence and the Macedonian Question.[69] Independence had now been attained. Winning Macedonia from Ottoman control, the nation's obsession and the chief preoccupation of the throne and of the political and military leaders since the Treaty of San Stefano, was however nowhere in sight. The Bulgarians demanded the whole of Macedonia on ethnic and historical grounds.[70] The Greeks and the Serbs disputed their claims for the very same

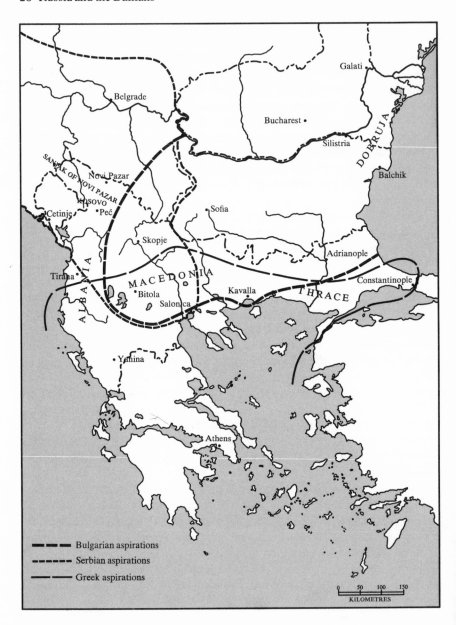

Conflicting claims in Macedonia and in Albania, 1912

reasons. Unlike Bulgaria, Serbia and Greece had more limited objectives. They aspired to portions of the area and were therefore willing to negotiate the division of Macedonia, but Bulgaria rejected outright any and all proposals for partition. In 1909, the Bulgarians preferred a united Macedonia under the temporary rule of the 'Sick Man' to a Macedonia divided between all the Balkan states.[71]

Theoretically, Bulgaria could have possessed Macedonia by two different means: either through direct annexation, or through absorption by way of autonomy as in the case of Eastern Rumelia in 1885–86. Annexation would have been possible after a victorious war; autonomy could have been imposed on Turkey by the signatories of the Treaty of Berlin.[72] In either case Bulgaria was doomed to fail without the support of Russia. For, to quote one Bulgarian authority:

On the way to its national unification Bulgaria would have inevitably been confronted by the open enmity of her Balkan neighbours and the Great Powers, Germany, Austria-Hungary and Italy. That is why the unification of the Bulgarian race could have been prepared and secured only with the assistance of Russia and her allies. Together they possessed the connections and influence necessary to remove all the perils to Bulgaria from its Balkan neighbours and the Great Powers, friends and allies of Turkey ...

Whoever attempted to unify the Bulgarians along different lines (or sought Macedonia without the support of Russia and her small and great allies) would have failed not only to realize our national unification, but would have also perpetrated a thoughtless adventure and caused a tragedy for the Bulgarian nation.[73]

In the aftermath of the Annexation Crisis, however, in order to win Russia's confidence and support, Bulgaria had to come, first of all, to an understanding with Serbia – the principal victim and foe of Austro-Hungarian expansion in the Balkans.

III

Relations between Serbia and Bulgaria had deteriorated drastically during the Annexation Crisis. 'By allying with Austria-Hungary, the enemy of Slavdom and particularly the Serbian nation.' declared N. Pašić in St Petersburg at the end of October 1908, 'Bulgaria had betrayed Slav solidarity.'[74] He sought an alliance with Turkey against all who threatened Serbia's national interests, including Bulgaria.[75] At a mass protest rally, held in Belgrade on the morning after the announcement of the annexation of Bosnia-Herzegovina, the crowds condemned Austria-Hungary and Bulgaria together. They cried out: 'Austria-Hungary is a medieval brigand land, Bulgaria her ally and Ferdinand – a Schwab agent.'[76]

The outburst of anti-Bulgarian resentment did not surprise the government in

Sofia. It was convinced that this was a temporary phenomenon that would pass once the Serbs accepted, as they must, the loss of Bosnia-Herzegovina and resigned themselves to the fact that they could not expect any aid from Europe. The Serbs will have to realize, wrote General S. Paprikov, the Bulgarian foreign minister, to A. Toshev in Belgrade, that:

in the future their glances will have to be turned toward Turkey and that Serbia will have to seek a way out of its predicament at the expense of Turkey. This will unavoidably force upon them an understanding with Bulgaria irrespective of the price. If in reality such a trend unfolds in Serbia, then it would be necessary to encourage its development. In the present political situation in the Balkans an alliance between Serbia and Bulgaria would be of the greatest significance.[77]

Without going into great detail General Paprikov also touched on the possible aims of Serbia and the Macedonian Question. For the time being, however, he only wished to know whether Serbia desired a 'sincere understanding' with Bulgaria, and if so, on what basis. He was anxious to learn whether such an understanding would require Bulgarian participation in a war with Austria-Hungary or call for a joint action against Turkey. 'If the basis is the latter proposition,' concluded Paprikov, 'then we must act fast.' He instructed Toshev to raise these matters with the Serbian leaders on his own initiative.[78]

All prominent political circles in Serbia were overwhelmingly in favour of an alliance with Bulgaria. Milovanović assured Toshev that there could be no serious talk of a lasting rapprochement with Turkey – the sacred policy of the small Balkan states aimed at the destruction of Turkey in Europe at the most convenient moment. Belgrade made it clear, however, that any Serbo-Bulgarian agreement must at the same time be directed against Austria-Hungary as well.[79]

The Bulgarians did not have any quarrels with Vienna, and were therefore disappointed with this conditional response from Belgrade. Paprikov commented pessimistically that nothing would come out of the talks with Serbia, but that Bulgaria could not afford to drop the unofficial contacts because she realized that the Macedonian Question would require a solution in the near future. Since Bulgaria was unable to impose her own solution on the other Balkan states, the government in Sofia had to reach an understanding with them, particularly with Serbia. It had to find out what the Serbian government thought, assumed, and planned for the future.[80]

However, when Toshev raised the Macedonian Question in Belgrade he received inconclusive and evasive responses. Milovanović was aware of Bulgaria's pretensions to the whole of Macedonia. He indicated to Toshev that Serbia looked toward Old Serbia and Macedonia, and did not specify the extent of her demands in the latter for he feared that Sofia might decide to put an end even to these informal contacts.[81]

At the end of January 1909, Sementovskii-Kurillo reported to St Petersburg that the Serbo-Bulgarian talks were 'hanging in the air' as a result of differing views on the Macedonian Question to which he referred as the 'stumbling block' in the negotiations.[82] The following month Izvol'skii assured King Ferdinand that Russia would help Bulgaria attain her national aspirations and urged him to follow a conciliatory policy toward Serbia.[83] In a letter to Sementovskii-Kurillo he outlined a proposal for the division of European Turkey which was to serve as a basis for the Serbo-Bulgarian understanding. He placed the region of Constantinople and the Straits in 'Russia's exclusive sphere of interest.' Bulgaria was given the right to expand to the limits of San Stefano Bulgaria and Serbia to acquire the regions needed for a territorial exit to the Adriatic Sea. Izvol'skii insisted that an alliance constructed on such a basis could be reinforced by a special military convention.[84] This proposal, however, was too vague to satisfy either Sofia or Belgrade. As far as is known, it was not used as a basis for further talks. In any event, Izvol'skii's direct involvement in the talks did ameliorate the distrust and suspicion between the two neighbours.

The counter-revolution in Constantinople in the spring of 1909 incited a new flurry of activities in Belgrade. On 14 April, the Serbian Foreign Office approached Russia, France, England, and Italy asking for their mediation and requesting them to bring their influence to bear upon Bulgaria. 'We are greatly concerned,' wrote Milovanović, 'as to the attitude Austria-Hungary will adopt if matters grow more involved and it becomes necessary for us to protect our national interests. A Serbo-Bulgarian union would be our first and most indispensable guarantee against fresh Austro-Hungarian surprises.'[85] At the same time Milovanović officially informed Sofia that, in view of the developments in Constantinople and the rising need for the defence of the common 'Bulgarian and Serbian interests, it would be advisable to establish greater contacts and a more intimate understanding between Bulgaria and Serbia.'[86]

The Bulgarian government agreed in principle, but declined to make any proposals. Through S. Simić, the Serbian minister, A. Malinov, the Bulgarian premier, informed Belgrade that, since the Serbian government took the initiative, Milovanović should specify in greater detail 'what issues he would like us to discuss, what immediate goals should we set up, and how does he think we will achieve them.'[87] The Bulgarians sought a definite and official statement of Serbia's position on the Macedonian Question before closer contacts could be established. This placed the Serbian government in a rather difficult situation. Having considered Serbia a '*quantité négligeable*,'[88] Bulgaria had consistently refused to make any concessions in Macedonia, and was still rejecting the whole idea of compromise. Consequently, Milovanović expected an 'exchange of strong words' on the Macedonian problem, but he was also convinced and repeatedly told Toshev that once Sofia agreed in principle to an alliance this and all other issues could be settled through negotiations. He assured him that Serbia's aspirations in Macedonia were modest and Bulgaria would in any event acquire the 'lion's share.'[89]

The Bulgarian government failed to respond and in July 1909 Milovanović took the initiative again. Before his departure for the cure in Marienbad he offered Toshev a two-stage plan: first, the conclusion of an agreement on all immediate and less important issues and, second, a treaty of alliance which would embrace all long-range Balkan problems. In a very careful and tactful manner Milovanović suggested a dual approach to the Macedonian Question. Personally he did not believe that an autonomous Macedonia was feasible, but he told Toshev that Serbia would accept autonomy. If it proved impossible to achieve, however, he sought a division of Macedonia which would cede to Serbia the area encompassing Skopje, Veles, Prilep, Debar (Dibra), and Ohrid.[90]

Toshev rejected the proposals and again emphasized that Bulgaria would not listen to any suggestions for the division of Macedonia. Autonomous administration for the region constituted the only expedient settlement of the Macedonian problem.[91] 'I know that your standpoint is autonomy for Macedonia,' replied Milovanović, and went on to say:

In the end even we could accept it. Personally, however, I have no confidence in autonomy. It would be superfluous for me to hide that one of our principal aims is Skopje. The largest part of Macedonia will, of course, be yours, but as far as Skopje is concerned, you must rightfully cede it to us. While for you that place has only secondary value, for us it is of capital importance. Only that way could we secure access to the Adriatic Sea ... Stated more clearly, we must reach a final agreement on the division in case autonomy proves impossible to realize.[92]

As far as the Bulgarian government was concerned the situation in the Balkans had not reached a critical stage. It believed time was on its side and was prepared to wait until Belgrade gave up all claims to Macedonia.[93] Although reluctantly, Milovanović had to concede that the conditions necessary for the conclusion of the Serbo-Bulgarian alliance had not yet materialized. Continual persistence on his part would only have complicated the future negotiations. It would have convinced Sofia more than ever that the alliance was totally indispensable for Serbia and in turn made her own attitude even more intransigent.[94] Milovanović, therefore, instructed Simić to avoid further discussions unless the question was first raised by the Bulgarian leaders.[95]

In the early autumn of 1909, the Bulgarians took the initiative and approached Belgrade. Dimitar Rizov, Bulgarian minister at Rome, arrived in the Serbian capital to begin a new round of discussions. Rizov was a Macedonian by birth and a long-time, vehement advocate of a Serbo-Bulgarian alliance. In the summer just ended, the Bulgarian government had sent him on a fact-finding mission through European Turkey. The widespread discontent in Macedonia and the explosive revolutionary situation in Albania convinced him that Bulgaria must hurry with the conclusion of an alliance.

In Belgrade he joined with Milovanović to establish a basis for an agreement. Rizov reiterated the Bulgarian contention that the partition of Macedonia was not acceptable. The two nations should instead co-operate and secure an autonomous Salvic Macedonia out of the vilayets of Salonica, Bitola (Monastir), and Kosovo, south of the Šar Mountains. Bulgaria would acquire the vilayet of Adrianople and access to the Aegean Sea at Dedeagach and Kavalla; Serbia the Sanjak of Novi Pazar, the Albanian coast around the mouth of the River Drim, and Old Serbia, north of the Šar Mountains.[96]

Milovanović had not changed his views on Macedonia. Given the expansionist aims of Bulgaria, Greece, and Serbia, Macedonia could not for long survive as an autonomous province. As in his earlier exchanges with Toshev, he again accepted the principle of autonomy, but he immediately suggested the delimitation of Macedonia into spheres of influence as a second alternative.[97] Not unlike Toshev, Rizov promptly rejected all notion of the partition of Macedonia.[98]

Actually, their stands were not all that different. Neither Milovanović nor Rizov held much hope for the survival of an autonomous Macedonia. The notion of annexation loomed large behind the designs of both Serbia and Bulgaria, but while the Serbs were thinking in terms of annexation through partition, the Bulgarians sought to annex the entire province once autonomy were proclaimed.[99]

Although Rizov's visit failed to bring the alliance closer to reality, the Serbian leaders were encouraged. It was one of the first serious indications that Bulgaria was sincerely interested in a rapprochement with Serbia.[100] Their relations continued to improve through the autumn of 1909 as the high-level contacts between them multiplied.[101]

In the mean time, in place of direct talks, Milovanović chose to pressure Sofia through the powers of the Triple Entente, and particularly Russia. As his latest biographer has pointed out, he had to convince the Russian government that the Balkan alliance he so earnestly sought to bring about was the only alternative for Russia's policy in the Near East. An official Russian endorsement of his ideas would have presented Sofia with a fait accompli that the Bulgarian leaders could ill afford to brush aside.[102]

Throughout the Serbo-Bulgarian talks the Russian government, or more precisely, those around Izvol'skii, who supported the alliance of the Balkan states, viewed sympathetically the Serbian endeavours. Officially, however, they assumed a cautious, neutral attitude toward both sides. They did not wish to alienate Bulgaria. The risk that the unpredictable King Ferdinand might turn around and conclude an entente with Austria-Hungary was ever present.[103] The Russian diplomatic representatives in the Balkans were advised to encourage the Serbo-Bulgarian rapprochement without playing 'too active' a part in the actual negotiations. The conviction that an Austro-Hungarian subjugation of Serbia would also endanger Bulgaria was gaining ground in Sofia. The Russians thought it wiser, and in the long run more effective, to let the rapprochement mature and spread on its own rather than through pressure from St Petersburg.[104]

The Serbian cause, as opposed to that of Bulgaria, gained additional solid support in official Russia in the autumn of 1909 with the arrival of N.G. Hartwig as the new Russian minister at Belgrade. Nicholas Hartwig was born on 16 December 1857, son of a military doctor stationed in Gori in the Caucasus, and grandson of a German doctor who had emigrated to Russia. He was educated in the universities of St Petersburg and Odessa. Though poor and lacking patrons, his brilliant scholastic record and remarkable diligence attracted the attention of the Asiatic Department of the Ministry of Foreign Affairs where he began his diplomatic career in 1875.[105] For a time he served as a regular correspondent for the influential *Novoe Vremia* and distinguished himself as a virulent critic of Russia's foreign policy. He attacked particularly his country's eastern policy for its lack of vigour and patriotism.[106] Early in his career his writings won for Hartwig the favour of the general staff and the elements in the court camarilla who shared his views.[107] Hartwig reached the peak in the diplomatic service at the turn of the century. He was Count Lamsdorf's right hand and under his administration he became Director of the Asiatic Department.[108] His ambition to succeed Lamsdorf was well known and rumour had it that his chances were good. Izvol'skii's appointment, therefore, represented a great personal set-back to Hartwig.[109] Besides the ministry of foreign affairs he aspired also to the embassy in Constantinople. The new foreign minister, however, did not want this clever competitor either in St Petersburg or in Constantinople, and dispatched him to Teheran. Hartwig considered this a personal humiliation and, at best, a diplomatic exile. He paid Izvol'skii back by virtually boycotting the negotiations with England which were taking place at this time. Hartwig's relations with his British colleague in Teheran were impossible. They did not speak to each other. In 1909 the two governments agreed to recall their ministers and Hartwig was appointed to head the legation at Belgrade.[110]

Hartwig was an unreserved proponent of an active Russian policy in the Near East, and an openly proclaimed foe of the Habsburg empire. He arrived in

Belgrade at the most suitable time, when Pevchevskii Most was adopting the course of policy he advocated.[111] He viewed the possible Serbo-Bulgarian alliance as an event of more than local Balkan significance. As a Panslav of the old type, he looked upon it as a potential tool of Russia's foreign policy and from the very outset of his tenure in Belgrade he became its most militant supporter. Unlike the Panslavs of the 1870s, however, Hartwig embraced whole-heartedly the Serbian and not the Bulgarian cause.[112] Hence, he secured for himself a position of unrivalled influence in Belgrade. Indeed, as Toshev pointed out, 'step by step he virtually took into his own hands the actual direction of the Kingdom.'[113] His extensive knowledge of Slavic affairs, gained during long years in the Asiatic Department, his excessive will-power, self-confidence, and Bismarckian ruthlessness and disrespect for morality in politics served him well in the small Balkan capital where he became convinced that his advice would not only be listened to but also followed.[114] Moreover, the confidence and support of the court and high military circles at home made it possible for him to carry out in Belgrade a personal policy which was neither initiated nor approved by Pevchevskii Most.[115] Three years later, during the war of the allied Balkan states against Turkey, Hartwig's British colleague, Sir Ralph Paget, complained to Sir Edward Grey of the dichotomy between Hartwig's and the official Russian policy. 'I regret that there are many reasons to suspect the Russian Minister is not acting straightforwardly,' wrote Paget; '... His position in the present crisis is consequently awkward and he seems to overcome the difficulty by carrying out his instructions officially, while privately encouraging Serbia to count upon Russian sympathy.'[116] Until his death, on the very eve of the Great War, Hartwig remained the centre of Russian political activities in the Near East.

IV

While the on and off contacts with Belgrade were taking place, the Bulgarian government initiated direct talks with St Petersburg. Only a few weeks after Russia recognized the independence of Bulgaria, King Ferdinand suggested a bilateral Russo-Bulgarian agreement in an interview with Sementovskii-Kurillo.[117] The Russian minister referred the question to Pevchevskii Most and was promptly informed by Izvol'skii that he would welcome concrete proposals from Bulgaria.[118] However, it appears that they did not agree on a basis for further talks until the autumn, when King Ferdinand convinced Belgrade and St Petersburg that he was sincerely interested in an understanding with Serbia.[119]

In a circular of November 1909, Izvol'skii described the agreement with Bulgaria, when concluded, as the first step toward the creation of a defensive alliance of the Balkan Slavic states aligned against Austria-Hungary.[120] But he actually proposed to Bulgaria only the renewal of the Military Convention of 1902, and this was promptly turned down by Sofia. Bulgaria was interested in a political alliance which would take into consideration Bulgaria's future borders, and the Macedonian Question and its resolution, in a manner most advantageous to Bulgaria.[121] Once such an understanding was reached, a military convention, which, as A. Malinov put it, should properly constitute only its annex, could easily be negotiated. A military convention by itself was of no great value to Bulgaria.[122] In December 1909, the Russian Ministry of War prepared a draft for a new secret convention.[123] Besides providing for joint Russo-Bulgarian military operations in a war against Austria-Hungary, Rumania, or Turkey, it also guaranteed Macedonia and Dobruja to Bulgaria.[124] Izvol'skii himself shelved it because it discarded completely the aims of Serbia and, therefore, threatened to undermine the Serbo-Bulgarian rapprochement and the envisaged Balkan alliance.[125]

In early 1910, King Ferdinand decided to intervene personally in the negotiations. He arrived in Tsarskoe Selo 'to take part in the funeral of a member of the imperial family,' and 'to thank Russia for the recognition of Bulgaria's independence.'[126] The negotiations took place in the Ministry of Foreign Affairs. A. Malinov and General Paprikov represented Bulgaria; Izvol'skii, Sazonov, and Sementovskii-Kurillo, Russia.[127]

Before the arrival of the Bulgarian delegation the ministries of Foreign Affairs and War reconsidered the earlier project for a secret convention. Then Izvol'skii handed the new draft to Malinov and Paprikov. They turned it down because, as Izvol'skii himself admitted, it was distinctly a one-sided affair expecting far too much from Bulgaria. Moreover, he agreed that the military convention should in any event be accompanied by a political agreement.[128] Malinov promptly outlined a project which he had brought along. It provided for the creation of San Stefano Bulgaria extending to the Enos-Media line in the east, Albania in the west, and including the port of Salonica on the Aegean Sea. Izvol'skii demurred that Salonica was not part of San Stefano Bulgaria, but reluctantly indicated that it might be included in the future Great Bulgaria.[129] No agreement was, however, reached on the maximum spread of Bulgaria in the east and west. The Russian government agreed with General V.A. Sukhomlinov and the entire general staff that Bulgarian control and possession of Adrianople and the mouth of the river Maritsa, let alone the Enos-Media line, were strategically most undesirable. On the question of the western boundary Russia remained completely non-committal. Izvol'skii declined to endorse autonomy for Macedonia or Malinov's border proposals – that was a strictly Serbo-Bulgarian affair.[130]

Malinov did not like Izvol'skii's attitude and told him bluntly that Russia was to blame for the failure of the talks between Sofia and Belgrade. Russia was in need of a powerful ally in the Balkans, Malinov argued, but it would be impossible to create a Great Bulgaria as well as a Great Serbia. Russia would have to choose between the two. 'Once you decide to go with us for the sake of your own interests,' Malinov continued, 'we will easily settle the Macedonian Question with the Serbs. As soon as this is understood in Belgrade – and you must make it clear in order to be understood – the Serbs will become much more conciliatory.'[131] Izvol'skii was not convinced. Russia was not prepared to take the chance of placing all her hopes in Bulgaria as she had done in 1878.

The Bulgarian delegation left for home on 3 March 1910. The meetings in St Petersburg, about ten in number, had failed to produce major results. The Bulgarians agreed in principle to seek alliances with Serbia, Greece, and Montenegro, provided that the annexation of Macedonia and Adrianople was guaranteed to them. Both sides also agreed that their direct negotiations would be continued in Sofia by Malinov and Sementovskii-Kurillo. The Russians, however, made it plain that the Russo-Bulgarian agreement was conditional on the conclusion of an understanding with Turkey and, particularly, with Serbia. Izvol'skii advised Malinov to raise and discuss with S. Simić the future boundary between Bulgaria and Serbia in the west.[132]

King Peter of Serbia visited Russia on the heels of King Ferdinand, and it became obvious that the Serbs did not intend to hand Macedonia over to Bulgaria and that Russia did not plan to pressure them into yielding. King Peter, accompanied by Pašić and Milovanović, arrived in St Petersburg on 22 March, and received a friendlier and warmer welcome. Unlike the Bulgarian monarch, King Peter enjoyed the confidence and trust of Nicholas II and court circles.[133] In the course of the discussions, both the government and the tsar blamed Sofia for the deadlocked Serbo-Bulgarian negotiations. Tsar Nicholas assured the Serbs that Russia was no longer bestowing special favours on Bulgaria at the expense of Serbia. Russia's foreign policy now sought to safeguard the independence and interests of all the Balkan states.[134] To the great satisfaction of the Serbian leaders, Izvol'skii for the first time confided, as the Serbs had maintained all along, that the Treaty of San Stefano was unfair to Serbia. To be sure, Russia could not denounce or discard this treaty altogether because it was her own creation. However, for the future Izvol'skii suggested a middle course. The Treaty of San Stefano would remain officially the basis of Russia's Balkan policy. At the same time, it would undergo certain changes 'to satisfy the interests and rights of Serbia, which were forgotten and abandoned at the time of its formulation.'[135] Izvol'skii also accepted two formulae which specified the demands of Serbia and promised to back them up in Sofia. The Serbs in turn undertook to continue the talks with Bulgaria and initiate discussions with Turkey.[136]

Leaving the Russian capital, on 26 March, the Serbian leaders had reason to be satisfied. Russia had accepted Serbian demands and, in effect, guaranteed that under no circumstances would the whole of Macedonia be given to Bulgaria. The policy of Milovanović 'was beginning to bear fruit.'[137]

The sojourns in St Petersburg, however, seem to have had a negative impact on the bilaterial Serbo-Bulgarian talks. The Bulgarians decided to place all their hopes in the negotiations with Russia. Indeed, as long as the conversations between Malinov and Sementovskii-Kurillo continued, Sofia declined Russia's promptings to renew the talks with Serbia, and turned a deaf ear to all the overtures from Belgrade. Hartwig did his best to ameliorate the Bulgarian fears by downgrading Serbia's claims in Macedonia. He assured Toshev repeatedly that the actual Serbian demands were modest and that the Serbs would be content with just that part of Macedonia required to secure an exit on the Adriatic. Claiming to speak in accordance with Izvol'skii's instructions he went so far as to suggest that if necessary they would abandon Skopje.[138]

In the summer of 1910 Milovanović instigated in Vienna and Paris rumours to the effect that an alliance had been concluded between Rumania and Turkey, two avowed opponents of Bulgaria.[139] Austria-Hungary and Turkey gave credence to the rumours by failing to issue denials.[140] It is not certain, but it might be safe to assume, that Hartwig, in view of his position in Belgrade, was Milovanović's accomplice. He used the occasion to warn Sofia that the alliance was not aimed at Russia, but against the 'South Slavdom.' He urged Bulgaria to advance a concrete plan for a Serbo-Bulgarian alliance and himself proposed a personal meeting between Malinov and Pašić and Milovanović in Belgrade. He was rebuffed by the Bulgarians, who 'considered such a meeting harmful in the present political situation.'[141]

S.D. Sazonov, who had in the mean time assumed the direction of Pevchevskii Most, was convinced that nothing was signed between Turkey and Rumania. He was equally certain, however, 'that there had been a verbal exchange of views with very much the same effect as if a written convention had been executed.' He thought and hoped that it would have the effect of bringing Serbia and Bulgaria together, and as he told O'Beirne, the acting British chargé d'affaires, he considered it Russia's task to endeavour to find a 'formula of agreement between Bulgaria and Serbia.'[142] When he raised the question with the Bulgarian minister, however, 'the latter speaking of the impossibility of coming to terms with the Servians had referred to Servian claims with regard to Usküb [Skopje]; upon which Mon. Sazonov had pointed out that it was foolish to speak of such quarrels when matters of vital importance were at stake.'[143]

During the last quarter of 1910, the Bulgarians used every occasion to snub St Petersburg and Belgrade. The newspapers in Sofia carried officially inspired articles commenting on the need for an Austro-Bulgarian agreement to divide Macedonia.[144] The Bulgarian government commenced secret talks with Greece and, in January 1911, A. Malinov made yet another visit to Vienna.[145] Official circles in Belgrade became convinced, and this conviction was shared by Sementovskii-Kurillo, that as long as the present Bulgarian administration remained in power further attempts to reach an agreement between the two nations would be futile.[146]

King Ferdinand was also disillusioned with Malinov's Democratic Party. For two years Malinov negotiated intermittently with Vienna, Belgrade, and Athens without scoring any real gains for Bulgaria. The bilateral talks with Russia were for all practical purposes terminated in January 1911, with the untimely death of Sementovskii-Kurillo.[147] On 22 March 1911, the king forced the resignation of Malinov's government and called on Ivan E. Geshov, leader of the National Party, to form a coalition government with the Progressive Liberal Party of Dr Stoian Danev. Geshov assumed the premiership and the post of foreign affairs, while Danev became chairman of the Narodno Sŭbranie (National Assembly).[148]

Both of these parties were traditionally strongly pro-Russian, and the new government was hailed in Russia and Serbia.[149] For Belgrade the change in Sofia appeared an open invitation to commence serious negotiations. On 15 April 1911, Milovanović called Toshev to the Ministry of Foreign Affairs and proposed immediate talks with Geshov, either in Sofia or Belgrade, or on foreign soil (i.e. the exposition in Turin). He did not suggest a plan for the talks, but only repeated what he had told Toshev on previous occasions: to win and maintain a territorial exit on the Adriatic Sea, which was a question of life and death for Serbia, the Serbs must acquire control of Skopje and Veles. All other issues would be settled very easily once serious negotiations commenced.[150] Responding to questions raised by Toshev, Milovanović defined the role of the alliance and its relation to the remaining Balkan nations: 'The alliance must take into account every possibility. Everything will depend on the situation in the Balkans. It is conceivable that the opportunity will come up when we shall be forced to accelerate the actual developments ... At the outset it would be necessary for us to agree on some definite clauses of the alliance; afterwards it would be possible to initiate into it other states.'[151]

Although the new Bulgarian government was preoccupied with domestic problems,[152] it had decided to attempt, perhaps for the last time, a repeat of S. Stambolov's successful pro-Turkish policy of the 1880s. It hoped to strike a bargain with Turkey that would safeguard Bulgaria's interests in Macedonia.[153] Consequently, Geshov did not respond to Milovanović's latest proposal. To forestall charges, especially from St Petersburg, that Bulgaria obstructed the negotiations with Serbia, he twisted, exaggerated, indeed falsified, Milovanović's views. He reported to Prince Urusov, the Russian chargé d'affaires, that Milovanović considered the moment propitious to incite and support a revolution in Macedonia so that the two nations might be able to take advantage of the ensuing turmoil to declare a war against Turkey and settle the Eastern Question once and for all. Furthermore, Geshov continued, 'Milovanović insisted that this proposal be kept secret from Greece and Montenegro. Only to Russia might something be reported.'[154] Prince Urusov concluded that the Serbs were not being completely honest with Russia, and that 'Milovanović aspired to resolve a problem that would stir up innumerable consequences without the knowledge and approval of Russia.'[155]

Infuriated, Milovanović protested to Hartwig that he would never again enter into talks with Bulgaria unless Russia took part as a witness.[156] Hartwig volunteered to go to Sofia to mediate these 'misunderstandings,'[157] but Pevchevskii Most considered such a move ill advised. 'Your personal trip to Sofia (for that purpose),' wrote the acting minister of foreign affairs, A.A. Neratov, is, in the present circumstances, liable to attract attention and excite suspicions about the existence of the talks for which absolute secrecy is the primary guarantee of success.'[158]

The Bulgarians seemed genuinely interested in a rapprochement with Turkey. Terrorist raids into Macedonia and Thrace were slowed down as much as possible. In late April 1911, the government sent the Bulgarian princes, Boris and Cyril, on a goodwill visit to Constantinople, and in Sofia, Geshov began serious negotiations with Assim Bey, the Turkish minister.[159] Speaking in Ruschuk, only a month after he had assumed the reins of government, Geshov declared that his policy toward Turkey was sincere. In order that 'it should not prove the ephemeral policy of our Cabinet but should become the permanent policy of Bulgaria, we hope that the neighbouring empire will facilitate our task by responding to our invitation to eliminate the causes that are at the bottom of our misunderstandings, and the motives which irritate public opinion in our country.'[160]

Sofia demanded concessions amounting to a virtual guarantee of exclusive Bulgarian influence in Macedonia, which in effect meant preparing the ground for her future annexation by Bulgaria. To be sure, the Ottoman Empire was the 'Sick Man of Europe,' weak and troubled by numerous internal problems. The Turks, however, did not wish to dig their own grave. They continued the policy of centralization of government and the suppression and Ottomanization of the nationalities of the empire.

The daily ravages perpetrated against the villages in Macedonia by the Turks, and the all too frequent border clashes between Bulgarian and Turkish soldiers,[161] infuriated the public in Bulgaria and, particularly, the large and extremely vocal and forceful Macedonian community there. Geshov's political opponents attacked his conciliatory policy.[162] He could not remain indifferent to this public outcry or 'ignore the open threats of the Turks.' In his book *The Balkan League*, Geshov wrote:

My manifest duty was to examine how Bulgaria could best be enabled to stop these excesses. Among the various methods that suggested themselves, the most important consisted in an understanding, not with Turkey, who rejected our advances, but with our neighbours.[163]

2

The making of
the Balkan system of alliances

By the autumn of 1911 a combination of factors led Bulgaria as well as the other concerned Balkan states to a greater appreciation of the need for unity. The Young Turk rule was entirely discredited and its ruthless anti-national measures provoked a reaction on all sides. The Albanian revolt, which broke out in 1910 and assumed considerable proportions in the following year, influenced the trend of events throughout Old Serbia and Macedonia and raised again the question of Turkey's control in the Balkans. But what really threw the entire Eastern Question completely into the open once again was the Italo-Turkish War. On 28 September 1911, the Italian government informed the Porte of its intention to carry out the military occupation of Tripoli and, when Turkey refused to consent within twenty-four hours, Italy responded with a declaration of war. In spite of the efforts of the great powers led by Russia and Austria-Hungary, it did not prove possible to confine the war and the fighting to Tripoli alone.[1]

The outbreak of this war had far-reaching repercussions. First of all, it affected the entire population in the Balkan peninsula, both Turkish and Christian, 'and aroused in it a bellicose mood which was encouraged by the comitadji activities and by the Albanian rising.'[2] The number and the violence of the disorders in Macedonia rose drastically. On 3 December 1911, a bomb exploded near Veles on the Skopje-Salonica railway. When government officials arrived to conduct an investigation a second bomb explosion rocked the police headquarters at the Veles railway station. The same day a dynamite explosion disrupted the flow of traffic on the Salonica-Seres railroad[3] and the following day a bomb exploded in the Turkish section of Štip inflicting heavy damage on a mosque and killing two Turks and one Christian. While the enraged Turks went on a rampage, which resulted in the death of 14 and the wounding of 157 Christians,[4] protest meetings were held throughout Bulgaria. The leaders of the Macedonian societies in Sofia called on the government 'not to stand there with crossed arms,' but to strike out against 'incorrigible Turkey.'[5]

In Albania, as a result of the failure of the Turks to fulfil their promises, tensions mounted and a new storm was brewing by the end of the year. The various scattered rebel groups agreed to co-ordinate their activities with the establishment of a Central Revolutionary Committee.[6] They also reached accord with the Macedonian organizations and with the Serbs operating in Old Serbia.[7] When, in May 1912, the Albanians raised the flag of revolution in Kosovo and appealed to Serbia, Montenegro, and the rest of the Slavic population of European Turkey for support, Harwig wrote to Sazonov that unless the Turks quelled the uprising quickly it would in a short time engulf the whole peninsula.[8]

Secondly, the declaration of war, as Ćorović pointed out, had a great moral effect on the Balkan states:

War had been declared on Turkey by a Great Power, one of those who had so far preached the doctrine of status quo; the peace of the Turkish empire was now being broken by the guardians of the existing order ... A Great Power had now come forward as the first partaker in the division of Turkish territory; tomorrow another might appear.[9]

Or as P. Carp, the Rumanian premier, reminded the Austrian minister at Bucharest on 2 October: 'Two lead off the dance, but many are in it at the end.'[10]

Russia tried to take advantage of Turkey's entanglement less than a month after the outbreak of war. In the middle of October, Charykov raised the question of free passage for Russia's war-ships through the Dardanelles. In return for this concession Russia was to guarantee to Turkey Constantinople and its hinterland and to restrain the Balkan states from acting against her.[11] On 9 December 1911, Sazonov disavowed Charykov's proposals and issued an official declaration to the effect that the 'Russian Government has no intention of bringing up that question at present.'[12] He did so, however, only after it became quite evident that the démarche to the Porte was not received favourably in the friendly capitals, let alone in Vienna and Constantinople.[13] Until then Charykov enjoyed the backing of his superiors at Pevchevskii Most including A.A. Neratov, who was in charge during Sazonov's absence due to ill health.[14]

Like St Petersburg, Vienna watched the Near Eastern situation very closely since Austria-Hungary wished to maintain Turkey as a bulwark against the expansionist aims of the Balkan nations, particularly Serbia. In case this proved impossible, which was not an unreasonable assumption at the end of 1911, she planned to intervene and seek a great autonomous Albania to serve the same purpose. With the creation of such a new anti-Slav and Austrophile state embracing the better part of Old Serbia and Macedonia, Austria-Hungary would have achieved her major aims: she would have gained an outlet on the Aegean Sea and at the same time she would have blocked Serbia's path both to the south and to the west, to the Aegean and to the Adriatic seas.[15]

The plans and attempts of the two powers, which steadfastly preached the preservation ot the status quo for the others, to draw advantages for themselves at the expense of the existing order were bound to produce alarm and resentment in the peninsula. The Balkan states considered Turkey's possessions in Europe as theirs, inasmuch as they had been taken away from them by force centuries before, and claimed that they were still inhabited by their co-nationals. The liberation of their 'brothers' across the borders, or simply pure territorial aggrandizement at the expense of the ancient common enemy, had been virtually their obsession since they regained independence. The internal turmoil in European Turkey and the Italo-Turkish War gave them an opportunity to strike against the weakened enemy.

These two factors – on the one hand, the threat of a great power intervention either to impose a European solution on the Eastern Question or to uphold the Ottoman Empire; and, on the other hand, the desire of the Balkan nations to make use of this favourable situation to force their own solution upon Turkey – stimulated, immediately after the outbreak of the Italo-Turkish War, a renewed and much more serious interest in the old idea of Balkan unity. Within precisely a year's time Bulgaria, Serbia, Greece,and Montenegro were bound to at least one other state by bilateral agreements. The Serbo-Bulgarian Treaty of Alliance was signed on 13 March 1912; the alliance between Greece and Bulgria was concluded on 29 May 1912. The continuing, and indeed, deepening crisis of the Ottoman Empire convinced the Balkan governments by the summer of 1912 to think not only in terms of unity but also of war. Bulgaria and Montenegro reached an oral understanding on 28 August 1912; Serbia and Montenegro concluded a treaty of alliance on 6 October 1912. Balkan unity became a reality and the fully mobilized allied states were ready and eager to challenge the empire of the sultans.

I

The utter failure of the talks with Turkey and the brewing storm over the Near East forced Bulgaria to seek a rapprochement with Serbia. Premier Geshov planned to go to Vichy after the Bulgarian general elections of 17 September 1911, and early in September he decided to meet with his Serbian counterpart, Dr Milovanović, on his return trip from France.[16] The meeting was to be arranged by D. Rizov, the Bulgarian minister at Rome, who enjoyed the confidence of both premiers and who happened to be vacationing in Sofia at this time.[17]

By the time Geshov reached the French resort town relations between Italy and Turkey had taken a most critical turn. On 29 September 1911, the Italian declaration of war gave the matter a new urgency. M.T. Teodorov, the Bulgarian minister of finance and, in Geshov's absence, acting prime minister, promptly sent Rizov to Belgrade to arrange the meeting and to sound the Serbian leaders on the main points of a political alliance.[18]

The Serbs agreed to the encounter between the two premiers, but Rizov's preliminary exchange of views with Milovanović, Pašić, and Hartwig made it obvious that the negotiations would be difficult and protracted. Neither side showed any indication of having changed its outlook on the 'stumbling block' of all the attempts to reach an understanding in the past – the old, troublesome problem concerning the division of Turkey's European domains.[19] Hartwig was fully aware of this and advised them to leave the question open for the sake of speeding the agreement on the political program which he considered much more important. 'The present moment should be recognized as being critical for your alliance,' he warned them. 'It is either now or never!'[20]

Rizov left Belgrade on 6 October and headed north to Vienna to meet with Geshov, who had cut short his stay in Vichy, and with D. Stanchov, Bulgarian minister at Paris, both of whom were expected to arrive there shortly.[21] According to I. Salabashev, Bulgarian minister at Vienna, who claimed to have been present at the talks,[22] they met in Stanchov's hotel room under the chairmanship of Geshov. During the overnight session Rizov presented a full account of his conversations in Belgrade. They then considered the question of whether allied Bulgaria and Serbia should take advantage of the Italo-Turkish conflict to strike against Turkey. Rizov, backed by Stanchov, came out decisively in favour of war. Salabashev argued against it and voiced strong reservations about placing too much trust in Serbia. Geshov did not express his point of view.[23]

Before the meeting adjourned they drafted a memorandum which embodied the Bulgarian premises for the projected alliance with Serbia. The Serbo-Bulgarian Treaty of 1904[24] was to serve as the basis for the negotiations. In the event that autonomous status for Macedonia proved impossible to achieve, the province was to be partitioned. The *casus foederis* was to arise in the following contingencies: if Serbia and Bulgaria were attacked by a third power; if Turkey attacked any of the Balkan states; if Austria-Hungary attempted to occupy Macedonia or Abania; or finally, if the internal troubles in Turkey threatened 'the peace and tranquility of the Balkan Peninsula' or the interests of 'Bulgaria or Serbia demanded that the question should be settled.' Montenegro was to be allowed to join the alliance and the concurrence of Russia was to constitute a condition sine qua non for the conclusion of the treaty.[25]

Geshov left Vienna on 11 October, and arrived incognito at the Belgrade railway station the same evening. He met with Milovanović in a special coach that was attached to the train, and during their three-hour meeting, while the train moved from Belgrade to Lapovo, they touched upon various problems of concern to both nations including the Italo-Turkish War and the Young Turk régime. Milovanović complained of Count Aehrenthal's schemes for the creation of an autonomous Albania, which was to embrace the vilayets of Bitola and Skopje and stretch all the way to the Bulgarian frontier. This was obviously not an acceptable design; and he suggested that in time, when the Balkan states settled their accounts with the Turks, the only feasible solution would be found in the annexation of northern Albania by Serbia and southern Albania by Greece. That time, however, had not yet arrived because the powers were resolved to localize the Tripolitan War and not to allow fresh complications in the Balkans. 'We must wait until the end of the war and try in the meantime to secure the backing of Russia,' continued Milovanović. 'Without her support nothing can or ought to be undertaken. But before turning to Russia we must come to an understanding and conclude a treaty in three copies, one of which will be handed to Russia.'[26]

The Serbian premier's provisions for the *casus foederis* were virtually identical with those contained in the memorandum drafted in Vienna. He proposed:

An absolutely defensive alliance against whoever attacks Bulgaria or Serbia; a defensive alliance against whoever attempts to occupy those parts of the Balkan Peninsula which shall be specifically mentioned: Macedonia, Old Serbia, etc.; an offensive alliance against Turkey with the object: a) of liberating Macedonia and Old Serbia in circumstances deemed favourable by both countries; b) of putting an end to the anarchy or massacres in the Turkish provinces when the vital interests of either contracting party are at stake.[27]

They were widely apart on the sensitive problem of the future of the areas that were to be conquered from Turkey. The Serbs had made up their minds that these areas would be divided among the victors. Milovanović readily assured Geshov that in connection with some of these lands there would be no arguments, or indeed a need for discussion. For instance, Adrianople belonged to Bulgaria, just as Old Serbia, north of the Šar Mountains, belonged to Serbia. He also conceded the greater part of Macedonia to Bulgaria, but maintained that a portion of northern Macedonia would have to be given to Serbia. For the time being, however, he suggested that perhaps the best way out would be to reserve the actual partition for the arbitration of the Russian tsar. 'Let us draw no dividing lines at present,' concluded Milovanović.[28]

Both Geshov and Milovanović had no illusions about the great difficulties they would have to resolve and overcome. But, in spite of this, they, as well as their monarchs and governments, appeared satisfied with the tone of these preliminary soundings and were intent on continuing the discussions on a higher level. Before the end of October the official negotiations for the treaty of alliance commenced in Sofia between Geshov and M. Spalajković, the Serbian minister.[29]

Russia knew of the Serbo-Bulgarian discussions as early as Rizov's departure for Belgrade; but at this time, she had no way of ascertaining exactly what the two countries were really after. Teodorov told A.V. Nekliudov, Sementovskii-Kurillo's successor at Sofia, that they sought a sincere understanding for the protection of the status quo in the Balkans from outside interventions, and that 'if worst comes to worst' Serbia and Bulgaria would be in need of Russian support.[30] The exact meaning of these words was not clear to the Russian minister. He admitted readily that the alliance would be of great help to Russia in the event of a war; and that a moment as favourable as this for the elimination of the traditional Serbo-Bulgarian animosities might not reappear again in the foreseeable future.[31] However, he also argued that once the alliance became a reality Russia might lose control over it. Serbia and Bulgaria might disregard her counsel and use their alliance offensively, for example, against Turkey or Austria-Hungary. In order to safeguard herself from such unwanted or unexpected dangers and surprises, Russia must be absolutely certain that Sofia and Belgrade understood the principles on the basis of which she would support the alliance and the occasions in which the allies could count on Russian assistance.[32]

Hartwig, who was directly involved in the talks from the outset, and indeed, was one of the guiding spirits behind the efforts for Serbo-Bulgarian unity, did not share Nekliudov's analysis and forebodings.[33] The reason for this was not so much that he thought Nekliudov to be wrong, but rather that he had an entirely different appreciation of Russia's foreign policy orientation and of the situation in the Balkans. Nekliudov spoke for Pevchevskii Most, for 'official' Russia. For Hartwig the demands of the Balkan nations were also the aims of the Russian people or of 'unofficial' Russia and he claimed to represent both. He argued forcefully that only through the unity of the two great Slavic Balkan states would these aims be achieved.[34] As a result Russia really did not have any alternative but to approve and uphold the negotiations between them. 'The present moment is such,' Hartwig wrote to Neratov on 6 October, 'that both states would be committing the greatest offense against Russia and Slavdom if they showed even the slightest vacillation.'[35]

Moreover, unlike Nekliudov, he opposed both Russian meddling in the negotiations and Russia playing a role in the alliance. Serbia and Bulgaria were to be allowed to negotiate their own terms and only when the alliance was concluded were they to submit it to the imperial government for approval.[36] Although he did not bother to explain his stand very clearly, the reasons for it seemed obvious. He suspected that as in the past, especially during the 1870s, St Petersburg would favour the Bulgarian side in the negotiations. But more significantly, he was afraid of and wished to prevent the very thing that Nekliudov hoped for: namely, that Russia would use her influence to tie the hands of the allies to complete inaction, as long as Pevchevskii Most deemed it necessary. He was too clever a diplomat not to see that once Serbia and Bulgaria reached a complete agreement and concluded the alliance the Russian government would have to go along and approve it whether it liked its provisions or not.

The official stand taken by Pevchevskii Most was somewhere between the

positions of Hartwig and Nekliudov. It approved of the Serbo-Bulgarian negotiations, in which Russia had no direct part to play, on the understanding that the
alliance, though close, would be defensive in character and would aim solely at the
preservation of the status quo.[37] An unprovoked attack on the part of the allies,
argued Neratov, would be suicidal because it would invite the immediate intervention of Austria-Hungary. Even if there were an obvious Turkish provocation the
allies should consult Russia before undertaking hasty and dangerous actions.[38]
Indeed, Neratov went so far as to suggest that the Serbo-Bulgarian alliance be left
open to the other Balkan powers, including Turkey.[39]

This represented a return to the idea of a Balkan confederation, which was
raised again in the second half of October by its old proponent, N.V. Charykov. It
continued to enjoy some favour in St Petersburg, but was wholly unacceptable to
either Sofia or Belgrade.[40] Hartwig warned St Petersburg bluntly that by insisting
on a 'Balkan Confederation headed by the Young Turks, who have shown their
political improvidence,' Russia would do irreparable damage to the Serbo-
Bulgarian alliance.[41] Neratov, however, continued to maintain that Turkey's
adherence to the alliance was desirable and must be kept in mind.[42] At the very end
of October, when Spalajković left for Belgrade to receive new instructions,
Nekliudov reiterated to him Neratov's views and reminded him that Russia sought
in the alliance a 'conservative block' to safeguard the status quo in the Balkans.
'You are of course right' – remarked Spalajković, 'and naturally the principal
condition of the Serbo-Bulgarian alliance must be, that the allies would not act
without the consent of Russia – nous considérons par contre la Russie comme le
depositaire et le garant de l'alliance.'[43]

Spalajković returned to Sofia with the first Serbian draft of the treaty of alliance at
the beginning of November. It contained eleven articles.[44] Hartwig thought it was
completely satisfactory.[45] Nekliudov objected very strongly to article 3 which
spelled out in detail the provisions for an offensive war against Turkey; and to
article 4, which specified the partition of the conquered Turkish lands. He again
reminded Spalajković that 'Russia did not wish to hear either about offensive
actions or about plans for the partition of Turkey; and that the alliance of Bulgaria
and Serbia must be purely defensive and must protect the status quo.'[46] Hartwig
refuted Nekliudov's objections by arguing that an offensive attack against Turkey
had to be taken into account in a situation so favourable to the Slavs and in view of
her nearing collapse.[47] Neratov sided with Nekliudov and instructed Hartwig to
demand the revision of the two articles. He rejected the idea of partition and
advised the two sides not to go beyond the simple definition of cultural spheres of
influence.[48]

The Serbian draft was not acceptable to Sofia either; Geshov rejected the third
and the fourth articles as well, but for entirely different reasons. With the third

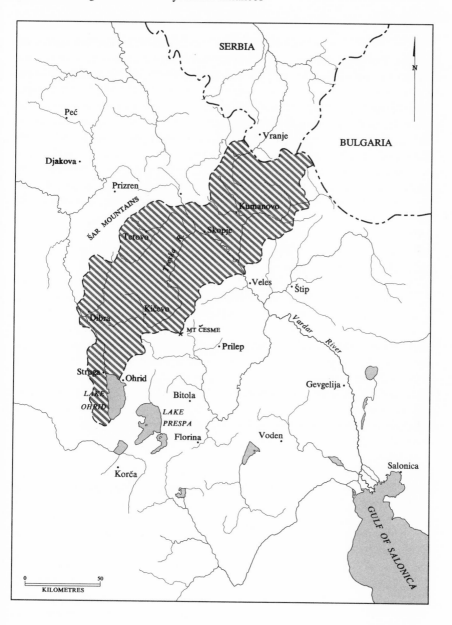

The contested zone in Macedonia according to the map annexed to the Serbian-Bulgarian treaty of alliance of 13 March 1912

paragraph of article 3 the Serbs were reserving for themselves the right to declare war without the tacit consent of the Bulgarians. More importantly, however, in article 4 they neglected to mention Macedonian autonomy, and in fact proposed that the vilayets of Salonica and Bitola, which were claimed by Bulgaria, were to be reserved for the arbitration of the Russian emperor.[49] Belgrade disregarded the Russian objections, but responded to Bulgaria on 7 November by introducing at least some modifications in the two disputed articles.[50]

According to Geshov, Sofia was satisfied with the changes in article 3, but the amended fourth article again did not provide for the autonomous status of Macedonia. Instead, it proposed to divide her area into three zones: an uncontested Serbian zone, a contested zone to be reserved for the arbitration of the Russian emperor, and an uncontested Bulgarian zone.[51] Although Geshov protested against both, 'the proposed partition and the systematic boycotting of the principle of Macedonian autonomy,'[52] the chief complaint of Bulgaria now concerned the size of the contested zone. Until the very end of the negotiations this constituted the main bone of contention between the two sides.[53]

The talks with Spalajković in Sofia failed to clear up this issue and Geshov approached Milovanović directly.[54] The latter was unable to respond immediately, however, because he was about to leave Belgrade and accompany King Peter on an official visit to France. In order to avoid unnecessary delays, and possibly to preserve the secrecy of the negotiations, Geshov commissioned Rizov and Stanchov to meet Milovanović in the French capital.[55] The two meetings in Paris, the first at l'Opéra and the second in the Bulgarian legation, did not advance the deadlocked negotiations either. Milovanović would only promise to do his best to persuade the other Serbian leaders to meet the demands of Bulgaria and then to summon Spalajković from Sofia and provide him with new instructions.[56]

On 28 or 29 December, Spalajković returned from Belgrade with a new Serbian draft. It proposed, and Geshov had agreed to it in advance, to exclude articles 3 and 4 from the main text and to incorporate them into a secret annex to the treaty of alliance. The Serbs accepted also Geshov's formula on the subject of Macedonian autonomy[57] and conceded two disputed towns to Bulgaria. However, as if they sought to be compensated for these concessions, the Serbs now asked that the boundaries of the contested zone be widened in the east and in the south.[58] And, to counter the opposition from Bulgaria, which they expected, the Belgrade government immediately approached St Petersburg to press Sofia to accept its latest draft proposal.[59] In spite of various Russian entreaties, however, the Bulgarians refused to yield. They considered the area of the contested zone as being far too wide.[60]

In early January 1912, both Nekliudov and Colonel Romanovskii, the Russian military attaché at Sofia, intervened actively in the talks between Geshov and Spalajković. In a short time they reached agreement on the eastern boundary of the contested zone which approximated very closely the last Serbian proposal. But they ran into unexpected difficulties over the final border point in the south, the town of Struga on Lake Ohrid, which Geshov in all honesty considered already conceded to Bulgaria.[61] The strongest opposition against the cession of Struga to Serbia came from the military. It maintained that in view of the topography of this contested area the boundary would be artificial and indefensible unless Bulgaria was in possession of the left bank of the River Black Drim and half of Struga.[62] Colonel Romanovskii accepted its views and incorporated them into what he believed to be a compromise proposal which he forwarded to Belgrade through Spalajković.[63]

The Serbs responded negatively, if not violently against it, blaming Romanovskii for completely disregarding the pressing needs of Serbia which required a substantial 'hinterland' north of Lake Ohrid as a barrier against the intrusions of the hostile Albanian tribes and to protect 'Serbia's life-line to the Adriatic Sea.'[64] Hartwig launched a vigorous attack on Romanovskii personally. Even though he himself played an important role in the negotiations on the Serbian side, Hartwig denounced Romanovskii for disregarding the policy of the imperial government and for disobeying its instructions by intervening in the disputes between the two parties. Furthermore, he chastised him for presenting his own opinion, the 'Romanovskii border,' as a Russian proposal and asked Sazonov to make it clear to Sofia that such a Russian proposal did not exist.[65]

The border quarrels between Sofia and Belgrade were beyond Russia's comprehension. They were petty, insignificant, and as Sazonov put it, 'secondary considerations.'[55] The Russians did not really care how they were resolved as long as the agreement between them was concluded. This lack of realistic appreciation of the 'secondary considerations' had far reaching repercussions. It helps explain Sazonov's vacillating attitude toward the two disputing parties at this stage of the negotiations.

At first Sazonov sided with Bulgaria and on 19 January 1912 he urged the Serbian government to accept the proposal worked out in Sofia with the help of Romanovskii.[67] Following Hartwig's attacks and denunciations of Romanovskii, however, Sazonov reversed his position and on 25 January pressed Sofia to accept 'the last proposal of Milovanović: to leave the question of the future of the borderline around Struga open.'[68] In other words, add it to the contested zone and submit it to the supreme arbitration of Russia. Sofia reacted negatively and promptly informed Sazonov that the 'Romanovskii border' was its last concession to Serbia. 'The Bulgarians now do not wish to hear of further concessions,' wrote Nekliudov on 30 January. 'In view of this I repeat that I consider the cause as finally having collapsed.'[69] The negotiations were and remained deadlocked for a time while the two governments focused their attention on other matters. Bulgaria was celebrating the majority of Crown Prince Boris.[70] Serbia was experiencing a government crisis caused by the sudden resignation of Milovanović on 31 January 1912.[71]

It appears that the return to power of Milovanović and his cabinet represented a victory for the moderates in Belgrade,[72] and this, in a way, made the successful completion of the talks certain. On 13 February 1912, Spalajković left for Sofia bearing conciliatory formulae concerning the disputed boundary north of Lake Ohrid. If all attempts at compromise failed the Serbs were prepared to take the risk of accepting the 'Romanovskii variant.'[73] But this was reserved for the very end; in the meantime they planned to squeeze some concessions from Bulgaria.[74] They appeared convinced that Geshov would not allow a rather small detail in the division of Macedonia to destroy the great achievements of the protracted and difficult negotiations 'which were of such a great significance for the whole Slavdom.'[75] Milovanović virtually begged him to reconsider his offer to postpone the decision on the disputed border until the actual division of the Turkish possessions took place.[76]

After prolonged deliberations the Bulgarian government approached Russia on 23 February with its own compromise proposal. Bulgaria expressed her readiness to go along with the Serbian offer to incorporate the small area north of Lake Ohrid in the contested zone. However, and this was the crucial point, in return she expected from Russia a 'confidential pledge that at the arbitration the town of Struga would be awarded not to the Serbs but to the Bulgarians.'[77] Committing Russia to either of the two parties on issues upon which they were unable to reach agreement was precisely what Sazonov wished to avoid. Therefore, in his reply to Sofia on 24 February[78] and in a dispatch to Belgrade of the same day,[79] he argued that the historical significance of the Serbo-Bulgarian alliance was to be found in the principles that it was to embody rather than in its immediate political importance or relevance. They should make use of the favourable moment to conclude the alliance as soon as possible and leave their border differences to the arbitration of Russia which had undertaken to safeguard the interests of both sides.

Such a non-committal attitude did not appease the Bulgarians and, as Nekliudov pointed out on 27 February, unless they received the pledge they requested from Russia, 'I am afraid the alliance will not materialize.'[80] He asked Sazonov to permit him 'to make to Geshov a verbal declaration, in a rather guarded manner, that at the final settlement Russia will award the eastern part of the town of Struga to the Bulgarians; that is, in the end she will insist on the Romanovskii border especially if the western bank of the Drim and of Lake Ohrid are secured for Serbia.'[81] On 1 March 1912, Sazonov backed down and empowered Nekliudov to make the verbal declaration, if he felt that such a move were required to secure the conclusion of the alliance between Bulgaria and Serbia.[82] The Bulgarians were now satisfied, and in order to mollify the Serbs, Sazonov requested Hartwig to explain to their leaders that on the question of Struga Russia had been bound to Bulgaria since the time of the Treaty of San Stefano. Russia had watered down the stipulations of that treaty and won significant concessions for Serbia. Consequently, Sazonov concluded, 'it would be unjust to find in our attitude on the question of Struga any sort of partiality.[83]

With the border problems out of the way the negotiations moved very quickly. Geshov and Spalajković ironed out the remaining differences and carried out the final editing of the documents.[84] On 11 March 1912, Spalajković brought to Belgrade the final drafts of the Treaty of Friendship and Alliance between the kingdom of Bulgaria and the kingdom of Serbia, the Secret Annex to the treaty of friendship and alliance, and the corresponding maps. King Peter and Dr Milovanović signed the documents at five o'clock in the afternoon of the same day.[85] In the evening Spalajković returned to Sofia where King Ferdinand and Dr Geshov signed them on 13 March (29 February *os*) 1912.[86] On 29 (16 *os*) April 1912, the two contracting parties concluded a military convention, which, as the treaty provided, was to be considered an integral part of the agreement.[87]

The achievement of Serbo-Bulgarian unity was welcomed with great satisfaction by the Russian and the two allied governments. This, however, did not mean that they were in complete accord in assessing the significance of the agreement which had just been concluded. Russia saw in the alliance an instrument that would put an end to the quarrels among the Slavic states of the Balkans and that would bring them into her own sphere of influence and, indeed, under her direct control. It assured Russia of a dominant position in the affairs of the allies and of the peninsula and thus guaranteed to her an extremely favourable strategic and diplomatic position vis-á-vis Constantinople and the Straits when the long awaited dissolution of the Ottoman Empire took place. Moreover, the defensive clauses directed against Austria-Hungary, which Russia considered the most crucial and most important in the agreements, provided Russia with valuable allies in the event of a future war with the Dual Monarchy or of a general European conflagration.[88]

The two allies, however, viewed their alliance in an entirely different light. To be sure, Serbia had reasons to appreciate the defensive clauses directed against Vienna as well, but Bulgaria had no quarrels with and consequently no fears of Austria-Hungary. What really caused Serbia and Bulgaria to unite were not common fears of Austria-Hungary, but their ambitious expansionist aims in European Turkey. The troubled state of the Ottoman Empire convinced them that the time was only too favourable for their plans and that they should put it to good use.[89] As far as the allies were concerned the offensive clauses directed against Turkey were the primary considerations of their alliance.[90] They were of far greater and more immediate importance than the defensive clauses aimed against Austria-Hungary.

Russia needed and wanted peace; she had no immediate designs against Turkey. Pevchevskii Most consented reluctantly to the inclusion in the treaty of these offensive clauses in order not to scuttle the negotiations, but also because it was satisfied that the consultation and arbitration clauses of the agreements gave the Russian emperor and government sufficient control to keep the allies in check.[91]

It would not be an exaggeration to suggest, therefore, that Russia and the two allies acted basically for their own selfish and not at all identical reasons. Russia encouraged and helped in the creation of the alliance because she needed and wished to use the two allies against Austria-Hungary, Turkey, or in a general European war sometime in the uncertain future. Bulgaria and Serbia sought to involve Russia in the negotiations so as to help them straighten out their own differences and, by means of the alliance, to use her in the forthcoming struggle against the Ottoman Empire: to protect their rear from Austria-Hungary and, if the war took an unfavourable turn for them, to bail them out without heavy losses.

II

The successful and, for all practical purposes, satisfactory completion of the negotiations with Serbia encouraged the Bulgarian government to turn sincerely to the serious overtures which had been coming from Athens for some time. In the past, in the late nineteenth century, the various attempts to arrive at a Greco-Bulgarian understanding directed against the Ottoman Empire had usually collapsed before the talks really got under way. The mutually ruinous strife of the Greeks and the Bulgarians in Macedonia, and the virulent antagonism caused by the schism between the Greek Patriarchate and the Bulgarian Exarchate, left no room for a political alliance.[92] More importantly, however, Greece did not appear a particularly desirable ally either to Bulgaria or to the other Balkan states around the turn of the century, especially after the humiliating defeat by Turkey in 1897. The all too frequent conflicts with the Ottoman Empire over the island of Crete had exhausted the nation and drained her resources and energies. Greece was ruled by weak and unstable governments, she faced unenviable financial difficulties, her military forces were inadequate, and her position in international affairs was completely shaken.[93]

The formation of the Military League in Athens in the late spring of 1909, and the arrival at its invitation of Eleutherios Venizelos from Crete as its political adviser, marked the beginning of a remarkable rejuvenation and regeneration of Greece.[94] Venizelos proved to be the man of the hour – the man who was able to face up to the troublesome situation of the mainland.[95] Born in Canea, Crete, on 23 August 1864, to a well-to-do merchant family, Venizelos studied law at the University of Athens and then returned to practice his profession in the capital of

Crete. Before he accepted the call of the Military League, at the age of 46, he went through a highly successful political apprenticeship in the turbulent affairs of his Mediterranean island home.[96]

A man of tremendous eloquence, energy, versatility, and diplomatic skill, Venizelos possessed a great force of character, independence of mind, and, most significantly, a remarkable sense of reality – qualities which 'raised him head and shoulders above the other Greek politicians who were his predecessors or his contemporaries.'[97] Soon after his arrival in Athens he initiated a reform program which transformed the life of the nation. He remodelled and strengthened the army and the navy; overhauled the administration; reformed and improved the educational system; and in general infused the nation with the spirit of pride and renewal.[98]

The hallmarks of his conception of foreign relations were his extreme practicality and realism. He was only too well aware that alone Greece could not attain her national aspirations either in his native Crete or to the north in Macedonia and Epirus. Greece needed allies and the natural, if not ideal, allies, in any struggle against the Turks, were the Slavic states of the peninsula, and especially Bulgaria. Venizelos was convinced, as were Geshov and Milovanović, that the Balkan nations would be able to deal with Turkey effectively only when they achieved unity and agreed to act in common.[99]

As early as 26 February 1910, even before he assumed the office of prime minister, Venizelos broached the idea of an alliance with Bulgaria to J.D. Bourchier, the *Times* (London) correspondent in the Near East. On that date Bourchier noted in his diary: 'Venizilos came to see me at 11:00 p.m. and stayed till 1:00 a.m.; unfolded all his views – even Bulgarian alliance.'[100] In the autumn of the same year D. Panas, the able Greek minister at Sofia, approached A. Malinov with a concrete proposal for a political alliance and a military convention. The latter concurred in principle and shortly thereafter submitted to Athens two conditions upon which all further talks were to be based. He asked the Greek government first, to inform Bulgaria of its maximal territorial aspirations, and second, to agree to enter into military operations immediately after the signing of the treaty of alliance and the military convention.[101]

It is conceivable that Malinov used this rather direct and blunt approach in order to test the sincerity of the Greek government and it is also possible that Venizelos declined to respond to Malinov's conditions because he distrusted his motives and intentions. In any event they agreed to continue the informal talks, and the frequent meetings between Malinov and Panas resulted in the exchange of draft proposals for a Greco-Bulgarian entente.[102] These proposals were vague, general, and almost identical.[103] They were not discussed further and were never signed, due to the collapse of the Malinov administration in Bulgaria.[104]

The Greeks renewed the campaign for a rapprochement with Bulgaria when the Geshov-Danev coalition assumed the reins of government. As has been shown, however, the new government in Sofia went through a pro-Turkish phase in its foreign policy orientation in the spring of 1911, and attempted to reach a direct understanding with Turkey on the Macedonian Question.[105] As long as friendly overtures were being made to the Porte, it abandoned the negotiations with Greece; and, indeed, turned down the recommendations favourable to the idea of a Greco-Bulgarian alliance contained in a memorandum prepared by the so-called 'Committee of Ten,' which had been appointed by the Greek government to review this question.[106] At the time Danev maintained that the memorandum paid too much attention to issues the solution of which he considered premature at best.[107]

In spite of such temporary set-backs neither side wished to see these talks terminated. Their mutual relations continued to improve throughout 1911 as evidenced by the frequent contacts between them. In April 1911 a group of Bulgarian students was received very warmly in Athens. It was remarkable to observe how during their stay there all themes that were helpful in bringing these two hostile nations together were played up; while the issues causing their centuries long antagonism were not even mentioned.[108] By the late summer of 1911 the Patriarchate and the Exarchate expressed strong desire for an understanding, and the two governments did their best to bring to an end the mutually destructive terror and atrocities in Macedonia.[109]

In the end, outside factors beyond the control or influence of either Athens or Sofia decided the issue and forced them to assume more amicable attitudes toward each other. Like Serbia and Bulgaria, Greece interpreted the Albanian and Cretan uprisings and, most of all, the Italo-Turkish war as definite symptoms of the approaching collapse of the Ottoman Empire. This in itself was sufficient to induce Athens to double its efforts in the search for an understanding with the Bulgarians. Bulgaria, however, now cured of the illusion that she might come to terms with the Turks, and frightened by the rumoured Austrian attempts to draw Greece into an anti-Slavic entente in the Near East, proved more receptive to the overtures from Athens.[110]

There was still widespread opposition in both countries to the idea of concluding an alliance. Venizelos's political opponents maintained that Greece would be better off to let the Slavic states break their heads against Turkey and then, at the most convenient moment, step in and help herself to whatever she wanted. Venizelos possessed a more realistic estimate of his country's capabilities. He argued that by herself Greece could hope to obtain only Crete and that she could not really expect to make any gains in the north and northwest by remaining on the side and allowing the three Slavic states to engage Turkey alone. Greece had absolutely nothing to gain from their defeat. As a result of their victory, however, Greece would have lost all chances of winning a share of Macedonia.[111]

The traditional distrust of the Greeks was still very pronounced in Bulgaria. But, at this particular time, other factors negated it and took precedence. As Danev put it, there were two major considerations. First of all, 'the Greek armed forces, although modest, were after all from the military-strategical point of view an additional element in the forthcoming difficult struggle against the common enemy.'[112] Furthermore, the Greek naval forces had as their task to disrupt and break the sea communications and connections of the Turks between Asia Minor and the shores of Thrace and Macedonia. Second, there were political reasons which were even more significant. The participation of Greece in the Balkan alliance was desirable in order to assure the success of the whole enterprise. It was necessary to win the sympathies of the entire world and at the same time to undermine the position and influence of the Turkophile officials and circles.[113]

To get the talks under way Panas approached Teodorov on 10 October 1911, and asked him directly how Bulgaria would react in the event that Turkey launched an attack against Greece. The acting Bulgarian premier assured him that in such a case Bulgaria would not leave Greece alone. However, Bulgaria intended to remain on the side if Greece launched an unprovoked attack against Turkey.[114] A week later Panas saw Geshov, who had just returned from the secret meeting with Milovanović, and in a very straightforward manner proposed what amounted to a defensive entente against Turkey. He told Geshov that if he would assure him of Bulgaria's 'willingness to intervene in the event of a Turkish aggression, he [Panas] was authorized by his government to declare to me [Geshov] that Greece in her turn will fight should Bulgaria be attacked by Turkey.'[115] Geshov replied that a simple exchange of declarations of this sort was not sufficient. The rights and obligations of each side would have to be specified in a formal defensive treaty of alliance.[116]

For various reasons neither side seemed prepared or willing to advance such a detailed proposal. Both sides were undoubtedly aware that their contradictory territorial claims in Macedonia would be very difficult, indeed impossible, to reconcile in a formal agreement. At the same time they could not count on the mediation or arbitration of Russia since St Petersburg was not as eager to see Bulgaria and Greece allied as it was for the conclusion of the Serbo-Bulgarian alliance. Nekliudov and Prince Urusov counselled Geshov to respond to the Greek overtures with extreme caution, if not with an outright rejection.[117] They argued that once the Greeks were assured of Bulgaria's support they were likely to adopt a more aggressive, and consequently, 'dangerous and egocentric policy' toward Turkey.[118] At the end of October Nekliudov wrote to Neratov: 'The addition of Greece to the Serbo-Bulgarian alliance would deprive it of its candor and wholesomeness; such a combination would be much more complicated and difficult to make use of in a given moment: "it is not handy,"'[119] Finally, Sofia did not wish to complicate or endanger its more significant negotiations with Belgrade. As long as they were in progress all serious talks with the Greeks had to be postponed.

Only when the alliance with Serbia was on the verge of being concluded did Geshov turn to Greece again. Through J.D. Bourchier, who was in Sofia for the celebration of Prince Boris's majority, Geshov invited the Greek government to renew the discussions.[120] On 24 February 1912, Panas saw Geshov to inform him that the Greek government was ready to conclude a treaty of alliance.[121]

The negotiations must have started well for in one month's time, before the end of March, Urusov was able to inform Sazonov of the major points of the proposed alliance. Sofia and Athens agreed on all the provisions to be included in the text of the treaty, but they ran into an impasse as soon as they took up the question of the division of the conquered territories.[122] The Greeks sought a precise division of Macedonia into Greek and Bulgarian spheres of influence. They argued that this was required, indeed indispensable, if future quarrels between them were to be avoided. But, more importantly, they wished to secure for themselves, in advance and in the form of an official treaty, a share of Macedonia against the claims of the two allied Slavic competitors to the north. The Bulgarians, however, refused to consider all suggestions aiming at the partition of Macedonia. They seemed quite convinced that it was not necessary for them to make concessions to Greece in Macedonia in order to win her for the struggle against the common enemy. Since they were doubtful about the power of the Greek armed forces, they were inclined to underestimate Greece's contribution to the war effort.[123] Furthermore, since they were allied with the Serbs and in complete agreement with them on the future of Macedonia, the Bulgarians probably felt that at the end of the war they would be in a position to dictate to the Greeks the terms of the Macedonian settlement. For the time being they wished to include in the treaty of alliance only clauses which provided for the future autonomous status of Macedonia.[124]

To break out of the deadlocked negotiations Venizelos decided to back down. In the second half of April he announced to his cabinet that Greece would not insist that terms providing for the division of Macedonia be included in the agreement. This did not mean, however, that he was abandoning the contested province to the Bulgarians. On the contrary, Venizelos told his ministers that when they reached the point of dividing the spoils of victory the fate of Macedonia will be decided by the force of arms. The Bulgarians forget that our armed forces are equal in strength ... The future military operations against the Turks will most probably take the following shape: The Bulgarians will concentrate their power toward Adrianople and the Maritsa; the Serbs toward Skopje. We will move against Salonica and Seres and in time we will get there. After that the division will be decided by the force of occupation.[125]

On 27 April Panas delivered to Geshov a new draft for a defensive alliance. Geshov again turned it down, but this time he did so not because it proposed the division of Macedonia, which it did not, but because it made no provision for Macedonian autonomy. To get over this difficulty Geshov proposed to Athens to include in the treaty of alliance a formula stating: 'Greece undertakes not to offer any opposition to the eventual demand by Bulgaria for administrative autonomy in Macedonia and the Vilayet of Adrianople, guaranteeing equal rights to the nationalities there.'[126]

As far as the Greek government was concerned the autonomy demanded by Sofia was to constitute nothing more than the first stage on the road of the eventual annexation of Macedonia by Bulgaria. Having abandoned their own demands for partition the Greeks were not going to sign Macedonia over to Bulgaria just like that. In rejecting Geshov's formula moreover Vnizelos made it clear that it was Bulgaria's turn to make concessions if the alliance was to be concluded. Geshov withdrew the above-mentioned formula and in its place proposed 'the use in the preamble and Article 2, which dealt with the rights of the Christian nationalities, of the words "conceded [by the Sultan]" and "deriving from the treaties."' Panas rightly surmised that Geshov had in mind primarily article 23 of the Treaty of Berlin, and told him frankly that this formula would not be accepted in Athens either.[127]

The final compromise, which paved the way for the conclusion of the negotiations, amounted to the following: Greece gave up her demand that provisions for the division of Macedonia be included in the agreement; Bulgaria abandoned her demand for an explicit declaration in favour of Macedonian autonomy.[128] This in effect meant that they failed to agree on the issue that divided them most. It was left open and to be somehow decided after the victorious war against Turkey.

With the Macedonian question out of the way the talks were speeded up. On the last day of April, Geshov informed Nekliudov that his discussions with the Greek minister were progressing well and that he expected the conclusion of the alliance soon.[129] Two weeks later, on 13 May, he read to him the French text of the draft submitted by Athens and expressed confidence that it would be approved by King Ferdinand.[130] The Treaty of Defensive Alliance between Bulgaria and Greece was finally signed on 29 (16 os) May 1912.[131]

The treaty was to be kept secret and to remain in force for a period of three years.[132] Although defensive in form, it was in reality an offensive instrument directed against Turkey. The treaty bound the two states to come to each other's assistance if one were attacked by Turkey,[133] but most importantly they promised to

support each other and to act together, both as regards the Turkish Government and towards the Great Powers, in all actions having for its object to secure the respect of the privileges deriving from treaties or otherwise conceded to the Greek and Bulgarian nationalities, and to obtain political equality and constitutional guarantees.[134]

The fact that the violation of the treaty rights, of which both Sofia and Athens were only too well aware, had become the rule rather than the exception in the Ottoman Empire transformed the agreement instantly into an offensive alliance.[135]

Even more than the alliance between Serbia and Bulgaria, the Greco-Bulgarian agreement was a consequence of new pressures and opportunities stimulated by events and developments beyond the frontiers of the two nations. These traditional adversaries were not brought together by a sincere desire for lasting friendship, but rather because they strongly suspected and, at the same time, needed and had to depend on each other. This, needless to say, was the greatest weakness of their alliance.

III

Throughout the summer of 1912 the Ottoman Empire was virtually in a state of chaos.[136] The government in Constantinople was unable to cope with the explosive situation, and one crisis after another threatened the complete collapse of order and authority in European Turkey.

There was no end in sight to the war with Italy. Indeed, in order to force the Porte to accept their terms and conditions, the Italians threatened to bring the war closer to home.[137] In the spring they engaged in talks with the representatives of the Balkan states in Sofia;[138] and, as an additional warning, an Italian naval force attacked the Dardanelles on the night of 23 July 1912.[139]

The Macedonian committees kept the fire burning in Macedonia. It will suffice to cite only one of many incidents and outbreaks that were taking place there. On 1 August 1912, bomb explosions in the town of Kočani killed 39 and wounded over 100 persons.[140] In the massacre that followed the death toll rose to over 120. These explosions, as well as many other acts of violence, were most probably the work of Macedonian terrorists. This fact, however, did not lessen the storm of public indignation arising out of the 'Kočani massacres.'[141] Protest meetings were held throughout Bulgaria. A great gathering in Sofia, which was organized by 30 Macedonian societies on 13 August 1912, called on the 'Government of the Bulgarian Kingdom to take all necessary measures to deliver Macedonia and the Adrianople region from Turkish slavery.'[142]

The revolt of the Albanian tribes, which broke out anew in May 1912, acquired the character of a Turkish revolution against the Young Turk régime. The officers of the Skopje, Salonica, and Constantinople garrisons showed great sympathy toward the Albanian movement.[143] Together, they demanded and forced the resignation first of Shevket Pasha, the grand vizier, on 10 July 1912, and, a week later, of the entire cabinet of the Committee of Union and Progress, which was headed by Said Pasha.[144] The new government, formed by the chief opponents of the Committee, was ill-equipped to deal with the situation. Its supporters were even less disciplined and not as well organized as the Young Turks.[145] It saw no other way out of the impasse in Albania except to try and mollify the rebels by granting them far-reaching concessions.[146]

On 9 August the Albanians presented their demands, in the form of 14 points,[147] to a commission which was sent from Constantinople to negotiate with them.[148] The failure of the Turkish government to respond promptly and favourably to their demands again set the Albanians in motion and in a short time they entered and occupied the towns of Prizren, Novi Pazar, and Skopje, where more than 15,000 armed Shiptars assembled.[149] By 20 August, Constantinople was forced to agree to the 14 points and in this manner handed over to the Albanians what amounted to virtual control of the vilayets of Yanina, Kosovo, Bitola (Monastir), and Scutari.[150]

Turkey's capitulation did appease the Albanians at least temporarily, but in the long run it aggravated the crisis in the Balkans. Bulgaria, Serbia, Greece, and Montenegro saw in the settlement a concerted attempt to establish Albanian autonomy and control over four important vilayets which, as far as they were concerned, belonged to them. They were determined to do away with Albanian autonomy no matter what the cost.[151]

In the summer of 1912, moreover, Turkey faced the possibility of a full-scale war with Montenegro over border disputes which resulted in serious armed skirmishes. On 11 July a joint Turkish-Montenegrin commission signed a border protocol which awarded to Montenegro a small stretch of land including a wholly Albanian-inhabited village. King Nikola ratified the accord promptly and insisted that the Porte follow suit without delay. The latter proposed to postpone the ratification until the situation in Albania had calmed down. The Albanian inhabitants apparently objected to being placed under Montenegrin sovereignty and the Turks feared that the ratification and execution of the protocol at this particular time would inflame the already highly dangerous situation in Albania.[152]

This was not acceptable to King Nikola, who appealed to the great powers to force Turkey to implement the provisions agreed upon by both sides, and threatened to take matters into his own hands unless they did so.[153] On 17 July the two opponents fought a six-hour battle on the border near Podgorica.[154] At the beginning of August the Montenegrin troops launched an attack against the Turkish positions and occupied a stretch of land in the vicinity of Gusinje.[155] Another armed clash took place on the eastern boundary near the town of Kolašina,[156] and Potopov, the Russian military attaché at Cetinje, reported that King Nikola was seriously contemplating an attack against Scutari and Gusinje.[157]

The Turks responded on 5 August with a twenty-four-hour ultimatum. They demanded a written declaration to the effect that the Montenegrin troops had been ordered to evacuate the occupied Turkish territory, and an official statement of regrets in writing.[158] The following day, after Cetinje declined to comply with these conditions,[159] the Turkish minister informed the Montenegrin minister of foreign affairs that 'beginning this evening Turkey does not have a representative at Cetinje.'[160]

Since neither Montenegro nor Turkey was in a position to fight they chose to ignore the dispute at this particular time.[161] However, as was the case with all the other issues mentioned earlier, this problem remained unresolved and in the end King Nikola utilized it as the main pretext to launch the war of the allied Balkan states against Turkey.

The great powers continued their attempts to bring the Italo-Turkish war to a close,[162] and Russia, in particular, repeatedly warned the Balkan states to avoid the temptation of disrupting the peace and the territorial status quo in the peninsula by exploiting Turkey's difficulties in Albania, Macedonia, and Old Serbia.[163] Although the Balkan governments were always mindful and, indeed, suspicious of the demands and interferences of the Concert of Europe, now they were especially perturbed by the aims and conduct of Austria-Hungary.

Anticipating the reaction of the Balkan states against its own involvement in Albanian affairs, Vienna raised the issue by attacking Serbia and Montenegro.[164] The Austrian government threw upon them the entire blame for the unrest and violence in Albania. 'The Belgrade Government should be the very last to play the part of agitator,' wrote Count Berchtold, 'for they have never missed an opportunity of slandering our policy, which aims exclusively at the maintenance of peace in the Balkans, and of ascribing to us – without being able to produce a shred of evidence – just such machinations among the Albanians as are now actually being carried out by Belgrade.'[165]

On 13 August 1912, Count Berchtold addressed a circular note to the capitals of the great powers in which he praised the Ottoman administration for its efforts to end the Albanian uprising by way of granting reasonable concessions; expressed surprise at the unfavourable reaction of the Christian population of the Ottoman Empire; and condemned in no uncertain terms the attempts of Bulgaria, Serbia, and Greece to exploit these concessions to advance their territorial pretensions in European Turkey. As far as Vienna was concerned the settlement reached between the Albanians and Constantinople did not encroach upon their interests and therefore should not cause any anxiety to them. Indeed, he believed that the Balkan Christians should even welcome 'this first step toward the decentralization of the administration.'[166]

Accordingly, he asked the great powers to support the Porte and the policy of administrative decentralization and to warn the Balkan states to refrain from anything that might inflame the situation and deprive Mukhtar Pasha of the necessary time to implement his program.[167] By the end of the month rumour had it that Count Berchtold planned to issue a call for a formal conference of the great powers to take up the Balkan crisis.[168]

The rumoured conference did not materialize, and nothing came out of Berchtold's proposals.[169] His initiative served no purpose except to antagonize further the Balkan governments which reacted vociferously by denouncing him and his contentions.[170] Paradoxically, they seemed to be in agreement with the grand vizier. The latter interpreted Berchtold's initiative as an attempt on the part of Austria-Hungary to impel the Albanians to seek complete autonomy, which they had not demanded until that time.[171] As J. Jovanović suggested, this represented 'a continuation of the policy of Count Aehrenthal who aspired to create an autonomous Albania out of the vilayets of Kosovo, Monastir, Yanina, and Scutari, which gravitate toward the four adjacent states. Therefore, these last can not react sympathetically to the news of Berchtold's proposal which is directed against their interests in Albania and is scarcely suited to contribute to the cause of peace.'[172] The three allied governments made it known, especially to Russia, that neither they nor their co-nationals in European Turkey would suffer Albanian controls over the four vilayets in question.[173] On 18 August 1912, the Bulgarian, Greek, and Serbian ministers at St Petersburg made a collective representation demanding for the Christian population of the Ottoman Empire the same rights and privileges as those granted to the Albanians.[174]

Austria-Hungary sought to win the backing of the Concert for her policies. But, contrary to his own expectations, Count Berchtold had raised issues which divided the great powers and tended to unite the Balkan states. Both the crisis-ridden condition of the Ottoman Empire and Austria-Hungary's diplomacy stimulated the trend which led to the completion of the Balkan system of alliances.[175] Unlike the negotiations that produced the alliances between Serbia, Greece, and Bulgaria, the talks which followed were carried out in complete secrecy, without the assistance and, indeed, without the knowledge of Russia. Moreover, the Balkan governments engaged in these talks with the definite and immediate aim of going to war against Turkey.

IV

This time the Greeks took the initiative. On 20 August 1912, the Greek government suggested to Belgrade, Cetinje, and Sofia that in view of the generally unsettled conditions in Albania, the renewal of the border conflict between Turkey and Montenegro, and, most importantly, Count Berchtold's recent initiative, the Balkan states should perhaps reconsider their positions and policies.[176] A few days later, on 25 August, Athens went a step further and proposed that they ask the great powers to force the Turks to introduce reforms in European Turkey and, if it proved necessary, they should be prepared to back up this demand by mobilizing. In the event that the border dispute between Turkey and Montenegro erupted into an armed conflict, the Greek note continued, then the other three Balkan states should enter the war on the side of the latter.[177]

Both the Serbs and the Bulgarians accepted the last point,[178] but they had serious misgivings about the reforms. Belgrade feared that a collective representation to the great powers might result in a reconciliation between Italy and Turkey, an understanding between Austria-Hungary and Turkey, and possibly an agreement between Italy and Austria-Hungary on the question of Albania.[179] Sofia, however, doubted the sincerity of the Greeks in making this proposal. It suspected that Athens was only interested in finding out what the two Slavic states to the north were up to. Moreover, even though Geshov looked upon the question of reforms as a perfectly good pretext for war, he thought it rather foolhardy to provoke Turkey into mobilizing before the Balkan states had completed all the necessary diplomatic and military preparations and made a final decision to go to war.[180]

The Bulgarians therefore decided not to waste any more time. On 26 August 1912, a crown council assembled in Cham Koriia, the hunting retreat of King Ferdinand. Besides the king, who chaired the meeting, the other participants were Geshov, Danev, Teodorov, and General N. Nikiforov, the minister of war. They resolved that once the diplomatic and military preparations were concluded, the allied Balkan states should confront Turkey with an ultimatum demanding the immediate and unconditional execution of article 23 of the Treaty of Berlin. In the event that the Porte rejected the ultimatum, they would mobilize and declare war. According to Toshev, Greece, Serbia, and Montenegro accepted the decision in principle.[181] Two days later A. Kolushev, the Bulgarian minister at Cetinje, who was in Sofia at this time, returned to his post to conclude an understanding with Montenegro.[182]

As early as May 1912, Danev broached the question of Montenegro's participation in the Serbo-Bulgarian alliance to Sazonov during his visit to Livadia.[183] Sazonov advised Bulgaria against it[184] in spite of the fact that the little kingdom was traditionally dependent on St Petersburg and was bound to Russia politically and militarily by the provisions of the military alliance of 1910.[185] The truth of the matter was that since the Annexation Crisis St Petersburg had grown extremely weary of King Nikola. The Russians disliked his independence of action, his persistent militancy, and his constant readiness to use every opportunity to stir up additional trouble in the Balkans. For instance, shortly after the outbreak of the Italo-Turkish War he attempted to come to an agreement with Italy.[186] When that failed, he became the most vocal and militant advocate of an offensive Balkan alliance against Turkey.[187] In both cases he was acting contrary to article 7 of the military alliance with Russia.[188]

Furthermore, the Russians were also suspicious of Cetinje's flirtations with Vienna and the apparent spread of Austrian influence in Montenegro.[189] At the end of October 1911, King Nikola threatened to enter into an alliance with Vienna if Austria-Hungary permitted Montenegro to expand to the south and southeast, into Albania and Old Serbia.[190] To stress the point he also told Arsen'ev, the Russian minister, that Count Aehrenthal had promised him a considerable increase in territory 'if Montenegro would march hand-in-hand with Austria-Hungary.'[191] In February 1912, discarding the vehement objections of Russia, Cetinje invited Austrian legal experts to supervise the reform of the courts and the judicial institutions of the kingdom.[192] The following month it became known that Austria-Hungary would build the strategic highway between Grahovo and Trubel. By autumn, when this project was to be completed, a well-developed and continuous highway was to run all the way from the Austrian port of Risano to Nikšić in the centre of Montenegro.[193] Miller, the Russian chargé d'affaires at Cetinje, who reported these developments, was convinced of the existence of a general political alliance between Austria-Hungary and Montenegro.[194]

For these reasons, Sazonov cautioned Danev, in Livadia, that in case Montenegro joined Bulgaria and Serbia the very existence of the alliance would 'inevitably become known to Austria in a very short time,'[195] and that in view of the continuing enmity between Serbia and Montenegro such an alliance would lack a sincere basis.[196] Finally, he warned him that the 'unprincipled' King Nikola might provoke and drag Bulgaria and Serbia into a war against Turkey, which Russia opposed most categorically.[197]

Either Danev refused to take Sazonov's warnings seriously or they came too late. In any case they did not influence Bulgaria's future policy or the more militant outlook of the Balkan states. On his return trip from Russia, Danev stopped in Vienna during the first week of June. King Ferdinand and Geshov were already there on an official visit, and they were joined by Teodorov, who arrived from Paris where he had been negotiating a loan, and by Rizov, who was summoned from Rome by Geshov.[198] When King Ferdinand left for Berlin on 3 June, the other Bulgarian leaders remained behind and engaged in important political discussions, the details of which are not known. According to both Geshov and Toshev they examined the question of war against Turkey and then went their ways. Geshov followed King Ferdinand to Berlin, and Teodorov returned to Sofia,[199] but Danev and Rizov stayed in the Austrian capital where King Nikola and his entourage were expected on an official visit.[200]

Shortly after their arrival Rizov approached *Brigadir* M. Martinović, the Montenegrin prime minister, with whom he was already acquainted, and arranged a meeting. Strangely enough this meeting, which marked the beginning of serious negotiations between Bulgaria and Montenegro, took place at the Hofburg in the suite of King Nikola.[201] It required only one short session for the two sides to agree on the main question. *Brigadir* Martinović declared unequivocally that Montenegro was ready to strike against Turkey immediately and without an official declaration of war as soon as Bulgaria agreed to provide financial subsidies toward the upkeep of the Montenegrin army.[202] Danev and Rizov were delighted, but before going any further they suggested that all the details would have to be worked out first by the two governments.[203]

After Vienna the talks were continued in Cetinje. In a conversation with Kolushev on 18 July, King Nikola pressed for the conclusion of the understanding. He reiterated that he was prepared to open the hostilities first but he sought assurances that Bulgaria would enter the war soon after.[204] The response from Sofia must have been favourable for before the end of the month King Nikola submitted a detailed eight-point draft for either an oral understanding or a formal treaty of alliance directed against the Turks.[205]

The available evidence indicates that the draft was on the whole acceptable to Sofia,[206] and Geshov decided to meet Kolushev personally to iron out the final details.[207] To avoid giving rise to rumours and suspicions, he planned the meeting for Munich and asked Kolushev to leave Cetinje on 17 August for the Bavarian capital.[208] There he was to find a dispatch with further instructions at the 'Hotel Continental.'[209] At the last moment Geshov changed his mind. On Tuesday, 20 August, the day of the planned meeting, he sent a telegram to Munich informing Kolushev that 'the person who wished to see you could not leave' and instructing him to 'Depart immediately for Sofia.'[210] Kolushev remained in Sofia until 28 August, that is, two days after the crown council of Cham Koriia, when he was sent back to Cetinje authorized to conclude an oral understanding with Montenegro.[211] On 3 September he reported to Geshov: 'Acted in accordance with your instructions. The King of Montenegro agrees to everything; [is] very much obliged, grateful.'[212]

The agreement povided [213] for an offensive war against Turkey to liberate the

Christian population, to free the Balkan peninsula from Ottoman control, and to enlarge the territorial boundaries of the two nations. Montenegro undertook to commence the hostilities at the latest by 14 September and to deploy 40,000 troops. Bulgaria promised to enter the war with all her military power no later than thirty days after and to pay Montenegro a subsidy of 35,000 levas a day for a period of three months.[214] They also agreed to enter into immediate discussions with Serbia, Greece, and the Albanian rebels.

V

While the agreement with Montenegro was being decided Sofia inaugurated urgent talks with Belgrade and Athens, the aim of which was to prepare the ground for the actual declaration of war.[215] On 31 August 1912, Geshov wrote Toshev to await a special emissary bearing a very important personal letter from him, and then to come to Sofia as soon as possible. The emissary, General I. Fichev, arrived in Belgrade on 3 September. The letter, dated 1 September, contained the Bulgarian project for the declaration of war.[216]

Geshov wished to know first of all whether the Serbs agreed to accept the question concerning the introduction of reforms in European Turkey as the principal ground and justification for the war. He thought, and the Greeks apparently shared the view, that this was necessary in order to win the nationalities of European Turkey, including the Albanians, and the public opinion of Europe and, further, to frustrate the possible intervention of Rumania against Bulgaria. Geshov did not object to Serbia raising other issues as well, but he hoped that Pašić would be persuaded to embrace article 23 of the Treaty of Berlin as the main cause: 'Without it there are dangers for us. Mr. Pašić must understand this.'[217] Secondly, Geshov dealt with the problem of which one of the allied nations would commence the hostilities. Spalajković had already made it known to him that Serbia could not undertake that responsibility. This eliminated Bulgaria also because Geshov himself maintained that the two should either start or enter the war together. Therefore, unless Greece accepted this burden, it would have to fall on Montenegro, and Pašić, who disliked and suspected King Nikola, would have to go along with such an eventuality.[218]

In the afternoon of the same day, 3 September, Pašić[219] joined Toshev and Fichev at the Bulgarian legation to examine Geshov's letter.[220] The following day, after he had received a detailed statement of Pašić's views on the topic from the Belgrade Foreign Office, Toshev left for Sofia.[221]

For Pašić, it was not a question of whether to accept the issue of reforms as a pretext for war – which he was prepared to do, but rather what kind of reforms Geshov had in mind. He did not believe that it was sufficient to demand merely the execution of article 23 of the Treaty of Berlin, because the article was not broad enough. More importantly, the Treaty of Berlin was the creation of the great powers and they might decide to take upon themselves the implementation of article 23 and thus deprive the allies of their chief excuse for the war. He proposed that the Balkan states should call instead for the introduction of wide-ranging reforms and demand equality with the great powers in deciding upon these reforms and overseeing their implementation. The allied governments would take such a step hoping that it would be turned down. If, however, it were accepted by Europe, then Bulgaria, Greece, Montenegro, and Serbia, supported by the powers of the Entente, would enjoy a commanding majority in settling the question of reforms. In the event that it were rejected, they would make a similar representation at Constantinople and use the negative response from the Porte as the most suitable pretext to launch military hostilities.[222]

Pašić would have preferred to see Greece begin the war, but he was prepared to go along with Montenegro on condition that King Nikola restrict the operations of his forces to Scutari and the other areas of northern Albania, which were inhabited by the Catholic Albanian tribes. He explained that this was a necessary precaution if they wished to avoid provoking the Muslim Albanians against both Montenegro and Serbia, which would have provided Austria-Hungary with an excuse to call for the creation of independent Great Albania. He agreed with Geshov's suggestion that Bulgaria and Serbia mobilize and enter the war at the same time. The final date for the war was to be decided while the mobilizations were in progress and was to depend on the reaction of Austria-Hungary, Rumania, and Russia. In case Rumania or Turkey or both attacked Bulgaria before the completion of the mobilization, Serbia was to come to her immediate assistance. Bulgaria was to do the same if Austria-Hungary attacked Serbia.[223]

When Toshev arrived at Sofia, he was taken straight to the premier's residence to meet with Geshov and Danev. Together they went over the Serbian proposals, and in the afternoon of the same day, 6 September, Toshev met Spalajković to discuss the remaining differences. The following day, in the presence of Geshov, Danev, and Teodorov, Toshev composed the final Bulgarian draft of the agreement with Serbia on the war.[224]

First of all, it declared that the two parties had reached the irretrievable decision to wage a war against Turkey 'together and at the same time.' For this purpose they agreed to undertake immediately and swiftly the necessary military preparations, which were to be followed, in the shortest possible time, by official mobilization and the opening of military operations. Second, it outlined the steps they planned to take to legitimate the outbreak of the war. The four Balkan states, Bulgaria, Greece, Montenegro, and Serbia, would make a representation at Constantinople demanding a binding official commitment that the Turkish government agreed to introduce in the shortest time the basic reforms defined by article 23 of the Treaty of Berlin throughout its European possessions. As a proof of her goodwill, and as a guarantee that these reforms would be promptly executed, Turkey would have to withdraw all her 'Asiatic' armed forces from these lands. A few days before the representation was to be made, the Greek government would call into session the Chamber of Deputies to seat the representatives from the island of Crete, and Montenegro would commence the fighting. Once the representation was delivered to the Porte, its terms would be communicated to the great powers, but only for their consideration. Finally, for the time being the agreement was to be kept strictly secret. When it became necessary it was to be made known to Russia, but only after each of the two parties consented.[225]

Toshev returned to Belgrade with the draft of the agreement amidst signs that Serbia would go along with its provisions. On 12 September, the caretaker cabinet of M. Trifković stepped down and what constituted virtually a war government was formed. N. Pašić became premier and minister of foreign affairs.[226] Two days later the crown council approved the Bulgarian draft of the agreement with only one additional recommendation to which Sofia acquiesced. This was a statement to the effect that the two nations would defend themselves with their entire common strength in the event that Rumania, Austria-Hungary, or both, invaded the territory of Bulgaria or Serbia with the aim of protecting Turkey.[227]

The talks between Bulgaria and Greece, which were taking place at the same time, did not fare so well. The Greeks vacillated on the question of war. They were still thinking, or made it appear that way, in terms of piecemeal reforms which were to be introduced in European Turkey under the direct supervision of the ambassadors of the great powers and the ministers of the Balkan states in Constantinople.[228] When Geshov showed to Panas an edited copy of the agreement with Serbia and asked Greece to adhere to it, he described its provisions as being identical with those advanced by Athens.[229] But L. Koromilas, the Greek foreign minister, could not have disagreed with him more. He protested to Sofia that while he sought reforms, the Serbo-Bulgarian agreement called for an offensive war. For, to demand that Turkey withdraw her troops from Europe, at a time when Montenegro had commenced military operations and Greece was seating the deputies from Crete, would certainly mean war, and the allies were not ready.[230] He pointed out that Greece had no alliance or any other agreement with either Serbia or Montenegro, and the talks for a military convention with Bulgaria were just beginning.[231] More importantly, and this was the crucial issue for the Greeks, they had not reached any agreement with the Bulgarians on the spheres of influence, or more precisely, on the partition of Macedonia.[232] Geshov argued then, as he did some years later, that there was no time to negotiate such an agreement.[233] It would be more correct to assume, however, that since their claims in Macedonia were so contradictory it would have been extremely difficult, if not impossible, for them to agree on anything.[234] In any event, the Greco-Bulgarian negotiations broke down. Only after Turkey began mobilizing did the Greek government agree to adhere to the terms of the Serbo-Bulgarian agreement and to act in common with her ally Bulgaria.[235]

VI

Meanwhile, once the new government in Belgrade decided in favour of war, it had really no alternative but to brush aside the traditional differences and animosities that divided Serbia from Montenegro, the other branch of the Serbian nation, and reach some sort of accommodation with Cetinje. The Montenegrin government had made frequent overtures to Belgrade in the past. Indeed, it came forth with a proposal for an understanding against Turkey at every opportune occasion. It did so in connection with the Albanian uprising,[236] the question of Albanian autonomy and Count Berchtold's initiative,[237] and again following the conclusion of the agreement with Bulgaria.[238] These advances were however either ignored or politely turned down.[239]

The truth of the matter was that the Serbs were even more suspicious of King Nikola than were the Russians. They were never certain of his real intentions, and of the degree of sincerity in his proposals; and they therefore feared that he might betray them to Austria-Hungary, Turkey, or the Albanian insurgents.[240] King Nikola was not unaware of the unfavourable views and opinions about him that prevailed in Belgrade. At the end of July he complained to M. Gavrilović, the Serbian minister at his court, against the 'obvious distrust of the Serbian Government toward him.'[241] But this did not deter King Nikola from trying. Around the time when Pašić, of whom he did not think well, assumed the reins of government at Belgrade, the Montenegrin king planned to make a direct appeal to King Peter.[242]

Such a move was not really necessary for although Pašić's appreciation of King Nikola was probably very modest indeed, there was no place for personal whims or dislikes in the political schemes of this long-time political boss of Serbia. One of his first undertakings as premier was to instruct Gavrilović to make it known to the king and government of Montenegro that the time had come to put an end to all the differences between Belgrade and Cetinje and to join hands for the good of the common cause.[243] The actual talks for the political alliances and the military convention commenced on 18 September 1912.[244]

To preserve the cloak of secrecy which surrounded the talks, both sides agreed to conclude them on foreign soil, in Lucerne, Switzerland. J. Plamenac, the minister of the interior, led the Montenegrin delegation; Colonel P. Pešić, an able high-ranking officer of the general staff, the Serbian.[245] On 25 September, shortly before his departure for Switzerland, Premier Pašić received Colonel Pešić and informed him of his mission. Pašić told him that a war against Turkey would break out sometime between 8 and 13 October. He was going to Lucerne to meet with J. Plamenac and *Komandir* J. Bećir, and to conclude in the shortest possible time a political alliance and a military convention. The main aim of the agreements was to establish that the two kingdoms would attack and fight Turkey with their entire common strength. Colonel Pešić did not have the power to accept, or even discuss, proposals for the division of the conquered Turkish domains. If Plamenac pressed this point Pašić asked Pešić to declare: 'Brothers, in case the war ends successfully – we will divide them very easily; but now it is very important to win against Turkey.' Finally, if Montenegro advanced a claim on the town of Prizren, he was instructed to turn it down; if Plamenac continued to insist, to break off the talks and return to Belgrade immediately.[246]

The Montenegrin delegates came to Lucerne armed with a detailed draft for a treaty. As long as they avoided the question of the future boundary between the two states the talks continued well and fast. Once Plamenac touched upon it, in the form of a proposal which was extremely generous to Montenegro, they ran into difficulties.[247] Colonel Pešić told him bluntly that his government's intention was to wage a war for the liberation of 'our brothers ... and not to bicker over the loot.' Unless they agreed to relinquish this particular issue until the end of the war, he threatened to break off the negotiations in which case the responsibility for the collapse of 'the talks for the Holy War against Turkey will fall on Montenegro and not on Serbia.'[248] The two sides remained deadlocked for several days, but in the end King Nikola backed down and Pešić had his way. The talks in Lucerne were successfully concluded on 1 October, and both the political and military conventions between Serbia and Montenegro were signed at Cetinje on 6 October 1912.[249] The political convention was more than an instrument of alliance – it was an agreement for an offensive war against Turkey. The third article bound the two signatories to enter into immediate talks if one of them deemed the situation in Turkey and Europe favourable to starting a war for the liberation of the Serbs from the Turkish yoke. But the following article went even further and declared:

As the governments of the Kingdom of Montenegro and the Kingdom of Serbia find the present situation in Turkey and the overall conditions in Europe exceedingly advantageous for an action with the aim of liberating the Serbs under the Turkish yoke, they agree that it is necessary to declare war against Turkey at the latest by October 1 [13] of this year.[250]

VII

Although the Russian government was not privy to the intensified diplomatic and military undertakings, it was of course aware of what had been taking place. Numerous reports coming from the allied capitals spoke of the rapidly growing pressures on the governments to opt for war and of the stepped-up pace of the war preparations.[251] 'The public opinion in Bulgaria is in an extremely bellicose mood,' wrote Colonel Romanovskii. 'Not only the entire press, but all social classes with minor exceptions demand war against Turkey.'[252] Bulgaria was not an exceptional case; this state of affairs prevailed in the other three allied nations as well.[253] The public did not concern itself with the outcome of such a war; it seemed confident that, in case it became necessary, Russia would bail the allies out of a disastrous war. This trust was based to a large extent on the reasonable premise that the preservation of the pro-Russian governments and of the Balkan alliances was in Russia's interest and that the survival of both depended on the outbreak of war.[254]

Emboldened by the near consensus on the issues of reforms and war, which they achieved after or perhaps as a result of Count Berchtold's initiative, the allies led by Bulgaria approached St Petersburg with their real designs. Geshov raised the question of reforms many times in his talks with Nekliudov, but he was repeatedly warned that Europe would not tolerate the disruption of the status quo in the Balkans.[255] On 7 September 1912, he instructed General Paprikov, now Bulgaria's minister to Russia, to ask Sazonov for a personal meeting and to make it clear to him that it was 'imperative that the Triple Entente support our demand for radical reforms and if need be, to allow the Balkan states to force them upon Turkey.'[256]

At the meeting, which took place on 16 September, General Paprikov told Sazonov bluntly that in view of Turkey's past and present stand on the question of reforms, the war of the allies against her was inevitable. If the great powers wished to prevent the outbreak of another war in the Near East, then it was up to them to coerce the Turks to satisfy the demands of the Balkan states.[257] Sazonov suggested that the allies would be embarking on a very foolhardy venture if they provoked the war. He pointed out that the Turks had a strong army of 350,000 men in the Balkans alone and further, that the very first move of the allies would invite the intervention of Austria-Hungary against Serbia and Rumania against Bulgaria. Paprikov responded by declaring that the Balkan states were strong enough to deal with the Turks. He asked Sazonov whether Russia was prepared and willing to permit Austria-Hungary to attack and occupy Serbia.[258] 'What do you expect of Russia?' retorted Sazonov. Russia would not wage a war against Austria-Hungary or anybody else just because the Serbs and the Bulgarians resolved to risk their own independence. Russia fulfilled her mission toward the Balkan Slavs and what she had already accomplished for them was sufficient. 'Do not expect more from us!'[259]

The talk with General Paprikov, his frankness and forthrightness, alarmed Sazonov as to the actual state of affairs in the Balkans. The alliances which he had helped create to serve as adjuncts, as obedient instruments of Russia, threatened to plunge her into an unwanted, unnecessary, and premature war.[260] Sazonov regarded the Bulgarian government and in particular King Ferdinand, whom the Russians never ceased to suspect, as the real culprits.[261] At the eleventh hour he tried to avert the threatening confrontation. First of all, he sought to undermine Bulgaria's prestige and influence by isolating her in the Balkans; and secondly, he attempted to persuade or force Constantinople to introduce reforms throughout European Turkey.

The day after he saw General Paprikov, Sazonov dispatched identical notes to his representatives at Athens, Belgrade, and Cetinje. He instructed them to urge most categorically the government to which each was accredited to dissociate itself from the Bulgarian war aims:

If it [the government] does not forewarn Bulgaria of its refusal to follow her, in our opinion, into a disastrous attack and takes the decision against which we repeatedly warned it, Russia renounces all responsibility for the consequences. The Balkan states can not count on her intervention in the impending struggle.[262]

The following day he directed another strong warning at Belgrade and Sofia. He reminded the two governments that Russia welcomed the Serbo-Bulgarian alliance because it promised to put an end to the fratricidal struggle between them. To facilitate the understanding the imperial government chose to overlook some of its provisions, which were clearly unacceptable to it, and agreed to arbitrate their future differences. However, continued Sazonov, Russia viewed the alliance in no other light except as a defensive instrument for the protection of their mutual interests:

In the event that in spite of our warnings the two states decide now to employ their alliance to launch a joint attack on Turkey ... and to expose their territorial integrity and independence to a ruinous ordeal, then we deem it our duty to warn them in advance that in such a case we will be guided solely by our concern for the direct and immediate interests of Russia.[263]

Sazonov's representations came too late. However, it seems very doubtful that they would have proven more effective at any time after the Serbo-Bulgarian alliance was concluded. As Hartwig suggested in one of his more balanced dispatches, since the signing of the treaty the governments in Sofia and Belgrade had only two alternatives. They could either disobey the representations of the 'powerful protectress of the Slavs' and let themselves be carried forward by the national wave for the sake of the 'holy Slav idea,' even at the expense of a possible defeat, or they could submit unquestioningly to the commands of Russia and, carrying the flag of Russophilism, fall victim to national indignation, and yield power to other elements who would undoubtedly redirect the course of political life in both states to the detriment of Russia and the Slavs.[264]

The Balkan governments chose the first alternative and decided to disregard Russia's commands and remain loyal to what they considered to be their nations' legitimate aspirations. Replying to Sazonov's representation, Koromilas stated that he could not renounce the binding ties of the Greco-Bulgarian aliance.[265] King Peter could not imagine 'how I could change the alliance with Bulgaria under which stands my signature.'[266] Only A. Giers, the Russian minister at Cetinje, who was not aware either of the Bulgarian-Montenegrin understanding or of Montenegro's commitment to commence the war, sounded an optimistic note. He did not think that King Nikola could afford to disregard the opposition of Russia or the situation in Montenegro and provoke a war.[267] However, Geshov was perhaps expressing the true outlook of all the allies when he told Nekliudov that he was 'deeply convinced that our interests and the interests of Russia are identical ... the warning does not perturb us!'[268]

Sazonov's push for the introduction of reforms did not produce results either. Winning peaceful reforms from the Turks had always been an excruciating experience, but the task was doubly difficult in periods of crisis, as was the case in September 1912, when the great powers of Europe were divided. Shortly after the encounter with General Paprikov, Sazonov saw the Turkish ambassador and impressed upon him the urgent need for reforms in Macedonia. The reforms that he had in mind were rather modest when compared to what the allies demanded: a guarantee for the safety of the Christian inhabitants and their property; equality before the law; and Christian participation in the administration.[269] He was anxious not to give the slightest impression that the Russian government was trying to pressure Turkey. Having cautioned his ambassadors in the capitals of the great powers to act likewise, he asked them to inquire whether the government to which they were accredited would consider it useful 'to charge its representative in Constantinople to make to the Porte a friendly representation in the sense of my aforesaid statement to the Turkish Ambassador.'[270] Sazonov was especially careful not to offend Austria-Hungary. In a private talk with Julius von Szilassy, special minister attached to the Austro-Hungarian embassy at St Petersburg, he suggested that in making this request he was inspired by the very same motives that influenced Berchtold's initiative the previous month and, consequently, hoped to have the strong backing of Vienna.[271]

The other powers, however, either did not see the need for Sazonov's proposed move or doubted its efficacy. Count Berchtold asked Pallavicini to pay a visit to the Porte even though he doubted the necessity of making the démarche because, as he put it, the suggested reforms had already been anticipated by the Turkish constitution.[272] Kiderlen-Wächter, German secretary of state for foreign affairs, held basically the same view. He indicated, moreover, that an agreement among the powers on the localization of the war, if and when it broke out, might serve a better purpose for it would influence the conduct of the Balkan states. Russia's partners in the Entente were no more receptive to the idea than her opponents in the Triple Alliance.[273] Sir Edward Grey at first declined to send the appropriate instructions to Sir C.M. Marling, and finally did so only after a meeting with Sazonov who was in London at this time.[274] Poincaré followed suit, hesitantly, shortly thereafter.[275]

Unlike the powers of the Triple Alliance and Great Britain, who did not wish to pressure Turkey, Poincaré held no hope for the success of the friendly démarches, because they were too mild and would most probably be altogether disregarded by the Porte.[276] He proposed instead formal discussions between France, Great Britain, and Russia to prepare a draft project of an agreement for the stabilization of the situation in the Near East around which all the great powers would unite.[277] As a basis for the discussions he proposed that: 1) The powers make immediately a collective representation in Sofia, Belgrade, Athens, and Cetinje to advise them to undertake nothing which might disturb the peace or affect the status quo in the Balkan peninsula. 2) If this advice were not followed the powers, while declaring their intention not to permit changes in the territorial status quo, would combine their efforts to localize the conflict and bring it to an end. 3) 'If the course of events necessitates the use of more energetic means, such as a military or noval demonstration, the Powers shall not undertake it without having concerted among themselves.' 4) At the same time that they carried out the démarche in the Balkan capitals, the great powers would make a representation at the Porte 'to advise it to execute, without delay, the administrative reforms which are legitimately claimed by the Christian population of the Balkan Peninsula.'[278]

Poincaré hoped that Great Britain and Russia would accept his four points and the three of them would try to win the approval of Austria-Hungary and Germany. But when, on 22 September 1912, P. Cambon presented the project to Grey and Sazonov in London,[279] the former voiced some serious misgivings about it. Although he was willing to embrace the first two points, Grey objected to the third because he refused even to entertain the notion that the great powers would intervene with force in the Balkan crisis. As for the fourth point, he considered it useless and unnecessary since Great Britain, France, Russia, and to a certain extent Austria-Hungary had already made a representation to that effect in

Constantinople.[280] Sazonov would have liked to retain the third point because, as Poincaré explained to Izvol'skii, the main objective behind it was to thwart the possible unilateral intervention of Austria-Hungary.[281] However, he backed down partly because of Grey's opposition, but also because he did not think it would be acceptable to Austria-Hungary and Germany. At this point, when the need for unity and unanimity was of the utmost importance, he did not wish to jeopardize the entire proposal or to provoke divisions among the powers.[282]

While the great powers were debating Poincaré's four points and before they reached any kind of agreement, the fast-moving developments in the Balkans took a radical turn for the worse.[283] Montenegro had been ready and eagerly awaiting the decision to go to war since she concluded the understanding with Bulgaria. On 13 September, King Nikola proposed to Sofia 27 September as the date for the opening of hostilities.[284] The other allied states were not yet ready to agree on the final date and the Bulgarians sent back evasive and inconclusive replies.[285] The delay was being caused by the still unfinished talks between the general staffs of Bulgaria, Serbia, and Greece.[286] More importantly, however, N. Pašić appeared to have some last minute misgivings about provoking the war.

Serbia was much more exposed to the threat of the possible intervention of Austria-Hungary and consequently in greater dependence on Russia's protection. Sazonov's repeated warnings and the recent urgent appeal by V.N. Kokovtsov, the Russian premier, not to risk a war until the outcome of Sazonov's talks in London and Paris became known were having an effect on the Serbian government.[287] Serbia was prepared to join Bulgaria and the other allies in mobilizing, but Pašić insisted that the date for the declaration of war be left open, to be decided only after the government in Vienna made its intentions clear. In case Austria-Hungary responded by mobilizing on Serbia's northern flank, the Serbs would have to defend themselves against her attack and must not be expected to join the other allies in the war against the Turks. Without being too explicit, Geshov, however, appeared to be arguing that the burden of checking Austria-Hungary's moves should be left to Russia. Once the ultimatums were presented to the Porte, all four allied states would have to enter the struggle.[288] A face-to-face meeting between Pašić and Danev, which was proposed by Geshov and took place on 21 September in Pašić's private coach on the train between Lapovo and Niš, failed to resolve the dissensions.[289]

In the end the Turks themselves provided the allies with the pretext to lay aside the remaining differences and step up the war plans. On 23 September the Turkish authorities in Salonica and Skopje detained 20 car-loads of war materials destined for Serbia. They comprised mainly ammunition which the Serbian government had ordered in France in the previous year,[290] and Constantinople had approved their transfer through Turkish territory only ten days earlier.[291] Around the same time the Turkish artillery on the island of Samos shelled the Greek ship *Rumelia* and the boat of the Greek consulate bearing the Greek flag.[292] The following day, 24 September, the Turks mobilized 100,000 men in the Adrianople vilayet, near the Bulgarian frontier, 'to help the Government [in Sofia] cool down the hot-heads in Bulgaria.'[293] This was followed by the call-up of ten reserve divisions throughout European Turkey.[294] With such actions, commented Neratov, 'Turkey flings a challenge at the Balkan states, which are even without it in a highly bellicose frame of mind in relation to her.'[295]

The Balkan states picked up the challenge immediately. On 25 September, the Bulgarian government decided to commence mobilization and appealed to Athens, Belgrade, and Cetinje to do the same in accordance with the terms of their 'defensive alliances.'[296] At the same time it requested the Serbian government to send an emissary to Sofia to sign the agreement between the two general staffs.[297]

Pašić agreed to join Bulgaria in ordering mobilization on 29 September, but he wished to do so under the disguise of carrying out military manœuvres.[298] This was not acceptable to Geshov, who persuaded him to justify it instead by referring to the holding up of the ammunitions and the Turkish mobilizations.[299] The general staffs agreement, the text of which was brought to Sofia by Colonel Pavlović, was signed by General Fichev on 28 September, and by *Vojvoda* Putnik on 29 September.[300]

The Greeks wanted to combine the mobilization with the annexation of Crete to Greece. But there was a danger that, if Greece joined the other allies in mobilizing and the great powers later forced them to demobilize, Greece might end up alone in a war with Turkey over the Cretan question. A special declaration attached to the treaty of alliance with Bulgaria freed the Bulgarians from all obligations to Greece in the event of a conflict over the island of Crete. Consequently, Venizelos now asked that, in return for mobilizing together with Bulgaria and Serbia, Bulgaria pronounce this declaration void and accept the Cretan problem as an integral component of the treaty of alliance.[301] When Geshov consented and communicated to Athens a declaration to that effect,[302] the Greek government agreed to start the mobilization with Bulgaria and Serbia on 29 September.[303]

The Bulgarian, Greek, and Serbian governments officially proclaimed a state of general mobilization on 30 September. Montenegro followed suit on 1 October; and Turkey responded on 2 October.[304] A few days earlier, on 28 September, Bulgaria had given King Nikola carte blanche to launch the attack which set off the war of the allied Balkan states against the Ottoman Empire.[305]

3

The war against Turkey

The mobilization in Turkey and the Balkan states represented a great set-back for Russia's drive to avert the outbreak of war in the Near East.[1] For the first time Pevchevskii Most had to concede that its influence over its Balkan protégés might not prevail. Russian diplomacy had helped them unite, but they now appeared to have chosen their own course of action. On 1 October 1912, A. Neratov told Julius von Szilassy, special Austrian minister at St Petersburg, that war seemed unavoidable. He doubted that it could be prevented even if Turkey accepted reforms. Bulgaria had decided on war. Serbia, Greece, and Montenegro would gladly partake in it.[2]

To be sure, the allied leaders insisted on their peaceful intentions. They maintained that the war would be averted if the great powers forced Constantinople to implement article 23 of the Treaty of Berlin, to appoint Christian *valis* (governors) from the neutral powers of Europe, and to establish an international police force in European Turkey.[3] But, as Nekliudov pointed out, they were not sincere and serious about the reforms. They raised the question in order to hasten developments and to engage the opinion of Europe.[4] 'To my great regret I consider the war inevitable' he wrote. 'The declaration of war will follow the mobilization and the military hostilities soon after the declaration of war.'[5] A. Giers reported from Cetinje on 1 October that in line with the obligations undertaken by the allies the military operations would begin on 8 or 9 October and perhaps sooner.[6]

Even at this late date, however, Sazonov had not given up all hope and remained confident that the powers could devise a scheme of reforms to appease the allies.[7] Until the last moment he continued to warn the allied governments that in a war against Turkey they would be embarking on a hopeless venture. Russia would not sacrifice her national interests to bail them out. 'You must not expect our aid,' he warned M. Madzharov, the Bulgarian minister in London. Bulgaria should not rely on the support of Greece and Serbia either as Greece had nothing to offer and whatever assistance Serbia could provide would be nullified by Austria-Hungary.[8]

Playing on Belgrade's fears of Austrian intervention, Sazonov again sought to isolate and disarm Bulgaria, which he viewed as the main culprit. He instructed Hartwig to act in common with the Austrian minister, and to advise the Serbian leaders that he has been reliably informed of Austria's plans to attack Serbia in the event of a war against Turkey.[9] Should Belgrade disregard Russia's friendly counsel the Serbs would be left to their own fate.[10]

Sazonov had tried to isolate Bulgaria earlier and failed. His failure this time was not less decisive. As Nekliudov pointed out, the attempts to isolate Bulgaria by intimidating her allies only stirred resentment against the powers among the Bulgarians. In any event, the great powers could not stop them from attacking Turkey because the Bulgarians were certain that at the first sight of bloodshed the Serbs and the Greeks would join with them.[11]

On 1 October 1912, Geshov dispatched a strongly worded telegram to Paris where Sazonov was expected to arrive from London. He asked D. Stanchov to

Inform Sazonov that we are surprised at today's declaration of Hartwig in Belgrade to the effect that he would act in common with his Austrian colleague. I hope that in accordance with Nekliudov's categorical assurances that if we ally with the Serbs there would be no understandings between Austria and Russia, the latter will not concur with the former to exert pressure against us, and would leave Austria, if she wished, to act alone. In a circular of July 23, 1908, Russia reserved for herself the right to return to the reforms agreed upon at Reval between her and Britain. The latter is today hypnotized by Kiamil Pasha, a man without a party, without a past and without a future, for whom no one could guarantee that he would not be overthrown by tomorrow. And to pamper him England is sacrificing the Balkan Christians, repeating the crime that she perpetrated at the Congress of Berlin. We beg Russia most cogently not to become accessory to that crime.[12]

To make his government's position doubly clear Geshov told Nekliudov and the other two Entente ministers at Sofia that 'Bulgaria would wage the war even if left alone.'[13]

During the first week of October the allied governments embarked on final preparations for the war. Serbia and Montenegro negotiated the last details of the plan for joint military operations, while Bulgaria and Serbia reached agreement for the transfer of Serbian troops and ammunition through Bulgarian territory.[14] On 2

October, the Serbs sent to Sofia and Athens their draft of the ultimatum which the allies planned to dispatch to the Porte.[15] The same day Cetinje informed the allied governments that Montenegro had decided to commence the war on 9 October.[16]

In addition to the direct representations and interventions in the Balkan capitals, Russia endeavoured to forestall the outbreak of the war and, if that failed, to localize it in collaboration with the other great powers. The new talks were again based on an initiative taken by the French premier. On 29 September, Poincaré suggested to Izvol'skii that in the event that a collective representation of all the great powers proved unfeasible, it could be undertaken by Russia and Austria-Hungary, as the two most interested powers, in the name of Europe's two power groupings.[17]

Neratov thought Poincaré's proposal offered the most suitable way out. On this basis Russia could reach an agreement with Austria-Hungary, the guiding principle of which would be the abstention by both sides from unilateral interventions in the Balkan crisis.[18] On 1 October, Sazonov had a meeting in London with Count A. von Mensdorff, the Austrian ambassador. He told him that Russia intended to limit herself to diplomatic measures to pacify the allies and expressed the hope that Vienna would act likewise and would not resort to the use of military force.[19] Berchtold concurred completely with Sazonov's views. However, he emphasized that the great powers should act jointly. They should make it absolutely clear to the Balkan states that they would not be permitted to derive any territorial advantages from a war against Turkey.[20]

A few days later Sazonov met Poincaré in Paris and reiterated Russia's readiness to make representations in the Balkan capitals, either with Austria-Hungary in the name of Europe or together with all the great powers. However, he maintained that warning the allies that the powers would not tolerate the violation of peace and changes in the territorial status quo if war broke out would be useless unless the great powers were prepared to facilitate the execution of reforms in favour of the Balkan nationalities.[21]

On the basis of his talks with Sazonov the French premier drafted the proposed representation and conveyed it to the other great powers.[22] It contained three major points informing the allied and the Turkish governments: 1) The great powers condemned all measures capable of violating the peace. 2) If in the end war broke out between the Porte and the Balkan states they would not tolerate any changes in the territorial status quo in the 'Balkans.' 3) In the interest of the 'Christian' nationalities they would 'take into their own hands' the execution of reforms in the government of 'European Turkey' based on 'Article 23 of the Treaty of Berlin' on condition that these reforms would in no way endanger the territorial integrity of the Ottoman Empire.[23]

Sazonov agreed to the proposed draft[24] and so did Kiderlen-Wächter,[25] while Berchtold suggested a few changes in the wording[26] which were accepted by the others.[27] The British government alone showed strong reservations to both the suggested procedure and the text. Nicolson thought that Austria-Hungary and Russia should be empowered to act only in the Balkan capitals and that the representation in Constantinople should be made by all the great powers.[28] Moreover, Whitehall considered Poincaré's draft unnecessarily strong as far as it concerned the Turks. It objected especially to the phrase 'They [the great powers] will take into their own hands,' because, as Nicolson put it: 'It eliminates the participation of Turkey ... and makes the concurrence of Turkey impossible.'[29]

Consequently, Grey proposed two different notes: one, containing the first two articles of Poincaré's draft to be delivered to the allied governments by the Russian and Austro-Hungarian representatives, the other, comprising a revised version of the third article to be delivered at the Porte by the representatives of the great powers.[30] Pressed by Russia and France,[31] on 6 October Grey and Nicolson dropped some of the objections in a meeting with Benckendorff and Cambon at the French embassy.[32] They accepted Poincaré's draft, as amended by Berchtold, as the final text of the démarche to be made by Russia and Austria-Hungary in the Balkan capitals.[33] As for the note to Constantinople, Grey again suggested a revised version of Poincaré's third point, which would take into consideration a recent declaration of the Porte of its readiness to put into effect the reforms foreseen in the Vilayet Law of 1880.[34] He also proposed that the great powers guarantee to Turkey the integrity of her European possessions. And, finally, to make it easier on the Turkish government, he favoured the milder, individual representations to a collective one.[35]

Sazonov thought that Grey was being unduly indulgent with the Turks. It was rather late to try to appease the Balkan governments by asking them to have faith in the Turkish government. They demanded guarantees from Europe that the reforms would be put into effect[36] but, in the end, Sazonov decided to go along with the British proposal. The final text, which was approved by the great powers,[37] merely states:

The five Powers notify the Porte that they take into consideration the public declaration of the Turkish Government of its intention to introduce reforms and that they would enter immediately into discussions with the Porte, – in the spirit of Article 23 of the Treaty of Berlin and the Law of 1880 – about the necessary reforms in the government of European Turkey. [They would also discuss] the measures required to secure their implementation in the interest of the nationalities on the indispensable condition that these reforms will in no way endanger the territorial integrity of the Ottoman Empire.[38]

The same day the text was approved, 7 October 1912, Sazonov informed the allies of the agreement and expressed confidence that the Porte would respond favourably to the demands of the great powers. Therefore, he warned them to avoid any sudden actions that might aggravate the situation and disrupt the peace. As he put it: 'there is no doubt that the Balkan states will not achieve, at the price of bloodletting, very heavy losses, and internal shocks, concessions greater than the ones that the Powers intend to extract from Turkey in favour of the Christian nationalities.'[39]

The consensus on the démarches reconciled at least temporarily the suspicions and adverse aims of the powers. Both Vienna and St Petersburg required a European guarantee of the territorial status quo in the Balkans: Austria-Hungary in order to justify a course of action she might deem necessary in the event of a decisive allied victory; and Russia to forestall the possible Austrian intervention against the allies, and to safeguard the territorial integrity of the Balkan states. Actually, the consensus represented a significant success for Russia's diplomacy since it meant that the war between the Balkan nations and Turkey would be localized. According to Neratov, the localization of the war was the most effective assistance that the allies could have expected from Russia in the then existing political situation.[40] However, to further insure the allies and thus safeguard Russia's national aims, direct talks with Vienna seemed necessary. Neratov was the chief advocate at Pevchevskii Most of some sort of bilateral agreement with Austria-Hungary.[41]

In a long letter to Sazonov on 6 September 1912, Nekliudov discussed the situation in the peninsula and put forth the course of policy he considered most suitable for Russia. Convinced that the war would break out before the spring of 1913, Nekliudov argued that the Russian Black Sea fleet should be prepared for every eventuality. Russia could then make it clear to all concerned that if Austria invaded Serbia, Russia would occupy temporarily the Black Sea coast between Burgas and the Straits until Austria evacuated her troops from the foreign soil. In this manner Russia would aid Serbia and at the same time assist Bulgaria by drawing a considerable part of the Turkish forces toward the Bosphorus.[42] Shortly after the mobilizations Nekliudov proposed the neutralization of the Black Sea for both Turkey and Bulgaria.[43]

On the basis of Nekliudov's recommendations Neratov advanced a scheme which tied together the questions of the Sanjak of Novi Pazar and the Black Sea. In a telegram to Sazonov in London he proposed that Russia should try to strengthen her position in dealing with the government in Vienna by making it clear that if Austria-Hungary occupied the Sanjak of Novi Pazar, Russia would undertake all necessary measures to protect the Black Sea basin from the Turkish fleet and, if need be, some action in the Caucasus.[44] Russia should also notify Turkey that she would not permit the spread of hostilities into the Black Sea. The neutralization of the Black Sea would safeguard the commercial interests of Russia and protect the undefended coast of Bulgaria from the Turkish navy. Any failure of the Turkish government to respect the neutralization would, however, provide Russia with an opportunity to dispatch her war-ships to the neighbourhood of the Straits.[45]

Sazonov was as eager as Neratov to secure a guarantee that Austria would not intervene in the conflict. However, he was not prepared to give Vienna a voice in the affairs of the Black Sea for the sake of the Sanjak of Novi Pazar.[46] Moreover, he did not wish to alienate Turkey by threats or by the actual use of force. But he asked Pevchevskii Most to study the question further and to submit to him the findings and conclusions before it was raised officially with the Porte.[47] Neratov doubted that friendly appeals would suffice to deter the Turks. Indeed, Turkhan Pasha, the Turkish ambassador at St Petersburg, made it clear that his government reserved for itself complete freedom of action in the Black Sea in the event of war.[48] The Black Sea was of great strategic importance for Turkey's war effort. Unless the Turkish navy took some sort of preventive action in its waters, Bulgarian torpedo-boats would provide a constant danger to the Turkish ships transporting men and supplies from northern Anatolia to European Turkey.[49]

Neratov seemed convinced, therefore, that only a strong declaration amounting to an ultimatum would force Turkey to back down. But, since such a strong measure involved the risk of provoking some of the great powers, he again urged Sazonov to reach a preliminary understanding with Vienna on the neutralization of both the Black Sea and the Sanjak of Novi Pazar. Armed with such an agreement Russia would be in a position to warn, and if necessary, to force Turkey to stay out of the Black Sea without risking the retaliation of Europe.[50] The Ministry of War and the general staff shared and supported Neratov's views.[51]

As events turned out, however, such an agreement proved unnecessary after all, because the Sanjak of Novi Pazar was, for all practical purposes, already neutralized. First of all it was not as important for the Serbian and Montenegrin military operations as Pevchevskii Most believed.[52] The Turks had moved most of their garrisons into Old Serbia and Macedonia; and the Serbs planned to send into the southern extremities of the Sanjak, far from the Austrian border, only a small contingent of troops during the first days of the war. Secondly, by early October, the Serbs were much less concerned with the possibility of an Austrian intervention. They held the view that if Austria really intended to intervene, she would have moved before they succeeded in arousing and secretly arming the population of the Sanjak.[53]

The Serbs were correct, for immediately after the mobilizations Vienna notified the Porte that Austria-Hungary would not protect the Sanjak of Novi Pazar.[54] Piecemeal reports of the decision reached Pevchevskii Most via the War

Ministry.[55] But it still remained in the dark as to the real intentions and plans of Vienna.

On 6 October 1912, N. Giers raised this question with Count Berchtold. He asked the Austrian government not to react even if Serbia decided to occupy the Sanjak. Such an occupation, he argued, would in any event be of a temporary nature, since the final settlement would be exclusively in the hands of the great powers and these had already reached an agreement on the need to preserve the status quo in the Balkans and to safeguard the territorial integrity of the Ottoman Empire. Berchtold assured Giers that Vienna would remain till the end loyal to the 'agreed-upon program and the localization of the war.' Austria-Hungary had no pretensions beyond her borders. But, as the Russian ambassador noted, throughout the conversation 'he did not once utter the words Sanjak of Novi Pazar.'[56] The following day Sazonov saw Szilassy who still gave him an evasive – but less ambiguous – reply. Szilassy told him that his acquaintance with Count Berchtold's views allowed him to think that Austria-Hungary would take calmly the Serbian military operations in the Sanjak. Her aims were confined to the protection of the general tranquillity in the region contiguous to the theatre of military operations.[57]

Sazonov passed this information confidentially to Belgrade. He advised the Serbs again not to extend the military hostilities too far to the north and thus provoke Austria to discard her neutral posture.[58] About the same time Sazonov responded to repeated requests from Sofia[59] and informed Turkhan Pasha that Russia was strongly opposed to all war activities in the Black Sea basin. Should Turkey disregard this warning, Russia would be forced to resort to drastic measures to protect her economic and commercial interests.[60]

II

When Sazonov returned to St Petersburg from his trip through the Western capitals the war in the Balkans appeared imminent.[61] On 8 October 1912, the ministers of Russia and Austria-Hungary made the representations to the allied governments.[62] Two days later the ambassadors of the five great powers at Constantinople handed identical notes to the Porte.[63]

The initial reactions of the individual allies left no doubt of what was to follow. Koromilas told Demidov, the Russian minister at Athens, that the allies had no confidence in Turkey's promises even when the great powers were behind the reforms. 'The Mürzsteg Agreement showed clearly the precarious nature of the unanimity of Europe.' He doubted if the apparent unity would prove more durable or more lasting this time. Greece intended to utilize the existing favourable conditions and place her entire trust in the solidarity of the Balkan states to win the needed reforms.[64] Geshov drew the attention of Nekliudov and Tarnowski, the Austro-Hungarian ambassador at Sofia, to the fact that the note of the powers contained neither a precise specification of the proposed reforms nor a guarantee that they would be put into effect.[65] Hartwig reported from Belgrade that by joining with Austria-Hungary Russia had made a rather disturbing impression on all the Balkan states and especially on Serbia.[66] Pašić warned him and Urgon, the Austro-Hungarian minister at Belgrade, not to expect a favourable reply; he no longer possessed the authority to forestall 'the fateful way out.' The state authority had passed into the hands of the military commanders. A return to a peaceful solution was no longer possible and further representations from the great powers, while undermining the prestige of Europe, would not secure the sought-after aim.[67]

Montenegro had already severed all relations with Turkey. On 8 October, the Montenegrin chargé d'affaires at Constantinople, after informing the Porte that 'the fortunes of Montenegro's arms' would 'decide the cause of the Montenegrins as well as their brothers, whose rights had been violated through centuries,' left the Turkish capital for home.[68] The government had already left Cetinje for military headquarters. A. Giers and Baron Giesl, Vienna's envoy at Cetinje, were received by King Nikola, who had stayed behind for this very purpose. 'I regret that the intervention of the Powers comes rather late,' replied the king after he listened to the representation. 'In the present moment the state of the Kingdom is such that even if our allies renounced their commitments toward us – which I do not assume for a minute – the mood of my peoples would force me to attack.'[69] After the audience King Nikola joined his government in Podgorica where he issued the official declaration of war against Turkey on the same day. The military hostilities commenced at 7 o'clock in the morning of the following day, 9 October 1912.[70]

Since the Russian leaders were not acquainted with the concrete plans and intentions of the Balkan states, they were not certain whether Montenegro had acted independently or in accord with her allies.[71] Neratov urgently advised Sofia, Belgrade, and Athens not to follow the lead of Cetinje.[72] 'Acting Minister of Foreign Affairs was today less pessimistic,' wrote Buchanan from St Petersburg on 9 October, 'and did not think it extinguished all hope of a peaceful termination to the crisis.' If Turkey at once announced her readiness to place the question of reforms in the hands of the powers, the governments of the three Balkan states might be able to hold back the popular movement in favour of war.[73]

Needless to say, even Neratov's restrained optimism was out of place at this time. On 12 October, the allies officially rejected the joint Russian–Austro-Hungarian representations.[74] In identical notes they argued that, because of Turkey's past failures to put into effect reforms which were recorded in international agreements, they felt obliged to obtain more binding and more radical reforms for the Christian population of the empire. For this reason they intended to address themselves directly to the government of His Majesty the Sultan.[75]

This allied note, which was really an ultimatum, had been prepared before the declaration of the mobilizations, and was handed to the Turkish representatives in Athens, Belgrade, and Sofia on 13 October.[76] The three allied governments called on Turkey to join with them and the great powers in elaborating and introducing in her European provinces immediate reforms based on the nationality principle as defined in article 23 of the Treaty of Berlin. The actual implementation of the proposed reforms was to be entrusted to a council composed of an equal number of Christians and Muslims under the direct supervision of the ambassadors of the great powers and the ministers of the Balkan states at Constantinople. They set a deadline of six months for the execution of all the reforms specified in the note and the explanatory annex that was attached to it.[77] Finally, as a proof of her assent, they requested Turkey to retract immediately the mobilization decree.[78]

Around the middle of October, Turkey rejected both the démarche of the great powers of 10 October and the collective note of the three Balkan states. To be sure, in its reply to the great powers of 14 October, the Turkish government reiterated its intention to introduce reforms. But this was to be accomplished without foreign interference and with the full approval and consent of the Ottoman parliament.[79] The reply to the Balkan allies was an unqualified rejection which was accompanied by the recall of the Turkish diplomatic representatives from Athens, Belgrade, and Sofia.[80]

In the mean time, even before they received the official replies from the allied and Turkish governments, the great powers were engaged in yet another last-minute round of talks to prevent the outbreak of war. When Nekliudov and Tarnowski delivered the representation at Sofia, Geshov inquired about the nature of the control of the great powers over the reforms.[81] Through Count Széczen, Vienna's ambassador at Paris, Berchtold requested Poincaré to respond to that enquiry and, on 11 October, the French premier proposed a conference of the powers and Turkey in Paris to consider the reforms proposed in the Vilayet Law of 1880.[82] In view of the demands of the allies a conference devoted to these mild reforms was doomed to fail from the start. Besides, as Sazonov pointed out, it was rather late to talk about reforms since Montenegro was already in a state of war and the other Balkan states were expected to follow suit shortly. Consequently, Sazonov asked Poincaré to propose, instead, a conference which would deal with the actual termination of hostilities.[83] In his four point proposal of 13 October, Poincaré attempted to take care of both eventualities.[84] He now called again for a conference of the powers and Turkey to draw up a program of reforms. In the event that Turkey declined and war broke out, the powers would take up the question of mediation. If the mediation proved successful they would meet and decide on the reforms. Otherwise, the conference would convene at the end of the war to decide the question of peace and the common interests of Europe.[85]

The powers, and particularly Russia and Austria-Hungary, accepted in principle the mediation and the conference. But, for the time being, that was the extent of their agreement.[86] The government in Vienna insisted on safeguarding the sovereignty of the sultan and the complete territorial integrity of his empire.[87] St Petersburg was prepared to go along with this in the event of a Turkish victory or a stalemated war. However, in case of a decisive allied victory Russia had to bear in mind the aims of the allies since the future of the Balkan system of alliances depended on the realization of their territorial aspirations.[88] Poincaré's last-minute efforts to bridge the differences between these two powers remained inconclusive.[89] They coincided with and were overshadowed by the actual outbreak of war.

On 17 October 1912, two days after the Porte rejected their collective ultimatum, Bulgaria, Greece, and Serbia broke off all diplomatic ties with the Ottoman Empire.[90] The declarations of war and the opening of military hostilities followed on the next day, 18 October.[91] All further talks between the powers had to be postponed pending the initial results of the armed struggle.

The outbreak of the war was welcomed in the Balkan states with an overwhelming public acclaim. Huge demonstrations in its support took place in the allied capitals and other cities and towns. In Sofia, Panas and Nenadić addressed crowds singing the patriotic *Shumi Maritsa*.[92] In front of the Bulgarian embassy at Belgrade the crowds shouted: 'Long live His Highness Tsar Ferdinand, Long live the fraternal Bulgarian nation and its valiant army.'[93] Never before and never again was the solidarity of the Balkan nations manifested so enthusiastically.[94] The traditional animosities seemed to have been forgotten. Leon Trotskii, at the time a correspondent for *Kievskaia Mysl'* in the Balkans, wrote that they had finally united around the slogan: 'The Balkans for the Balkan peoples.'[95]

During the slightly more than two weeks separating the mobilizations from the declarations of war the allies had completed the necessary military preparations. On the eve of the war the Bulgarian army numbered 366,000 men,[96] the Serbian 190,000, the Greek 120,000 plus a considerable navy, and the Montenegrin 40,000.[97] According to the plan of the Turkish general staff, in a state of full mobilization Turkey expected over 1,000,000 men under the colours. In reality, however, she succeeded in mobilizing only 420,000 men to face the enemy.[98]

The allies did not possess a joint plan for military operations. Separate agreements existed only between Serbia and Bulgaria and Serbia and Montenegro.[99] The bulk of the Bulgarian army was engaged on the eastern front in Thrace. The

Serbian army, reinforced by two Bulgarian divisions, and the Greek and Montenegrin armies operated in the west in Macedonia, Old Serbia, Epirus, and Albania. The small Bulgarian navy protected the Black Sea coast and the Greek fleet engaged the Turks in the waters of the Aegean Sea.[100]

The main Turkish plan of operations, which was prepared in September, had divided the Turkish army into two groups: the eastern numbering about 183,000 and the Adrianople garrison of 70,000 men, and the western comprising about 156,000 men. It called for an all-out offensive in the east and a defensive war in the west until the Bulgarian forces in Thrace were crushed.[101] In spite of the overwhelming numerical superiority of the allies in the west, a last-minute revision of this plan, on 16 October, ordered offensive operations on both fronts.[102] Consequently, the plans of both belligerent camps called for an all-out offensive war.

Already in the course of the first week of the war the Turks suffered costly defeats at Mustafa Pasha (Svilengrad), Gerkenli, Selioulu, Erikler. Demoralized and panic-stricken, they were pushed back and on 24 October the Bulgarians occupied Lozengrad.[103] The mass retreat of the enemy enabled the Bulgarians to begin the siege of Adrianople which was completed by 12 November.[104] The failure of the third Bulgarian army under General R. Dimitriev to pursue the panic-stricken Turkish forces after the fall of Lozengrad provided them with an opportunity to stop the retreat and regroup along the line Liule Burgas–Bunar Khisar.[105] This breathing space was, however, all too short. By the end of October the Bulgarians resumed their drive and after four days of heavy fighting – probably the bloodiest of the Balkan wars – they captured Liule Burgas. The defeated Turkish troops were hurled back and did not stop their disorderly retreat until they reached the Chatalja line of fortifications.[106] In the south the Bulgarian units occupied one town after another and advanced toward the Aegean Sea. On 5 November, they captured Drama and cut off the strategic railway connection between Salonica and Constantinople. On 27 November, they routed a large Turkish force at Sverkhomūl' and occupied Dedeagach (Alexandropolis).[107] In just over a month of fighting the Bulgarians were entrenched on the Aegean, the Sea of Marmara, and stood at the Chatalja line of fortifications only forty kilometres from the Ottoman capital.

The Turkish armies did not fare better in the west. On 8 October, the small Montenegrin army had moved into the Sanjak of Novi Pazar and toward Scutari. It advanced quickly through the Sanjak taking Bijelo Polje on 24 October, and Plevlje, the last fortified Turkish point in the north, on 29 October. In the south Berana fell on 14 October, and Plava on the 19th, and it moved into Old Serbia toward Peć (Ipek). The battle of Scutari began on 10 October. The initial set-backs suffered by Montenegro forced King Nikola to blockade the city, and to complete the seige he had to await the arrival of additional Montenegrin and Serbian reinforcements.[108]

The Serbs advanced into the Sanjak on 19 October, and occupied Novi Pazar on the 23rd and Kosovska Mitrovica on the 25th. Their attempt to capture the town of Peć, the ancient seat of the Serbian patriarchal see, was frustrated by the Montenegrins on 30 October. By the end of the first week of November the Sanjak of Novi Pazar and the Vilayet of Kosovo-Metohia were under the control of either Serbia or Montenegro.[109]

In the heart of the Balkans, in Macedonia, the Turks faced the bulk of the Serbian army in the north, two Bulgarian divisions in the east, and the Greek army in the south and southwest. When the Serbs crossed the frontier and advanced toward Ovče Pole in the night of 19–20 October, the Turks attempted to drive them back but failed. The Serbs then resumed the attack and on 24 October destroyed the Turkish positions at the great battle of Kumanovo. The defeated Turkish army evacuated Skopje and withdrew toward Bitola (Monastir).[110] Meanwhile, in the east the two Bulgarian divisions moved south and without encountering heavy resistance occupied Štip, Strumica, and Demir Hisar. On 1 November, the Bulgarian high command ordered them to make a dash for Salonica before it fell into the hands of the Greeks.[111]

The Greek army under the command of Crown Prince Constantine was concentrated in northern Thessaly. A smaller force destined for offensive operations in Epirus and southern Albania had been assembled near the Gulf of Arta. At the outset the task of the Greeks in Macedonia, where they faced only four weak Turkish divisions, was not difficult. They captured Elasson on 19 October and three days later routed the Turks at the Pass of Sarandaporo. Tahsin Pasha, the Turkish commanding officer, regrouped some of his troops at Enidže Vardar, to protect the approaches to Salonica, and the remaining Turkish forces retreated toward Bitola.[112]

Since the capture and occupation of Salonica was of crucial importance for the future territorial settlement in Macedonia, Crown Prince Constantine was determined to get there before the small Bulgarian force. Consequently, he sent only one division to pursue the retreating Turkish army and pushed east with the bulk of his forces. On 3 and 4 November he stormed the Turkish positions at Enidže Vardar but was repulsed. Two days later the attack succeeded and the Turks were driven into the city.[113]

The Bulgarians were approaching Salonica as well, but on 8 November, when they were within ten kilometres of it, Crown Prince Constantine informed them that the Turks were negotiating with him and therefore he no longer needed their assistance. The same evening Tahsin Pasha surrendered Salonica to Constantine.

The Bulgarian advance units arrived the following day. The Greeks had won the race to Salonica but the Bulgarians were by no means ready to renounce their own claims. For the duration of the war against Turkey they shared the joint, but extremely uneasy, occupation of this prized possession.[114]

From Salonica most of the Greek troops moved west toward Kožani and Florina (Lerin) to assist their defeated and retreating compatriots and to ease the pressure on the Serbian positions around Bitola. After the battle of Kumanovo one Serbian division was sent to help the Bulgarians in the siege of Adrianople. The rest pushed south toward Bitola, capturing Tetovo, Prilep, and Kičevo on the way. The Turks had taken strong fortified positions north of Bitola and were determined to stand their ground. In the battle, which lasted five days, the Serbs led by Crown Prince Alexander inflicted a devastating defeat on their enemy and entered Bitola. The Greeks captured Florina on the same day. All that remained for the allies in the western theatre of war was to march through Albania to the Adriatic Sea and to complete the siege and force the surrender of Scutari and the fortress of Yanina in Epirus.[115]

In the relatively short time of a month and a half the allies had conquered nearly the whole of European Turkey from the Adriatic Sea to the Chatalja line of fortifications. When the armistice agreement was concluded on 3 December 1912, Turkish resistance west of Chatalja was restricted to the fortified positions of Adrianople, Yanina, and Scutari.

When the war broke out neither the great powers nor the belligerents were able to foretell its eventual outcome. Russia and her partners in the Entente hoped for and at the same time dreaded the consequences of an allied victory. Austria-Hungary and the other powers of the Triple Alliance wished for and appeared confident of a Turkish victory. In any case they had all agreed on the need to localize the war and to discuss at an opportune moment the question of mediation. What constituted *un temps opportun* was, of course, left in the air because of their divergent expectations.

Destined to bear the entire burden of bailing out the allies from a disastrous defeat, Russia envisaged a great powers intervention after the first decisive encounters in the field.[116] Even the allies, and particularly Bulgaria, which faced the best and most numerous Turkish forces, considered this alternative before the outbreak of the war.[117] When S.S. Bobchev left Sofia on 17 October to become Bulgaria's minister at St Petersburg, he was instructed to work for the immediate intervention of the powers.[118] A few days after hostilities had commenced Buchanan reported to Grey that Sazonov 'was most anxious that the Powers should intervene in the war at the first possible moment and according to a report just received from the Russian Minister in Sofia, that moment might present itself shortly, perhaps within a week.'[119]

To prepare the ground for it the Russian government sought to initiate preliminary consultations with London and Paris. 'It was most necessary that there should be no divergence of views between the Powers of the Triple Entente in any discussion in which all the Powers were engaged,' Neratov told Buchanan.[120] The Foreign Office agreed, but believed it best if Pevchevskii Most submitted a scheme of reforms to serve as a basis for the discussions.[121]

In consultation with Grey and Nicolson, Count Benckendorff, the Russian ambassador in London, prepared and conveyed to Sazonov on 21 October a project that reflected the views of the British government and which he thought might take the place of Poincaré's last four point program. It proposed that Russia and Austria-Hungary be empowered by Europe to intervene in the Balkan conflict whenever they deemed it feasible, while the powers backed this move at Constantinople. At the same time it advanced to the two belligerent sides the following general conditions for the conclusion of peace: first, direct control over Constantinople and the adjoining region by Turkey; second, nominal Turkish sovereignty over the rest of European Turkey where fundamental reforms were to be introduced under the direct control of the great powers; third, no changes in the territorial possessions of the belligerents.[122]

Sazonov appreciated the recent improvement of relations with Vienna: it made possible the agreement on the localization of the war. However, in connection with the mediation and the questions that would arise at the end of the war, he preferred to work closely with France, Britain, and Italy.[123] In response to Count Benckendorff's proposal he drew up and sent to London and Paris a program of reforms;[124] this restated with some minor modifications the provisions of the Vilayet Law of 1880. Such reforms were to be put into effect in a number of autonomous regions to be created, under the formal sovereignty of the sultan, west of the line stretching from the mouth of the Maritsa through Adrianople to the Black Sea. As Benckendorff had suggested, the area to the east of this line, namely, Constantinople and the adjoining regions, was to remain under the real sovereignty of the sultan.[125]

This proposal represented Russia's final gesture in support of the pre-war territorial status quo. The battles of Lozengrad, Kumanovo, Liule Burgas, and so on demonstrated the superiority of the allied arms and left no doubt as to the final outcome of the war.[126] The press and public opinion in Russia were, as was to be expected, vehement in their support of the demands of the allies. The influential *Novoe Vremia* was undoubtedly voicing the opinion of the great majority of politically conscious Russians when it asked: 'If the Slavs and the Greeks prove victorious, where is the iron hand that will preserve the *status quo* and that will snatch from them the fruits of victories which they will have purchased with their blood?'[127] They attacked Sazonov's pro-status quo and hence pro-Austrian policy as a direct act of hostility against the Slavs. They called for Sazonov's resignation and, indeed, there were rumours that he would be forced to resign.[128]

Pevchevskii Most could not remain oblivious to the critics, who had no difficulty in showing the short-sightedness of the pro-status quo line. They pointed to the fact, which was well known in St Petersburg, that Austria-Hungary was engaged in intrigues and pursued a double-faced policy in the Balkans. Vienna officially preached the status quo and opposed the aims of Serbia; but after the initial successes in the field it secretly offered Sofia material and financial aid and promised to support Bulgaria's territorial acquisitions.[129] It was obvious that Austria sought to draw Bulgaria away from Russia and Serbia and back into her own sphere of influence and in this way secure her interests in the direction of Salonica and the Aegean Sea. In short, she was attempting to destroy Russia's influence and assure her ascendancy in the Balkans by disrupting the Balkan system of alliances.[130] In these circumstances, as Sazonov put it, it was 'psychologically' impossible for Russia to oppose the Balkan states and their territorial expansion at a time when another power supported them.[131]

The combination of all these factors – the allied victories and demands, the pressure of public opinion and the press, Austria's policy, and to some extent the apparent support of Britain and France[132] – marked a turning point in the outlook and commitments of Russia. A policy aimed at depriving the Balkan states of all their conquests seemed highly unrealistic. 'It was clear to all that it would be impossible now to use the same language to the victors as was employed when their own strength and the hopeless weakness of their antagonist had not yet been exposed,' wrote Sazonov in his memoirs. 'It was necessary to find new formulas corresponding to the new situation.'[133] Or, as Izvol'skii told Poincaré, the powers would inevitably have to renounce the principle of status quo and allow territorial changes in favour of the allies.[134]

The demands of the allies, which were already known in St Petersburg,[135] amounted to the virtual exclusion of Turkey from Europe. Further talk of reforms at this time was useless, wrote Geshov on 1 November. 'The only acceptable solution ... would be the liquidation of European Turkey and its partition among the allies.'[136] Bulgaria claimed, and refused to be satisfied with anything short of, the San Stefano borders. Serbia wanted the Vilayet of Kosovo, the Sanjak of Novi Pazar, and northern Albania, in order to secure her place on the Adriatic Sea. The Montenegrins had their eyes set on the Vilayet of Scutari and the Greeks on southern Albania (or northern Epirus, as they liked to call it). However, Greek pretensions to parts of Macedonia were not as yet officially advertised. The allies had also made it clear that they were resolved to uphold all these demands even by the force of arms.[137]

Not long after Sazonov telegraphed his program of reforms to London and Paris, he accepted in principle the right of the allies to divide the conquered territories.[138] He told Buchanan that the reforms could now apply only to 'those portions of territory with a Christian population which were left to Turkey.'[139]

This change of heart surprised Buchanan as well as most foreign observers. On 30 October, he wrote to Grey:

Circumstances have now proved too strong for him [Sazonov]. After treating the Slavist propaganda carried in the press as a purely personal attack against himself, he has now made a complete *volte-face*, and has at the eleventh hour adopted the policy of his critics. Not only has he abandoned the idea of maintaining the principle of the *status quo*, but he will find himself forced to support the extreme territorial claims of the Balkan states before Europe. He is moreover, so impressed by the anti-Austrian utterances of the press that, while anxious to keep in close contact with Vienna and to come to a friendly understanding with Austria as regards the eventual settlement of the Balkan question, he declines to be seen keeping company with her in public and prefers that France, and not Austria and Russia should lead the concert.[140]

Sazonov's volte-face must also have come unexpectedly to the Russian representatives abroad, for at the end of October he deemed it necessary to explain to them Russia's past policies and the reasons for the change and to chart the new course. He acknowledged that the government had been attacked by the press and public opinion for discarding the legacy of the past, for entering into an understanding with Austria-Hungary, for selling out the interests of the Slavs, and for virtually having taken upon itself the responsibility of depriving the Balkan states by force of the fruits of their struggles and sacrifices. While dismissing some of these charges outright, he stressed that Pevchevskii Most had made good use of the apparent split between official and unofficial Russia. By pointing to the difficult situation created by the pressure of public opinion at home, St Petersburg was able to affect the views of the European chancelleries.[141]

From the very beginning of the deepening crisis in the Balkans, Sazonov continued, the imperial Foreign Ministry had sought to prevent the war. Having exhausted all means for achieving a peaceful resolution of the impending conflict, it then undertook all possible measures for the localization of the war. In attempting to achieve either of these two alternate goals Russia found it essential to establish direct contacts with Austria-Hungary, the power that would otherwise have intervened against the allies. At the same time Russia secured for the allies the neutrality of Rumania[142] as well. 'In this manner Russia succeeded peacefully in eliminating the danger of serious complications which threatened the allied Balkan states simultaneously on two fronts.'[143]

When Sazonov came to discuss the change of Russia's policy, its departure from the declaration of the inviolability of the territorial status quo, he put forward a new, but not very convincing, explanation. While until the outbreak of the war he had held the Bulgarian government responsible for it, he now threw the entire blame for failing to agree on reforms and consequently for the war itself on Turkey. Sazonov argued that the declaration in favour of the preservation of the status quo was inseparably tied to the condition that the powers would take into their hands the execution of the reforms. 'Who prevented them from carrying out this mission?,' Sazonov asked. 'The Balkan states? No, because ... they only requested a more precise elucidation of the guarantees included in the mentioned formula. On the contrary, Turkey ... replied that she would not permit foreign interference and that she would carry out the necessary reforms alone.' Once the second part of the formula – the execution of reforms by the powers – was rejected by the Turks, the first part – the declaration of the inviolability of the territorial status quo – lost its validity.[144]

Consequently, since the question of the status quo was no longer of chief significance, Russia would insist in future that, if it were violated, the following fundamental principles be observed: 1) the disinterestedness of the great powers in the territorial changes; 2) the division of the conquered territories among the Balkan states to be undertaken in accordance with the agreements which preceded their alliance. Sazonov included one additional condition, namely, that the region of Constantinople, east of the line from the mouth of the Maritsa via Adrianople to the Black Sea must remain under the real sovereignty of the sultan. In conclusion, Sazonov stressed that the above stipulations constituted the guiding principles of Russia's policy on the questions of mediation and the liquidation of the war. The Russian government could count on the support of Britain and on the timely initiative of France.[145]

The French initiative came immediately. In accordance with the principles enunciated by Sazonov, Poincaré[146] proposed, on 31 October 1912, a four point mediation procedure.[147] In a separate protocol, which had already been approved by London and St Petersburg, he asked the powers to declare their complete disinterestedness. The formula simply stated:

Recognizing that the moment feasible for the mediation between the belligerent sides in the Balkan Peninsula is nearing, and, preoccupied above else with the preservation of peace in Europe, the Powers declare that they enter upon this common task in the spirit of complete disinterestedness.[148]

Germany, Austria-Hungary, and Italy replied on 4 November, with identical notes. While they admitted the need for mediation, they were of the opinion, nonetheless, that it should be undertaken only when one of the belligerent sides requested it.[149] The notes made no reference to the principle of disinterestedness – Berchtold had rejected it earlier in a conversation with the French ambassador at Vienna.[150] Poincaré therefore had no alternative but to scrap the proposal for the time being, at least, that is, until one of the belligerents requested the mediation of the great powers.[151]

III

The collapse of Poincaré's initiative was a great set-back for St Petersburg for, as soon as Russia renounced the status quo in favor of the allies, she exposed herself to severe complications unless the powers agreed to bring the war to an immediate end. At this particular time, the beginning of November 1912, when the Bulgarian armies were poised at the Chatalja fortifications and the Serbs were pushing toward the Adriatic, the most explosive issues were those of Constantinople and the Straits and of Serbia's future presence on the Adriatic Sea. The former pitted Bulgaria against Russia; the latter, Serbia and, out of necessity, Russia against Austria-Hungary.

In almost all past negotiations with the Bulgarians dating back to the Treaty of San Stefano and the Congress of Berlin successive Russian governments had always stressed that, as long as the Ottoman Empire survived, they would not tolerate another power, great or small, at Constantinople and the Straits. When the 'Sick Man of Europe' passed away the region was to come under the control of the Russian Empire. This was made quite clear in the negotiations between Russia and Bulgaria in 1902 and 1910 and in the Serbo-Bulgarian negotiations of 1912.[152] On the eve of the war Pevchevskii Most reminded Sofia that, according to mutually accepted commitments, Bulgaria did not have the right to operate against Adrianople because it belonged within the sphere of Russia's influence.[153]

Neither the overwhelming success of Bulgarian arms in the east nor, as has been shown, the change in Russian policy in connection with the renunciation of the status quo principle altered Russia's attitude. After the earlier Russian declarations this should not have come as a surprise to the Balkan states, wrote Sazonov in the circular of 31 October.[154] Russia hoped that the Bulgarian government would take her interests into consideration and would not create difficult and embarrassing situations by attacking the Chatalja fortifications. For, although the allies, including Bulgaria, could count on the support of Russia for reforms and territorial acquisitions, Bulgaria must not encroach on the area around Constantinople and the Straits.[155] 'Be content with San Stefano Bulgaria and do not enter Constantinople under any circumstances,' Sazonov told Bobchev, Bulgarian minister at St Petersburg, 'because you will otherwise complicate your affairs too gravely.'[156] He warned that the occupation of Constantinople would provoke widespread riots and disorders which would force Turkey's creditors, especially Great Britain and France, to intervene to protect their interests in the Ottoman Empire. This would be disastrous for the allies, for without the backing of London and Paris it would be extremely difficult for Russia to defend their interests against Austria-Hungary and Rumania.[157]

It appears that Sazonov intentionally exaggerated the danger of Franco-British retaliation. Indeed, both the Quai d'Orsay and Whitehall considered Russia's attitude too rigid and disagreed with Sazonov: Poincaré feared that it might force the Bulgarians to rely on the powers of the Triple Alliance.[158] There was indeed something to this because Austria-Hungary and Germany, who were soliciting a break between Russia and Bulgaria, encouraged Ferdinand to move into the Ottoman capital.[159] Grey thought that the Bulgarians might find it essential to occupy Constantinople, at least temporarily, in order to prevent the re-forming of the Turkish army at Chatalja.[160] But he advised the Bulgarian government to try and convince St Petersburg that it did not intend either to remain in or to retain indefinitely Constantinople.[161]

The governing civilian and military circles in Sofia were divided on this issue. The extremists or 'romantics,' as Rizov called them, who were grouped around King Ferdinand, were determined to enter Constantinople. The moderates or 'realists' did not wish to alienate Russia, but they wanted to utilize the question of Constantinople to strengthen Bulgaria's position at the peace negotiations.[162] They asked Russia and the other powers to guarantee to Bulgaria as favourable a peace settlement as she could demand if her army captured Constantinople.[163]

The Russians were at first taken aback by these demands. They found it difficult to comprehend how Bulgaria could demand and expect more than the San Stefano boundaries which Russia had already promised.[164] But they could not maintain their stand for very long without the backing of the other powers. At a meeting between Premier Kokovtsov, Sazonov, and the ministers of war and the navy on 3 November, the military advisers acknowledged that Adrianople did not command the strategic importance vis-à-vis Constantinople which they had ascribed to it until then.[165] They agreed to cede it to the Bulgarians and suggested a new line of demarcation between the allies and Turkey in the east. It ran from Enos at the mouth of the Maritsa along the course of the Erkene to Media on the Black Sea, giving Bulgaria control over both banks of the Maritsa.[166]

This was not enough to appease the 'romantics' in Bulgaria or to satisfy Paris and London. Poincaré again criticized the 'Sazonov-Izvol'skii policy of opposing the Bulgarian demands – barring, of course, the retention of Constantinople – as very short sighted.'[167] On 6 November, he informed St Petersburg that Grey was ready to propose the neutralization and internationalization of Constantinople and Salonica along lines similar to those worked out by the powers for Tangiers.[168] As far as the Russians were concerned permanent international control over the Straits and Constantinople was worse than a temporary allied occupation.[169] Consequently, the same day Sazonov reversed his position and informed London and Paris that Russia would not oppose the entry of the allies into Constantinople, but she would be obliged to send a naval squadron to remain there for the duration of the occupation.[170] 'He has, much to his regret, tacitly consented to the temporary occupation of Constantinople and he now acquiesced in the retention of Adrianople as a fortress, as well as in a frontier line that will bring the Bulgarians much nearer to Constantinople than he had at first indicated,' wrote Buchanan on 13 November. 'This last concession as he told the Bulgarian Minister was his final word on the subject.'[171]

It was quite evident that Sazonov made this concession unwillingly and hoped that Bulgaria would not take advantage of it. Geshov and his followers, including generals I. Fichev and R. Dimitriev, were ready to follow the counsel coming from St Petersburg;[172] having won guarantees over Adrianople and the Enos-Media line they assured Sazonov that Bulgaria had no designs on Constantinople.[173] The Russians, however, correctly suspected the motives and intentions of the vain, ambitious, and unpredictable king of the Bulgarians.[174] For King Ferdinand it was not just a question of entering Constantinople: ever since his arrival in Bulgaria he had 'contemplated placing upon his head the Crown of Byzantium.'[175] And now, impressed by the brilliant performance of his armies and by the reports of various western observers to the effect that the fall of Constantinople was imminent, he was not prepared to let this opportunity slip away. Neither King Ferdinand nor the western observers, however, bothered to examine the extremely hazardous situation of the Bulgarian armies before Chatalja. Their lines of communication were already drawn very thin; they suffered from shortages of food, clothes, and ammunition; and they were disease-ridden and lacked even the most elementary medical and sanitary aid.[176] Moreover, the Russians and some Bulgarians warned that the Turks were ready and able to mount a fierce and determined resistance.[177]

This was the situation when on 13 November Kiamil Pasha proposed to Bulgaria that talks for an armistice and preliminary peace commence immediately after Sofia had consulted with its allies.[178] 'In the name of the honour of our fatherland,' King Ferdinand felt forced to forbid Geshov 'to convey the request of the Grand Vizier to our allies before I have consulted my advisers and the Commanders of the three armies.'[179] The following day, 14 November, King

Ferdinand instructed General S. Savov to order the storming of the Chatalja fortifications as soon as possible.[180] Only then did he permit Geshov to inform the allies and to enquire about their demands.[181]

The attack commenced on 17 November and from the very beginning it became quite clear that this undertaking was a mistake, that it had no chance of success, and that Bulgaria would pay a heavy price for it.[182] As early as the next day King Ferdinand authorized Geshov to inform the Porte that Bulgaria accepted Kiamil Pasha's proposal.[183] Two days later Danev, who was with King Ferdinand at military headquarters, demanded from Russia 'the most energetic measures for the conclusion of the armistice.' In the event that the talks for the termination of the hostilities failed, he threatened Russia that the Bulgarians would not only enter Constantinople, but would also move the line of demarcation further to the east from the prescribed Enos-Media line.[184]

Danev's words and warnings now carried little if any weight in either St Petersburg or Constantinople. On 25 November General Savov himself notified King Ferdinand that the demoralized army was no longer able to continue the war. He warned of dire consequences within its ranks unless the armistice were concluded immediately.[185]

The brilliant Bulgarian victories before the attacks against the Chatalja lines had forced Turkey to appeal for an armistice and for peace. Bulgaria was then in an especially strong position to dictate her terms. But the collapse of the attacks revealed the exhausted state of the Bulgarian army and created a radically new and less favourable situation.[186] 'We must regret that the talks were not concluded before these attacks,' wrote M. Giers, shortly after he conveyed to the Porte Bulgaria's acceptance of the grand vizier's proposal for armistice talks.[187]

IV

At the time when the Bulgarian threat to Constantinople subsided, Russia was deeply involved in an acute crisis resulting from Austria-Hungary's determination not to permit Serbia to acquire a territorial outlet on the Adriatic Sea. Not unlike St Petersburg, Vienna was unable to formulate a precise Balkan policy before the outbreak of the war. Even its long-range general aims underwent change with the evolution of the crisis.

The chief objective of Austria-Hungary was to prevent armed conflict between Turkey and the Balkan states and see to it that everything in the Near East remained unaltered. In regard to Serbia specifically, Vienna would have liked to see Belgrade return to the policy of the reign of King Milan when Serbia was dependent on Austria-Hungary and bound to her by a secret alliance. This, however, seemed unlikely. No Austrophile party existed in Belgrade either in government circles or in the public at large.[188]

But if, in spite of Vienna's wishes, the break-up of the Ottoman Empire commenced, Austria-Hungary did not intend to remain passive. According to Count Berchtold, Austria-Hungary could not allow Serbia to expand to the west because that would bar her way to Albania where she possessed 'traditional rights and obligations which she could not abandon.'[189] Moreover, a Great Serbian state created by the coming together of Serbia and Montenegro in the Sanjak of Novi Pazar would present a grave danger to the South Slav provinces of the Dual Monarchy.[190] Berchtold, of course, realized that it would be premature for Vienna to act alone at this particular time. Hence he recommended a 'wait and see' policy for the time being.[191]

A couple of days before the outbreak of the conflict on 16 October 1912, the departmental heads in the Ballplatz met to scrutinize Austria's Balkan policy. They agreed that Austria-Hungary would resort to force only if one of the great powers attempted to establish itself on the eastern shores of the Adriatic and Ionian Seas, and that it was in the interests of the Danubian monarchy to obtain certain corrections of her frontier, but not to acquire more territory in the Balkans. Concerning the Sanjak of Novi Pazar they recognized that it would not be advisable or practical to either possess it or award it to Albania. Austria-Hungary should instead reach agreements on rights of communication which would be operative not only in the Sanjak but throughout Old Serbia and beyond. The mere possession of the Sanjak without such agreements would be of no advantage whatsoever. They also conceded that the Sanjak was losing its importance as a corridor separating Serbia from Montenegro as these two kingdoms might unite somewhere to the south of the Sanjak. Consequently, instead of forcibly resisting this union they suggested other means to protect Austria-Hungary from the Greater Serbia idea – for instance, the strengthening of the strategic position against Montenegro in the Boka, the regulation of the frontier 'as a compensation for our [Austria's] consent to the aggrandizement of Montenegro to the south,' or 'an economic union with the monarchy of Montenegro or Serbia or possibly both.'[192]

The day after the declaration of war a fresh conference convened in the Ballplatz. The participants reiterated their stand that changes in the existing territorial status quo were undesirable but had to be taken into account. They also again upheld the line that the monarchy should conclude a customs union with Montenegro and that she should allow Montenegro to acquire the Sanjak of Novi Pazar and some other small districts in return for the rectification of the Austrian frontier at Lovčen and in the Sanjak.[193]

A further conference held sometime between 25 and 30 October decided that

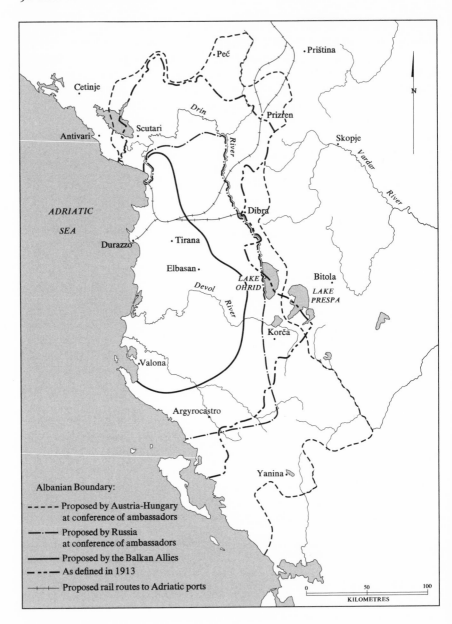

Albania and Serbian aspirations on the Adriatic coast

Austria-Hungary must prevent, if need be at the cost of war, any great power or even a smaller state, for instance Serbia, from establishing itself on the eastern shores of the Adriatic Sea. It considered the creation there of a large Albania as being very much in the interests of the Dual Monarchy. The new state was to be extensive. In the Yanina Vilayet, Greece was to receive only Yanina and the district to the south, and in the Bitola Vilayet the Albanian frontier was to stretch to the watershed between Lake Ohrid and Lake Prespa. The Albanians were also to acquire the Sanjak of Elbasan, the greater part of the Sanjak of Dibra, and the 'purely Albanian' territory of the sanjaks of Prizren and Peć in the Kosovo Vilayet. In the Vilayet of Scutari, Montenegrin gains were to be limited to Malessia and the town and valley of Scutari. In return for the possible enlargement of Serbia, which would not include Albanian territory and an outlet to the Adriatic Sea, Austria-Hungary was to demand special compensations of an economic nature. Belgrade's insistence on an outlet on the Adriatic Sea, it was asserted, would only prove that Serbia did not care for the friendship of Austria-Hungary.[194]

On 27 October, Count Berchtold instructed Urgon to inform the Belgrade government that the Dual Monarchy would not oppose the extension of Serbia, 'if Serbia on her part offered guaranties as to the permanent security of our economic interests. The closer the economic relations established between Serbia and Austria-Hungary, the more friendly will be the attitude of the Viennese government toward the above mentioned matter.'[195] When J.M. Jovanović, secretary of the Foreign Office, inquired as to what would constitute closer economic relations, the Austrian minister replied that he had a customs union in mind.[196] Dr Vladan Đorđević, a former Serbian minister who was close to the Belgrade Foreign Office and in touch with persons close to the Ballplatz, reported the offer of a customs union from Vienna as well.[197]

About this time, in the first week of November, Professor J. Redlich arrived in Belgrade. As an emissary of Count Berchtold he came to remove the difficulties standing in the way of the Austro-Hungarian–Serbian understanding.[198] According to Pašić's own account of the wide-ranging discussions, he told Redlich that Serbia wished to include within her frontiers the Sanjak of Novi Pazar and the Vilayet of Kosovo with the Adriatic coast from Durazzo (Drač) to San Giovanni di Medua. He insisted that the outlet on the sea was a vital question for Serbia. Without it she would be 'stifled and stewed as in a caldron with the lid on.' On the question of the customs union Pašić suggested that the time was not ripe for it and before it could even be discussed Serbian mistrust of Austria's Balkan policy must be removed. This could be accomplished only if Austria-Hungary responded favourably to the territorial demands of the Balkan allies and especially in regard to the question of the outlet on the sea. 'It is an opportune moment for Austria-Hungary to win the sympathy of the Balkan states and to create the basis of her economic rapprochement with them. It is up to Austria-Hungary to make possible the formation of a customs union with Serbia and the other Balkan states.'[199]

Pašić maintained that in the drive to the Adriatic Sea the Serbs did not seek the illegitimate subjugation of any foreign elements. He advanced the traditional Serbian claim that 'the Albanians on the northern littoral were of Serbian blood but had changed their religion under the persecution and pressure of the Turkish authorities ... How far that region had been Serbian in the Middle Ages could be judged from geographical names, customs, historical remains and from the fact that King Vladimir was venerated as a saint by all the Albanians in that region, both Catholic and Orthodox.'[200] To seek both a Great Albania and, at the same time, a rapprochement with Serbia, as Vienna seemed to be doing, appeared to Pašić inconsistent and contradictory.[201]

The differences between Austria-Hungary and Serbia were difficult to reconcile. Austria-Hungary demanded – and the other powers, including Russia, accepted at least in principle – the creation of an autonomous or independent Albania. In the final outcome even Serbia would have gone along with this. What really made the crisis acute, and an understanding between Austria-Hungary and Serbia impossible, was the determined and unyielding opposition of Vienna to a Serbian outlet even at the northernmost point of the Albanian coast where the population was mixed. This was also a clear-cut indication that Serbia alone could not succeed against her formidable opponent without the full backing of Russia.

From the very outset, therefore, the question of Serbia's outlet on the Adriatic Sea was in the hands of the great powers. Indeed, gradually it assumed all the trappings of a trial of strength and prestige between Austria-Hungary and Russia not unlike that of the Annexation Crisis.[202] Sazonov had this in mind when he told Pourtalès, the German Ambassador, that Russia would not tolerate a situation similar to that of 1908–09 and that she would not let herself be humiliated a second time.[203]

As in the case of the Annexation Crisis, Vienna now appeared assured of the unwavering support of Berlin and Rome. Publicly the Russian government promoted the aims of the allies, including Serbia, on the question of the outlet on the sea. But it remained to be seen how far Russia was prepared to go with or without the backing of London and Paris, whose views on this matter she had not fully explored.

On 4 November, after the powers of the Triple Alliance rejected the 'disinterestedness' formula, Poincaré enquired at St Petersburg whether 'the Imperial Government would respond as antagonistically as we toward any annexing of Ottoman possessions by the Great Powers and whether it was disposed to discuss with

France as well as England measures to forestall this danger.'[204] Sazonov was slow in replying. Poincaré was, of course, concerned with Austria-Hungary and must have been disappointed when St Petersburg did not readily grasp this overture. This was true of Izvol'skii as well. In a telegram and a long letter of 7 November, he tried to explain to Sazonov the significance of the French move. He wrote that until the beginning of November the French had not wished to be drawn into what the Quai d'Orsay considered a purely local Balkan affair. By taking this new step France recognized that any territorial conquests by Austria-Hungary would constitute a breach of the European equilibrium and affect France's vital interests. To be sure Vienna had repeatedly declared that it did not seek additional territories in the Near East. But Izvol'skii stressed that Vienna's declarations were not unconditional in character. In the event of a determined Serbian drive toward the Adriatic or a strong opposition to her economic claims Austria-Hungary would, in spite of the declarations, occupy the Sanjak or parts of Serbia and Albania. Izvol'skii urged Sazonov to take advantage of this new outlook of the Quai d'Orsay immediately to secure the backing of both France and England for the future.[205]

On the whole Sazonov concurred with Izvol'skii's reasoning. St Petersburg wished to be assured that France would not 'choose to remain indifferent if Russia found herself forced to intervene against Austria-Hungary.'[206] Nevertheless, he pointed out that the situation in the Balkans was changing rapidly. The Bulgarians were threatening Constantinople and the Straits, and he could not write off entirely a Russian intervention to stop them. Consequently, he advised Izvol'skii to omit from his reply to Poincaré the total condemnation of the intervention of the great powers in the armed conflict because 'it might be applied against Russia in the region of the Straits.'[207] Izvol'skii's communication to Poincaré merely stated that, like France, Russia could not accept with indifference the territorial enlargement of Austria-Hungary in the Balkans, and that the imperial government was ready to discuss and to reach an agreement on the necessary course of action with the French and British governments.[208]

Before the discussions got off the ground the Serbs threw the question of the outlet on the Adriatic Sea into the open rather tactlessly and prematurely. On 7 November, M. Bogićević, the Serbian chargé d'affaires at Berlin, saw Kiderlen-Wächter to whom he made some far-reaching assertions: he told him that Serbia needed the outlet and would force her way to the Adriatic even against the opposition of Austria-Hungary. When Kiderlen suggested that Serbia would face both Austria-Hungary and Italy, Bogićević declared that the allied plans for the division of European Turkey were approved by Russia. In case of a conflict Serbia had the promise of full backing from Russia and Bulgaria. Then Bogićević asked him point-blank what Germany's attitude would be in a war between Serbia and Austria-Hungary. Kiderlen issued a warning that if Serbia received military assistance from Russia, Germany would march with her ally. He was not certain whether Bogićević expressed the views of St Petersburg; however, he seemed convinced that Izvol'skii and Hartwig were inciting the Serbs. If war were to be avoided Pevchevskii Most should discipline its representatives in Paris and Belgrade.[209]

According to Ćorović, Bogićević's move had not been authorized by Belgrade.[210] But it appears that Pašić, who declined to reprimand his envoy, had a hand in the affair. Through this incident he hoped to force Russia to support Serbia more energetically by placing her in a position from which she could not easily back down.[211] Pašić was undoubtedly inspired by Hartwig who disapproved of Sazonov's policy and encouraged Belgrade to believe that unofficial 'Slavic' Russia would compel Sazonov to go along with Serbia's demands.[212]

If, indeed, this was Pašić and Hartwig's intention it backfired, for, when confronted by Pourtalès, Sazonov rejected Bogićević's contentions. He let it be known in Belgrade and the capitals of the great powers: 'Russia has an Ambassador in Berlin through whom the Russian Government communicates with the German Government, and the Serbian representative had no business speaking as he did.'[213] Granted, the pressure of public opinion was felt at St Petersburg, but the influence of this unofficial Russia was not as decisive as Hartwig made it out to be. Moreover, Sazonov was inclined to give greater credence to other factors.

Neither France nor Great Britain was prepared to go to war merely on account of the Adriatic port sought by Serbia.[214] As Buchanan told Sazonov, Serbia's economic interests would be sufficiently safeguarded if the old idea of a trans-Balkan railway with a terminus at a port on the Adriatic Sea and with guarantees for Serbian commercial access to it were revived.[215] Germany had suggested this project at one time or another during the crisis,[216] and Austria-Hungary had actually proposed to Serbia neutral railways to the Adriatic and Salonica to serve the commercial traffic of both.[217]

Russia resisted such proposals because they were not acceptable to the Serbs. They demanded a territorial outlet to the sea through a narrow belt of their own land.[218] But now, having sounded London and Paris, and virtually using Buchanan's exact words, Sazonov warned Belgrade that Russia would not allow herself to be dragged into a war with the powers of the Triple Alliance. 'The interests of Serbia would be equally well satisfied if she were to be allowed the use of a neutral railway, such as Austria-Hungary was to have to Salonica.'[219]

In a long dispatch to Belgrade on 9 November, Sazonov tried to explain Russia's overall position in a more conciliatory manner. 'We are prepared now as we were earlier,' he wrote, 'to render Serbia the most energetic diplomatic support together with France and England.' But Russia could not disregard the well-known fact that Germany and Italy together with Austria-Hungary were determined to prevent the establishment of a Serbian territorial presence on the shores of the Adriatic Sea. For this reason, Sazonov continued, Russia had to distinguish between final aims and the means for realizing them. The widest possible guarantee of Serbia's economic independence remained the final aim; the Serbian exit to the Adriatic Sea the means toward that end. This could be achieved either by a territorial acquisition to and on the seaboard or by a guaranteed free communication to one point or another on the sea. A more flexible Serbian stand on the question of the Adriatic port, which in effect meant opting for the last alternative, would provide Russia with an opportunity to demand additional gains for her elsewhere. Otherwise, Serbia might very well jeopardize all the great achievements of this short war about which she could not even have dreamed only a short time earlier.[220] In an additional note to Hartwig he warned that Belgrade's continued intransigence might force Russia to dissociate herself from Serbia publicly.[221]

In a move obviously designed to isolate Serbia, Sazonov virtually begged the Bulgarian government, 'the head of the Balkan Alliance,' to use its influence in Belgrade to bring an end to the Serbian struggle for territorial acquisitions on the Adriatic Sea. It is imperative that 'Serbian diplomats stop talking of annexing northern Albania down to Durazzo.'[222] At this time, however, Bulgaria could hardly afford to oppose Serbia's demands. The two nations were bound by treaty obligations. Serbian units were assisting Bulgaria at Adrianople. The government in Sofia, moreover, counted on Serbia in its dispute with Rumania over Dobruja and in the growing differences with Greece over the future partition of Macedonia. Most significantly, however, the Bulgarians feared that, deprived of her territorial ambitions in the west, Serbia would seek compensation in the direction of the Aegean Sea, in Macedonia, and would thus come into conflict with Bulgaria's territorial pretensions.[223] For these reasons Sofia turned a deaf ear to the pleadings from St Petersburg. Indeed, Geshov warned Pevchevskii Most that only the powers that prayed for the breakdown of the Balkan alliance wished to see Serbia advance toward the Aegean Sea. 'Under no circumstances could we accept such a proposal. We will insist that Serbia be given a port on the Adriatic Sea ... We will stand together with Serbia just as she is sticking with us at Bucharest and Athens.'[224] When Pašić inquired at Sofia whether Serbia could depend on the assistance of Bulgaria in the event of an Austro-Hungarian attack, Geshov replied, on 13 November, that he considered the question of Serbia's outlet on the Adriatic 'the most important of all Balkan questions. Serbia can count on the complete solidarity of Bulgaria and the support of her army.'[225]

Sazonov was alarmed by Geshov's uncompromising stand and militant language.[226] He viewed the Balkan scene strictly through his own narrow prism of Russia's national interests. Since Russia was not prepared for war his chief aim was to avoid risking an armed conflict with the Dual Monarchy. This is why, as he told Bobchev on 12 November, he thought 'it would be madness on Bulgaria's part to join Serbia in attacking Austria if the latter occupied Durazzo or any other port on Turkish territory with the object of forestalling Serbia.'[227] Sazonov could not really comprehend Geshov's and, for that matter, the other allied leaders' fears and concern about the future while the differences and the potentially explosive conflict between them remained under the surface. Eventually, he realized how serious these were, but by then the foundations of the Balkan system of alliances had been undermined.

Although officially Russia continued to pay lip-service to the Serbian territorial outlet on the Adriatic Sea[228] Sazonov's refutation of Bogićević's declarations was a clear indication of Russia's real position. This was undoubtedly taken into account by the officials at the Ballplatz and, indeed, was probably responsible for the stiffened attitude of Austria-Hungary. On 10 November, after his return to Belgrade from Bucharest where he met Count Berchtold, Urgon communicated to Pašić officially his government's determination not to allow Serbia an outlet to the Adriatic Sea through territory inhabited by Albanians.[229] Strangely enough Vienna justified this policy by invoking the principle of nationality and the slogan 'the Balkans for the Balkan peoples.' In accordance with this principle Vienna had firmly resolved to prevent Serbia from acquiring any portion of Albania; Austria-Hungary and Italy wished to see Albania either as an autonomous state under Turkish sovereignty or as a fully independent state. Serbia could seek an outlet on the Aegean Sea or in Dalmatia. Austria-Hungary would not oppose Serbia if she tried to reach the Adriatic by railway either through Montenegro or by way of the new Albanian state. The Austrian minister made it clear that his government's declaration had the backing of Germany and Italy.[230] Speaking for himself, Pašić told Urgon that the views of Austria-Hungary and Serbia were altogether irreconcilable. He promised an official reply after he had consulted with the king and with Serbia's allies.[231]

Two days later, on 12 November, Baron W. Giesl, the Austro-Hungarian minister at Cetinje, delivered a similar verbal communication to King Nikola. He declared that Austria-Hungary would place no obstacles in the way of Montenegro's military operations against San Giovanni di Medua and Alessio (Lješ). A permanent occupation of the Albanian coast by either Serbia or Montenegro would not be in harmony with the creation of the Albanian state, which Austria had in view;[232] however, he indicated that Vienna was prepared to bargain over other issues. Austria-Hungary hoped to see Scutari remain Albanian because it was of great importance to her as well. However, if Montenegro agreed to cede to Austria a part of Lovčen 'as a very small pledge of her future friendly policy which was to include no aggressive plans,' Vienna would readily meet the wishes of Montenegro in Scutari. In addition, Giesl proposed a customs union and other commercial ties which would have in effect placed Montenegro economically at the mercy of the Dual Monarchy.[223]

To be sure, the Montenegrins were determined to acquire and annex Scutari, but not at the expense of their independence. King Nikola therefore promptly told the Austro-Hungarian minister that he considered his government's representation as '*nul et non avenue.*'[234]

Shortly after Urgon's visit Pašić turned to Russia, France, and England to seek their advice.[235] To avoid Urgon he left immediately for Skopje on the pretext of having to confer with the king. He did not reappear in Belgrade until 16 November.[236]

The British and French leaders were gradually assuming a more critical attitude toward the Serbs, who, according to Poincaré, 'at present are suffering from swelled heads.'[237] Serbia, noted Nicolson, 'has become so inflated with her own importance and military strength as to believe that she could dictate to the whole of Europe.'[238] Officially Britain and France counselled moderation at Belgrade. Serbia and the other allied states should not discuss their claims until they had formulated the terms of peace in common. At the same time, the allied governments should not deny rudely to the great powers, who were most interested in the pending changes of the map of Europe, a say in the matter.[239]

These cautious warnings to Belgrade were in harmony with the line taken by Pevchevskii Most after the Bogićević affair. In the mean time, and to the great surprise of Whitehall and the Quai d'Orsay, a complete reversal of Russia's attitude took place.[240] Sazonov now informed them again, as he had done before 7 November, that Russia might have to intervene against Austria-Hungary if the latter attacked Serbia. He wanted to know the views of these two friendly governments.[241]

This sudden volte-face is difficult to explain. In his memoirs Sazonov wrote: 'Certain circles in St. Petersburg connected with the court and the whole of the national press in the capital which had been hostile to the Foreign Ministry carried on a noisy campaign against Russia's Foreign policy.'[242] Sir George Buchanan agreed with the German and Austro-Hungarian ambassadors who put the blame for it on the intrigues at the court. On 17 November, he wrote to Grey:

I can not explain sudden change in Sazonov's language. My Austrian colleague and my German colleague who seemed uneasy after their interview attributed it to some powerful influence brought to bear on the Emperor. They told me that Grand Duke Nicholas, who will have chief command in case of war, had recently been summoned at Spola and that Rasputin had been summoned there during Czarevitch's illness. Latter has an extraordinary influence over the Empress and may, they think, have been employed for political purposes by two Montenegrin Grand Duchesses, [who] purchased him.[243]

In any event the responses from London and Paris were evasive. Grey thought that the question Sazonov just raised was an academic one and 'one could not give a decision about a hypothetical contingency which has not arisen.'[244] Poincaré, who had experienced in the past similar changes in Russia's outlook, wished to know first of all what the Russian government proposed to do. Otherwise, as he told Izvol'skii, by 'taking the initiative the French Government would run the risk of embracing a position which did not agree with the intentions of its ally.'[245]

On 14 November, Sazonov informed Paris and London that Serbia intended to reject the Austrian representation, and he suggested that they use the question of Albanian autonomy or statehood to extract concessions from Vienna.[246] He argued that in this question the Triple Entente had a powerful weapon for exerting pressure on the Ballplatz. Without the sanction of Russia, England, and France, who were signatories of the Treaty of Berlin, Austria-Hungary and Italy could not create an Albanian state out of an area which was still an integral part of the Turkish Empire. The least that Austria-Hungary should do in return for their agreement would be to consent to a Serbian port, without which, as Kokovtsov put it, 'Serbia could not live any more than the lungs could breathe without air.'[247] Two days later Sazonov proposed to the powers specifically to allow Serbia to retain San Giovanni di Medua with a narrow strip of land connecting it with Prizren or some other point on the territory of Serbia, on condition that the Serbs would neither fortify the port nor keep war-ships there.[248] Both Sazonov and Kokovtsov emphasized in dispatches to London and Paris and in their talks with the British and French ambassadors that Russia counted on the support of Britain and France. The Triple Entente was not a negligible quantity, Kokovtsov told Buchanan. It 'should exercise all its influence in Vienna and Berlin to obtain satisfaction for Serbia.'[249]

This hoped-for support, however, did not materialize. The British and French governments feared that their intervention in Vienna might further rigidify the already existing divisions between the powers on this issue and make its peaceful settlement even more difficult. Thus, they preferred to see a direct understanding between Russia and Austria-Hungary.[250] But, in spite of the fact that Sazonov was in constant contact with Vienna, such an agreement was nowhere in sight. The latter would not consent to ceding Medua to Serbia and refused to consider all proposals which favoured even a symbolic rather than real Serbian presence on the Adriatic Sea.[251]

In a meeting with the German and Austro-Hungarian ambassadors on 20 November, Poincaré suggested that Serbia might be appeased with an exit to the Adriatic Sea by way of a neutralized strip of land to a neutralized port between

Montenegro and the territory which was to be allotted to Albania.[252] At about the same time Italy proposed two commercial, though not territorial, routes for Serbia. One, by a railway through Scutari, would go to Montenegro, to the port of Antivari (Bar), and the other through Albania to Medua and possibly to Durazzo. The railways and the ports were to be neutralized.[253] The Austro-Hungarian government turned down both proposals. Concerning the former Vienna claimed that a Serbian territorial exit would interfere with the commercial rights of the monarchy; that it would provoke disputes between the Serbs and the Albanians over the neutralized strip of land; and, finally, because a commercial port would sooner or later become a military port.[254] Vienna rejected the latter, the Italian, because it allotted Scutari to Montenegro.[255] The impasse continued.

In the mean time, Pašić had returned to Belgrade. The Serbian cabinet met on 15 and 16 November to decide on a reply to the Austrian representation of 10 November, and to assess its future policies in light of the latest moves of the great powers. On the whole the participants agreed to follow the counsel of the friendly powers and to avoid, whenever possible, bilateral talks with Vienna; the questions raised by Urgon were to be left to the general peace settlement at the end of the war.[256] They also agreed, however, that an outlet on the Adriatic Sea would remain Serbia's primary aim. The best way to achieve it was to partition Albania with Greece and Montenegro. But, since the great powers were of one mind on the question of autonomy for Albania, Serbia would also accept this, at least in principle, on condition that she would be allowed an outlet on the sea. What this meant, of course, was that Serbia would continue the struggle for a piece of northern Albania, and in return for that area she would accept autonomy for the rest of Albania to the south.[257]

In all official dealings with the European chancelleries, Belgrade continued to oppose Albanian autonomy.[258] On various occasions, when the Serbian armies were pushing through Albania toward the Adriatic, Pašić made conflicting claims and purposely left the great powers to guess Serbia's real aims and intentions.[259] Paget complained that he found it

difficult to give any useful account of the present situation here, as owing to many conflicting statements going about, one does not quite know what to believe. For instance, last Saturday M. Pašić told me that Serbia must insist on having Durazzo and would take nothing less whilst two days later the *Times* correspondent understood from him that they only had San Giovanni di Medua in view and the Austrian Minister gave the same information yesterday, but this morning M. Pašić in speaking to me again insisted on Durazzo ... Just at present the Servians seem to be relying on the probability that if they open their mouths wide enough at first they are sure to get something or other in the end ... I question very much whether the Servians look upon the operations of their troops on the Adriatic coast as provisional. It looks to me as though Austria could be met with a *fait accompli* and who will then expel the Servian troops from Durazzo and other parts of Albania?[260]

On 25 November Pašić completely confounded the great powers by a signed communication which appeared in the London *Times*. 'It is essential that Serbia possess about fifty kilometers from Alessio to Durazzo,' it stated. 'This coastline would be joined to what was formerly Old Serbia, approximately by the territory between a line from Durazzo to Ochrida Lake in the south, and one from Alessio to Djakova in the north ... For this minimum Serbia is prepared to make every sacrifice, since not to do so would be false to her national duty. No Serbian statesman or government dare betray the future welfare of the country by considering for a moment even the abandonment of this minimum.'[261] The leading article in the same issue of the *Times* typified the hostile reaction of the powers. Deprecating the appearance of Pašić's declaration as being unlikely to assist efforts to preserve peace in Europe it warned that it was not 'an hour when M. Pašić could expect his very sweeping proposals to be accepted calmly by his nearest neighbour.'[262]

Pašić's 'trial balloon,' as Đorđević called this declaration, represented his last desperate effort to win Russia's unqualified backing for the territorial outlet on the Adriatic Sea. It was his final attempt to force Russia to end her vacillation and take a definite stand against Austria-Hungary.[263]

Time was running out for Serbia. Her relations with Austria-Hungary were rapidly deteriorating and an armed clash between them could have erupted at any time. As Serbian troops moved into Old Serbia and Albania on the way to the Adriatic, they were met with suspicion and open hostility by the local Austrian representatives. The latter deliberately spread biased reports about the Serbian army, incited the local Albanian population to resistance against the Serbs, and supplied them with small arms.[264] In agreement with the authorities in Vienna they actively supported the movement for Albanian independence or autonomy which was Austria-Hungary's chief argument against the Serbian outlet on the sea. With the aid of the local Austrian representatives, and the encouragement of Vienna, an Albanian national congress actually met in Valona and proclaimed Albanian independence on 29 November, the very day the Serbs occupied the port of Durazzo.[265]

The Serbian military leaders in the area felt obliged to retaliate and, in the case of Austrian consuls von Tahy in Mitrovica and Oscar Prochaska in Prizren, they resorted to restricting their freedom of movement.[266] The press in Vienna and Budapest used the 'consular affairs' to launch a violent anti-Serbian campaign. It accused the Serbian authorities of alleged atrocities in the occupied territories and against the Austrian consuls. Although the Austrian government had been informed of the well-being of Prochaska and the others, it not only did not deny, but initiated and spread, some of these false reports of violence perpetrated against the consuls.[267] Indeed, as Ćorović showed, these incidents were welcomed and deliberately exploited by Vienna. They could easily be used against the Serbs when the penetration of the Serbian army to the sea became a fait accompli and Austria decided to dislodge it at any price from the conquered territories on the Adriatic.[268]

The diplomatic and political offensive against Serbia was accompanied by intensified military undertakings. The initial military moves of Austria-Hungary at the beginning of the war were insignificant. The troop concentration in Bosnia-Herzegovina was no more than a warning to Serbia and Montenegro. The military successes of the allies, and especially Serbia's penetration into Albania and her rejection of the Austro-Hungarian demands, however, altered the entire situation. By the middle of November the military preparations along the Russian and Serbian frontiers were stepped up. Three classes of reservists were called out in Cracow, Graz, Pressburg, Koshau, Przemysl, Lemberg, Agram, and Temesvar.[269] The northern border corps and several cavalry divisions in Galicia were placed on standing orders.[270] On 27 November the British military attaché reported to the director of military operations that Austria had 110 battalions with a total strength of all arms of 125,000 to 150,000 men. The military preparations were to be completed in eight days. Austria-Hungary planned to employ against Serbia 300,000 men including 14 mountain brigades, under the command of General Potiorek.[271]

On 22 November Archduke Francis Ferdinand and General Schemua, the chief of staff, held military conversations in Berlin. Kaiser Wilhelm II agreed that Austria-Hungary could under no circumstances allow Serbia a port on the Adriatic Sea. If the prestige of Austria-Hungary came into question, he told Francis Ferdinand, 'he would not be afraid of a world war and that he would be prepared to go to war with all the three Powers of the Triple Entente.'[272] Similar discussions were held at the end of the month in Bucharest where General Conrad von Hötzendorf reached an agreement with General Avarescu, the Rumanian chief of staff.[273]

All these measures were not aroused simply by the question of the Serbian outlet alone. Influential quarters in Vienna, particularly the military, were thinking in terms of the whole South Slav question which they viewed as a thorn in the flesh of the monarchy. 'We shall see how Russia responds to our measures,' General Auffenberg, the war minister, told Tschirschky on 21 November. 'If she takes it quietly, we shall have a free hand in regard to Serbia. We need at least half a century of peace in the Monarchy to bring the South-Slavs to order, and that peace we can only have if the South-Slav hopes of Russian help are finally removed. Otherwise, the Monarchy will go to pieces.'[274] The same sentiment was echoed by Hötzendorf. In his memoirs he wrote:

The crux of the matter was to smash Serbia who was, with Russia's help, the uncompromising, stubborn enemy of the Monarchy, and thus safeguard the existence of the state, which was then threatened. All other questions, such as those of Albania, the port, the Danubian Adriatic Railway, etc., were secondary and derivative.[275]

Russia had put into effect certain military measures as well.[276] On 10 November, while in Spola, the military leaders had persuaded the tsar to order the retention on active duty till the end of December of the recruits usually discharged at the end of October.[277] At the same time supplementary credits to strengthen Russia's defences on the Austro-Hungarian frontier were sanctioned, against opposition from the Council of Ministers.[278] Needless to say, however, in view of the deepening crisis between Austria-Hungary and Serbia, and when compared to the general military preparedness of the former, these measures were obviously insufficient and inadequate. As Pašić repeatedly tried to impress on St Petersburg, Russia had to take a stand. She could either come out openly in support of Serbia and take the necessary diplomatic and military measures to sustain this position, or desert Belgrade and throw the question of the Serbian outlet on the Adriatic Sea into the lap of Europe. The decision reached in the end at St Petersburg was not the one Pašić hoped for.

Russian military leaders favoured tough measures directed against Austria-Hungary. They succeeded in winning the tsar to their point of view at least temporarily after his return from Spola to Tsarshoe Selo in the third week of November. At a conference which met on 22 November and was chaired by the tsar, the commanders of the Kiev and Warsaw military districts decided to mobilize the entire Kiev district and part of the Warsaw district and to prepare to mobilize the Odessa military district.[279] This decision was taken without the knowledge of the civilian leaders in the government. Even after it had been reached, General Sukhomlinov did not bother informing the Council of Ministers. As he later told Kokovtsov, 'he believed it best that we [the civilian ministers] should learn from the Tsar himself what he had in mind.'[280]

The following day the tsar called a meeting at his study in Tsarskoe Selo. The participants, besides the tsar, were V.N. Kokovtsov, S.D. Sazonov, S.V. Rukhlov, and generals Sukhomlinov and Zhilinskii. The tsar tried to impress them with the need to increase substantially the numbers of troops stationed near the frontier and then informed the civilian ministers of the decision reached the previous day. 'I wish to stress particularly the fact that this refers exclusively to our Austrian frontier and that we have no intentions whatever of taking any steps against Germany,' the tsar continued. 'Our mutual relations (with Germany) leave nothing to be desired and I have every reason to hope for the support of Emperor William.' In conclusion he told them that the telegrams pertaining to the mobilization had been prepared and that he had asked the minister of war not to dispatch them immediately because he 'wanted to discuss the situation with those ministers who ought to be appraised of it before the final orders were given.'[281]

The civilian officials were flabbergasted. Struggling to retain his composure, as he wrote in his memoirs, Kokovtsov denounced the projected mobilization. He pointed out that it would throw Russia into a war with both Austria-Hungary and Germany at a time when Russia's national defences dictated extreme caution. Since they were bound by a treaty of alliance, Austria-Hungary and Germany could not be treated separately. Furthermore, Russia owed certain obligations to France and, according to the terms of the Franco-Russian Treaty of Alliance, Russia had no right to order and carry out a mobilization without having reached an understanding with her ally. Finally, Kokovtsov reminded the minister of war that he did not possess the authority even to discuss such a matter without a preliminary agreement with the head of the government and the minister of foreign affairs.[282] Supported by Sazonov and Rukhlov, Kokovtsov at the end carried the day. The mobilization orders were shelved, and their place was taken by Kokovtsov's proposal to lengthen by six months the term of service throughout Russia (which increased the numerical strength of Russia's standing army by one-fourth).[283]

Confronted with the real possibility of war the Russian government capitulated, as it had in the crisis of 1908–09, and pushed aside the Serbian demand for a territorial outlet on the Adriatic Sea. Sazonov denounced Pašić's declaration in the *Times* as a 'provocation' which 'could only do damage to Serbia.' He warned the Serbian prime minister to refrain from making statements incompatible with the policy of Russia.[284] This was also the message given to the Austro-Hungarian ambassador by the tsar on 26 November in an audience especially arranged by the minister of foreign affairs. Tsar Nicholas assured Count Thurn that Russia was not committed to any one particular solution of the Serbian port question. There was no reason why the great powers, into whose hands this question was to be placed, could not agree on a peaceful solution by means of friendly discussions.[285]

Russia's latest volte-face assured Austria-Hungary of a favourable solution to the Serbian port question but Vienna was not appeased. It continued to seek and demand the public capitulation of Serbia. The propaganda campaign against Serbia was mounting, and the military preparations on the southern borders were being accelerated. The exaggerated and, indeed, false reports surrounding the consular affairs were arousing public opinion against Serbia.[286] Responsible circles in Vienna were calling for a war against her. 'In all classes of society here,' wrote Cartwright on 4 December, 'especially in industrial and financial circles feeling is growing that it would be better to take action at once against Serbia and so put an end to the present suspense.'[287] *Gröss Österreich*, the organ of Francis Ferdinand, declared openly that 'war against Serbia was unavoidable.'[288] Berchtold, Czernin, Szápáry, and other officials at the Ballplatz, as well as intellectuals such as H. Friedjung and A.F. Pribram, who were close to it, shared this view.[289]

At the end of the first week of December confirmed reports reached Belgrade that the Austro-Hungarian government intended to send an ultimatum to Belgrade.[290] Sazonov considered such a step unnecessary because the powers had already agreed to take up this question at the London conference which was preparing to start its work.[291] Berchtold argued, however, that the public in Austria-Hungary demanded advance guarantees of Serbia's future attitude and conduct.[292] The powers of the Triple Entente, to whom Pašić turned for advice,[293] urged Belgrade to submit if and when the ultimatum were presented. Sazonov at first advised Belgrade to reply that Serbia had decided to leave the entire question to the powers of the Entente.[294] But in the end he went along with Paris and London, which, in order to avoid divisions in the ranks of the powers, preferred to have Serbia place it in the hands of all the powers.[295]

Abandoned and pressured by Russia on the one hand, and threatened with war by Austria-Hungary on the other, Serbia had no alternative but to back down. Already at the end of November Pašić had written to St Petersburg that the Serbs

do not desire to enter alone into the question of our outlet to the sea, but that the decision be left to the Great Powers when the war is over and the peace concluded. We shall not in the end be opposed to the creation of autonomous Albania, if Europe is agreed on that point. But we think that an autonomous Albania will not make for the peace which is necessary both to the Balkan allied states and to the whole of Europe. Our wish is to have an outlet to the coast and to possess a port on our own territory but we leave that question to the Great Powers for settlement when they settle all the other questions which will arise after the conclusion of peace.[296]

The leaders of all the political parties in Belgrade agreed with Pašić and the government that war with Austria-Hungary was out of the question, and that in the end, if it proved necessary, Serbia would back down. However, for the time being this decision to capitulate was not made public.[297] They still hoped that something might be salvaged before the question was placed in the hands of the powers. Moreover, they preferred to wait until the conference of ambassadors in London had assembled. For, as Ćorović put it, 'It seemed more dignified to Serbia to bow to the will of Europe than to the will of Austria-Hungary alone.'[298]

4

The peace negotiations

The allied Balkan states would much rather have negotiated a direct peace settlement with Turkey without the interference, or indeed the assistance of, the great powers. In line with this, Geshov, after receiving the official Turkish request for armistice and peace,[1] promptly notified the representatives of the great powers in Sofia that their mediation was no longer essential.[2]

It is doubtful, however, if either Geshov or the other allied leaders did really believe that Europe would permit them to dictate to Turkey the entire final settlement of the centuries-old Eastern Question. The magnitude of their victory necessitated the complete redrawing of the map of southeastern Europe. The powers of the Triple Alliance, and Austria-Hungary in particular, were not prepared to sit idly by while the allies were encroaching on what they regarded as their rights or spheres of influence.[3]

In any event, even if the allies had been able to agree on a settlement satisfactory to all of them, which was an extremely difficult task in itself, it would not have been acceptable to the Dual Monarchy. The unresolved differences between Austria-Hungary on the one hand, and Serbia and Montenegro on the other, had now reached a critical stage; there was a real danger that Vienna might resort to the use of force. Thus, for the first time since the Annexation Crisis, Europe faced the possibility of an Austro-Hungarian–Russian or, indeed, a general European confrontation.

The threat by itself transformed the war from a purely Balkan (if it ever was only that) into a European crisis that could have been resolved peacefully only through the concerted efforts of all the great powers. As has already been shown, since the beginning of the crisis the great powers attempted to work in unison. At first they declared in favour of the preservation of the status quo; then ensued the Russian formula for the disinterestedness of the powers, which was rejected by Vienna and its allies; and finally came the proposals for mediation by the powers advanced at various times by Paris, Berlin, and, at the end, by London.

In calling for mediation they envisaged a separation of issues considered to be of only Balkan interest from those that were viewed as being of European concern or, more precisely, from those that supposedly infringed upon the interests of some great powers. The former were to be taken up directly by the allies and Turkey, while the latter constituted the preserve of the powers and their decisions were to be presented to the two belligerent sides.[4]

I

The collapse of the attempt to storm the Chatalja fortifications left Sofia no alternative but to accept the Turkish overtures for armistice negotiations.[5] Belgrade and Cetinje followed suit and authorized the Bulgarian delegates to act on their behalf as well.[6] The Greeks refused to go along; they insisted that the armistice talks should await the fall of Yanina, the imposing Turkish fortress in Epirus.[7]

The real reason behind Greece's dissension, however, was much more serious. For quite some time before the negotiations had commenced, the Greek government had demanded from Bulgaria an agreement on the partition of Macedonia. Their opinions on this problem had not changed at all since they signed the treaty of alliance. Indeed, one could say that Sofia assumed an even more intransigent stand now that the Greeks had captured the city of Salonica. Although Geshov tried to give the impression that the time was not ripe for such an agreement because it would take too long to negotiate, it would be more accurate to suggest that he recognized the chances that they could agree on anything were more or less non-existent. Accordingly, the Bulgarian government decided to disregard the objections from the Greeks and begin the talks without them.[8]

On 20 November 1912, Geshov conveyed the terms of the armistice to the Porte through the Russian embassy at Constantinople. The allies asked the Turks to: 1) surrender Adrianople, the Chatalja fortifications, Yanina, Dibra, and Scutari; 2) to abandon the entire peninsula to the west of the Chatalja lines, which were to constitute the lines of demarcation separating the two armies; and 3) to raise the blockade of the Bulgarian ports.[9] Turkey at first rejected these conditions, but eventually, as a result of some rather strong and energetic Russian representations, agreed to send delegates to the armistice talks.[10]

The armistice conference opened on 25 November, in the village of Plaiaa, on Lake Biuuk Chekmedzhe. The allies, Bulgaria, Serbia, and Montenegro, were represented by Danev, General Savov, and General Fichev; the Turks by Nazim Pasha, minister of war, Reshid Pasha, minister of agriculture and commerce, and Colonel Ali Riza Bey. Panas and Major Francis, who was attached to the headquarters of the Bulgarian army, represented Greece as 'official observers.'[11]

The talks turned into a prolonged 'oriental pazarlik,' lasting an entire week. The armistice protocol, which was signed on 3 December, avoided all controversial questions and only reflected the uncompromising positions taken by both sides.[12] Its main terms provided merely that: 1) the belligerent armies were to remain in their positions; 2) the besieged fortresses were not to be revictualled, or supplied with ammunition; 3) the revictualling of the Bulgarian army and the replenishment of its ammunition were to be carried out only by way of the Black Sea and Adrianople, beginning ten days after the signing of the armistice; and 4) the peace negotiations were to commence in London on 13 December.[13]

When they signed the armistice agreement, the allies had no illusions about either their ability or their freedom to impose their own final settlement upon Turkey. On the day of the first meeting at Plaiaa, the Ballplatz let it be known that it would not accept any agreement concluded by the two belligerent sides without the approbation of Europe.[14] The notion that the great powers might or ought to partake in the reestablishment of peace in southeastern Europe was raised by Poincaré on 15 October 1912, even before the war had commenced. With the mounting tension between Austria-Hungary and Serbia, and the resulting deterioration in relations between Russia and Austria-Hungary, the other powers accepted Poincaré's suggestion as the only effective way to prevent a European war.[15] They still had to decide and agree on the manner in which they were to intervene in the peace settlement.

On 18 November 1912, Kiderlen-Wächter proposed to London and Paris that the great powers agree in advance on the resolution of the major issues. He thought that questions relating to Albania, Adrianople and Constantinople, Mount Athos, the Mediterranean islands, and the rectification of the Rumanian-Bulgarian frontier ought to be reserved for the great powers.[16] On the whole, the French and the British governments responded favourably.[17] But, since there were no major difficulties between Russia and Bulgaria over Constantinople, Adrianople, and Mount Athos, Grey was inclined to believe that it might not be necessary to raise these points unless, of course, Russia wished to do so herself.[18] In a further exchange of views with the Quai d'Orsay on 22 November, Grey suggested a conference of the delegates of the powers and that the ambassadors at the capital chosen might be the delegates. The capital city that he had in mind was Paris.[19]

Afflicted by persistent disagreements with Bulgaria, and unable to take a stand on the Serbian–Austro-Hungarian dispute, the response of Pevchevskii Most to Grey's suggestions and enquiries reflected the great uncertainty and vacillation that prevailed in St Petersburg. On 22 November, Sazonov told Buchanan that he 'entirely concurs' with Grey's views. Russia would not bring up the question of Constantinople provided it remained Turkish.[20] Three days later he endorsed the idea of the ambassadorial conference in Paris and singled out the questions of Albania, the Serbian port, the islands, and Mount Athos as the main problems that would confront such a conference. He also indicated that he might propose

the neutralization of all Albanian ports under an international guarantee so that Serbian commerce would be placed on the same footing as that of all other countries. She might be given access to them by means of an international railway, on the administration of which she would be represented with a guarantee against any differential rates.[21]

Sazonov must have known that such a solution would not meet with approval in Belgrade; and it is hard to explain why he made the suggestion in the first place since he was not prepared to stick to it. For, when Grey pressed him to make an official statement to the same effect,[22] Sazonov backed down.[23] 'M. Sazonov is a sad wabbler,' commented Robert (later Lord) Vansittart.

It is disappointing to find him now inclined to back down about the consultation between the Ambassadors in Paris and about his own suggestion respecting the neutralization of Albanian ports. It was of course obvious at the beginning that the solution would not meet all Serbia's pretentions, but one would have thought that he had realized this.[24]

Shortly afterwards Sazonov changed his mind again, embraced the idea of the conference of the six ambassadors, and asked Poincaré to propose it officially.[25] The French premier, however, advised him to invite Grey to take the initiative, since it would have appeared rather awkward for him to call a conference that was to meet in his own capital.[26]

Once he was assured of the consent of St Petersburg and Paris, Grey instructed Sir W.E. Goschen, the British ambassador, to inquire at the Wilhelmstrasse:

How would the German Government view a proposal that instructions should be sent to the six Ambassadors at one of the capitals – I suggest Paris if that would be generally agreeable – to consult together and to submit to their Governments propositions on three points?

He put forward three questions: 1) 'To what extent are the allies free to change the map of Europe without any stipulations being made by [the] Great Powers?'; 2) 'On what points must the Great Powers reserve their right to have some say in the settlement?'; and 3) 'What settlement on each of these points would secure the assent and support of [the] six Great Powers?'[27] Goschen was to ascertain whether Kiderlen-Wächter shared Grey's views and, if that was the case, to ask him to sound out the Austro-Hungarian government. Before this was effected the British newspapers reported Grey's proposal and the Foreign Office sounded the Ballplatz directly.[28]

Although Kiderlen-Wächter was on the whole well disposed to the proposal, he expressed preference for London as th seat of the conference.[29] Austria-Hungary was committed to Albanian autonomy and had made declarations to that effect at Belgrade, Athens, and Cetinje. Count Berchtold now informed Grey that Austria would participate in the conference, but that she was not prepared to go beyond the simple exchange of views to secure the commercial '*débouché*' of Serbia on the Adriatic. The Austrian ambassador 'could under no circumstances join in a discussion which would have the object of a territorial extension of Serbia to the Adriatic, or the acquisition of a port.'[30] Grey did not consider this either a justified or a legitimate condition for the non-committal conversations. He therefore reminded Count Mensdorff that 'if some Powers were prepared to accept unreservedly, and other Powers made conditions – especially if they made them publicly – the conversations might never begin at all.'[31] In his reply Count Berchtold emphasized that he did not wish to restrict the subjects that were to be discussed at the meetings of the ambassadors. Nevertheless, he took the trouble to reiterate the Austrian position on the question of the Serbian exit to the Adriatic Sea. In regard to the place of the conference Berchtold, like Kiderlen-Wächter, favoured London over Paris.[32]

Either of these two capitals was acceptable to Pevchevskii Most, but both the Russian and the British governments 'feared that it would be a bitter disappointment to [the] French President of the Council if the meetings did not take place in Paris, as the latter had set his heart on presiding at an international conference.'[33] In order to soothe Poincaré's feelings, once the powers accepted London as the seat of the preliminary ambassadorial conference, Grey suggested to Berlin and Vienna to indicate to the Quai d'Orsay that, should a formal conference take place, they would agree to Paris.[34]

The instructions forwarded to their ambassadors in London by the respective governments foreshadowed the course of the forthcoming conversations. Sazonov singled out Serbian access to the Adriatic Sea and the status of Albania as the two most serious problems to be discussed.[35] The principal aim of Russia, wrote Sazonov, was the political and economic emancipation of Serbia. Albania should be brought into being as an autonomous province under the sovereignty of the sultan: Turkey would be granted the right to keep a limited number of troops there. To make certain that the creation of Albania did not place in jeopardy the interests of Serbia, Sazonov advised Benckendorff to bear in mind and to be constantly guided by three principles. First of all, he stressed the need to neutralize Albania and her sea coast as a means of preventing the interested powers, primarily Austria-Hungary, from transforming the area into an exclusive sphere of influence. Secondly, he emphasized the necessity to recognize and accept the right of Serbia to free communications with the sea through Albanian territory on the railway lines connecting Serbia with the Adriatic ports. The complete freedom of movement was to encompass the transport of military hardware to and from Serbia. Finally, Sazonov instructed both Benckendorff and Izvol'skii to acquaint Whitehall and the Quai d'Orsay with Russia's position and to secure in advance their approval and assistance.[36]

The views of the British and particularly the French governments were identical or at least very similar to the ones held by St Petersburg. Poincaré emphasized the significance of the Balkan alliance for the future and stressed the point that Austria-Hungary should not be permitted to derive any commercial or other advantages from the peace settlement.[37] As was to be expected, Vienna's position was diametrically opposed. Austria-Hungary not only saw Albania as a prospective sphere of influence, but also as a convenient tool to be used to strike down the interested allied states. Mensdorff was to struggle to cut to complete insignificance the acquisitions of the allies in the west through the establishment of Great Albania. On the Serbian access to the sea Berchtold merely restated by now his all too well-known opinions.[38] Berlin and Rome embraced the stand taken by their ally and instructed their ambassadors in London, Prince Lichnowsky and Marquis Imperiali, to follow Mensdorff and support the Austro-Hungarian program.[39]

Hence, even before the actual deliberations began it was obvious that at the conference the ambassadors would be divided and would represent not so much their home countries as the two power blocks of Europe. Count Benckendorff, spokesman for the Triple Entente, was to defend the aims of the allies with the backing of Cambon and Grey. Count Mensdorff, assisted by Lichnowsky and Imperiali, championed Great Albania – the cause of the Triple Alliance.[40]

II

The conference of ambassadors, or 'the Reunion of the Ambassadors of the Six Great Powers, signatories of the Treaty of Berlin,' was inaugurated at the Foreign Office in Whitehall on 17 December 1912.[41] Edward Grey was chosen chairman and throughout the conference, which lasted until August, acted the role of 'honest broker' between the two groups. The conference was extremely informal. The ambassadors met irregularly 'when occasion required,' which meant, in effect, whenever they received instructions and were ready to discuss particular issues. The proceedings where kept secret. Official 'communiques' to the press were made only when it was 'judged opportune' to do so.[42]

In the opening session the ambassadors agreed to take up first the Albanian question. Count Mensdorff proposed the creation of an Albanian state that would be autonomous and 'viable,' meaning large enough to sustain independent existence. In order to prevent Austria-Hungary from turning it into an exclusive sphere of influence in the future, Count Benckendorff suggested that Albania should remain under the sovereignty of the sultan, while the six great powers would guarantee her autonomy.[43]

The fixing of the boundaries of Albania presented the conference with its most difficult task, since the Austro-Hungarian schemes clashed with the proclaimed territorial goals of Serbia, Greece, and Montenegro. The Serbian government had already intimated privately that it would submit to the decision of the conference, which meant in effect that Serbia was abandoning her demand for a territorial exit to the Adriatic Sea. However, it was the function of the ambassadors to finalize and make public Serbia's access to the sea and to decide the details of Albania's boundary lines with the three allied nations.

To placate Austria-Hungary, and perhaps hoping to prepare in this way the ground for some future compromises favourable to the allies, Benckendorff closed the question of the Serbian territorial exit to the sea during the first session of the conference by proposing a common boundary between Albania and Montenegro in the north. At the same time, the ambassadors resolved, again on Benckendorff's initiative, to guarantee Serbia a commercial outlet in a free and neutral Albanian port, served by an international railway protected by an international gendarmerie under European control.[44] At the third session, on 20 December, Benckendorff also proposed to grant Belgrade the right to select the route of the railway and its terminal point and a share in the international control of the line and the port. Since only Russia and Austria-Hungary showed direct interest in this issue, it was left to them to decide.[45]

On the same day, Grey conveyed the resolutions of the conference to Belgrade and to the press. S. Gruić, the Serbian chargé d'affaires in London, in his turn handed Grey an aide-mémoire declaring Serbia's intention to abide by the decisions of the powers.[46] The Russian and Serbian governments capitulated; Austria-Hungary had scored an impressive victory.

The press and public opinion in both Russia and Serbia were disenchanted and reacted bitterly. They denounced the conference and the policy of the imperial government for, as far as they were concerned, Russia's capitulation fell nothing short of being another 'diplomatic Mukden.'[47] Or, as *Novoe Vremia* put it in a violent article entitled 'Austrian triumph,' Russia had suffered a worse humiliation than in 1909. 'If any further concessions have to be made to Austria at the expense of [the] Balkan Slavs,' warned Buchanan, 'the Government will be placed in a difficult position.'[48]

There is no doubt that in return for the clear-cut and prompt capitulation, St Petersburg and Belgrade expected greater consideration and pliancy from Vienna.[49] Hence, they must have felt shocked and disappointed when, on 20 December, Count Mensdorff submitted a map proposing for Albania a territory far larger than the allies had even thought possible. It assigned to her Scutari, Peć,

Djakova, and Dečani in the north, Yanina in the south, and Prizren, Dibra, and Ohrid in the east. This proposal, which Count Benckendorff rejected categorically,[50] also astonished all the other ambassadors and brought the conversations on the boundary problem to a standstill.[51]

In the mean time, the conference dealt with other issues affecting the peace settlement. During the second session, on 18 December, the ambassadors discussed the future of the islands in the Aegean Sea. Greece claimed all the islands and neither France and Britain nor the powers of the Alliance raised strong objections against it.[52] Although Russia was also prepared to go along with Greece in regard to most of the islands, she took exception to the four – Imbros, Lemnos, Tenedos, and Samothrace – controlling the entrance to the Dardanelles. Pevchevskii Most preferred to see them remain under Turkish rule with autonomous institutions for the protection of the Christian inhabitants.[53] When Grey raised a few enquiries and suggested that such an arrangement would only recreate in the future a Cretan problem, Benckendorff did not have sufficient instructions to respond and promised to refer the question to St Petersburg. In the end, leaving the question unsettled, the conference recorded the unanimous decision about the neutralization of the islands.[54]

Soon afterward, the Quai d'Orsay persuaded Pevchevskii Most that effective neutralization of the four islands, even if they went to Greece, would accomplish Russia's objective, which was solely to prevent the blockage of the exit from the Straits. On 21 December, Sazonov informed Benckendorff that Russia acquiesced in the cession of the four islands to Greece, provided that they were fully neutralized and the fortifications there destroyed, that Greece promised not to fortify them again, and that she would not extend to any power the right to possess or use the islands. In return, Russia expected the Greek government to relinquish its claim to sovereignty over the Holy Mountain – Mount Athos.[55]

During the first three sessions the conference reached 'the maximum of agreement that the instructions and the information in possession of the Ambassadors rendered possible.' To give time to the governments to 'digest' the decisions already agreed upon and to the ambassadors to obtain further instructions, the conference was adjourned until 3 January 1913. It was hoped that in the course of the recess direct contacts between Austria-Hungary and the Balkan allied states and Russia would elucidate and disentangle the acute disagreements surrounding the question of Albania's boundaries.[56]

No matter what informal contacts took place during the recess they did not contribute much toward the resolution of the problem. Neither Montenegro nor Serbia (and consequently Russia, at least for a time) were prepared to give way and capitulate again. In spite of the strong warnings from Vienna, King Nikola maintained that he would not succumb under pressure and would fight all attempts to prevent Montenegro from acquiring Scutari.[57] His delegates to the peace conference had definite instructions not to sign the peace treaty without Scutari.[58] To be sure, Vienna advertised, as did Count Mensdorff at the second session of the ambassadorial conference, the notion that Austria-Hungary would agree to extensive concessions being made to Montenegro in case the latter relinquished Scutari to Albania.[59] Although Count Mensdorff did not specify the concessions he had in mind, it was rather obvious that Vienna was not going to compensate Montenegro with the port of Spizza or another port on its own territory. In this respect Mensdorff's offer represented just another Austro-Hungarian effort to divide the allies, this time to drive Serbia and Montenegro to each other's throat.[60]

Russia saw this very clearly and Sazonov rejected the offer and termed 'inadmissible' any further attempt to appease Montenegro at the expense of Serbia.[61] Russia's endeavours to bolster Montenegro, however, were constricted by the fact that the Turks defending Scutari, though beseiged for a prolonged time, held fast and refused to capitulate. Writing to Giers on 24 December, Sazonov emphasized that at that moment the Russian government was more concerned about the ability of the Montenegrins to capture the fortress than with the Austrian opposition to its annexation by Montenegro.[62]

Unlike Montenegro, Serbia had captured and held towns such as Prizren, Peć, Djakova, Ohrid, and others, which Vienna demanded for Albania. Moreover, most of them were old historic Slavic towns, surrounded by predominantly Serbian or Macedonian populated areas, and it would have been awkward and extremely hazardous for Russia to press 'the return to Albanian control of the Slavic population liberated by the Serbian armies.'[63]

On 22 December, Harwig communicated to St Petersburg the Serbian project delineating the boundaries of Albania. It proposed a line running south of the River Drim in the north; west of the Black Drim to a point west of Kapra in the east; and from there north of Argyrocastro to the Gulf of Valona in the south. It left Scutari, Medua, and Lješ to Montenegro; Dečani, Djakova, Prizren, Dibra, and Ohrid to Serbia; Yanina, Korča, Argyrocastro, and the island of Corfu to Greece.[64] Belgrade implored the Russian government to champion this project at the conference of ambassadors. Another capitulation to the demands of Austria, warned Pašić, would endanger Serbia's internal stability and the monarchy, and would disrupt relations between Russia and Serbia.[65]

The Serbian project was not altogether different from a previous rough Russian scheme which was conveyed to Benckendorff on 9 December 1912.[66] It remained to be seen whether Sazonov could persuade the other powers to accept a solution approximating the Serbo-Russian proposals. Although Great Britain was less concerned than France as to who should become the possessor of Scutari or the other contested towns, both of them were ready to follow Sazonov in order to avoid weakening or impairing the understanding with Russia.[67] Early in the conversations Grey indicated to the ambassadors of the Triple Alliance that having promoted an agreement on the question of Serbian access to the Adriatic Sea so favourable to Austria-Hungary he would have to support Russia on the question of Scutari and some other towns. He asked Lichnowsky and Imperiali to do the same and to bring their influence to bear upon Austria-Hungary to get over the difficulties.[68]

Dealing with Austria-Hungary, however, proved a most arduous proposition. The direct contacts between St Petersburg and Vienna which were envisaged when the conference adjourned did not materialize. Austria-Hungary carried out military preparations and the Russian government did not deem it feasible to enter into talks while she was deploying troops along the Russian and the Serbian frontiers. Sazonov pointed to the impropriety of such measures at the time when the conference was taking place,[69] but Vienna maintained that they were essential as long as there were differences of opinion between the ambassadors.[70] They were necessary in order to insure that the decisions of the conference would be put into effect as, according to Berchtold, Vienna suspected the true intentions of the Belgrade government.[71] Pašić's official declarations in Vienna and London that Serbia would respect the will of Europe and retire from Albania as soon as peace was concluded, as well as appeals from the tsar, King George V, and M. Poincaré, did not move the government in Vienna.[72] Consequently, when the conference reconvened in early January 1913, Russia and Austria-Hungary were still deadlocked. Nicolson described the actual state of affairs acutely when he observed: 'Count Berchtold said that he would put away his revolver when all questions as to Albania & Co. had been solved, and M. Sazonov said that he did not want to discuss Albania till the revolver had been put away.'[73]

To break out of the impasse Grey proposed to isolate the question of Scutari from the rest of the Albanian boundary problem and to deal with it first.[74] As stated earlier, had Montenegro captured Scutari before the opening of the conference it would in all probability have remained in her possession. At the outset Russia and Italy backed Montenegro. They were supported by Great Britain and France. Germany did not exhibit any strong interest in the future of Scutari. Austria-Hungary at first opposed Montenegro, but in November, Vienna proposed to Cetinje that it trade Lovćen to Austria-Hungary in return for Scutari. King Nikola rejected the offer and from that point on the Ballplatz resolved to deny Montenegro the town.[75] More significantly, however, the Austro-Hungarian offer marked a turning point in the position held by Italy. Rome was categorically opposed to the cession of Lovćen to Austria and, to forestall the possibility of a Lovćen-for-

Scutari bargain in the future, the Italians insisted vehemently that Scutari be included in Albania.[76]

Consequently, now in January, Grey's appeals to Vienna and Rome to concede Scutari to Montenegro or to find some other way of satisfying King Nikola fell on deaf ears. In an interview with Grey on 7 January, Count Mensdorff reiterated Austria-Hungary's determination to go to war rather than hand over Scutari to Montenegro.[77] He also indicated that his government was all in favour of compensating Montenegro without again spelling out what he had in mind. He merely implied that once the Scutari question was resolved in a manner satisfactory to Vienna, a settlement of Albania's eastern frontier, that is, the boundary with Serbia, would not be difficult to arrange.[78]

Russia's conduct in regard to the Scutari problem approximated very closely the manner in which she had capitulated on the Serbian exit to the Adriatic Sea. Once Austria-Hungary stiffened in her outlook Pevchevskii Most began to wobble and retreat. As late as 9 January, Sazonov maintained that Russia would agree only to a solution satisfactory to Montenegro.[79] But only a few days later, he informed Grey privately that Russia might give way on the question of Scutari if the Serbian line were adopted for the eastern boundary of Albania.[80] After the session of 22 January, at which Count Mensdorff rejected decisively the Russian arguments in favour of Scutari being awarded to Montenegro,[81] Sazonov abandoned Montenegro altogether. He instructed Benckendorff to tie the question of Scutari to the delineation of the eastern boundary of Albania, to demand Djakova for Serbia and, if it proved essential, to bargain away Scutari for Djakova.[82]

During the session of 25 January, Benckendorff proposed that Djakova be given to Serbia. But Mensdorff, although prepared to cede Dečani, the historic monastery located in the neighbourhood of Djakova, to Serbia, insisted that the town itself remain in Albania.[83] In such a manner Vienna and St Petersburg set the stage for a possible Scutari-for-Djakova swap, and Lichnowsky and Imperiali volunteered to work on a compromise proposal.[84] Sazonov was for all practical purposes abandoning King Nikola, although the latter was not yet fully aware of this situation. Russia was on the verge of capitulating to Austria-Hungary on the question of Scutari.

III

While the ambassadors were absorbed in the Albanian boundary question, the peace negotiations between the allies and Turkey, which were taking place simultaneously, passed the stage of possible compromises and were breaking up. The representatives of the belligerent nations assembled in St James's Palace on 16

December 1912. S. Danev, S. Novaković, E. Venizelos, and L. Mijušković headed the Bulgarian, Serbian, Greek, and Montenegrin delegations respectively. Reshid Pasha was the chief Turkish delegate.[85] Grey opened the proceedings and was nominated *president d'honneur* of the 'St. James's Peace Conference.'[86]

The entire first week of the talks was taken up by sharp exchanges, attacks, and mutual recriminations. The Turkish delegates refused to treat with the Greeks until they received new instructions and an authorization from Constantinople, because Greece had not signed the armistice agreement. This was a handy delaying tactic since Turkey had nothing to lose by prolonging the negotiations. Indeed, the Turks hoped to win time to recoup their strength and to excite the latent disagreement between the allies.[87]

On 24 December, after this approval arrived from Constantinople, the allies presented collectively their peace terms. They required Turkey to relinquish to them the entire area west of the line extending from a point on the Sea of Marmara east of Radosto to a point in the Gulf of Malatra on the Black Sea to the east of Media (except the Gallipoli peninsula), the islands in the Aegean Sea, and, finally, to renounce all her rights to the island of Crete.[8]

The Turks dismissed these demands as unrealistic and exaggerated[89] and submitted a counter-proposal, the aim of which could not have been anything but to try the will and patience of their opponents. Rejecting all the territorial claims of the allies, they proposed for Macedonia an autonomous administration headed by a Protestant prince to be selected by the allies from a neutral state, and for Albania an Ottoman prince ruling under the sovereignty of the sultan. The Vilayet of Adrianople and the Aegean islands were to remain under direct Turkish control, and the future of Crete was to be determined by the great powers and Turkey.[90]

Such concessions were adequate to satisfy the 'public' grievances which were used by the Balkan governments as pretexts to justify the war. Having defeated Turkey, however, they were no longer concerned merely with the well-being of their 'enslaved brothers.' Every allied nation had far-reaching territorial ambitions as well as schemes for their attainment and therefore saw no reason why it should even listen to the Turkish designs for the conquered territories. In view of the subsequent tragic disagreements between the allies over the division of Macedonia, the Turkish proposal does not appear unreasonable. In any event, the allies rejected it as they did two other Turkish offers containing a few additional minor and relatively insignificant concessions.[91]

On 4 January 1913, the allied delegates put forward a declaration requesting Turkey to renounce her rights over the island of Crete, to give up the Aegean islands, and, finally, to indicate a line of demarcation in the east which left the city of Adrianople to them. They warned that a failure on the part of the Turkish government to come up with a new proposal embodying these demands by 6

January would result in the break-up of the peace negotiations.[92] Although the Turks again refused to go along, the great powers prevailed upon the allied governments not to terminate but only to suspend the negotiations temporarily, and to await the results of their intervention in Constantinople.[93]

When the conference of ambassadors considered the measures that the great powers ought to take to avert the renewal of hostilities, Grey suggested a collective representation to be made to the Porte. Cambon went a step further and proposed to reinforce the representation with a naval demonstration. Benckendorff agreed, but Grey, Mensdorff, Lichnowsky, and Imperiali thought that such a show of force was premature and unnecessary.[94] After a prolonged delay caused by disagreements over the nature and text of the collective démarche, it was delivered on 17 January.[95] The great powers drew the attention of the Turkish government to the grave complications that would confront the empire if the negotiations failed and the war were resumed. Turkey would not be able to rely on their assistance for the protection of her capital or the Asiatic provinces. Accordingly, the great powers advised the Turks to part with Adrianople, to leave the future of the Aegean islands in their hands, and to depend upon them for the safety of Constantinople and the protection of Muslim interests in Adrianople.[96]

On 22 January, the grand vizier summoned the Divan, the council of the chief religious, civil, and military dignitaries, to consider the problem and to prepare a reply. The government urged compliance with the demands of the powers; and the Divan, with only one negative vote cast, resolved in favour of concluding peace.[97] For the Committee of Union and Progress, whose influence and prestige were growing with every humiliating defeat at the hands of the allies, this decision represented treachery.[98] In the afternoon of the next day a group of Young Turks, led by Enver Bey and Talaat Bey, forced their way into the Porte. They killed Nazim Pasha, the minister of war, and, with the sultan's consent, ousted the senile Kiamil Pasha. After six months in the political wilderness, the Committee was back in power with Mahmud Shevket at the helm.[99]

The successful coup d'état in Constantinople strengthened the position of those allied civilian and military leaders who advocated the renewal of the war. The Bulgarians, particularly King Ferdinand, General Savov, and Danev, were the most militant on this issue, even though they were obviously aware that if the war were renewed Bulgaria would have to bear the brunt of the fighting. They pressed Geshov and his more moderately minded colleagues to discard the counsel of Russia and the other friendly powers and use this 'most convenient moment,' as Danev put it, to denounce the armistice and to begin military operations.[100]

Premier Geshov tried to resist by pointing out that Bulgaria as well as her allies would have to stick to the promise made to the great powers. Like Sazonov,[101] he argued that the coup in Constantinople had not altered the situation for them, for, no matter who occupied the Porte, the Turks would have to respond to the note of the powers. He also cautioned Danev that Bulgaria did not possess the right alone to denounce the armistice without the consent of her allies.[102] However, Danev was already enlisting the support of the other peace delegates. The Greek and Montenegrin representatives agreed quickly, but the Serbs hesitated for a while. They had very little to gain from the resumption of hostilities and were therefore more interested in impressing the great powers, who were deciding Serbia's western boundary, with their peaceful intentions. When Danev approached them they claimed at first to be without instructions,[103] but eventually, on 27 January, joined in the drafting of the note to end the peace negotiations,[104] which was delivered to the Turkish delegation on the 29th.[105] The following day the allied governments announced that the armistice would be denounced in the evening and military hostilities would recommence four days later, at 7 pm on Monday, 3 February.[106]

Only hours later, in the afternoon of 30 January, the Porte finally replied to the collective note of the great powers. Politely, but definitely, the Turkish government rejected all the recommendations. It refused to cede the part of Adrianople on the left bank of the river where the mosques, the graves of the sultans, and other historical and religious memorials were to be found, or to relinquish the Aegean islands which it considered vital for the protection of the capital and Asia Minor.[107] In other words, the new nationalistically minded administration at Constantinople was not prepared to place the fate of Anatolia and whatever was left of Rumelia in the hands of Christian Europe. It chose instead to accept the challenge of the allies and decided on the resumption of the war. In the evening of the same day, General Savov notified the Turkish commander in chief that the armistice had been terminated and that hostilities would be resumed in four days' time.[108]

During the course of the truce the Turks had improved their situation only slightly: they reinforced the Chatalja fortifications and organized an entire new army in the Gallipoli peninsula. Although the Turkish army was still holding to Adrianople in the east, and Scutari and Yanina in the west, these fortified strongholds were besieged and isolated.[109]

The Bulgarian war plan provided for a defensive stand at Chatalja and offensive action against Adrianople. Assisted by two Serbian divisions, the Bulgarians intended to take Adrianople by storm on 23 February, but owing to unfavourable weather conditions and almost daily snowstorms, which took a heavy toll of allied lives, the attack was postponed from day to day. However, around the middle of March reports reached the Bulgarian command that the defenders were highly demoralized and on the verge of capitulating as a result of hunger and the spread of a typhus epidemic. And, on 24 March, General Savov ordered generals Ivanov and Vazov to attack the frontal Turkish positions. The following night they assaulted the main line of fortifications and, on 27 March, Adrianople capitulated.[110]

From the available Bulgarian sources it is not clear whether King Ferdinand contemplated another attempt against the Chatalja lines. In any event, Russia was vehemently opposed to it and chiefly for this reason condemned the resumption of the war and chastised the Bulgarian government for having taken the initiative. 'We are astonished at the conduct of the Bulgarian Government,' Sazonov wrote Nekliudov on 31 January. 'The resumption of the military hostilities, in our opinion, threatens Bulgaria with new, probably considerable sacrifices while it does not guarantee to them [Bulgarians] any further gains.'[111] On 2 April, after the fall of Adrianople, he warned Sofia: 'The additional extension of Bulgaria and her craving to secure an outlet on the Sea of Marmara will encounter all-out opposition from our side. We can not leave the freedom of passage through the Straits to the discretion of Bulgaria.' He objected to having to submit his country's 'strategic interests' to the whims of whatever cabinet happened to be in power in Sofia.[112]

To make Russia's determination absolutely clear, Sazonov also asked Britain and France to join her in making a collective representation at Sofia; if that came to naught, the imperial government intended to dispatch the Russian fleet to protect Constantinople.[113] In the end events evolved in such a way that Russia did not have to resort to the use of force against one of the allies, for, if King Ferdinand seriously contemplated advancing against Constantinople, he changed his mind. The fall of Adrianople signified the virtual end of the war for Bulgaria.

Aided by two and, after the unsuccessful all-out attack of 7 February, by three Serbian divisions, the Montenegrin army continued the pressure against Scutari. It kept up the assaults throughout March and most of April: the starving and dispirited defenders did not capitulate until 23 April.[114]

The task of the Greek forces besieging Yanina was much easier. With the resumption of the war they were reinforced by three divisions, which were transferred from Macedonia, and the newly formed Epirus army of 70,000 men stormed the fortress by surprise on 4 March. The next day Yanina was under Greek control.[115]

The Serbs did not engage in major military operations during the second phase of the war against Turkey. Their actual involvement was limited to the two infantry divisions aiding the Bulgarians at Adrianople and the two infantry and one heavy artillery divisions participating in the siege of Scutari.[116] The entire attention of the Serbian government focused on the conference of ambassadors and the renewed deliberations on the Albanian boundary question.

IV

The parties most concerned with the Albanian boundary problem held the following positions toward the end of January 1913. King Nikola insisted that Montenegro would not give up Scutari.[117] Pašić maintained that neither the military commanders nor the Serbian people would ever accept the inclusion of Peć, Djakova, Prizren, and Dibra in the new Albanian state and nothing short of force would bring the withdrawal of Serbian troops from these places.[118] Russia, as Buchanan pointed out, had gone far on the path of concessions and her prestige in the Balkans suffered accordingly. She was ill-equipped to apply additional pressure against either Montenegro or Serbia.[119] The strong situation of Austria-Hungary was weakened a bit, partly because even her allies, Germany and Italy, came to view the entire affair as not worth a major crisis, let alone a war, and therefore sought to induce Vienna to allow some modifications in its originally proposed boundary line.[120] More importantly, however, the renewal of the war provided Austria-Hungary with telling arguments in favour of a more flexible approach. For, if the Montenegrin and Serbian forces had captured Scutari and presented Europe with a fait accompli she would have lost ground. Hence, it was only rational for the Ballplatz to assume a more conciliatory stand on some of the disputed boundary points in order to win Russia's approval for Scutari to remain in Albania whether Montenegro took it or not.[121]

As early as the beginning of February, the government in Vienna took some steps to mollify Russia. Emperor Francis Joseph dispatched Prince Gottfried zu Hohenlohe-Schillingsfürst, a former military attaché and person well thought of at St Petersburg, on a special mission to Russia. On 4 February, he was received by the tsar to whom he delivered a very friendly personal letter from the emperor.[122] In the second half of the month Count Berchtold himself took the initiative to propose to Russia a mutual reduction of troops on both sides of the Galician frontier.[123] However, genuine concessions on the Albanian boundary were very slow in coming. The ones that Vienna eventually did make were 'the outcome of almost incredible oriental haggling.'[124]

On 6 February, Lichnowsky tendered to the conference his compromise which proposed to leave Hoti and Gruda to Montenegro; Plava, Gusinje, Peć, and Dečani to Serbia; and Djakova, Dibra, and Scutari to Albania.[125] Count Berchtold immediately announced that it contained the very maximum concessions that Austria-Hungary was prepared to make.[126] As far as Russia was concerned this was hardly a compromise. Sazonov had pointed to a Scutari-for-Djakova arrangement, but he was in no position to concede Scutari to Albania and, at the same time, deprive Serbia of both Djakova and Dibra. In rejecting the so-called compromise, Count Benckendorff for the first time left Scutari completely out of the picture and demanded Dibra and Djakova for Serbia and the entire Lake Scutari, Mount Taboraš, and the Luma Plain for Montenegro.[127] This did not satisfy Count Berchtold but, if the rest of the Austro-Hungarian line were approved, he offered Dibra as the 'very last sacrifice.'[128] The future of Dibra and Djakova became the center of the whole dispute.

The Serbian monarchy and government had placed their prestige on the acquisition of the two towns. Pašić refused to budge and vowed that he would under no circumstances withdraw the troops from there. After an interview with the premier, Paget wrote on 18 February that

in the matter of Djakova and Dibra Servia could not and would not give way. Even if he himself was inclined to cede it he would not be permitted by the public and the army. Should Austria resort to force, Servia would resist. And if no assistance came from Russia and the Servians were consequently worsted, they would make the best of a bad bargain and go over entirely to Austria for the future.[129]

In a message for St Petersburg, which he himself drafted, Pašić grieved that:

Serbia had been obliged to withdraw from the littoral at Austria's insistence and be shut again on all sides. Albania is being created on her frontier with the aid of paid agents; commitadji bands are being organized, armed and assisted against Serbia. Scutari has been taken away from Montenegro, which had been fighting for its life for the last two hundred years, only for the sake of creating a Greater Albania. The territory and holy places of Old Serbia are being taken from her to be given those who ravaged them in the past. Djakovica is left in doubt. A new impulse is being given to foreign agitation, the Serbian people are being reduced to despair ... The Bulgarians and Greeks are not treated so ruthlessly. The Balkan alliance is stabbed in the heart![130]

At this point Russia could not do otherwise but stand solidly behind Serbia. On 20 February 1913, Sazonov empowered Benckendorff to inform the next session of the conference that for various reasons, many of which were of an ecclesiastical nature, Russia would not consent to the exclusion of Djakova and Dibra from Serbia.[131] She could yield Taboraš, Luma, and Radomir but would not go beyond that.[132]

The refusal of Russia to back down and capitulate again and, more significantly, the arrival around this time of the Serbian forces to the assistance of Montenegro against Scutari induced Vienna to compromise. Accordingly, on 5 March, Count Mensdorff proposed to the ambassadors that the great powers make representations in Belgrade and Cetinje to put an end to the siege of Scutari and to bring about the withdrawal of all allied forces from Albania. He indicated that in return Austria-Hungary would agree to refer the question of Djakova to an international commission.[133] Grey promptly seized the opportunity to urge Sazonov to 'make it quite clear that if the question of Djakova is settled, he would join in preventing Montenegro from going to Scutari and securing the recall of [the] Serbian troops from territories agreed to be Albanian.'[134] On 12 March, Sazonov handed to Buchanan a written reply declaring that:

The Imperial Ministry would be disposed to consider the question of pressure being applied at Cetinje and Belgrade with regard to Scutari in close connection with the question of Djakova. More especially if Austria consents to exclude Djakova from the limits of Albania, the Imperial Government on its part would instruct its representatives in the said capitals to make the most energetic representations with the object of raising the siege of Scutari.

The imperial government would make no objections to similar steps being taken at Belgrade to secure the evacuation of territories recognized as Albanian, continued Sazonov, 'provided that Djakova be assigned to Serbia as, according to all accounts, the Serbian Government would never be able to withdraw its troops from that town.'

Hence, Sazonov asked the Austrian government to give Russia in advance 'an assurance that the town would in principle be assigned to Serbia' and that the international commission 'should at the same time elaborate certain guarantees especially of economic character with regard to that town.'[135]

Vienna at first objected to Sazonov's definition of the prerogatives of the international commission. As Mensdorff argued in London, it was up to the commission to decide to whom Djakova ought to belong; but if it chose to exclude the town from Albania, it would have to secure economic and other guarantees for the protection of its non-Serbian inhabitants.[136] Sazonov, however, refused to agree to the international commission even after Count Thurn indicated to him privately that by proposing it Austria-Hungary was merely seeking an expedient way to save face. He insisted that Russia would have to be assured in some manner that its decision would assign Djakova to Serbia.[137]

On 21 March Vienna dropped the idea of the international commission and backed down. Count Mensdorff informed Grey of his government's decision to give up Djakova on the understanding that there would be a promise to secure effective protection for the Albanian and Catholic minorities in the territories going to Serbia, and that the rest of the line of north and northeast Albania would be settled according to the last Austrian proposal. More importantly, however, Austria proposed that the six great powers demand and secure the immediate cessation of hostilities and the evacuation of the territories allotted to Albania.[138]

The following day the conference of ambassadors accepted the Austrian conditions. It issued a resolution calling on the great powers to authorize their representatives at Belgrade and Cetinje to invite the Montenegrin and Serbian governments 'to raise the siege of Scutari, to end the hostilities in the territories abandoned to Albania, and to proceed rapidly to the evacuation of this territory.'[139] Sazonov immediately instructed Benckendorff to announce to Mensdorff that Russia would consent to the inclusion of Scutari in Albania and would agree to join the other powers in making a declaration to that effect at Belgrade and Cetinje as soon as Mensdorff declared that Djakova would be excluded from Albania.[140] This completed and sealed the Scutari-for-Djakova bargain.

V

In resolving to call on Serbia and Montenegro to cease all military operations, the great powers disregarded a highly significant consideration, namely, that the fighting around Scutari constituted an integral part of the war of the allies against Turkey. As Sazonov informed Grey: 'The Serbians could not be asked to retire from Durazzo, etc., till the war was over, while they consider themselves bound to stand by Montenegro till Scutari falls.' It was therefore rather unreasonable on their part to raise such demands before armistice and peace had been concluded.[141]

The moves aiming at a second cease-fire got under way approximately a month after the resumption of hostilities. On 28 February, Tewfik Pasha informed the conference of ambassadors that Turkey was ready to accept the proffered mediation of the great powers.[142] Due to the disagreements that divided them,[143] the allied governments failed to respond until 14 March, when they presented the great powers with a collective note containing their peace terms. In addition to the conditions they put forth before the break-up of the St James' conference, for instance, the Radosto-Media line in the east, the Aegean islands, and Crete, they now also demanded military and other reparations, the right to decide and include in the peace treaty questions relating to the status of their co-nationals in Turkey and trade relations with the Ottoman Empire, and that the military hostilities should not be terminated before the conclusion of peace.[144]

The powers viewed these conditions, some of which encroached upon the authority and the work of the ambassadors' conference, as far-fetched. They agreed on and stipulated their own provisions for the peace negotiations in identical notes which they delivered to the Balkan governments on 23 March. In the east they suggested the line from Enos to Media following the course of the rivers Maritsa and Erkene as the western boundary of the Ottoman Empire. They proposed to leave the entire territory to the west of this line, except Albania, as well as the island of Crete at the disposal of the allies. But they reserved for themselves the right to decide the future of the Aegean islands, and although they were ready to allow the belligerents to participate in the work of the international commission for the settlement of all financial questions, they rejected the demands of the allies for military indemnification. Finally the powers insisted that once the Balkan nations accepted these conditions, military operations must cease immediately.[145]

After Adrianople capitulated to the Bulgarians, on 27 March 1913, Sofia sought greater acquisitions in the east and brought up again the Radosto-Media line. The Russians, however, made it clear, as they had done on many previous occasions, that they would not allow under any circumstances the presence of Bulgaria on the Sea of Marmara.[146] But Danev, who was in St Petersburg at this time, persuaded the Russian government at least to accept, as Bulgaria's very last demand on the question of Turkey's western boundary, a straight line from Enos to Media, which gave Bulgaria a larger area of land, instead of the line running along the courses of the Maritsa and Erkene rivers.[147] When Sazonov secured the approval of the other powers for this modification,[148] the straight Enos-Media line, together with the other conditions for the preliminary peace contained in the identical notes to the allied governments of 23 March, were presented collectively by the great powers to the Porte on 30 March.[149]

Although the Turkish government promptly acceded to their proposal[150] a cease-fire could not be effected. The allies refused to go along with the Turks and, moreover, had great difficulties in agreeing on a common reply to the powers. While the Bulgarians appeared relatively appeased, Montenegro refused to accept Europe's views on the question of Scutari, and Serbia and Greece wanted to know the exact boundaries of Albania before agreeing to the peace deliberations.[151] On 29 March, Geshov attempted to draft a compromise reply designed to mollify them,[152] but succeeded only with the Greeks.[153] The Serbs and Montenegrins were now asking for the surrender of the scattered Turkish garrisons in Albania and the capitulation of Scutari.[154]

Indignant and already tired of waiting, the great powers made on 5 April a new collective representation in the Balkan capitals demanding prompt acceptance of the terms for the preliminary peace.[155] The allied governments responded the same day with Geshov's compromise proposal of the previous week, which restated their by now well-known objections. To repeat them again, the allies asked that the Enos-Media line be viewed merely as a basis for the negotiations and not as the final boundary; that Turkey relinquish to them the Aegean islands; that they be informed in advance of the projected borders of Albania, which ought to conform to their own proposals; and that their requests for military reparations be accepted in principle.[156] The great powers had already rejected such demands and it seemed that there was nothing else left for them to do but wait.

The failure of Europe to force the allies to back down collectively, however, did not exhaust all the possibilities. Russia, for one, now focused her attention on

Bulgaria. Partly because the Bulgarians felt the brunt of the war most, but also, and probably more significantly, because as long as the war continued they threatened Constantinople and the Straits, Russia was applying strong pressure on Sofia and the Porte to conclude a separate truce. The day Adrianople capitulated Sazonov advised the Bulgarian government in no uncertain terms to seek a cease-fire without delay, and there were further exchanges on this topic between them.[157] Although not every detail of what was said is known, there are some very strong indications that Sazonov committed Russia to sticking to the letter of the secret annex of the Serbo-Bulgarian treaty of alliance when the question of the partition of Macedonia came up, as the Bulgarian government demanded, if Bulgaria would conclude immediately an armistice with Turkey.

In the first week of April, M. Giers, the Russian ambassador at Constantinople, informed the Turks that the Bulgarians were ready to terminate hostilities and advised them to take the initiative and approach Sofia. Thereupon, on 7 April, General Izzet Pasha, commander of the Turkish forces, invited General Savov to designate the meeting for the armistice talks.[158] Before the Bulgarians responded to the invitation, Geshov wrote to Bobchev on 11 April:

Note that I have an official promise from Nekliudov to carry out exactly our agreement with Serbia, if we attempt to end the military operations at Chatalja. We are trying, and if the task is delayed the responsibility belongs to the Turks ... Explain this to Sazonov so that he knows that we have taken note of the official promise of the Russian Minister for the literal execution of our agreement.[159]

The following day, when he authorized General Savov to appoint a Bulgarian general for the meeting, he also sent him a copy of a recent telegram from Giers to Nekliudov which stated:

The Grand Vizier advised Izzet Pasha to send tomorrow, Sunday, at 12 o'clock in the afternoon, one Turkish general to General Savov without any letter. The Turkish general will communicate orally the following explanations: The Turks learned from the Russian Ambassador that the Bulgarians yielding to the counsels of Russia would be prepared to enter into talks for the termination of the military hostilities. It is well known to the Turks that there have been no overtures for the termination from the Bulgarian side. Nevertheless, the Turks are ready to commence such talks.[160]

On 13 April, General Toshev met General Ziya Pasha east of Chatalja and agreed orally on a truce between Bulgaria and Turkey. It went into effect at noon of the following day and, renewed every ten days,[161] it remained in effect until 30 May, when the Peace Treaty of London was signed. Since the truce was reached without the knowledge and approval of the other allied governments, Bulgaria had acted contrary to the terms of her agreements with Greece, Montenegro, and Serbia. For this reason Geshov requested St Petersburg to keep it secret until he found an opportune occasion to announce it to them.[162]

Around this time and undoubtedly in connection with the Bulgarian-Turkish armistice, the powers rejected the note of the allies of 5 April and reiterated the terms for the preliminary peace which had been included in all their earlier representations.[163] Having concluded a separate cease-fire, Bulgaria was naturally inclined to accept the recommendation.[164] Serbia, Greece, and Montenegro continued to oppose the terms and only after prolonged discussions, which took place in an atmosphere of mutual suspicion and distrust, did they reach an agreement. In a collective reply, on 21 April, the allied governments restated all their objections but at the same time accepted the mediation of the powers on condition that they would reserve for themselves 'the right to debate with the Great Powers, during the course of the negotiations, the questions pertaining to the islands and the fixing of the boundary in Thrace and all the boundaries of Albania.'[165] A few days later, the conference of ambassadors, 'taking note of their acceptance of the mediation of the Powers on the basis proposed by the latter,'[166] invited the belligerents 'to cease hostilities immediately and to designate their plenipotentiaries and the place where the peace negotiations were to be held.'[167] In such a manner, without direct contacts with Turkey, Serbia and Greece joined Bulgaria in the second armistice. Only the kingdom of Montenegro chose to continue, at least for a while, to defy the will of the Concert of Europe by openly refusing to abandon Scutari, which was now in its possession.

VI

Since 22 March 1913, when the ambassadorial conference resolved to award Scutari to Albania, the Russian government repeatedly urged Montenegro and Serbia to give up the struggle and abide by the will of the great powers.[168] Although the Serbs saw the situation as clearly as the Russians did, Pašić argued that there was very little they could do beyond advising Montenegro to yield. Serbia was bound to aid Montenegro by treaty obligations and her army at Scutari was under the command of King Nikola. The final decision as to whether the siege of Scutari would be raised or not rested not with Serbia but with the king and government of Montenegro.[169]

While the Russians found some rationale behind the Serbian position, they did not or could not understand the rigid attitude of King Nikola.[170] For a long time he was *persona gratissima* in St Petersburg. Tsar Alexander III had referred to him as 'his best and most loyal friend.'[171] But by now he had lost the popularity and confidence that he once enjoyed there. In a conversation with D. Popović, the Serbian minister, Sazonov went so far as to call King Nikola 'the enemy of the Serbs, the Russians and the Slavs; he is Austria's friend only!'[172]

The truth of the matter was that for King Nikola Scutari had become an affair of personal and national honour. He was determined to possess the town no matter what the cost. When the Cetinje government rejected the resolution of the powers, it also made it absolutely clear that 'it did not consider it possible to end the military operations as long as Scutari does not surrender or is not captured.'[173] By adopting such a course of action King Nikola chose to disregard the counsel of Russia, including a curt message from Tsar Nicholas to the effect that the struggle for Scutari was futile; and he thus placed Russia in the embarrassingly difficult position of having to support Austria-Hungary's stern measures against Montenegro, a Slavic state and a member of the Balkan system of alliances.[174]

On 31 March, the conference of ambassadors resolved on a naval demonstration to force Montenegro to back down.[175] Although Russia approved the decision, she declined to commit her ships for the task on the feeble ground that she had no ships in the Mediterranean.[176] However, Sazonov besought England and France to prevent Austria-Hungary from acting the major role by sending their own ships;[177] and to make the task of explaining their participation easier for them, Pevchevskii Most issued an official communiqué stating that they were taking part at the express wish of Russia.[178] By 4 April, all the great powers, except Russia, had instructed their war-ships to proceed toward the coast of Montenegro.[179] The naval demonstration alone proved ineffective and, in order to hold off the Serbian military transports, it was soon transformed into a blockade of the entire coast from Antivari to the mouth of the river Drim.[180]

The blockade, coupled with Austria's open threats of war, gradually produced the desired results, at least as far as concerned Serbia. On 8 April, to escape coming into contact and hence into conflict with the fleet of the great powers, the Serbian government decided to stop transporting additional reinforcements to Scutari. The following day, responding to rather grave representations from the Russian tsar and government, it announced that the Serbian forces would cease immediately all operations against Scutari and would withdraw from Albania altogether once the peace were concluded.[181]

Montenegro, however, refused to back down. King Nikola dismissed both the naval demonstration and the blockade as flagrant violations of the promised neutrality of the great powers.[182] When the conference made attempts to buy off Montenegro with offers of financial compensations, Cetinje rejected them as 'insults which neither the King nor Montenegro would ever accept.'[183] Thus, the

Montenegrins stuck to their undertaking and continued to struggle till the end: until 22 April, when the starved defenders surrendered and placed Scutari at the disposal of King Nikola[184]

Needless to say, the capitulation itself did not alter the basic positions of the great powers. Only a day later the conference of ambassadors declared that the occupation of Scutari had in no way affected the previous decisions of the powers and called upon Montenegro to hand Scutari over to them as soon as possible.[185] To make their determination felt they tightened and expanded the blockade to Durazzo (Drač),[186] and Austria-Hungary, supported by Germany and Italy, began to press for a direct military intervention.[187]

The Russian leaders, who had resorted to some vulgar words of reproach against Montenegro before the fall of Scutari, again found themselves in a delicate situation. For, no matter what Austria-Hungary and her allies suggested, they could not after all disregard entirely the jubilant reaction of public opinion at home.[188] And they could not neglect the fact that two of King Nikola's daughters were married to influential Russian grand dukes with strong army and court connections.[189] However, they could not very well demand now that Scutari be left in the possession of Montenegro; it was rather late for that. Hence, they tried to appease Cetinje in the only way left open to them: namely, they requested territorial and other compensations for Montenegro in return for Scutari.[190] Soon thereafter Russia prevailed upon Montenegro to accept such a point of view as well. The Cetinje government itself gave the first indication that it would yield peacefully on the last day of April when its minister at London called on Grey to enquire about the territorial and financial compensations Montenegro could expect to obtain.[191]

However, due to the violent opposition of Austria-Hungary, which rejected the idea of territorial concessions or for that matter any sort of compensation, King Nikola was left with very little besides hope. For in spite of Sazonov's feverish appeals to the other powers to help influence Vienna, Austria-Hungary refused to be moved.[192] Indeed, as Berchtold explained on 2 May, the question of Scutari now involved her entire Balkan program and the prestige of the monarchy. He left no doubt whatsoever that for the sake of both, Vienna was prepared and willing to dissociate itself from the other powers and embark upon a war with Montenegro and perhaps Serbia.[193]

As a result of strong pressures coming from all sides, from friends and enemies alike, in the end Montenegro took the advice of the ambassadorial conference and resolved to leave the matter of compensation in the hands of the powers.[194] On 4 May, King Nikola conveyed the decision to Grey in his role of chairman of the conference. As if copying the example set by Serbia, when she capitulated on the question of the territorial exit to the Adriatic Sea, King Nikola stated that his own honour as well as that of his people did not allow him to bow to the wishes of a single power. Therefore, he chose to place the fate of Scutari in the hands of all.[195]

VII

With the resolution of the Scutari crisis Montenegro joined in the unofficial cease-fire; the belligerents and the great powers turned to the task of reaching a peace settlement. On 28 and 29 April, separately and independently of each other, the Bulgarian and Turkish governments requested Grey to prepare a draft treaty of peace.[196] Grey obliged in the name of the ambassadorial conference and when he accomplished the work he handed copies of the project to ambassadors M. Madzharov and Tewfik Pasha.[197]

Grey's draft did not offer or demand anything new but merely restated the conditions contained in the last collective representation of the powers. Turkey had already agreed to those terms and, on 3 May, the Porte conveyed to the great powers its readiness to appoint delegates to the peace parley for which it again recommended London as the meeting-place.[198]

Just as in the case of the armistice agreement, Bulgaria did not inform her allies of the request to Grey. Greece, Montenegro, and Serbia learned about the draft on 5 May when the conference of ambassadors took it up.[199] The next day the Serbian legation at Sofia lodged two official protests with the Ministry of Foreign Affairs, accusing Bulgaria of having contravened the terms of the treaty and the military convention on both occasions.[200] In his reply Geshov argued that the Bulgarian government had not concluded a formal armistice, but had agreed only to a cease-fire, and that Bulgaria had as much right to stop hostilities against any fortified Turkish position as Serbia had had in terminating her operations against Scutari. In respect to the request to Grey for the draft treaty for preliminary peace, Geshov rejected the implied charges that Bulgaria had acted in collusion with the enemy, insisting that she acted alone and that she was not aware of the similar Turkish overture.[201]

Geshov's explanations did not suffice to heal the ill-feelings that divided Bulgaria from her allies or to hasten the peace. The divisions were, in any event, caused by much more consequential disagreements and disputes concerning the post-war territorial arrangements in the Balkans. Greece and Serbia were secretly concocting an alliance against Bulgaria for the division of Macedonia. Their positions there were very strong, for while the bulk of the Bulgarian armies were tied up needlessly in Thrace, the Greek and Serbian forces were concentrated on Bulgaria's western and southern frontiers and were in control of most of Macedonia, which had been assigned to Bulgaria by the terms of the Serbo-Bulgarian agreements.[202] Accordingly, the Bulgarians wanted to conclude peace and to free themselves from Turkey as soon as possible in order to claim, by force if necessary, their share of Macedonia. The Greeks and the Serbs, however, had nothing to lose by delaying the peace. Indeed they hoped to gain valuable time to entrench themselves even further in the disputed areas.

Consequently, when they began to deliberate Grey's draft for the preliminary peace, they were unable to arrive at a consensus. The Bulgarians were on the whole satisfied with the draft. They asked for a few insignificant changes in the Enos-Media line and when Sazonov indicated that these would be possible,[203] Sofia informed Grey that Bulgaria was ready to sign the preliminary peace.[204] The modifications sought by Serbia and Greece were more controversial since they infringed upon issues that the powers had reserved for the conference of ambassadors. For instance, Serbia demanded the inclusion of firm guarantees for a free port on the Adriatic Sea and the railway connections to it, as well as for the freedom to import and export all kinds of goods free of custom tariff or other duties.[205] The Greeks insisted on the inclusion of provisions for a general amnesty and on safeguards for the free passage of their vessels through the Straits.[206]

In order to prevent delays in the signing of the preliminary peace, Russia urged the allies to place these and all their additional demands in the protocols of the ambassadorial conference.[207] However, they refused because they feared that nothing would come of it. They accepted instead a Greek proposal to instruct the delegates to the peace conference to take up with the ambassadors or the Turkish representatives Grey's draft for preliminary peace and to insist that the objections and the additional demands of the allies be added to it at least in the form of an annex.[208]

In any case, when the Balkan governments announced officially, on 14 May, that they were ready to begin the peace talks,[209] they were promptly rebuffed. Europe was no longer interested in any peace talks or negotiations. The powers were asking the allies to sign the preliminary peace but discovered that only the Bulgarian delegates were authorized to do so.[210] Their Greek and Serbian counterparts refused to sign until they were informed about the decisions in regard to the islands, the Albanian frontiers, and the nature of the Paris conference which was to arrange the final financial settlement.[211] On 21 May, Novaković saw Grey and in the name of the Serbian, Greek, and Montenegrin delegations asked that these matters be included in the draft treaty. Grey turned him down and in his written reply declared that the conference of ambassadors would not permit any changes in the text and insisted that it must be signed the way it was. Thereupon the chief Serbian delegate threatened to leave for home unless changes were made.[212]

Meanwhile, at Sofia, Geshov found himself caught in the middle between the allies, on the one hand, and the court and most of the generals at home, on the other. While the former were delaying the peace, the latter pressured the government to conclude it immediately and, if necessary, to sign a separate peace with Turkey.[213] Geshov wished to prevent such an open violation of the treaties, but it was becoming more and more difficult for him to resist.[214] Unless the powers forced the signing of the preliminary peace, he wrote to St Petersburg, the Bulgarian government would have no alternative but to desert its allies.[215]

Although Russia was equally eager to see the war ended and peace reestablished in the Balkans, Pevchevskii Most refused to endorse a move which threatened the very existence of the Balkan system of alliances. Sazonov promised to work for the earliest peace but warned Sofia:

If the Bulgarians manifest unwarranted haste and conclude peace without awaiting the allies, they take upon themselves the responsibility for the rupture of the alliance, after which they could not count on Serbia to honor the treaty of alliance.[216]

In reply Geshov sent to Bobchev in St Petersburg a copy of a telegram from London; in it M. Madzharov argued that in view of the existence of a Greco-Serbian alliance directed against Bulgaria, Sofia must conclude peace with Turkey. If Sazonov wanted the continuation of the alliance, continued Madzharov, he should employ his influence more effectively. Finally, Geshov instructed Bobchev to see Sazonov and declare to him most categorically that if the allies refuse to sign, Bulgaria 'would be forced to present them with a time deadline in which to sign.'[217]

At this critical stage, Grey, who had impatiently watched the goings on between the allies, intervened and saved Geshov from having to resort to an ultimatum. On 27 May, he received individually on behalf of the ambassadorial conference the heads of the peace delegations, declaring to them that those delegates who were ready to sign the treaty as it stood had better do so at once and those who were not prepared to sign should leave. 'I would be ready to go to St. James Palace next Friday morning, the 30th instant, to be present at the signature of the Treaty.'[218] And on this date the representatives of all the belligerent states duly showed up and signed the Peace Treaty of London, which ended the war of the victorious Balkan allies against the Ottoman Empire.[219]

As far as the powers were concerned, peace had returned to the Near East: the war that threatened their interests and the peace of Europe was over. It was up to the allies now to settle the growing disagreements among themselves and decide whether in fact peace was destined to prevail in the Balkan peninsula as well.

5

The Bulgaro-Rumanian dispute

Rumania remained outside the Balkan system of alliances because neither of the two major conditions that helped unite the other four Balkan nations – fear of Austria-Hungary and antipathy toward the Ottoman Empire – affected or concerned the Rumanians. Rumania did not share a common boundary with Turkey. Her direct involvement in the Macedonian problem or the Eastern Question did not extend beyond the 'official' concern for the fate and well-being of the Kutso-Vlachs, a nomadic group of shepherds in the mountainous areas of Macedonia and Thrace, who spoke a Latin tongue akin to modern Rumanian. Shortly after the Congress of Berlin, Bucharest concluded a secret treaty with Vienna and moved into the orbit of the Triple Alliance.[1] This in effect predetermined Rumania's future relations with the Ottoman Empire, on the one hand, and Russia and her Balkan protégés, on the other.

The estrangement between Russia and Rumania began at the Congress of Berlin where the Rumanians, having fought side by side with Russia against Turkey before Plevna, were forced to 'retrocede' southern Bessarabia to Russia.[2] Rumania received northern Dobruja, but this did not appease successive governments in Bucharest. Her disillusionment was completed in 1880, when, due to Russia's persistence, the international commission on the delimitation of the Dobruja frontier between Rumania and Bulgaria awarded the town of Silistria to the latter.[3] These experiences instilled in governing circles in Bucharest 'distrust and fears' of Panslav expansion. In the consequent search for a powerful ally 'King Charles' dynastic and national sentiments pushed him toward the Central Powers, and his soldier's instinct in favour of the strongest military power in Europe impressed his all too realistic ministers.'[4] On 30 October 1883, Rumania concluded a secret treaty of alliance with Austria-Hungary, to which Germany adhered by a special protocol. While the other Balkan states drifted from one great power to another, Rumania remained loyal to the Triple Alliance through the years before the Balkan wars, indeed, until her entrance into the Great War in 1916 on the side of the Allied Powers.

Rumania's fear of Panslavism extended to the newly created principality of Bulgaria, which was virtually a vassal of Russia during the initial stage of its existence. Relations with Bulgaria were further complicated by Rumania's refusal to accept as permanent the Dobruja frontier established by the international commission.[5] The renewed rapprochement between St Petersburg and Sofia, following the fall of the pro-German Stambolovist régime, coupled with the impressive rise in Bulgaria's military posture in the Balkans in the first decade of the new century, only accentuated Rumania's enmity.

Unlike the other Balkan states Rumania stood for the preservation of the status quo in the peninsula: when the power of Turkey in Europe collapsed, all the Balkan states were to be compensated equally.[6] For the Rumanians this meant extension into Bulgarian Dobruja. They were determined not to permit 'any one-sided aggrandizement of Bulgaria.'[7]

Conscious of the ever-present threat from the immediate north, successive governments in Sofia looked for protection to Russia, the nation's liberator. Tradition, past commitments and assurances, and most recently the signing of the treaty of alliance with Serbia, made the Russophile Geshov-Danev coalition confident that Russia would indeed be on its side in case of danger from Rumania. Under Sazonov's leadership, however, Pevchevskii Most decided on an ambivalent course of policy. The special moral obligations that Russia assumed toward the Balkan allies, including Bulgaria, did not deter Sazonov from simultaneously wooing Rumania. In his memoirs, Sazonov wrote:

One of the first questions that seriously attracted my attention on my appointment as Minister of Foreign Affairs was that of our relations with Rumania. I knew that not only was she favourably inclined towards the Powers of the Triple Alliance, but she was actually bound by treaties to two of them, and therefore belonged to the camp of our political opponents. I was also aware of the reasons which rendered her policy hostile to Russia. Speaking generally, her attitude was due to the feeling of irritation inherited from the political leaders who played a great part in the war of 1877, and who were indignant with Russia for recovering, at the conclusion of the war with Turkey, the three southern districts of Bessarabia – which we had lost by the Treaty of Paris – in spite of our promise to Rumania to keep her territory intact.[8]

To win Rumania from the Triple Alliance Russia had to equal the 'brilliant prospects offered to her by Vienna and Berlin.' From a close connection with Russia and the Triple Entente Rumania might expect 'the realization of her national unity by the absorption of a population of nearly five million Rumanians, who were under Magyar yoke, and sincerely desired reunion with their brothers across the frontier.'⁹ Russia could advance this generous offer in the event of a direct confrontation with Austria-Hungary or between the Triple Entente and the Triple Alliance – a confrontation such as the Great War, which raised the entire question of the future of the Habsburg empire.

This was not, however, the situation in 1912. The offensive clauses of the accords concluded by the Balkan states were not aimed at Austria-Hungary, but at the Ottoman empire. The allies were not mediating the nationality problems of the Dual Monarchy, but planning to put an end to the Turkish presence in Europe.

Under these circumstances the attention of Rumania was not focused on Transylvania, but on southern Dobruja, and her designs were well known in St Petersburg. On 1 March 1912, Giers wrote to Sazonov that the views of the Rumanian ruling circles had not changed since his arrival in the Rumanian capital nine years earlier. Should Bulgaria make gains at the expense of Turkey Rumania would demand territorial concessions.¹⁰ The extent of the demands was not known on the eve of the war, but there was not any doubt that an allied victory would confront Russia with a terrible dilemma because both countries looked to St Petersburg for support: Bulgaria to safeguard her territorial integrity against a Rumanian invasion; Rumania to expand into southern Dobruja at the expense of Bulgaria.¹¹

I

After the conclusion of the treaties with Serbia and Greece, Bulgaria sought an accommodation with Rumania. However, her peaceful overtures and professions of friendship were largely ignored in Bucharest because, as T. Maiorescu, the Rumanian premier and foreign minister, pointed out in a conversation with the Bulgarian chargé d'affaires, as long as the status quo in the Balkans remained intact, he could not foresee any cause for serious differences between Rumania and Bulgaria and consequently talks between them were not necessary. Only in the event of a 'cataclysm' in Turkey requiring the resolution of the Eastern Question 'we shall encounter difficulties in the course of two or three weeks. During that time we would have to come to an agreement with the Bulgarian leaders, the Russians and the Austrians ... Only the Turkish problems could divide us.'¹²

On 2 August 1912, Geshov instructed Ikonomov to find out from Maiorescu what possible moves Rumania would consider if Bulgaria, as a result of such a 'cataclysm,' were 'forced to defend her interests and perhaps her very existence.'¹³ Maiorescu did not wish to pursue the topic any further at that particular time. 'We do not have the capacity to foresee that which has not occurred,' he told Ikonomov, 'we do not have the right to prepare, even theoretically, a revision of the *status quo*. Let us leave events on their natural and normal course of evolution.'[14] 'The fatal hour has not set in. It is still far away and there is no need for us to begin searching and allying. The Eastern Question has not exploded.'[15] Later in the month Geshov again raised the question of a possible rapprochement. He asked Ikonomov to suggest privately an 'exchange of views' between Sofia and Bucharest,[16] but Maiorescu declined this offer as well. He did not consider the situation sufficiently explosive to demand definitive talks with Bulgaria 'on matters that could still be easily settled or averted.'[17]

The Rumanian premier was only too well informed of the latest developments in the Balkans. By mid-summer 1912 he was convinced that an armed conflict was unavoidable,[18] but Rumania, tied to the Triple Alliance, could not join an anti-Turkish, indeed, anti-Austrian coalition, especially since the outcome of the approaching war looked extremely uncertain. The government in Bucharest underestimated the military might of the allies. It was inclined to believe that Turkey was still powerful enough to deal a decisive blow to any coalition of the small Balkan states.[19] Consequently, it did not wish to tie itself prematurely to either side. It preferred to remain free to manœuvre between Bulgaria and Turkey and at the most appropriate moment to present Sofia with its 'bill of particulars,'[20] in the form of a demand for the rectification of the common frontier in Dobruja.[21]

By the beginning of September the Bulgarian government had concluded that a basis for the settlement of the Bulgaro-Rumanian differences did not exist, but the preparations for war continued. Indeed, at this time the final decision rested no longer with Bulgaria, but with all the allies. The prevailing feeling among them was that the conditions for a victorious war against Turkey were too favourable to be missed.

Bulgaria's northern frontier was left unprotected, but the government in Sofia remained confident that the Rumanians would not intervene. It calculated that the formal representations to the Porte demanding the execution of reforms in Macedonia, in accordance with article 23 of the Treaty of Berlin and subsequent international agreements, would have a restraining effect in Bucharest; especially since the great powers themselves insisted on these reforms.[22] Furthermore, the Bulgarians took comfort in the fact that the alliances were concluded with the approval and assistance of the Russian government. The Rumanians were not certain of Russia's obligations toward the allies in general and Bulgaria in particular. Before undertaking any hostile action against her southern neighbour, Rumania, because of this uncertainty, had to take into consideration the possible reaction of Russia.[23]

The Bulgarians were taking a calculated, but a highly dangerous, risk just the same, since under the terms of the treaties, Russia was not obliged to come to the aid of Bulgaria against Rumania. In May 1912, in Livadia, Sazonov told Danev that the Russian government would try to convince the Rumanian government to remain neutral; but, if they refused to heed Russia's advice, Russia could not and would not resort to the use of force.[24]

More significantly yet, the Russian government was openly courting Rumania's favour. Early in September 1912, N. Shebeko arrived in Bucharest as the new Russian minister with the task of dissipating 'the misunderstandings' and achieving 'a *rapprochement* with Rumania which is united to Russia by a common faith and a mass of common interests.'[25] On 30 September, the very day the allied governments officially proclaimed mobilization, the Russian emperor appointed King Carol of Rumania 'General-Field Marshal of the Russian army on the occasion of his fifty years of military service.'[26]

Sofia, however, placed its hopes and confidence in 'unofficial' Russia. General I. Kholmsen, the Russian military attaché at Constantinople, reported to the general staff on 12 September: 'The Bulgarians count strongly on the public opinion in Russia; they reckon that if the worst came to the worst, Russia will prevent Rumania from intervening and from concluding an alliance with Turkey.'[27] Public opinion, as was shown during the Annexation Crisis, was a potent force in Moscow and St Petersburg, and the press and Slavophile circles were sensitive to developments in the Balkan peninsula. It would have been embarrassing, indeed extremely difficult, for the imperial government to observe 'the General-Field Marshal of the Russian army' intervene against unprotected southern Dobruja at a time when the Bulgarian army was engaged in an open war against the ancient common enemy.[28]

II

The quick and overwhelming victories of the allies took Bucharest by surprise. They destroyed whatever hopes the Rumanians might have entertained about independently assuming the role of 'honest broker' between Bulgaria and Turkey. Already, before the end of October, they found it necessary to apply to the great powers to uphold their as yet unspecified demands. The Rumanian government promised to preserve complete neutrality for the duration of the war, but trusted that the great powers would invite its participation at the peace conference.[29]

On 30 October, Shebeko informed Sazonov that Bucharest planned to demand territorial compensation, but he was still uncertain of its extent.[30] Gradually, however, this began to emerge in a confused and haphazard fashion. Shebeko was told that the demands were very modest, requiring slight changes in the boundary with Bulgaria and some guarantees for the rights of the Vlach population in Macedonia.[31] Prince Fürstenberg, the Austrian minister, reported that Rumania sought a rectification of the frontier in Dobruja 'without the inclusion of the cities of Russe and Varna.'[32] Shebeko and Ristić, the Serbian minister, heard that Rumania demanded a rectification that would include the cities of Balchik and Silistria.[33]

On 2 November, Take Ionescu, Rumania's minister of the interior, sent a personal friend of Premier Geshov on a special mission to Sofia. The following day, in a private conversation, he informed Geshov that Rumania would demand the territory from Tutrakhan to Balchik as compensation for her benevolent neutrality during the war.[34] This raised an extremely serious problem that had to be considered by the entire cabinet. The ministers, Geshov told him, were not likely to listen to any claims on Bulgarian territory at a time when the Bulgarian army was scoring impressive victories in the field.[35] Through Nekluidov he let St Petersburg know that Bulgaria would under no circumstances consent to territorial demands from Bucharest.[36]

Austria-Hungary stood solidly behind Rumania. Vienna was prepared to advance Rumania's demands for compensation, and even though the great powers had not yet decided whether a peace conference would be held, Count Berchtold assured Bucharest of the support of Austria-Hungary.[37]

Russia's position was not so clear-cut. Shebeko had told Maiorescu that his government intended to support the rectification of the border in Dobruja.[38] When Bobchev inquired about the nature of Russia's commitment Sazonov replied that he had only advised Russia's representatives abroad to bear in mind the possibility of a border concession. He thought it best if the two governments reached a direct bilaterial agreement.[39]

On 8 November, Geshov sent to St Petersburg a proposal containing, as he put it, Bulgaria's maximum concessions. Sofia was prepared: 1) to accord extensive cultural and economic guarantees to the Kutso-Vlachs in Macedonia; 2) to promise under the guarantee of Russia or the powers not to seek additional territory in Dobruja, and not to maintain any troops except border guards in Silistria and on the Rumanian border in Dobruja; 3) to concede to Rumania one or two strategic points around Silistria, but would not consent to be deprived of a larger piece of land.[40]

The same day Danev left Sofia to plead Bulgaria's cause in Austria-Hungary. Through Berchtold, with whom he planned to meet in Budapest, he hoped to bend Rumania into disclaiming her intentions to seek territorial compensation.[41] He received a flattering reception in Budapest. Emperor Francis Joseph and, particularly, Archduke Francis Ferdinand seemed well disposed toward Bulgaria. It was very clear, however, that the Bulgarians could not depend on Vienna in their dispute with Rumania. 'Only in respect to Rumania,' Danev telegraphed King Ferdinand, 'the Emperor recommended that we concede something small because the position of the King has become much more difficult.'[42] Before the parliamentary commission of inquiry in 1914, Danev explained that he became convinced in

Budapest that Austria-Hungary would support Rumania's claim to expand at the expense of Bulgaria: 'It might be said that I was, at least partially, satisfied only in regard to one consideration, namely, that Austria would strive to influence Rumania not to resort to extreme measures and to be moderate in her demands.'[43]

Meanwhile, on 9 November, Maiorescu officially requested the mediation of the Russian government 'to clear up, by way of confidential friendly talks, the attitude of Bulgaria toward the question of the possible rectification of the Rumanian-Bulgarian border from Tutrakhan to the Black Sea with the inclusion of Silistria.'[44] Shebeko interpreted this move as a convincing indication that Rumania was drawing away from Austria and into the Russian sphere of influence.[45] The outcome of the Russo-Austrian rivalry for the allegiance of Bucharest hinged on their contributions toward the achievement of Rumania's aims.[46] Hence, he urged Sazonov to respond favourably and without delay to Maiorescu's request.[47] Bobchev, however, begged Sazonov not to undertake any commitment until the attitude of his government became known. Geshov feared that Russia's consent to mediate the dispute might be taken in Bucharest as tacit approval of Rumania's claims. Through Nekliudov he asked Sazonov to decline the role.[48]

Russia was not anxious to get directly involved in the dispute as long as this complete divergence of views persisted and an agreement was not in sight. But, given Russia's goal of attaining a rapprochement with Rumania, Sazonov could not easily reject Maiorescu's request.[49] Sazonov again chose a safe and middle course. In principle he agreed to mediate the dispute, but urged both sides, particularly Sofia, to continue seeking a direct understanding.[50]

In view of the rumours pertaining to an imminent intervention from the north, which were in fact altogether unjustified, Nekliudov pressed Sofia to respond to Rumania's demands,[51] and on his own initiative advised Geshov to send Danev on a special mission to Bucharest.[52] 'It would be extremely important,' he wrote to Sazonov, 'to ward off any kind of rash actions from Rumania ... until the question of Danev's trip is decided.'[53]

The Bulgarian government agreed and, having received King Ferdinand's approval, Geshov informed St Petersburg of Danev's impending visit to the Rumanian capital.[54] To G. Kalinkov, his minister at Bucharest, who was not consulted at all, Geshov wrote: 'In order to prove our high appreciation of Rumania's friendship we have decided to send Danev to Bucharest for exploratory talks ... Convey this strictly confidentially to the Rumanian Minister of Foreign Affairs. Be cautious not to raise hopes for a rectification of any kind.'[55] Kalinkov was taken completely by surprise. Only three days earlier, on 13 November, Maiorescu had told him that the time was not ripe for Rumania to put forth '*notre petite note.*' 'I believe that moment will soon come and then, *sans violer la susceptibilité réciproque*, we will not neglect the occasion to prove that we are good friends and excellent neighbours.'[56] He considered Danev's visit untimely and hazardous and, before informing Maiorescu, he decided to await further instructions from Sofia, warning Geshov:

In view of the categorical declaration of the Minister of Foreign Affairs that for the time being Rumania wants nothing from us and does not make any proposals to us, I consider Danev's coming here premature and very harmful. It would senselessly agitate the public opinion and the rather tranquil and correct behaviour of the governing circles who will direct ... at the special emissary questions relating to the [border] rectification and its magnitude. If his replies prove to be negative, our relations will deteriorate sharply.[57]

Kalinkov was, of course, right. With Rumania demanding, and Bulgaria denying, her right to territorial compensation there was no basis for direct talks. By accepting Nekliudov's advice, Sofia committed a tactical blunder and now sought to throw the main responsibility into the lap of the Russian government. Bobchev conveyed to Sazonov Kalinkov's objections and showed him a telegram from Teodorov, minister of finance and Geshov's chief confidant, proposing to surrender the entire dispute into the hands of Russia.[58]

The Russians, however, refused to accept this task. They were already committed to support, at least in part, the Rumanian claims. Sazonov, as well as Shebeko and Nekliudov, had endorsed Rumania's claim to compensation. The assumption of the role of mediator, at this point, entailed forcing Bulgaria to make the necessary concessions. Moreover, Sazonov had already notified Maiorescu of Danev's impending visit. Its cancellation would have been viewed as a slap in the face by the Rumanians. Consequently, Sazonov impressed upon Bobchev that Russia considered the visit desirable and necessary.[59]

Under these circumstances the Bulgarian government did not have any alternative. 'In view of the insistence of all the friendly Powers,' Geshov wrote to Kalinkov, 'we shall send Danev to exchange views and not to negotiate.'[60] He was authorized to pledge Bulgaria's readiness to safeguard Dobruja to Rumania 'with whatever earnest guarantees she desired, short of territorial concessions.'[61]

Danev stopped in the Rumanian capital on 8 December 1912, while on his way to London for the peace negotiations.[62] He met with Maiorescu and Ionescu and was received by King Carol. Shebeko reported that his thirty-six-hour stay made a very favourable impression.[63] The Rumanian leaders complimented Sofia for having selected 'for such a delicate mission perhaps its best and most conciliatory man.'[64]

From the talks with Danev, Maiorescu claimed to have understood that in principle Bulgaria accepted Rumania's right to compensation and that an agreement would be possible. Moreover, he contended that they agreed that formal negotiations on this and all related topics would commence immediately in London and that Sofia would make the initial proposal.[65] The negotiation's were to be conducted simultaneously with the peace talks by Danev and N. Mişu, Rumania's very able minister at the Porte, who was shortly transferred to London for this very purpose.[66]

The Rumanian leaders either misunderstood Danev, or intentionally publicized assumptions calculated to throw doubt on the sincerity and honesty of the Bulgarian side in order to force its hand in future negotiations. In any event these contentions and assumptions were denied by the Bulgarians and proved wrong by subsequent developments. In his memoirs Kalinkov wrote:

Mr. Danev left Bucharest the following day convinced that he did not agree on anything with his interlocutors, and that he promised nothing positively except full legal church and school rights for the Kutso-Vlachs in Macedonia.[67]

As he had cautioned Geshov, Danev's visit did not contribute toward the settlement of the dispute. On the contrary, it complicated all future negotiations. 'From this point began our fatal misunderstandings with the Rumanians,' concluded Kalinkov, 'as a result of which Mr. Danev ... became [for them] a most despicable man and a worthless diplomat.'[68]

III

Anticipating a specific proposal Maiorescu authorized Mişu to begin the negotiations immediately.[69] Before the end of the month, he was joined by T. Ionescu, who came to London supposedly on a vacation, but in reality to direct the negotiations from behind the scenes.[70]

Since they lived under the constant threat of a possible invasion, the Bulgarians could not reject the talks altogether.[71] They strove, however, to conduct them on 'a wider basis,' one that would not involve the cession of populated areas.[72] Danev was only permitted to meet and hear from Mişu Rumania's minimal demands;[73] when he asked for additional instructions from Sofia, they were not readily available. Consequently, the meetings turned into meaningless and embarrassing affairs. 'I used to meet with the Rumanian delegates,' stated Danev, 'but I either did not talk at all, or tried to avoid talking under whatever pretext. Well, one could say once that he does not have instructions, but the second time – there is no reason why the instructions could not have arrived.'[74]

On 28 December 1912, Danev took the initiative. He prepared a proposal containing four points and asked Count Benckendorff to communicate them to St Petersburg. They provided for: 1) church and school autonomy for the Kutso-

Vlachs in Macedonia; 2) the razing of all forts and fortifications in Silistria and, in the last resort, the cession of the strategic position Medzhidie-Tabia; 3) rectification of the frontier involving the cession of about twenty villages to Rumania; and 4) a guarantee for the inviolability of Rumanian Dobruja.[75] Unaware of this move, Geshov instructed Denev on the following day to propose to the Rumanians to take up the sovereign rights over Mount Athos in place of the rectification of their common frontier.[76]

When Sazonov turned to Bobchev for a confirmation of Danev's four points, the Bulgarian minister told him that he had not been informed of any proposals submitted by Danev,[77] but he handed Sazonov Geshov's plan for Mount Athos. Russia planned to turn the Holy Mountain into a completely autonomous region, and Sazonov dismissed Geshov's scheme as not being worth his serious consideration.[78] However, he seemed highly impressed with Danev's four points,[79] which represented a radical departure from Bulgaria's previous stand, and he advised Bucharest to utilize them as a basis for an agreement. 'The stated principles in our opinion embody serious guarantees of the Rumanian interests,' wrote Sazonov to Shebeko. 'We hope very strongly that the Rumanian Government will find it suitable to accept the proposal.'[80]

Sofia followed suit and empowered Danev to begin official negotiations on the four points.[81] In case the Rumanians rejected them, and the Danev-Mişu talks collapsed, Bulgaria asked the Russian government to mediate the dispute using the four points as a basis.[82] Teodorov was dispatched to St Petersburg to win the support of Russia.[83]

On 3 January 1913, during the first formal meeting, Mişu rejected the four points, because they offered too little. He told Danev that Rumania's minimal territorial demands extended along the line from a point west of Silistria to the Black Sea, south of Balchik.[84] In the mean time, in Paris and London, Ionescu spread public accusations that Danev did not act honestly and that he broke all engagements and promises made during his short stay in Bucharest.[85] Wounded by these baseless and unjust attacks, Danev refused to continue the negotiations and recommended the appointment of M. Madzharov, the Bulgarian minister at London, as the chief negotiator.[86] King Ferdinand and the Council of Ministers, however, refused to accept his resignation and urged him instead to seek an explanation from Ionescu or Mişu.[87] When Danev approached them, both Rumanian delegates feigned complete surprise; Ionescu denied making such statements and told Danev that he regretted the incident.[88]

The government in Bucharest reacted differently. On 7 January, it notified St Petersburg, Vienna, and Sofia, that in view of Bulgaria's refusal to consider seriously Rumania's claims, her troops would occupy the demanded area within the next few days without a declaration of war.[89] Russia and Austria-Hungary protested.[90] Sazonov warned Bucharest that such an inexcusable step would stir strong resentment in Russia.[91] When Danev was persuaded to continue the talks, the Rumanian government changed its mind and promised to refrain from invading northern Bulgaria as long as the talks continued.[92]

In the meeting of 10 January, the Rumanians scaled down their demands from the line Tutrakhan-Balchik to Tutrakhan-Kavarna and asked for a counterproposal.[93] The Bulgarian government had placed its hopes in Teodorov's trip to St Petersburg and awaited his arrival there before forwarding Danev new instructions.[94] Teodorov's chief aim was to persuade the Russian government not to abandon the four points.

The Rumanian threats of intervention had a strong effect on Russia. By the time of Teodorov's arrival in St Petersburg Sazonov had altered his stand; he urged Sofia to forget the four points and accept a new line that was in the mean time presented to him by Nano, the Rumanian minister.[95] Hoping that Sazonov would be persuaded to return to his former position, Sofia resorted to delaying tactics. Instead of sending Danev new instructions Geshov asked him to seek again an official reply to the four points and to emphasize that Russia strongly recommended their acceptance.[96] This time Danev did not even get an opportunity to see Mişu. The centre of the negotiations had shifted for the moment to the Russian capital.

On 13 January 1913, Bucharest forwarded to the Russian government a new proposal which demanded the territory north of the Silistria-Kavarna line, including those two cities. The Rumanians were particularly insistent on acquiring Sisistria. This proposal embraced a smaller area than the original Rumanian line Tutrakhan-Balchik, but larger than what Nano had suggested only a few days earlier. Should Bulgaria accept this proposal, Rumania promised military, economic, and financial assistance in her struggle against Turkey.[97]

Since his arrival in St Petersburg Teodorov had made at least some progress by swaying the Russian leaders to his point of view. He argued that a sincere rapprochement between Bulgaria and Rumania, which Russia sought to bring about, could not be achieved by forcing Bulgaria to sacrifice populated areas. Such concessions would not be approved by the Grand National Assembly, and occupation by force would result not in rapprochement, but in permanent enmity between the two nations. At least for the time being Teodorov persuaded Sazonov to return to the proposal made by Naño, which did not claim any Bulgarian towns, and promised to win his government's approval. A measure of Teodorov's successful lobbying was Sazonov's outright rejection, on 15 January, of an Austrian proposal for a joint representation at Sofia.[98]

The Rumanian dispute and Teodorov's latest recommendations from St Petersburg were taken up on 15 January by the crown council which met in Mustafa

Pasha. Sensitive to the reaction of public opinion and unwilling to assume the burden of responsibility, the civilian ministers remained opposed to any territorial concessions.[99] They consented only after the six participating generals – Savov, Ivanov, Kutunchev, Dimitriev, Fichev, and Kovachev – signed a protocol suggesting a rectification of the Rumanian-Bulgarian frontier as the only means of forestalling a Rumanian occupation of northern Bulgaria.[100]

The government worked out a project incorporating all the main points contained in Nano's proposal.[101] Bulgaria agreed to cede Medzhidie-Tabia, make some concessions on the northeastern boundary, and cede a small stretch of the Black Sea coast, south of the Rumanian port of Mangalia. Geshov instructed Teodorov to convey the plan to Sazonov and inform him that it contained Bulgaria's maximum concessions. It was being made, Geshov added, on the following conditions: 1) Bulgaria would receive Adrianople; and 2) Russia would (a) side with Bulgaria if Rumania rejected it and demanded additional concessions, (b) support Bulgaria's further expansion in the east if the war against Turkey were resumed, and (c) support Bulgaria if Greece rejected the principle of commensurability and Serbia attempted to circumvent the terms of the treaty of alliance dealing with the division of the conquered territories.[102] Sazonov assured Teodorov that Russia would do everything possible to persuade Rumania to renounce her claims to Silistria and the use of force to occupy it. Thereupon, Teodorov declared: 'the occupation of Silistria would inevitably result in a war, and ... in such an event we expect the aid of Russia in accordance with the Convention of 1902 and the force of historical traditions.' Sazonov replied: 'The Convention of 1902 does not exist. His Highness King Ferdinand renounced it before Izvol'skii and the Emperor and this is well known to Malinov and Paprikov. As for the historical traditions, they oblige us to help you, and we are doing that.'[103]

Teodorov's activities in St Petersburg again raised the fear of Panslavism in Bucharest. The Rumanians now changed their minds and no longer wished to see Russia involved in the dispute.[104] Indeed they threatened to counter the Bulgarian request for the mediation of Russia by bringing in all the great powers. Politely, but firmly, Sazonov reminded them that they were the first to seek the mediation of Russia, and Bulgaria had only followed their example. He viewed Bulgaria's assent to cede Medzhidie-Tabia as a major concession and asked Bucharest not to insist on the town of Silistria.[105] In an equally polite manner Maiorescu turned down Sazonov's recommendations and rejected the mediation of Russia. Rumania preferred to stick to the bilateral negotiations until the two sides reached a 'dead end' by way of mutual concessions.[106]

The talks in London, however, were not making progress at all. While Ionescu and Mişu awaited new Bulgarian proposals, Danev feared meeting them because he did not have anything to propose.[107] On 14 January, Ionescu sent him a letter in which he threatened to return home immediately unless Danev met him and renewed the deadlocked talks.[108] Danev had not been informed of the crown council or of the latest scheme worked out by Sofia and consequently, to prevent another embarrassing confrontation, he put forward what he termed a final proposal explicitly stating that Bulgaria could not cede Medzhidie-Tabia, because of its strategic location vis-à-vis Silistria. Ionescu expressed the hope that this was not Bulgaria's final word, and the following morning headed for Bucharest.[109]

Meanwhile, Geshov sent Danev a new five-point proposal, which was in effect the last made by Sofia in London. It reiterated the guarantee of the inviolability of Rumanian Dobruja and the school and church rights of the Kutso-Vlachs in Macedonia. It conceded to Rumania Medzhidie-Tabia, a piece of Bulgarian land in the north embracing about 20 villages, and a strip of the Black Sea coast, six versts (approximately 6.4 kilometres) in length, to the south of Mangalia. Mişu again rejected this proposal because the territorial concessions were not sufficient.[110]

As far as the Rumanians were concerned the talks in London failed. They blamed the failure on Bulgaria's intransigence and threw the whole responsibility for it into Danev's lap. They wished to avoid any further dealings with him and suggested transferring the talks to Sofia or Bucharest.[111] The Bulgarian government, however, considered Danev, who had been engaged with the dispute from its very outset, as the best qualified person. If the Rumanian government did not wish to continue the talks in London, their resumption would have to wait until Danev was freed from his task as Bulgaria's chief delegate at the peace conference.[112]

Before the break-up of the peace talks, a crown council held in the royal palace in Bucharest decided to approach Danev for the last time.[113] 'You have the necessary instructions,' wrote Maiorescu to Mişu, 'which contain our demands in respect to the border question: maximum Tutrakhan-Dobrich-Balchik, minimum Silistria-Balchik without Dobrich. Compel Danev to fix Bulgaria's final offerings and communicate them to us immediately.'[114] Mişu saw Danev the same day, 25 January, and proposed the minimal line, Silistria-Balchik, but Danev argued that this line had already been disavowed by Ionescu as excessive and, when Mişu persisted, he told him that Bulgaria's reply was a categorical rejection.[115] In the final instruction to Mişu on 26 January, Maiorescu authorized him to sign a protocol wrapping up the talks:

If [Danev's] proposals offer a borderline leaving Silistria and Kavarna to Rumania and Bulgaria does not require any compensations or aid from Rumania, you may accept and sign a protocol constituting an agreement. If, however, Danev does not offer Silistria and

Kavarna you must establish in the protocol that we demand the line Tutrakhan-Balchik and that you did not reach an agreement. Please hurry up and finish.[116]

During the last meeting in London Danev again submitted Bulgaria's five points. Mişu rejected them, and, in accordance with Maiorescu's instructions, reintroduced Rumania's very first and maximal proposal. To wrap up the unsuccessful talks the two chief negotiators agreed to draw up a protocol recording Rumania's demands and Bulgaria's offerings.[117] It was signed on 29 January 1913,[118] with the understanding that the talks would be continued. [119] A few days later the two governments agreed to renew the talks in Sofia, though neither side showed any hope for a bilateral understanding. Prince Ghika, the minister at Sofia, represented Rumania; S. Danev and M. Sarafov, a former minister at Bucharest, represented Bulgaria.[120]

IV

At the beginning of the dispute, Russia, eager to draw Rumania into her sphere of influence, viewed benevolently and indeed encouraged the Rumanian claims. But, when after the renewal of the war against Turkey, it became obvious what a disruptive role Bucharest could play in the Balkan system of alliances, St Petersburg found out that it was too late to reverse or even modify this course of policy.

The outcome of the second stage of the war against Turkey was not certain. The allies were already quarrelling about the spoils of victory. The possibility that Rumania might take advantage of the divisions to strike against Bulgaria could not be wholly discounted. Sazonov continued to refute Geshov's contentions that the Russo-Bulgarian Convention of 1902 was still in force and to claim that Russia was not obligated to come to the aid of Bulgaria.[121] But, as Izvol'skii told Danev in Paris, 'Russia could not allow the amputation of Bulgaria, even if there was no convention.'[122]

At the end of January, when the talks in London broke down, Sazonov deemed it necessary to direct a warning at Bucharest. The Bulgarian concessions, made on the insistence of the imperial government, Sazonov wrote, were sufficiently serious and extensive to satisfy Rumania:

A Rumanian attack or military occupation of Bulgarian lands without a declaration of war before the latter settled her accounts with Turkey would incite in our public opinion an outburst of sympathy toward the Bulgarians to which the government would not be able to remain indifferent. Moreover, we are compelled to remind Rumania that in the present negotiations she has departed completely from the original demands for a strategical rectification of the border.[123]

In the course of a long interview with Shebeko, Maiorescu confessed that the proposal included in the protocol did not represent Rumania's genuine claims.[124] In Mişu's words, 'it was thrown in for bargaining.'[125] Maiorescu emphasized, however, that Rumania would continue to insist on the cession of Silistria. Reporting the interview to Sazonov, Shebeko wrote that Maiorescu left him with the impression that Rumania would not resort to the use of force for the moment and might even be content with Bulgaria's last five points if the coastal strip were extended to include Kavarna or Kaliakra.[126] Sazonov grasped this suggestion and advised Sofia to accept it as the only way by which Silistria could be saved.[127]

Geshov did not share Sazonov's optimism. He doubted that Rumania would be satisfied with just another bit of the Black Sea coast. Moreover, he feared that new concessions offered directly by Sofia, after the hostilities against Turkey had been renewed, would be interpreted in Bucharest as tokens of Bulgaria's weakened position and would only stimulate further demands. Therefore, Geshov asked Sazonov to persuade Rumania to accept the mediation of Russia alone or, if necessary, of Russia and another power, and to impose his recommendations on both sides.[128]

Sazonov was elated with Geshov's conciliatory response. He declined the role of official mediator because, as he wrote Shebeko earlier, it 'involved great risks,'[129] but he conveyed the proposal to Bucharest and urged its acceptance.[130] Either Shebeko's impressions were erroneous, or the Rumanian government again altered its position. A larger strip of the Black Sea coast was no longer adequate. Maiorescu now stated that the Rumanian government decided to ask for the town of Silistria. This was a final and irreversible demand.[131]

The same day, 12 February, at the first official meeting of the bilateral talks in Sofia, Rumania demanded an area of 3,200 square kilometres stretching from Silistria to Balchik, and Prince Ghika set a deadline for the Bulgarian reply.[132] In Bucharest, Maiorescu informed Kalinkov that if Sofia failed to meet the deadline and refused to cede Silistria, his government, the last one committed to a peaceful settlement of the dispute, would certainly resign.[133]

Sazonov had not informed Sofia that the proposal embodying his own recommendations had already been turned down by Bucharest. Consequently, when Geshov appealed to him to press that proposal,[134] Sazonov told Bobchev: 'You are very late in making this proposal ... I would very much like to help you, but I do not know how.' He advised Sofia to give its utmost attention to the cession of Silistria.[135]

This unexpected twist in Sazonov's position dismayed governing circles in Sofia. 'On the basis of Mr Bobchev's previous dispatches,' wrote Nekliudov, 'they assumed that Russia would never ask them to cede Silistria to Rumania and see in this sudden change the bankruptcy of their own policy.'[136] Geshov instructed Bobchev to declare to Sazonov: 'It is a great fallacy to think that by giving away Silistria Russia would win Rumania. Russia will not win Rumania, but will lose Bulgaria.'[137]

This prophetic warning was uttered by the head of the Russophile government that had finally committed Bulgaria to Russia and to the cause of Balkan unity. However, it did not have any effect on Sazonov. He rejected all Bulgarian pleadings and appeals for Russia's direct intervention in the dispute;[138] instead, he put the squeeze on Bulgaria by requesting London and Paris to press Sofia to cede the line Silistria-Shabla.[139] Tsar Nicholas and the Russian Council of Ministers shared Sazonov's reasoning:

One Silistria does not merit a war just as neither Scutari nor Djakova were worth a war. Bulgaria and Serbia should have avoided placing Russia constantly in danger. Russia, after all, has her own distinct national interests which she cannot sacrifice anytime it suited someone else. As far as vital Slavic interests are concerned, Russia has the right to choose for herself the time when to act.[140]

At the second session of the Sofia negotiations, on 15 February, Prince Ghika reiterated Rumania's last proposal, while the Bulgarians advanced the line Med-zhidie-Tabia-Shabla.[141] Sazonov spoke in favour of this line at Bucharest, but Maiorescu rejected it because it did not include either Silistria or Kaliakra.[142]

By now both sides recognized that the continuation of the bilateral talks had become useless. Out of sheer desperation and helplessness, and without a trace of enthusiasm, the two governments consented to leave the dispute in the hands of one, two, or all the great powers.[143]

V

On 14 February 1913, the conference of ambassadors in London pondered the Bulgaro-Rumanian dispute. Marquis Imperiali, the Italian ambassador, proposed a great power mediation.[144] Taking up this initiative, Sazonov went one step further and instead of simple mediation recommended a great power resolution of the dispute. The other powers agreed and, on 19 February, the representatives of the great powers at Sofia and Bucharest officially requested the two governments to leave their dispute to the decision of the great powers.[145]

Bulgaria consented without any reservations.[146] To counterbalance the favour-able disposition of both power blocs toward Rumania, Geshov and Teodorov commenced secret talks with Count Tarnowski. In return for Austrian support in the disputes with Rumania, Greece, and Serbia and at the peace negotiations with Turkey, the Bulgarian government promised to hand over to Austria-Hungary control of the railway lines Skopje-Salonica and Salonica-Bitola as well as a free zone in Salonica should that city be annexed by Bulgaria.[147]

The Rumanians were careful to make the distinction between great power mediation and settlement. They preferred the former because it appeared less binding but even here their acceptance was not immediate or unconditional. Before responding to the great powers, Maiorescu proposed to Russia to arbitrate the dispute alone or with another power, possibly Italy, with either Great Britain or Germany in the role of supreme arbiter. As an integral part of this proposal Maiorescu demanded in advance a pledge that Silistria would be awarded to Rumania.[148] Only when Sazonov, insisting that the powers of the mediators should not be restricted by any conditions, rejected the proposal,[149] Bucharest accepted, on 23 February, the 'mediation' of all the six powers.[150] Geshov took exception to the use of the word 'mediation' instead of 'settlement,' but Maiorescu appeased him and the powers by arguing that the difference constituted a pure formality, since both Bulgaria and Rumania would find it extremely difficult to turn down the mediatory decision of the six great powers.[151]

Originally Sazonov intended to delegate the dispute to the conference of ambassadors in London,[152] but he and Geshov accepted[153] a Rumanian suggestion to call another conference in St Petersburg.[154] The participants, besides Sazonov, were the ambassadors of the five great powers of Europe at St Petersburg.

The procedural format of the conference was the following: Rumania was asked to present her demands and conclusions, and then Bulgaria to make her rejoinder; whenever it was deemed necessary the conference requested additional submissions and explanations; finally it concluded its work in secret sessions.[155] There was a controversy on how the final decision would be reached. After a prolonged debate all agreed to Count Berchtold's suggestion that it would have to be approved unanimously.[156]

Neither Rumania nor Bulgaria was permitted to participate in the sittings of the conference, their presentations being submitted in writing. To avoid behind-the-scene intrigues and complications instigated by appeals to the local press and public opinion, Sazonov asked Sofia and Bucharest not to send any delegates.[157]

The question of Silistria was the focal point of the dispute. Even before the deliberations of the conference commenced, Russia and Austria had agreed privately and indicated to Sofia that Silistria could not be saved.[158] The main task of the St Petersburg conference, therefore, was to determine whether concessions other than Silistria would be made to Rumania, and to decide if and how Bulgaria would be compensated.[159]

The first session of the conference was held on 31 March 1913. The discussions, Buchanan wrote, were 'conducted on purely party lines – the Ambassadors of the Triple Alliance taking the side of Rumania, while the cause of Bulgaria was pleaded by Sazonov, Delcassé and myself.'[160] The ambassadors of the Triple Alliance advanced the line Silistria-Balchik. This was rejected by their Entente counterparts since it required unreasonably large concessions from Bulgaria.[161] Later they were joined by Pourtalès and Carlotti in opposition to Count Thurn's proposal to award Salonica to Bulgaria as compensation.[162]

At the second session, on 4 April, the Triple Alliance scaled down Rumania's demands and argued specifically in favour of ceding Silistria. Buchanan, a former minister at Sofia and Bulgaria's chief defender at the conference, spoke at first in opposition, but eventually joined Sazonov in support of a compromise proposal presented by Delcassé. The Entente representatives were ready to accept the cession of Silistria provided that the other territorial demands of Rumania were abandoned and that the Rumanian government compensate those inhabitants of Silistria who wished to leave the town and move into Bulgaria.[163]

During three subsequent sittings, on 7, 11, and 15 April, Count Thurn continued his efforts to win compensations for whatever sacrifices Bulgaria might be called upon to make and, together with Carlotti and Pourtalès, sought greater territorial gains for Rumania. The Entente objected on both counts. This apparent deadlock was overcome only when the latter agreed to assign to Rumania, as a final concession, the area within a three-kilometre radius of Silistria.[164]

On 17 April, the decisions of the conference were summarized into a four-point proposal.[165] With the exception of a few minor and insignificant additions, it comprised the final draft of the St Petersburg Protocol, signed by Sazonov and the five ambassadors on 8 May 1913.[166] Two days later, Sazonov handed Bobchev and Nano sealed copies of this document. At the request of the Bulgarian government[167] he asked Bucharest to delay its publication until the peace negotiations in London were concluded.[168]

The Russian government was elated with the settlement. It had placed itself between two disputing parties with irreconcilably contradictory aims, and strived not to alienate either; a settlement forced upon the disputants by all the great powers provided the best possible way out of the dilemma. It appeared that neither Rumania nor Bulgaria could blame Russia if she deemed the decision unjust. In his memoirs Sazonov wrote that the results of the conference 'should have been recognized as satisfactory, for they obviated the possibility of fresh complications at a time which was clearly sufficiently disturbing and dangerous.'[169] In reality, however, the decisions embodied in the St Petersburg Protocol satisfied neither Bulgaria nor Rumania.[170]

Engaged in critical disputes with Greece and Serbia, Bulgaria had to swallow the bitter pill, and feeling let down by Russia she began to seek to be in the good graces of the other great powers. The Russophile Geshov-Danev government did not view the outstretched helping hand of Austria-Hungary with complete confidence, but the only other alternatives open to it were the abdication of power or a frightening diplomatic isolation.[171]

For the Rumanians the settlement was altogether inadequate and they regarded it as a temporary solution at best. As King Carol explained to the German minister: 'Silistria was not owed to the good will and sincere desire of the Bulgarians, but to the authority of Europe.' He expected now a voluntary *beau geste* from the Bulgarian side.[172] In Bucharest the opposition Conservatives led by P. Carp were soon joined by the governing Liberals in the public clamour against the St Petersburg Protocol.[173]

Most significantly, however, the Rumanian government encouraged the tempting overtures from the Greeks and the Serbs, who were concocting an alliance against Bulgaria for the defence of their conquests in Macedonia. 'Here they follow with strenuous attention the wranglings between the allies,' reported Shebeko, 'taking up exclusively the side of the Greek and Serbian aspirations. Rumania would undoubtedly take advantage of an armed conflict between Serbia and Bulgaria to realize all her claims.'[174] Needless to say, these were ominous developments for the Balkan system of alliances, the survival of which was a primary aim of Russia's foreign policy.

6

The uncoupling of
the Balkan system of alliances

In the course of the great powers' deliberations on the peace settlement in southeastern Europe, the St Petersburg government endeavoured, alone or with whatever support it was able to muster from its partners in the Triple Entente, to uphold the aims of the allied Balkan states. However, confronted with the determined and united opposition of the Triple Alliance led by Austria-Hungary, Russia surrendered on the most crucial issues – the Albanian question and the Serbian territorial exit on the Adriatic Sea, Scutari, and the Bulgaro-Rumanian dispute. By so doing Russia avoided a possible European war for which she was not prepared and thus attained one of her major foreign policy aims. But, at the same time, and largely as a result of it, Russia placed in jeopardy her other primary aim – the preservation of the Balkan system of alliances.

For with the collapse of Serbia's ambitious pretensions on the Adriatic Sea, Belgrade sought an effective recompense in Macedonia where it encountered the intransigent and unyielding opposition of Bulgaria. The consequent territorial conflict between these two allied nations intensified the already existing dispute between Bulgaria and Greece and vice versa. More significantly, the divisions among the allies provided Rumania with a welcome opportunity for diplomatic manœuvring between them which gave the Bulgaro-Rumanian dispute a much more serious and destructive character.[1]

In its attempts to resolve the inter-allied disputes peaceably the Russian government exhibited an even greater degree of hesitancy and indecision than in the dispute between Bulgaria and Rumania. At one time or another Sazonov promised to support the irreconcilably contradictory aims of each of the disputing parties. This constant wavering and inconsistency dispirited the Balkan governments. Each suspected Russia of favouring its opponent's point of view and became convinced that she would not be able to come up with and impose a rational

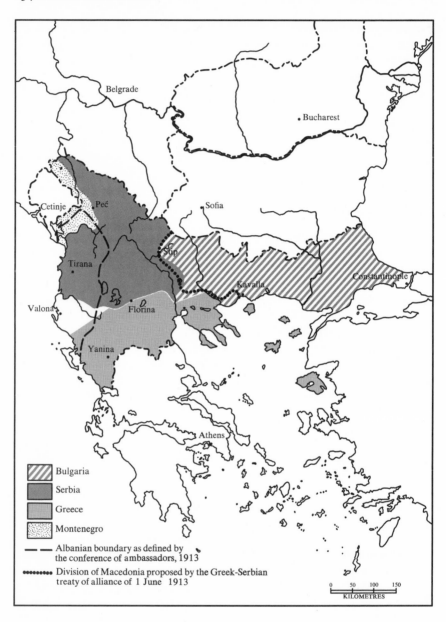

Regions occupied by the belligerents by the end of April 1913

solution, one that would satisfy its own selfish interests. Consequently, they commenced their own search for simpler and more satisfactory solutions, a search which intensified the mutual antagonisms and produced the Inter-Allied War.

I

Greece entered the system of Balkan alliances with the conclusion of the treaty of alliance and the military convention with Bulgaria. Neither of these two agreements, however, made any provision for the future common Greco-Bulgarian border in Macedonia. Venizelos made various overtures on this subject, but the Bulgarian government either rejected them or ignored them altogether. After the wars Geshov argued that his administration did not and could not devote to this question the serious consideration that it deserved because of lack of time.[2]

This does not seem entirely convincing in view of the fact that a period of five months separated the signing of the treaty of alliance from the declaration of war. The real reason for the failure to reach an understanding, as Toshev pointed out, was rather the highly contradictory nature of the Greco-Bulgarian pretensions and claims in southern Macedonia. Even a simple discussion of this topic might have jeopardized their alliance without which the war against Turkey would have been unthinkable.[3] Moreover, as far as Sofia was concerned, the agreements with Serbia had already taken care of the future of Macedonia. The Bulgarians were confident that in the event of a territorial dispute with Greece they would enjoy the unreserved backing of Serbia, their foremost ally.[4]

The Greeks, in contrast, placed their hopes on the favourable strategic position of Greece vis-à-vis the contested area. Venizelos appeared certain that the regions conquered by the Greek army would remain under Greek control. In any event, both Bulgaria and Greece entered the war fully aware that their alliance was more ephemeral than real.[5]

During the initial stage of the war both sides avoided entirely this and all other related problems. They concentrated instead on the victories and conquests in the field to fortify their respective bargaining positions. The Athens government raised first the issue of the common border in Macedonia. But it did so only after its forces captured the strategic bridge guarding the approaches to Salonica, and when this city, which lay at the heart of their rivalry, appeared safe within their grasp.

On 31 October 1912, Koromilas, the Greek foreign minister, broached to Mishev, the Bulgarian minister at Athens, the extent and nature of his country's pretensions. He told him that in spite of the fact that Greece had always looked on the River Mesta (Nestos) as the most appropriate eastern boundary, she would be willing to cede Kavalla to Bulgaria. But on a nearby map he also singled out the town of Bitola in the west and, of course, the entire Aegean coast west of Kavalla as belonging to Greece.[6] A few days later, on 3 November, Athens drew up and sent to Sofia a detailed project for the future Greco-Bulgarian frontier. It proposed a line which started to the west of Kavalla and headed in a northwesterly direction to Demir-Kapija and then continued westward to Kruševo and Lake Ohrid and ended at Valona on the Adriatic coast of Albania.[7]

King Ferdinand did not think it represented a serious move worthy of a Bulgarian counter-proposal.[8] Geshov was completely surprised and startled by it. He instructed Mishev to see Venizelos and to inform him that Koromilas's project made a 'crushing impression' in Sofia.[9]

When Mishev visited the Greek premier, Venizelos told him that he did not share all of his foreign minister's views. The submission, at this time, of such a detailed proposal was premature, according to him, because the two governments had not even reached an understanding on the basic principles that were to guide them in the actual delimitation of the frontier. For this he advanced four points which were to serve as the guiding principles. Briefly stated, he proposed that in the negotiations the two sides must bear in mind the balance of power in the Balkans, natural frontiers, the neutralization of the Straits and the Turkish capital, and finally, the exchange of populations, that is, the exchange of Greeks for equal numbers of 'Bulgarians' (ie Macedonians).[10]

The last point was the most crucial. To put it simply, what it really meant was that Venizelos was proposing to Bulgaria to keep Thrace with its large Greek population, and in return Greece would keep a large part of Macedonia with a predominantly Slavic Macedonian population. In the end they would swap the Thracian Greeks for an equal number of Macedonians. The total population in the part of Macedonia claimed by Greece was far larger than the Greek population in Thrace; but this the Greeks seemed to argue was only for the good, because it promised to bring close to par the pre-war population ratio of the two countries which favoured Bulgaria. 'The principle guiding the delimitation of the future frontiers should aim at the attainment of power equilibrium in the Balkans,' Koromilas told the Russian minister. 'No single nation should end up being more powerful than two other Balkan states together.'[11]

Needless to say, the Greek reasoning and arguments in favour of the establishment of a balance of power in the Balkans were not acceptable to Sofia. The Bulgarian government advanced and pressed the adoption of the principle of commensurability. It argued that the pre-war population ratio which favoured Bulgaria by 43 to 27 should be maintained and perpetuated.[12] Geshov also proposed that factors such as losses in man-power and material suffered in the course of the war, rights recognized by international accords, the commercial value of the conquered territories, and the economic potential of the liberated population must be considered in the territorial settlement between Bulgaria and

Greece.[13] With Athens pressing for a power equilibrium and Sofia insisting on a settlement corresponding to the pre-war power ratio, the mutual wranglings and recriminations between them commenced.

In spite of the Bulgarian objections, Koromilas forwarded to Sofia on 18 November 1912, a list of *kazas* (districts) that Greece claimed on the basis of Venizelos's proposal and recommendations. He conceded that it did not represent Greece's final word, but he also made it quite clear that there could be no bargaining over Salonica. Koromilas declared bluntly to Mishev that he would 'sooner cut off his head than relinquish Salonica' and the hinterland necessary for the city.[14] In the event that this proposal was not to the liking of Sofia, he asked Geshov to make a counter-offer and thus get the negotiations moving.[15]

The Bulgarians refused even to entertain the notion of abandoning Salonica and the other Macedonian cities claimed by the Greeks. Yet, they were fully aware that if an armed conflict developed, they would find themselves in a hopelessly difficult position. While most of the Greek forces were concentrated in Macedonia where the Turkish resistance had collapsed, the Bulgarian troops were still engaged on the distant Maritsa front where fierce fighting persisted. Consequently, Sofia seemed to have no alternative but to prolong the negotiations for the time being. Geshov argued at first that Bulgaria would be unable to make a definitive offer as long as her eastern boundary and Greece's island acquisitions remained undecided.[16] Then, on 26 November 1912, knowing in advance that the Greek government would not agree, he changed his mind and instructed Mishev to tell Venizelos that he was prepared to make a proposal if Greece accepted his principle of commensurability and the conditions that went along with it.[17]

Although the Greek premier was not willing to accept Geshov's views entirely, he wished to force Bulgaria to concede that Greece was entitled to part of Macedonia, which she had not yet done. He told Mishev that he was ready to compromise on his principles and conditions if Geshov would do the same, or, even better, to set them aside altogether for the time being. He suggested that a statement of Bulgaria's maximal demands might result in a compromise agreement. Otherwise, he threatened to take the defence of Greece's interests outside the alliance.[18] Even though Geshov protested that it would not be wise or appropriate to throw their 'family problems' into the lap of the great powers,[19] both sides were already trying to convince Pevchevskii Most of the mischievous conduct and disloyalty of the opponent. Koromilas accused Sofia of intentionally boycotting the discussion of pertinent proposals and wasting time with generalities;[20] Geshov complained that the excessive demands of the Athens government represented a grave danger to their alliance.[21] 'The Greco-Bulgarian discord,' wrote Demidov, 'hangs over the Balkan Alliance like a menacing cloud darkening future perspectives at the very moment, when more than ever before, the allies stand in need of concerted actions and conciliatory efforts for the completion of their task. *Quos vult perdere Jupiter, dementat.*[22]

The Russian government was perturbed and perplexed by the deepening dispute between the two allied nations. Officially Sazonov wished both sides a quick and peaceful adjustment of their differences, but he refused to go beyond restating the Greek grievances at Sofia and the Bulgarian complaints at Athens. He admonished the Greeks to scale down their demands, and the Bulgarians to avoid delaying serious discussions. However, he rejected requests to undertake the 'thankless tasks of an honest broker.'[23] But in the very important unofficial and behind-the-scene dealings Russia appeared more responsive and more sympathetic to Greece, partly because of the services of her minister at Athens, who was close to the Greek government and in complete agreement with Koromilas's views.[24] But also, and more significantly, as Mishev reported after an interview with Prince Urusov, the Russian chargé d'affaires: 'It should not be forgotten that the [Greek] Queen is a Russian Grand Duchess and that the wife of Prince Nicholas, the present military commandant of Salonica, is also a Russian Grand Duchess ... I was left with the grievous impression that Russia would hardly support us on [the issue of] Salonica.' Indeed, the Russian consulate general in Salonica had already been placed under the direction of the Russian legation in Athens.[25]

On 25 November 1912, Demidov advised the Bulgarian government frankly to forget about Salonica and hinted very strongly that in return Greece would be prepared to make concessions or indeed back down on other disputed issues, such as the towns of Kavalla, Drama, Seres, and Bitola.[26] Geshov took Demidov's advice in earnest and, on 1 December, asked him to secure from the Greek government a formal declaration to the effect that Greece renounced all disputed towns except Salonica.[27] Demidov had acted on his own initiative: he was not authorized by the Greek government and nothing came of this except further complications. In any event, Geshov did not have to wait long for such a declaration. The very same day the Greek chargé d'affaires handed him a strongly worded note requesting the Bulgarian government to draw its own line of delimitation on a map and proposing to refer all points of disagreement to the arbitration of the powers of the Triple Entente.[28] Geshov now reverted to his earlier stand and again proposed the postponement of all negotiations until the allies concluded peace with Turkey and Bulgaria's eastern boundary and Greece's island acquisitions became known and final. He agreed to consign the settlement of their dispute to the heads of state of Russia, France, and Great Britain only if they failed to reach a complete understanding.[29]

The postponement of the negotiations until after the conclusion of the peace treaty with Turkey held no advantages for Greece in this dispute. Even now the position of Greece seemed weaker as a result of Bulgaria's treaty of alliance with Serbia which remained intact, in appearance at least, as far as the Greeks were concerned. After the war Bulgaria could improve her posture further by redeploying her superior military man-power from Thrace into Macedonia.

Consequently, on 6 December 1912, Athens proposed an early personal meeting between Venizelos and Geshov. Since, at this time, the allied premiers were contemplating going to London for the peace talks, this encounter could have taken place there. Venizelos ascribed great importance to it and must have been disappointed and, indeed, slighted, when at the last minute Geshov, following the example of his Serbian and Montenegrin counterparts, changed his mind and decided not to go to London.[30] The Bulgarian delegation was headed instead by Danev who met with Venizelos several times.

Danev raised the Greco-Bulgarian dispute, and particularly the question of Salonica, during his stop-overs in the European capitals on the way to London. He was 'favourably impressed' in Germany and Austria-Hungary. From Berlin he telegraphed Geshov that Kiderlen-Wächter supported Bulgaria's claim to Salonica and the island of Tassos, and that Berchtold recommended a joint Greco-Bulgarian condominium over the city.[31] Affected by these vague and, as it turned out, exaggerated overtures, Geshov instructed Bobchev to seek the support of Russia. 'In the presence of such assurances from Germany,' wrote Geshov, 'continue to insist before Sazonov that Russia also be just toward us in regard to Macedonia and convince Greece to accept the principle of commensurability and, more importantly, not to demand the division of the conquered territories before the conclusion of peace with Turkey.'[32]

Visits to Berlin and Vienna by Bulgarian public figures, now as in the past, were liable to stir grave suspicions in St Petersburg. Geshov's statements, moreover, sounded like blackmail. They irritated the Russian leaders and in the long run were bound to do damage to Bulgaria's cause in Russia. Sazonov instructed Nekliudov to point out to Geshov very strongly that:

recently the Bulgarian Government has not been showing consistently the frank and faithful attitude to which we have become accustomed at Sofia. Not from words, but rather from our deeds, the Bulgarians themselves could have become sufficiently convinced that our entire policy up till now originated from the recognition of the solidarity of the interests of Russia and Slavdom.

The Bulgarian government was flattered by the insincere advances of its imaginary friends who were striving to embroil the Bulgarians with Russia, continued Sazonov. But Russia was not in a position to build her relations toward the Slavs on such false grounds. 'Our special situation imposes upon us the unpleasant respon-sibility of having to remind each of the Balkan states of the necessity of reciprocal flexibility.'[33]

Meanwhile, the few meetings between Danev and Venizelos in London did not clarify or ameliorate the dispute. Venizelos admitted again that the Greek propos-als were inflated, but he insisted that Bulgaria should present her own line.[34] Danev did not possess a detailed and precisely worked out proposal and only suggested that Sofia would be content with an ethnographic line in southwestern Macedonia which would award Salonica to Bulgaria.[35] This was clearly not acceptable to Venizelos, and he bluntly warned Danev that public opinion at home would not permit the Greek government or the Greek king to abandon Salonica. 'Only the arbitral decision of the friendly powers could provide a different solution.' However, he put forth a new line, one that demanded for Greece a smaller portion of Macedonia than the previous proposals submitted by Koromi-las. Starting at Praviško, to the west of Kavalla, the new line ran to the River Struma (Strimeon), then north to Lake Takhino, from there across the River Vardar to Giumendže and north through Enidže-Vardar and Voden to the south-western corner of Lake Prespa and on to Korča in Albania. He promised to instruct Panas to convey this new proposal officially to Sofia.[36]

On his return trip to Athens, at the beginning of February, Venizelos responded to Geshov's invitation and stopped in Sofia. The two leaders met, rehashed their old views, and parted without deciding on a next step.[37] Although the negotiations were not broken off officially, for all practical purposes they were discontinued.

The crux of the matter was that the Greek government no longer had to press and hurry with the talks. The peace negotiations collapsed and, in the mean time, the war against Turkey had been renewed. The Greek government now could afford to procrastinate in the negotiations and await detailed proposals from Sofia, while Bulgaria was preoccupied and burdened by the war effort in the east, the threat of military intervention from the north, and, most significantly, the rapidly escalating territorial dispute with her foremost ally, Serbia.

II

Unlike the Greco-Bulgarian treaty of alliance, the agreements concluded between Bulgaria and Serbia made specific provisions for the partition of Macedonia. These arrangements appeared, at least at the time they were made, satisfactory to Sofia and to M. Milovanović and his supporters in Serbia, who saw the alliance as a promising beginning for long-lasting co-operation between the two Slavic neigh-bours. There were, however, political circles and leaders in Belgrade who did not view the alliance as favourably as its founder. They believed that Milovanović had paid too high a price in order to win Bulgaria's friendship. N. Pašić, the *spiritus rector* of Serbia's politics, raised serious objections even while the agreements were being negotiated.[38] Soon after Milovanović's death, J. Jovanović, the new foreign minister and one of Pašić's closest associates, complained to Toshev privately that Milovanović had allowed himself to be deceived by the Bulgarians and that with his passing the treaties should be considered void unless they underwent certain revisions.[39]

In a highly confidential circular of 15 September 1912, Pašić provided the first inklings of the contemplated changes and corrections. In connection with Count Berchtold's proposal for the decentralization of European Turkey, Pašić instructed Serbia's representatives abroad to seek autonomous reforms for what he termed Old Serbia. He included in it not only Old Serbia proper and the Serbian zone, as defined by the terms of the secret annex to the Serbo-Bulgarian treaty of alliance, but also the entire contested zone and the towns of Prilep, Kičevo, Ohrid, and their environs, which were located in the Bulgarian zone.[40]

Although clearly dissatisfied with the territorial arrangements of the accords, Belgrade at first watched the progress of the war and for a time refrained from raising the issue with Sofia. The swift advances of her armies in the west brought Serbia to the Adriatic Sea. The primary national aspiration – political and economic independence and hence the end of dependence on Austria-Hungary – appeared close to being won. Only when it became clear that the Dual Monarchy would not permit a Serbian presence on the Adriatic Sea, and Russia would not back Serbia at the risk of war, did the Serbian government begin to broach publicly the revision of the treaty of alliance and to demand additional compensation in the south, in Macedonia.

In the middle of November 1912 rumours in official circles in Belgrade questioned the future of certain Macedonian towns such as Skopje, in the contested zone, and Prilep and Bitola, both of which were situated in the Bulgarian zone. When confronted with enquiries from the Bulgarian legation, Pašić usually responded that all differences could and would be settled easily. He expected some difficulties over Prilep, but as Hartwig declared to Toshev: 'Even this problem is simple. You will help the Serbs win an exit on the Adriatic and they, on their side, will not create for you headaches in the south.'[41] To be sure, Bulgaria, disregarding Russia's counsel, promised Serbia her complete support even in the event of a war against Austria-Hungary.[42] But in the end Vienna had its way. Even before the amabassadorial conference convened, Serbia found herself on the verge of having to capitulate.[43]

On his way to London for the peace talks, S. Novaković, the Serbian chief delegate, paused in Paris. In his talks with Poincaré and Izvol'skii he explained that if Serbia were definitely blocked from acquiring a territorial exit and a sovereign port on the Adriatic, she would be forced to seek compensation beyond the limits set by the Serbo-Bulgarian treaty of alliance. He pointed to the area along the course of the River Bregalnica to Lake Ohrid and including the towns of Prilep, Bitola, and Ohrid.[44]

His statements threw Sofia into confusion. Toshev was summoned home for consultations. The government started drafting a categorical protest which threatened to throw the dispute and the disagreements into the open. The idea was dropped only when Russia, counselling patience, assured Sofia that the final settlement in Macedonia would be carried out in strict accordance with the terms of the agreements.[45]

Sazonov rebuked Belgrade for bringing up the question of territorial divisions before the peace negotiations were concluded. Moreover, through Hartwig he warned the Serbs that:

the violations of the delimitation agreed upon by the two states with such great hardships can neither be viewed with sympathy nor supported by our side. The renewal of the discord between Serbia and Bulgaria would imperil all their common achievements and would be utilized by Austria-Hungary and Turkey. We hope that Belgrade realizes that if we counsel Serbia to show flexibility on the question of the [Adriatic] port, we are guided not by indifference to the interests of Serbia, but by a deep conviction that it represents an unavoidable necessity.[46]

In his dispatches Hartwig argued that Novaković was not familiar with the terms of the Serbo-Bulgarian agreements, that his conversation in Paris was of only academic significance, and that he was not authorized to make such statements by his government.[47] Hartwig purposely minimized the incident and in doing so was misleading his superiors at Pevchevskii Most. His explanations obviously did not correspond to reality.

There was no doubt at all that Novaković put forth the real aims of Serbia and the views of Pašić as well as Hartwig. Only a few days later, on 14 December 1912, Hartwig himself informed Toshev that he would be asked soon by Serbia to intercede on her behalf in connection with the question of Prilep.[48] In early January 1913, Teodorov, who was travelling to St Petersburg, had a short meeting with Pašić in Pirot. The Serbian premier, while trying to assure his guest that the Belgrade government would uphold the terms of their treaty, stressed the fact that it would also expect territorial concessions at the final settlement.[49]

Novaković's Paris performance appears to have been yet another of Pašić's 'trial balloons.' His purpose was to test the reaction to the Serbian demand for the revision of the territorial clauses of the Serbo-Bulgarian treaty of alliance. The alarming responses of the Russian and Bulgarian governments convinced Pašić of the need to delay the contemplated official representation to Sofia until a suitable pretext for it was found. For the time being he turned to Greece to strengthen Serbia's bargaining position.

From the outset of the Greco-Bulgarian dispute over Salonica, the Greeks had been wooing Belgrade.[50] They offered Serbia military aid in case she encountered complications on the Adriatic, even though the Serbs were well aware that Greece would not partake in an armed struggle with either of the two Germanic powers. In return they asked Belgrade to intervene in Sofia in favour of a 'just agreement between Greece and Bulgaria in connection with the line of delimitation in Macedonia.' Indeed, Athens requested Pašić to present to the two disputing parties his own project for the settlement of the dispute.[51]

Pašić accepted only too gladly the Greek overtures and secret Greco-Serbian negotiations commenced in London. Very little of what transpired between Venizelos and Novaković is known. It appears certain, however, that these talks paved the way for the encounter in Salonica, on 24 January 1913, of Crown Prince Alexander of Serbia and King George and Crown Prince Constantine of Greece.[52] There they established the real basis for the future Greco-Serbian alliance against Bulgaria.[53]

Returning from London Venizelos stopped in Belgrade on 5 February 1913, and for the first time discussed with Pašić the future common boundary of Greece and Serbia. Half apologetically Hartwig claimed that they considered only the common frontier in Albania. Evidence suggested, however, that they commenced what proved to be lengthy talks on a new partition of Macedonia. Subsequently, the negotiations were continued by M. Bošković and J. Alexandropoulos, the Serbian minister at Athens and the Greek minister at Belgrade respectively.[54]

This promising opening in the relations with Greece emboldened Belgrade to bring into the open its grievances against Bulgaria. On 23 January, Pašić talked to Toshev about the 'absolute necessity' to reconsider and rectify their border agreements.[55] J. Jovanović, now minister at Vienna, publicized Serbia's pretensions to Ohrid, Bitola, and Veles in an article in the *Neue Freie Presse*.[56] But as long as these demands were not made officially at Sofia the hands of the Bulgarian government were tied. It could not do much beyond taking its complaints to St Petersburg. On 26 January 1913, Geshov instructed Bobchev to:

Protest to Sazonov against these official Serbian statements and declare to him that we are not denouncing them publicly in order to avoid giving the world the wistful spectacle of allied quarrels before the conclusion of peace, but that we must protest against them to our protector. We would in no way consent to a violation of the line of delimitation specified in our agreement with Serbia which is well known to Sazonov.[57]

When the war against Turkey was resumed, the fighting continued almost exclusively on the eastern front, with the exception of the siege of Scutari and a few other isolated points in the west of the peninsula. While Serbia and Greece were able, and actually began, to consolidate their presence in the conquered and occupied lands, the Bulgarian armies carried the entire burden of the war. They were exhausted and in great need of supplies. Most of all they were in need of heavy siege artillery for the storming and seizure of Adrianople.

For this reason the Bulgarian government turned to Belgrade and asked for help.[58] On 13 February 1913, the Serbian government responded favourably, agreed to loan Bulgaria siege artillery on condition that the guns would be returned to Serbia in case of great need, and specifically proposed to leave the settlement of the question of indemnity to a later date.[59] The vague but explicit reference to the indemnity frightened the Bulgarians. Suspicious of Pašić's motives and eager to avoid future disagreements, they immediately offered financial compensation and asked Belgrade to determine the amount.[60] Spalajković rebuffed Geshov for even having considered such a suggestion. The Serbs feigned to have been gravely offended and a serious diplomatic incident followed over what might have appeared on the surface an insignificant misunderstanding.[61] It was precisely the occasion created by this incident that the wily Serbian premier utilized to present to Sofia Serbia's grievances and to request formally the revision of the territorial clauses of the Serbo-Bulgarian treaty of alliance.

On 22 February 1913, Pašić dispatched to Spalajković a long memorandum and instructed him to hand a copy to Premier Geshov personally.[62] In its introduction Pašić rejected outright Geshov's offer of monetary compensation for Serbia's assistance in men and arms in the struggle for Adrianople. He explained that until now the Serbs had purposely avoided discussion of the nature and the magnitude of the compensation to which Serbia was entitled. They did not intend to raise this question even now because they preferred to postpone its consideration until later, when the allies discussed the whole problem of the division of their commonly held conquered territories. But, since the question of the very nature of the indemnity had now been raised by the Bulgarian side, said Pašić:

I consider it my duty to acquaint the Bulgarian Government through you [Spalajković] with the point of view held by our Government not only in regard to the compensation for the siege artillery, but also in connection with the overall indemnity which Serbia has the right to demand ... Consequently, I entreat you Mr. Minister to, please, make a representation to the Royal Bulgarian Government to rectify in our favour the boundary foreseen in the Serbo-Bulgarian Treaty of Alliance.[63]

The treaty of alliance, Pašić went on, was negotiated and concluded under fancied suppositions. Reality had, in the mean time, shown that these were unfounded and that the agreement must undergo changes so that it would correspond to the real situation. Serbia wished to see the gains of the war justly divided in conformity with the real effort and the sacrifices of each party.[64]

On that basis Pašić raised four principal reasons to justify Serbia's demand for the revision of the treaty of alliance:

1 He argued that the terms of the treaty and the military convention obligated Bulgaria to deploy 100,000 men in the Vardar theatre of military operations. Her failure to do so had forced Serbia to raise double the number of troops agreed and to fight and defeat the Turks alone, without the aid of her ally. By so doing, Serbia enabled Bulgaria to concentrate all her forces on the Thracian front.

2 Furthermore, in spite of Bulgaria's failure to fulfil her military obligations, Serbia, without being bound to do so by formal commitments, dispatched 50,000 men in October and siege artillery in February, to assist Bulgaria.

3 Pašić emphasized that in spirit the treaty provided that the uncontested zones, if and when conquered, would automatically remain under Serbian or Bulgarian control. The Serbian army conquered the Vilayet of Scutari or, more precisely, the Adriatic coast with Durazzo, which belonged to Serbia. However, Austria-Hungary threatened war if Serbia did not renounce and evacuate the vilayet, and in the event of such a war Bulgaria was bound to come to the aid of her ally with 200,000 men. To avoid the attack from Austria-Hungary, which threatened to nullify all the successes of the war, Serbia, for the sake of her own as well as Bulgaria's interests, agreed to leave this question to the conference of ambassadors and was eventually dispossessed of the Vilayet of Scutari and the Adriatic coast. Thus, Serbia sacrificed a most valuable part of her zone in the interests of both and this loss should therefore be shared by Bulgaria in the form of additional concessions to Serbia in Macedonia.

4 Finally, he stressed the fact that at the time of the negotiation and conclusion of the treaty Bulgaria disclaimed Adrianople because it was located in the area of Constantinople and the Straits. In the course of the war, however, changes took place and Bulgaria's pretensions extended to Adrianople and even further to the east. This would not have been possible without Serbia's assistance. 'Serbia has thus won for herself a fourth reason for the enlargement of her territory in Macedonia.'[65]

Pašić's démarche startled the government in Sofia. Geshov telephoned Toshev to instruct him to ask the Serbian premier to rescind it and to set out for home immediately. Pašić declined the suggestion and, when Toshev turned to Hartwig for aid, the Russian minister feigned complete ignorance on the matter.[66]

At the beginning of March 1913, Geshov drafted a detailed repudiation of Pašić's four major arguments and the demands based upon them. Like the Serbian note, it was in the form of a memoir from Geshov to Toshev in Belgrade.[67] In the preliminary passage Geshov wrote:

The Bulgarian Government, motivated solely by its intense longing to see the alliance, concluded between the two neighboring states, invigorated and strenghtened ... finds that this could be accomplished only if the agreements upon which the alliance is based are safeguarded sacredly and inviolably by both sides ... We consider it the duty of both sides to make constant efforts to abstain from everything that could in one way or another ... reflect harmfully on our alliance ... or undermine its very essence.[68]

Geshov made it a point to remind Pašić that the conditions of the alliance were agreed upon in three different sets of documents: the treaty of alliance between the kingdom of Bulgaria and the kingdom of Serbia; the military convention between the kingdom of Bulgaria and the kingdom of Serbia; and four agreements between the Serbian and Bulgarian general staffs. According to Geshov, these agreements could not be viewed individually and separately, but as an interrelated and, indeed, indivisible whole. Together they defined the relations between the two allies – their rights and obligations.[69]

Geshov then proceeded to refute, one by one, Pašić's principal arguments. He admitted that the military convention obliged Bulgaria to leave 100,000 men at the disposal of Serbia, first in case Turkey attacked Serbia or secondly if Serbia and Bulgaria jointly declared war against Turkey. But he pointed out that the former did not apply to the present war, because it was not defensive; and that the latter was superseded by the agreements concluded between the two general staffs on 23 August (4 September) 1912, and on 15(28) September, 1912. Article 2 of the latter stated: 'the entire Bulgarian army will operate in the Maritsa valley, while leaving at the beginning of the war one division along the line Kustendil-Dupnica.' Hence, Bulgaria was bound to send to the Vardar front not 100,000 men, but only one division, and even that only for the initial period of the war. Bulgaria's seventh division remained on the Vardar front until the fall of Salonica and was only subsequently transferred to the east. In any case, 'nowhere and at no time was there any talk about partitioning Macedonia on the basis of the military contributions made by both allies in the Vardar theater of operation in a war against Turkey.'

Moreover, Geshov emphasized that while article 2 of the secret annex to the treaty of alliance made clear and detailed provisions for the future settlement in Macedonia, none of the agreements specified what portions of the lands around the Adriatic Sea would go to Serbia, or the part of the Vilayet of Adrianople that would be annexed by Bulgaria. Consequently, neither side was entitled to special privileges or obligations by the fact that Serbia consented to renounce her claim for a territorial exit on the Adriatic Sea, or by the fact that the Vilayet of Adrianople might eventually come under Bulgarian control.

As far as Serbia's assistance to Bulgaria went, Geshov made the point that both allied nations were obligated to assist one another with all the forces that they could spare. He pointed to article 7 of the general staff agreement of 23 June (2 July) 1912, which provided specifically for the transfer of troops from the Vardar to the Maritsa theatres of operation and vice versa, depending on the requirements dictated by the fortunes of the war. Hence, Serbia did no more than fulfil her obligations as an ally and could not justify territorial claims greater than those prescribed by the treaty.

He concluded by stressing the fact that the agreements did at no place state that Adrianople and the area to the east were outside Bulgaria's sphere; and by the same token, they did at no place state that Serbia would renounce the Sanjak of Novi Pazar or the Adriatic coast.[70]

This memoir, which reflected the official position of Sofia, did not reach Belgrade; the Bulgarian government wished to avoid irritating the Serbs before the fall of Adrianople. Moreover, Sazonov advised them not to send it.[71] He castigated Pašić and the Serbs for putting forth demands 'contradicting the obligations undertaken by the Serbian Government,' and assured Sofia of Russia's full support.[72] The memoir was marked 'not sent' by Geshov himself and remained in the Sofia archives.[73]

When Toshev returned to Belgrade on 19 March 1913, he approached Pašić personally and through Harwig to retract his note. Pašić again refused and argued that he was provoked by the Bulgarian offer of financial compensation for the siege artillery.[74] On 1 April 1913, Toshev read to him a very short note from Geshov, which, for the time being, constituted Bulgaria's official reply. It declared:

We would not wish, Mr. Minister Toshev, to debate the question raised by Prime Minister Pašić, because its debate cannot pass without leaving harmful effects on the stability of our alliance with Serbia ... However, if such a debate is imposed upon us I reserve for myself the right to give subsequently and in detail all our arguments in defense of our point of view.[75]

Pašić expressed his satisfaction with this reply, but at the same time he told Toshev that he was in an extremely difficult situation and unless the treaty were revised he might not remain in power for very long.[76]

III

The Bulgarian government had resolved not to discuss, let alone permit, any changes in the territorial arrangements with Serbia. This was partly the result of what proved to be a rather mistaken belief that Bulgaria enjoyed the full backing of Russia. It was also due to the government and King Ferdinand's striking lack of appreciation of the country's exposed and vulnerable position in the Balkans and in Europe.

To be sure, it was not difficult for Premier Geshov to declare, as he did to Toshev: 'We shall not grant to the Serbs territorial concessions. We would rather reach an agreement with the Greeks by ceding Salonica.'[77] However, to conclude an understanding with Greece was no longer such a simple affair. The Greco-Serbian negotiations had, in the mean time, progressed very far. Indeed, reports reaching Sofia at the beginning of March revealed the existence of a Greco-Serbian agreement for the partition of Macedonia.[78] Pašić denied the validity of these reports or of what he described as rumours inspired by Austrian intrigues.[79] But, his denials notwithstanding, an incident, one of many which took place in Salonica at this time, symbolized more correctly the actual state of the relations between Serbia and Greece. General Khesapchiev reported on 9 March 1913 that:

Yesterday and the day before yesterday, in one restaurant, in the presence of many Greek, 15 Serbian and 10 Bulgarian officers, one of the Greek officers carrying the Serbian flag and a Serbian officer carrying the Greek flag, entered and crossed the flags while their comrades welcomed them with hurrahs and with shouts of 'Long live the Greco-Serbian brotherhood.'[80]

Greece and Serbia were not as yet bound by a formal treaty of alliance, but the relations between them had become sufficiently intimate to give the Greek government carte blanche whenever Sofia decided to take up the negotiations again. On 4 April 1913, King Ferdinand chaired an important conference devoted to the dispute with Greece in a railway-car near the Adrianople station. Later, in a book written in defence of his policy, Geshov was to state that at this meeting he recommended very strongly the acceptance of the Greek proposal to hand over the dispute to the arbitration of the great powers.[81] Since most, if not all, the great powers were more sympathetically inclined toward Greece on the question of Salonica, this would have meant in effect that Bulgaria was ready to abandon her aspirations to that city. Geshov claimed that his suggestion was at first approved and then rejected at the conference. Even though he did not explain who opposed him, it would be safe to assume that his line of policy was not acceptable to King Ferdinand.[82]

In any event, the only thing this conference agreed on was to approach Athens again. On 16 April, Geshov notified Venizelos that Sofia was prepared to enter into talks if the Greek government advanced a satisfactory boundary line.[83] Venizelos at first complained that he had not yet received a reply to the second Greek proposal which he himself expounded to Danev in London,[84] but on 22 April he communicated a new proposal and a new line. This, the third put forward by Athens, was much more exacting than the previous two. If the islands were taken into account, it claimed for Greece an area with a total population of 2,043,000, and left to

Bulgaria an area with a population of 1,401,000. On this count alone it was rejected by the Bulgarians. Geshov also complained that it was too vague and that it could hardly be used as a basis for further negotiations. He asked for a new and more concrete proposal, the terms of which were to approximate the line which was unofficially suggested by the Russian minister at Athens.[85] Venizelos was in no mood either to defend his old proposal or to make new ones. He bluntly told Mishev that Sofia should not expect anything from Athens. Bulgaria had to choose between two alternatives: accept his proposal for the arbitration of the great powers or put forward her own project and boundary line.[86]

Since the Sofia government gave no indication at all that it planned to do either, the talks were again deadlocked. The allies, Greece and Serbia on the one hand, and Bulgaria on the other, began preparing for a possible armed conflict for the spoils of victory, while the war against their common enemy was still on. After the fall of Yanina the Greek government gathered most of its forces in the disputed areas in Macedonia and fortified Greece's position around the strategically important towns such as Nigrita and Giumendže.[87] Venizelos explained to Demidov that these moves were necessary because the designs of the Bulgarians to capture Salonica made armed conflict between them unavoidable.[88] The Greek navy was at the same time transferring Serbian troops from the Adriatic coast to Macedonia following Serbia's withdrawal from the siege of Scutari. On 28 April 1913, General Khesapchiev reported from Salonica that a few days earlier 20 steamships were dispatched to the Albanian ports for this purpose and that the Greeks were making all the necessary preparations for the immediate transfer of the Serbian troops from Salonica to Bitola and Veles-Skopje.[89] Although the bulk of the Bulgarian armies was still actively engaged in the east, the Bulgarian government redeployed some of its forces in Macedonia as well.[90]

Disturbed by this new twist in events, Russia pointed repeatedly to the dangers for the Balkan system of alliances in these undertakings.[91] The Russian government, and Sazonov in particular, however, failed to rise to the requirements of the occasion. Instead of pursuing a consistent course of policy, one that might have and could have gradually developed into a serious alternative to the military solution of the disputes, Pevchevskii Most vacillated for a long time between the demands of one or the other of the antagonists.

Having at first rebuffed Belgrade for demanding the revision of the treaty of alliance, by the end of March Sazonov changed his mind and pressed Sofia to make territorial concessions to Serbia.[92] Then, only a week later, Danev, who was in Russia in connection with the St Petersburg ambassadorial conference, reported that 'Sazonov promised to uphold our stand.'[93] This was restated in a more binding and categorical fashion by both Sazonov and Nekliudov after the Bulgarian government agreed to follow Russia's advice and conclude a separate armistice with Turkey.[94]

In the Greco-Bulgarian dispute Russia had counselled Sofia for a long time to give up Salonica, for, as Sazonov kept pointing out, Russian, German, and British court circles supported Greece on this question. However, this did not prevent Sazonov from assuring Danev that Russia had not yet taken her final stand. Russia, Sazonov continued, would not interfere in the settlement of the Salonica problem, which ought to be resolved between the Greek and Bulgarian governments.[95]

The failure of the Russian government to come up with a definitive and consistent policy had far-reaching consequences. It emboldened the allied governments to cling to their rigid and uncompromising stands. Furthermore, in view of the fact that each one of the allies looked to Russia for support, the absence of such a policy created a vacuum which permitted her ministers in the Balkans to formulate and push their own courses of policy. In the long run this proved detrimental for Russia because, like Shebeko in Bucharest, the independently minded, ambitious, and energetic ministers in Belgrade and Athens, more often than not, represented the views and interests not of Russia but of the governments to which they were accredited.[96] Moreover, since Nekliudov lacked the self-reliance of either Hartwig or Demidov and hardly ever took the initiative, he placed Sofia in an awkward and almost perpetually defensive position which heightened Bulgaria's alienation and mistrust of both Russia and her allies.

Around the middle of April, Hartwig and Demidov took the initiative and brought forward proposals acceptable to the Serbian and Greek governments. Hartwig suggested the formation of a commission composed of two or three representatives from each allied nation to decide all the disputed issues;[97] Demidov proposed a meeting of the four allied premiers.[98] St Petersburg received favourably the latter proposal and on 22 April 1913 Sazonov urged Geshov to agree to meet with Pašić and Venizelos.[99] Otherwise, he warned, in an armed conflict with her present allies Bulgaria would lose everything she had won. He also argued that if it really came to such a conflict Turkey would undoubtedly renew the hostilities and Rumania would enlarge her demands severely and might even resort to the most extreme measures against Bulgaria:

In the event of a fratricidal conflict of the Bulgarians with the Greeks and the Serbs, even our public opinion will turn its back on Bulgaria and the Imperial Government will remain ... a disinterested observer of the ruin of the Bulgarian cause, confining itself exclusively to the protection of the interests of Russia. The Bulgarians must by no means overlook also the fact that in case of an armed conflict with the Serbs, and together with it, will collapse the entire agreement of 1912 upon which are based the Bulgarian rights of delimitation in Macedonia.[100]

In spite of Sazonov's warnings, however, Sofia turned down the proposal. Bulgaria resisted all initiatives, such as Hartwig's and Demidov's, that suggested even vaguely the joint resolution of the two disputes. This was to be expected. First of all, in view of the very close relations between Serbia, Montenegro, and Greece and the Serbo-Greek agreement for the partition of Macedonia, Bulgaria would have been completely isolated in a conference of the four allied nations. Secondly, and more significantly, Bulgaria had insisted all along that the settlement of the Serbo-Bulgarian dispute must be based on the strictest interpretaion of the terms of the secret annex to their treaty of alliance. Since neither Montenegro nor Greece were parties to that agreement, it could not possibly have been used as a basis for the settlement of all the disputed issues between the allies.[101]

On 26 April 1913, Geshov threw the burden of responsibility back on Sazonov. He raised article 4 of the secret annex and requested Russia to decide the dispute with Serbia. The Russian emperor had agreed to act the role of supreme arbitrator as provided in article 2.[102] Although Sazonov could not therefore easily reject the request he still hoped that Russia would not have to get directly involved in the dispute.[103] In a long dispatch of 30 April 1913, Sazonov tried to define Russia's role in it. He wrote that as far as he was able to tell neither of the two parties questioned the validity of the treaty of alliance. The differences that divided them concerned the question of its interpretation. Without embarking upon an analysis of the existing differences, and with an attitude of complete neutrality toward both sides, Sazonov continued:

We consider it a duty to emphasize one important condition, which under any interpretation of the treaty could not lose its force, and namely, that all controversies relating to the question of interpretation or execution of the treaty as well as the military convention, are to be left up to the decision of Russia as soon as one of the sides makes it known that it is impossible to reach an agreement through direct negotiations.[104]

For the time being he disregarded Geshov's request and asked the two governments to bind themselves that 'the disagreements between them will be settled in the ways which were foreseen in the treaty and not by the force of arms.'[105]

Naturally, neither Bulgaria nor Serbia declined to renounce the use of force; but this did not lessen their differences or alter their basic stands. Geshov continued to insist that Bulgaria would not agree to any revisions of the treaty.[106] Moreover, he asked Bobchev to point out to Sazonov that the functions of the arbitrator, as they were defined by the fourth article of the secret annex, did not include even the examination of the question of revision, and that any territorial compensation, no matter how small, which was contrary to the line set in the treaty, would amount to a revision of that treaty.[107] Sazonov now again embraced Bulgaria's position.

Bobchev reported from St Petersburg that Sazonov declared solemnly that he had always believed that Bulgaria's view of the treaty was entirely right. He assured him that as an arbitrator Russia would undoubtedly pronounce a judgment favourable to Bulgaria.[108]

Reporting Pašić's reaction from Belgrade, Hartwig wrote that Serbia had never sought or intended to destroy the treaty. However, in view of the developments that had taken place, the Serbian government felt that it was necessary to subject it to an amicable reexamination. If a direct understanding proved impossible to attain, then the Serbian government would be prepared to submit its claims and interpretations to the judgment of the imperial government.[109] In an interview with Toshev, on 7 May 1913, Hartwig argued that a meeting between Pašić and Geshov should take place before Russia intervened in the dispute. Toshev, however, maintained that since the agreement was so clear and so precise the encounter of the two premiers was not necessary. When Hartwig threatened that Pašić, who did not sign the agreement and openly disagreed with Milovanović, might denounce it in its entirety, Toshev replied that in that case, King Peter, who was a signatory, would have to carry the whole burden of responsibility for the act.[110] In a dispatch to St Petersburg on the same day, Hartwig again pressed Sazonov to call a conference of the four premiers. He claimed that an exchange of views between them would simplify Russia's task as arbitrator and would help preserve the contacts with the Greeks who possessed the same interests as the Serbs.[111]

As has been shown, the common Greco-Serbian interests that Hartwig had in mind concerned primarily the future partition of Macedonia. After prolonged negotiations the two governments reached complete agreement on this most important question. On 5 May 1913, Koromilas and Bošković signed in Athens a 'Protocol Concerning the Conclusion of a Treaty of Alliance Between Greece and Serbia.' The two partners agreed on a common border and decided their boundary lines with Bulgaria (article 2). If Bulgaria declined to accept such a territorial settlement, they agreed to uphold it by supporting each other diplomatically and, should the need arise, militarily (articles 3 and 4). Most significantly, they bound themselves 'to conclude and sign a treaty of amity and a defensive alliance within the period of twenty days from the signature of the present instrument'' (article 1).[112]

Even before they had finally resolved their differences over the division of the spoils both Athens and Belgrade sought assistance against Bulgaria outside the Balkan system of alliances. On 13 March 1913, Vnizelos called on Berlin to bring its influence to bear upon Rumania to conclude an understanding with Greece. As Venizelos explained to the German minister, Greece counted on Serbia for the time being, but in the long run he did not believe it possible to collaborate with the

Slavic Serbs.[113] King George of Greece raised the same issue with the Rumanian minister in Athens at the end of March.[114] In the first week of April King Carol of Rumania spoke wistfully of closer ties between Rumania, Serbia, and Greece to Ristić, the Serbian minister. On 15 April, Pašić authorized Ristić to propose a treaty of alliance to Rumania; the Greek government followed suit a month later, on 15 May.[115]

Although the Rumanian government welcomed, and indeed encouraged, these overtures, for the time being it declined to sign formal treaties. The Rumanians believed that it was still premature for them to join formal alliances against Bulgaria before the Balkan system of alliances collapsed. They feared that such steps might drive the Bulgarians into making concessions to the Greeks and the Serbs which could have revived and strengthened the existing alliances. As Maiorescu told King Carol, it was best for Rumania to stay on the side, await the outbreak of the war between the allies, and then intervene in the conflict.[116]

Moreover, Rumania's patrons in the Triple Alliance naturally objected to the possible alliance with Serbia. Austria-Hungary continued to work for a tripartite agreement between Bulgaria, Rumania, and Turkey.[117] This was not unacceptable to Rumania, but as a price for the alliance with Bulgaria she demanded territorial concessions which went beyond those stipulated in the St Petersburg Protocol.[118] Count Berchtold urged Sofia to respond to these demands and to surrender voluntarily the sea coast south of the port of Mangalia. He argued that this was a price worth paying. With Rumania as her ally, Bulgaria would be assured of a victory in the event of a war with Serbia, especially since Russia would have to remain neutral in a war between the two Slavic nations. He also promised that Austria-Hungary and Italy would assist Bulgaria to acquire the towns of Seres and Kavalla and would persuade Germany to support Bulgaria's claim to Salonica.[119] H. von Tschirschky, the German ambassador at Vienna, seconded Berchtold on every point. He assured I. Salabashev that the alliance between Bulgaria and Rumania would force Serbia to capitulate without a war.[120]

The alliance with Rumania, as portrayed by Vienna, held enticing possibilities for Bulgaria. Indeed many of the pro-German–minded leaders in Sofia were ready to begin the talks, but neither they nor their Russophile colleagues wished to make additional territorial concessions. The Geshov-Danev Russophile government moreover, suspected the sincerity of the promises coming from Vienna and Berlin.[121]

Confused and uncertain what to do or where to turn next, at the end of April Premier Geshov naïvely suggested to Bucharest not to enter into agreements with Greece and Serbia until he consulted Danev and Teodorov, both of whom were away, in London and Paris respectively.[122] Danev had always tended to oversimplify complex issues in a peculiarly arrogant manner. This time he urged Geshov to open immediately talks with the Rumanians, while he rejected the very notion of further territorial concessions.[123] Teodorov, who was more sensible and more circumspect, pointed out very clearly the difficult predicament of the Geshov-Danev administration and the alternatives open to it and, for that matter, to Bulgaria. On 29 May 1913, he wrote from Paris:

> we can not buy Rumania's dubious friendship at the price of new territorial concessions. I repeat that after a victorious war against the Greeks and the Serbs we could find ourselves in an even more unfavourable position in regard to the pretensions of Rumania and Turkey, if ... we are not supported effectively by Russia or the Triple Alliance. You must communicate Kalinkov's telegrams to Russia and we must try to win Russia's backing or resign from power and let others take the dispute into the enemy camp.[124]

Geshov agreed to make a final attempt to settle the allied disputes with the aid of Russia.

IV

As already indicated, at the end of April, Belgrade and Sofia responded to Sazonov's call to refrain from resorting to the use of force and to leave the resolution of the dispute to the arbitration of Russia. Sazonov, however, did not make it clear whether Russia planned to assume its task as arbitrator immediately after she was asked by either of the two parties, or whether she would first insist on direct talks between them. The Bulgarians favoured the former and the Serbs the latter alternative.[125] When Nekliudov inquired about it, Sazonov replied that they were ready to begin the arbitration after either to the two sides requested it.[126]

In view of Bulgaria's well-known eagerness to see Russia in the dispute as soon as possible, Pevchevskii Most found it necessary to inform Sofia of what Prince Trubetskoi, head of the near eastern section of the Foreign Office, called the basic principles of Russia's Balkan policy in its newest phase.[127] The Russian government acknowledged that the Serbo-Bulgarian treaty of alliance was clear and that formally and legally Bulgaria ought to receive everything in accordance with its provisions, which would have to be carried out. However, Trubetskoi argued that beyond and outside the limits of the agreement there existed certain moral obligations which gave Serbia reason to ask for some concessions. In order to facilitate and hasten the arbitration of the dispute, the imperial Russian government wished to know: 1) whether the Bulgarian government could agree to make a territorial correction and if so, what kind? and 2) whether it could agree to conclude new economic agreements with the Serbs which would give Serbia concessions on Bulgaria's Aegean and Black Sea coasts?[128]

On 19 May 1913, without even referring to the memorandum of Trubetskoi, Bulgaria informed St Petersburg that a direct agreement with Serbia appeared improbable and requested Russia to assume the functions of the court of arbitration.[129] Sazonov replied that Russia accepted the request on condition that the alliance with Serbia would be renewed. Furthermore, he demanded assurances that both the Bulgarians and the Serbs would submit to the arbitration; that the Serbs, the Bulgarians, and the Greeks would demobilize to one-third or one-fourth of their present strength; and finally, that the Greco-Bulgarian dispute would be put to arbitration as well. For the latter he recommended the Triple Entente. Both arbitrations were to begin soon after the conclusion of peace.[130]

Serbia had at no time rejected or declined the arbitration of Russia. At the same time, however, she had not yet agreed explicitly to accept it either. Both Pašić and Hartwig continued to insist that the meeting between the two premiers, and possibly between the four allied leaders, should take place first.[131] As long as Serbia questioned the timeliness of the arbitration and there was the slightest chance that the decision might be turned down by either side, the Russians shied away from fulfilling their obligations. Sazonov preferred to cast the responsibility to the disputants even though it was quite obvious that they were unable to agree on anything.[132]

Since Russia either did not try very hard, or if she did, did not succeed, in bringing Belgrade to accept the immediate arbitration of the dispute, the Bulgarians again approached Pašić directly. In mid-May Toshev asked Geshov to send to Belgrade D. Rizov – 'perhaps the most outstanding warrior for our allying with Serbia' – hoping that he might have greater success 'with his old friends in the Serbian capital.'[133] Geshov agreed and instructed Rizov to impress upon Pašić that the best and only way out of the dispute was to be found in the terms of the Serbo-Bulgarian agreements and conventions.[134]

However, on the basis of his talks with Pašić and other public figures in Belgrade, Rizov became convinced that the Serbs were determined not to be dislodged from the lands they occupied.[135] He was equally convinced that Hartwig was to blame for Serbia's intransigent attitudes. 'Hartwig enjoys such an unlimited influence in the Serbian government and society,' wrote Rizov in his report to Geshov, 'that his [diplomatic] colleagues privately call him "the Regent", for, in reality, he fulfills the functions of the ailing Serbian King.' Before he left for home Rizov warned Hartwig that 'if it now comes to a war between us and Serbia, the principal and indeed the only culprit would be you, Hartwig.'[136]

Shortly after his arrival at Belgrade, Pašić confided to Rizov that he planned to send to Sofia a second official representation for the revision of the treaty of alliance.[137] This note, dated 15 May 1913, was presented to Geshov verbally by Spalajković on 26 May.[138] Pašić used this occasion again to advance the arguments that he gave in the note of 22 February 1913 to prove that both the basis and the procedure for the liquidation of the 'allied condominium' established by article 2 of the secret annex were breached and were, for all intents and purposes, virtually destroyed. The new basis for the division of the conquered lands must be determined by common agreement of the four allies. Pašić insisted that, in addition to the part of the contested zone that belonged to Serbia, this new agreement must grant to her four territorial concessions, or, as he put it, four 'pieces' of territory. They were to idemnify Serbia: for the failure of Bulgaria to fulfil her obligations during the war; for the Serbian sacrifices on behalf of Bulgaria which were not called for by the terms of their agreements; for Bulgaria's extensive gains in the east which supplemented her share of the contested zone; and finally, for the Serbian territorial losses in the west which included the Adriatic coast.[139]

Two days later, on 28 May, Pašić brought the dispute completely into the open. In a major foreign policy exposé in the Skupština, he reiterated all his arguments in support of the demand for the revision of the treaty with Bulgaria. He declared that since Serbia was barred from the Adriatic, her life interests dictated and made indispensable a common boundary with Greece in the south. He maintained, moreover, that, in return for the renunciation of Albania and the Adriatic coast, Serbia was offered the entire Vardar valley including Salonica.[140]

Although Sofia looked upon the latest note as a 'new Serbian provocation, a proof of Serbia's treacherous conduct,'[141] Geshov began to ponder seriously the possibility of making concessions to Serbia in the contested zone. Most of his colleagues in the cabinet did not agree, but at the same time they were unable to formulate and concur on a course of policy that the government was to pursue.[142] In the end they empowered Geshov only to accept Pašić's long-standing invitation for a personal encounter between them. The decision was transmitted to Belgrade and by mutual consent the meeting was to take place in the border town of Tsaribrod on 31 May 1913.[143]

The Bulgarians made some new overtures to Greece as well. In mid-May Sofia informed the Greek government that it planned to send M. Sarafov to join Mishev in Athens and to resume the talks. But the Greeks were no longer interested in bilateral negotiations. Panas told Geshov that the quickest way to settle their quarrels was through talks between the premiers of the four allied nations, a 'Conference à quatre.'[144] Geshov objected to this and pointed out to him that as far as the quarrels with Serbia were concerned there were provisions for arbitration; and that the other allies had no right to interfere in the controversies between Greece and Bulgaria. Thereupon Panas declared that his government would commence negotiations with Mishev and Sarafov only if it could keep the other allies informed of their progress. Geshov protested to Athens and accused the

Greeks of having concluded secret alliances with Serbia and Montenegro.[145] Koromilas did not even bother denying this charge. He just reiterated his government's resolve to settle all the disputes in a conference of all the allied states.[146] The Bulgarians again turned down the proposal.[147]

On 21 and 22 May the Greek and Bulgarian armies engaged in violent bloody clashes around Angista and Nigrita, which raised the spectre of an all-out war.[148] The following day Belgrade notified Athens of its latest representation to Sofia. The Greek government welcomed the Serbian action because it represented the final and complete break between Sofia and Belgrade. Shortly thereafter Venizelos instructed Alexandropoulos, the minister at Belgrade, to hasten the negotiations and sign the treaty of alliance with Serbia without delay.[149]

Since the signing of the protocol of 5 May, and particularly after 14 May, when they signed a military convention that was not ratified, the Greco-Serbian negotiations remained bogged down.[150] The Greeks wanted a defensive alliance and a military convention which was directed only against Bulgaria. The Serbs, however, demanded that both agreements be directed against an attack from any third power, which meant Bulgaria or Austria-Hungary. The deadline for the conclusion of the treaty was 25 May. At the last minute Greece agreed to the Serbian demand and the negotiations were completed.[151] The treaty of alliance between the kingdom of Greece and the kingdom of Serbia was signed on 1 June 1913, in Salonica, by J. Alexandropoulos and M. Bošković. The new military convention was signed, the same day and in the same place, by X. Stratigos and colonels P. Pešić and D. Tufegďić.[152]

The first article of both the treaty and the convention bound the two parties to assist each other in case of an unprovoked attack by a third power and 'not to conclude peace subsequently except jointly and together.' The rest of both agreements were aimed solely at Bulgaria. The treaty of alliance provided that at the division of the territories of European Turkey, after the conclusion of peace, 'the two high contracting parties bind themselves not to come to any separate agreements with Bulgaria, to afford each other constant assistance, and to proceed always together, upholding mutually their terriotiral claims and the boundary lines hereafter indicated' (article 2). They agreed on their common boundary west of the River Vardar, 'based on the principle of effective occupation,' (article 3); and 'the Greco-Bulgarian and Serbo-Bulgarian boundary lines shall be established on the principle of actual possession and the equilibrium between the three states' (article 4). The fifth article was the most crucial. It ran as follows:

Should dissension arise with Bulgaria in regard to the frontiers as indicated above, and every settlement became impossible, the two high contracting parties reserve to themselves the right to propose, by common agreement, to Bulgaria, that the dispute be submitted to the mediation or arbitration of the sovereigns of the Entente Powers or the chiefs of other states. In case Bulgaria shall refuse to accept this mode of peaceful settlement and assume a menacing attitude against either of the two kingdoms, or attempt to impose her claims by force, the two high contracting parties bind themselves solemnly to afford assistance to each other with all their armed forces and not to conclude peace subsequently except jointly and together.[153]

The ratifications of both documents were exchanged in Athens on 21 June 1913.

7

The Inter-Allied War

The signing of the Greco-Serbian treaty of alliance, for all practical purposes, marked the end of the Balkan system of alliances. In 1912 the Balkan states united and went to war against Turkey. Their officially proclaimed aim was to liberate the Christian population still under Turkish control. In reality, however, they only sought to conquer and to expand into the remaining Turkish possessions in Europe.

The newly concluded alliance between the Greeks and the Serbs had really nothing in common with either of these two aims. Indeed, its primary objective was to subvert the territorial settlement agreed upon between Bulgaria and Serbia in 1912, and to impose upon Bulgaria, if necessary by force of arms, the new Greco-Serbian arrangement.

At the same time it undermined whatever value or significance the meeting between Geshov and Pašić or the proposed conference of the four allied premiers might otherwise have had. It left no room for debate or for a negotiated settlement between the allies. Bulgaria was to be presented with what amounted to an ultimatum, a fait accompli. If she did not accept it, there was to be war.

The Greco-Serbian treaty of alliance was to be kept strictly secret. Neither of the two contracting parties, nor, so far as is known, Hartwig or Demidov, bothered to inform St Petersburg. The Russians, whether they suspected its existence or not, continued in their efforts to bring the allies together to iron out their differences voluntarily because they wished to escape the difficult task of arbitrating the disputes and alienating one or the other disputant.[1] The failure of this policy made unavoidable the Inter-Allied War which destroyed and buried the Balkan system of alliances of 1912.

I

The personal encounter between Geshov and Pašić, which was postponed at the last minute from 31 May to 1 June 1913, was for a long time Sazonov's main preoccupation. On its eve he instructed his ministers in the Balkans to convey to the allied governments Russia's great satisfaction that it was finally taking place. 'From the very outset of the disagreements between the allies we insisted on personal meetings between the Premiers,' Sazonov wrote. 'Consequently, we welcome the impending meeting of Mr. Geshov with Mr. Pašić, and we urgently counsel that a meeting between Mr. Geshov and Mr. Venizelos take place as well.'[2] In the event that these meetings did not produce the sought-after direct negotiations, Russia invited the Bulgarian, Greek, and Serbian premiers to St Petersburg to 'determine with the aid of Russia the basic principles necessary for the re-establishment of peace and the strengthening of the alliance in the Balkans.'[3]

Needless to say, Sazonov was overly optimistic. The meeting in Tsaribrod was to take place only hours after the treaty of alliance between Greece and Serbia had been signed in Salonica. The Greeks and the Serbs had already agreed on the partition of Macedonia, and Pašić was obviously not going to Tsaribrod to negotiate. But, even if he had been able to do so, Geshov's hands were tied.

Premier Geshov was one of the most moderate and one of the few political leaders in Bulgaria who was disposed to enter into discussions and perhaps make some small territorial concessions in order to avoid the tragedy of an inter-allied war.[4] However, his influence in Sofia had recently been steadily on the decline. The military high command opposed all concessions and attacked Geshov's peaceful inclinations.[5] They pressured the government to make use of what they considered to be a most favourable time for a war against Serbia and Greece, 'to secure the primacy of Bulgaria in the Balkans.'[6] General Savov called publicly for a change in Bulgaria's foreign policy orientation by replacing the Geshov-Danev coalition with the pro–Triple Alliance minded Stambolovists.[7]

The crown, the leaders of the opposition parties, and, to a certain extent, some members of the coalition shared the views of the soldiers. King Ferdinand regarded Geshov as a weak person who was unable to act courageously and energetically. Like General Savov, the king was dissatisfied with the pro-Russian leaders and their course of policy and began to seek and listen to the counsel of those leaders of the opposition who advocated a tougher stand toward the allies.[8]

Since the disputes with Greece and Serbia had come into the open, Geshov placed Bulgaria's case in the hands of Russia. For a long time he remained confident that the arbitration of Russia would follow closely the terms of the treaty of alliance with Serbia and would therefore be satisfactory to the Bulgarians. By the end of May, however, it was becoming apparent to Geshov as well as to his political opponents at home that Sazonov had embraced the position of Serbia. For instance, shortly before the Tsaribrod meeting he urged Sofia to cede voluntarily to the Serbs the towns of Struga, Kruševo, Veles, Kratovo, and Egri Palanka.[9]

Feeling let down by Russia and more and more isolated at home, Geshov saw that his position had become untenable and decided to step down. On 29 May 1913, without having informed the cabinet, King Ferdinand received the leaders of all the opposition parties for a wide-ranging discussion of Bulgaria's position in the crisis. The following day, S. Dobrovich, King Ferdinand's *chef de cabinet*, advised Geshov of the meeting and informed him that the king was entirely satisfied with the views and counsel of the opposition. Convinced finally that he no longer enjoyed the confidence of the crown and that he was no longer in agreement with the leaders of the other parties, Geshov handed to Dobrovich the resignation of his government on the same day, immediately after the news reached Sofia that the peace treaty had been signed in London.[10]

Geshov, accompanied by D. Rizov, A. Toshev, and M. Spalajković, travelled to Tsaribrod to meet Pašić in the capacity of a 'lame duck' prime minister. 'The encounter of the Prime Ministers of the two "fraternal and allied" nations was conspicuously cold,' wrote Toshev.[11] In spite of Rizov's incessant attempts to bring a certain measure of intimacy into the meeting by invoking the 'Slavic ideals,' the 'community of interests,' and the 'brilliant future of the two brotherly nations,' the talks failed to get off the ground.[12] In order to shorten the anguish of this embarrassing situation, Toshev proposed a second meeting in Salonica where they were to be joined by Venizelos. Pašić and Spalajković agreed; but expressed a preference for St Petersburg instead of Salonica. In the end they left the question of the meeting-place to be decided at a later date.[13] Before they left Tsaribrod they issued a communique which voiced the 'favourable disposition on the part of both sides to resolve their misunderstandings.'[14] Needless to say, this was hardly the case, or to use Toshev's remark in regard to the communique: 'We resembled priests who listened to the liturgy, but did not believe in God.'[15]

Only the Russians appeared pleased and satisfied that the allies had finally accepted their outlook. In Sazonov's absence, Neratov used the occasion to advise Belgrade, Athens, and Sofia to announce in advance that the meeting in Salonica was to be the first, but by no means the last; and to make arrangements for the future talks that were to be held elsewhere.[16] At the same time he informed them that on the basis of a Russian proposal the conference of ambassadors in London adopted a resolution calling on the belligerents to demobilize.[17]

All further work on both these issues – the future meetings and talks and the demobilization – had to be postponed until after the settlement of the government crisis in Sofia. When Geshov resigned, the Sūbranie deputies from his own party urged him not to reject the mandate to lead a new government if the king offered it to him again.[18] Geshov was ready and willing to preside over a national coalition, which would have meant in effect that the crown and the leaders of the other political parties had accepted his course of policy.[19] This did not happen, however, because King Ferdinand disregarded Geshov and asked A. Malinov to form a coalition government with the several liberal parties. When Malinov failed, because he was not acceptable to N. Genadiev or the other liberal chiefs, King Ferdinand authorized S. Danev to form a new government. Denev at first attempted to create a wide coalition that was to include Malinov, Genadiev, V. Radoslavov, and D. Tonchev, but did not succeed. In the end, on 14 June 1913, he presented the new government, which was made up again only of the two parties in Geshov's coalition, his own Progressive Party, and Geshov's National Party. Danev assumed both the premiership and the portfolio of foreign minister.[20]

Although Geshov and Danev had in a way shared the leadership of the former coalition, there was a marked difference in their outlooks. Danev claimed that his and Geshov's aims were the same since both of them sought a peaceful settlement of the disputes. This might be true, but there was a great difference both in their approaches and in their tactics. Danev himself was very critical of Geshov because he found him too flexible and overly hesitant in acting.[21] They differed, as Danev put it, in 'temperament' and in 'tact.' What he really meant, specifically, was that in order to cancel out the impression made at St Petersburg by the Serbs whenever they 'raised their voice,' the Bulgarians should 'raise the tone of their voice' even higher.[22] Stated otherwise, the Bulgarians were to assume gradually a more militant attitude until Russia backed down and embraced Danev's point of view.

II

On 6 June 1913, shortly after his resignation became public, Geshov made it known to the allies and the interested great powers that 'as a result of the resignation of the ministry – the meeting with the allied Prime Ministers is postponed until the termination of the crisis.'[23] In the mean time, relations between the allies were going from bad to worse. Serbia and Greece threatened to annex formally all the lands that they conquered and occupied. They, as well as Bulgaria, were completing the last stages of the redeployment of the troops into Macedonia and the other military preparations.[24]

The seriousness of this highly explosive situation did not escape the attention of St Petersburg. Indeed, as Sazonov wrote in his memoirs, it drove him 'to resort to the extreme course of intervention by the Emperor in the form of a personal appeal to the Kings of Serbia and Bulgaria to cease their contest and leave the problem in his hands.'[25] Sazonov explained to the tsar that all other means for the peaceful resolution of the Serbo-Bulgarian quarrel had been tried in vain and that his personal intervention had been forseen when the treaty was signed between the allies. The appeal or intervention took the unusual form of personal identical telegrams from the tsar to the kings of Serbia and Bulgaria. They were signed and dispatched from Moscow on 8 June 1913.[26]

The Russian tsar regretted very deeply that the agreed meeting of the four allied premiers had not yet materialized and that the 'Balkan States are apparently preparing for a fratricidal war' which was liable to destroy all the great achievements of their common victories. He reminded them that in the treaty of alliance, both nations, the Bulgarian and the Serbian, left up to Russia the decision of every controversy concerning the execution of the clauses of the treaty and the other related agreements:

I beg Your Majesty to remain loyal to the obligations you have undertaken and to rely on Russia for the solution of the present dispute between Bulgaria and Serbia ... I consider it necessary to declare that the state which will start the war will be held responsible before Slavdom; and that I reserve the absolute right to determine what stand Russia would take up in relation to the possible consequences of such a criminal war.[27]

The replies to the tsar's appeal reflected and reiterated the divergent outlooks, the deep division between the two allies. King Ferdinand accepted the arbitration of Russia on condition that it be carried out in accordance with the terms of the treaty of alliance, which, as he suggested, justified Bulgaria's claims in Macedonia. Furthermore, he added, Bulgaria could not renounce her special obligations to the population of Macedonia, which through the years 'were recognized even by Russia.'[28]

King Peter did not mention the term arbitration explicitly. The Serbs were willing to discuss all the issues, but it was obvious that they were not ready to accept a decision based solely on the terms of the treaty of alliance. His main point was that the revision of the treaty was necessary. It was required and dictated by the very life interests of the Serbian nation. 'I hope Your Majesty will manifest justice toward us by recognizing that we did not cause the difficulties in question,' wrote King Peter, 'but that they were foisted upon Serbia by the force of circumstances.'[29]

On the basis of the two replies Sazonov somehow drew the conclusion that both governments hoped to utilize the assistance of Russia 'to come out of the present critical situation peacefully and with the alliance preserved.'[30] He invited the prime ministers of Bulgaria, Greece, Serbia, and Montenegro to come immediately to St Petersburg 'where all questions relating to the disagreements and to the modes of their resolution will be subjected to discussions.'[31]

Greece accepted the invitation on 14 June,[32] and Serbia followed suit the next day.[33] The Bulgarians took exception to the fact that Sazonov omitted the term arbitration in his note; Danev sought assurances that there would be arbitration and not just discussions and that the discussion would be within the confines of the treaty.[34] He also demanded a definite commitment from Belgrade that Serbia should agree unconditionally to the arbitration.[35] Furthermore, on 11 June, Serbia proposed the simultaneous reduction to one-fourth of the allied military strengths and Sazonov insisted that it be carried out immediately.[36] Danev agreed but only on the condition that Serbia consent to a joint Serbo-Bulgarian occupation of Macedonia until the decision of the arbitration was pronounced.[37]

Danev's tactics exasperated Sazonov. He argued that an acceptable basis for the arbitration and the demobilization would be found in St Petersburg. For the moment, the most urgent concern was the immediate arrival of the prime ministers.[38] In point-blank fashion he demanded a 'yes' or 'no' answer as to whether Danev intended to come to St Petersburg or not.[39]

In an equally blunt manner, Danev expressed deep puzzlement that Bulgaria, having accepted the tsar's appeal for arbitration, was now being asked to come to the Russian capital to engage in plain discussions with the other Balkan states. 'This procedure is incomprehensible to us,' Danev continued:

All discussion with the Serbs concerning the territorial problems is a useless waste of time, because ... a direct agreement is not possible ... If the Imperial Government wishes to ease the conflict between Bulgaria and Serbia ... there remains nothing else except to notify us immediately that Serbia accepts the arbitration in accordance with and within the bounds of the treaty.[40]

As Danev hoped, Bulgaria's unwillingness to compromise had the sought-after effect on Russia. On 18 June, Sazonov tried to reassure Sofia that Russia was not inviting the premiers only in order to make it possible for them to talk to each other, but because the Russian government wished to talk to them as well. The arbitration was the prime responsibility of Russia and she intended to carry it out. Most significantly, as he pointed out, once in St Petersburg 'Pašić will not be able to decline it.'[41]

The same day Sazonov informed Belgrade that Danev refused to make the trip to St Petersburg as long as he was not convinced that Serbia was ready to submit to the arbitration of Russia. He added that a pledge of this nature was equally necessary for Russia. For this reason he suggested to Pašić to communicate to St Petersburg a declaration stating:

Once in St. Petersburg, Mr. Pašić agrees to discuss also the treaty arbitration and he hopes that these talks will lead to the realization of Russia's supreme power of arbitration between Serbia and Bulgaria.[42]

The following day Sazonov again asked for 'a clear and unequivocal answer' from Pašić.[43] Hartwig reported from Belgrade, however, that he had failed to persuade the Serbian government to accept unconditionally the arbitration of Russia. 'The prevailing sentiment here is that we wish to force Serbia to surrender to all the demands of Bulgaria' wrote Hartwig.[44] To prove this point and to impress upon Russia that there were limits beyond which he was not prepared to go, Pašić resorted to one of his old tricks. He offered to resign, but, as was to be expected, he was easily persuaded by King Peter not to do so.[45]

Influenced by Sazonov's representation at Belgrade for which he undoubtedly claimed credit, Danev raised his demands. In addition to the public declaration of Serbia that she agreed to submit to the arbitration of Russia, he now maintained that it was impossible for him to go to St Petersburg so long as the demobilization had not commenced. In order to start demobilizing, Serbia had to agree to a joint Serbo-Bulgarian occupation of Vardar Macedonia.[46]

Sazonov turned down the attempt to combine the two issues – unconditional acceptance of arbitration and joint occupation of Macedonia – as prerequisites for the encounter in St Petersburg. He protested that:

If Serbia comes forth with a satisfactory assertion on the question of arbitration, then we do not see the need for another guarantee in regard to the commencement of the demobilization ... The wisest decision would be to begin demobilizing without any conditions except the agreement in principle of the Serbian Government to the arbitration of Russia.[47]

Danev again refused to yield and condemned Russia for failing to realize that, in spite of the proposed conference, a war might break out unless it were accompanied by the demobilization. In a strongly worded telegram of 20 June, he closed the door to the conference in the event that Serbia did not respond favourably to Bulgaria's demands. He instructed Bobchev to see Sazonov and tell him that this was the decision of the ministerial council which met and reviewed the entire situation during the previous night.[48] Neratov, who received Bobchev in Sazonov's absence, asked the Bulgarians to ponder all the possible consequences before they made such a rash decision and warned them that the meeting of the premiers, which had been agreed to by everyone except Bulgaria, provided the only rational way out of the allied disputes.[49]

In the mean time, Sazonov seemed to have made some progress in his dealings with the Serbian government. On 21 June, he informed Sofia that in a recent conversation with Hartwig, Premier Pašić had declared that the Serbo-Bulgarian differences on the treaty of alliance did not prevent Serbia from accepting the invitation to go to St Petersburg and from handing over the disagreements to the court of arbitration. Sazonov believed that these words of the Serbian premier were sufficiently binding to satisfy Sofia, and he assumed that the Bulgarians now joined the ranks of the other allies in agreeing to the meeting at St Petersburg. To set the stage for the actual talks he asked the two governments, the Serbian and the Bulgarian, to supply Russia in four days' time with memoranda which presented and defended their respective positions and demands. For the liquidation of the Greco-Bulgarian dispute he proposed simultaneous, but separate, arbitration.[50]

On Sunday, 22 June, when Nekliudov received Sazonov's telegram, Danev chaired the meeting of the cabinet which reviewed the entire question of the arbitration. Danev himself seemed convinced that Serbia would in no case accept an unfavourable decision, that is, a decision based on the terms of the treaty; and this in itself made a war between them unavoidable. As far as he was concerned, the main task facing Bulgaria was to decide the most opportune moment for the outbreak of the war: whether it should come before or after the decision was pronounced in St Petersburg. The ministers representing Geshov's party were opposed to such a war and refused to entertain the possibility that Bulgaria might provoke it. They felt certain that the Russian tsar would pronounce a decision favourable to Bulgaria and that it would be up to the Serbs to decide on the next move. If they opted for war, then the entire blame and responsibility for wrecking the alliance would fall on them. Their views prevailed at the meeting and, after it had ended, Danev left to report to King Ferdinand.[51]

In the afternoon of the same day another meeting, which was chaired by King Ferdinand and involved Danev, Teodorov, Dobrovich, and General Savov, convened in the king's summer residence at Vrana. King Ferdinand was already familiar with Danev's views and asked Teodorov to speak first. He defended very ably the views of his supporters, the *Narodniaks*, and the decision reached at the morning session.[52] Neither King Ferdinand nor General Savov seemed to have rejected his presentation. However, both of them stressed the point that the army could not remain in a position of full readiness for any length of time; they could not exclude the possibility of serious border clashes if the arbitration decision was long delayed.[53] General Savov was ready to guarantee only that the army could wait for about ten days.[54]

In the end they resolved to inform the Russian government that Bulgaria was prepared to send her representative to St Petersburg on condition that the dispute with Serbia were decided in accordance with the terms of the treaty, and to request the Russian government to make the decision known within seven days.[55] After the meeting adjourned, Danev, Teodorov, Savov, and Dobrovich met Nekliudov in the chamber of the Council of Ministers and asked him to convey the resolution to Sazonov.[56] In the final draft, which was edited by Teodorov, the deadline was extended to eight days and the Bulgarians also asked St Petersburg to let them know no later than Tuesday, 24 June 1913, whether their request had been accepted. In the event of an affirmative response, Danev planned to leave for Russia on Wednesday, 25 June.[57]

The deadlines made a very bad impression on St Petersburg because they were viewed as ultimatums. As Demidov told Mishev, 'They gave grounds for believing ... that one of the other Great Powers encouraged Bulgaria.'[58] In a telegram to Nekliudov, Sazonov wrote that the Russian government preferred to think that the latest Bulgarian request was never made,[59] and that Russia awaited the memoranda from Belgrade and Sofia.[60] When Nekliudov saw Danev, the Bulgarian premier told him that he planned to telegraph the memorandum to St Petersburg, but he forewarned him that Sazonov's rejection of the deadline would meet with the resolute opposition of the generals.[61] Later in the day, after he consulted King Ferdinand, Danev instructed Bobchev:

[The Bulgarian] formula for the arbitration and the seven days' time limit for the announcement of the decision were our last proposal ... Sazonov's reply amounted to a rejection because it did not specify the time when the decision would be handed down. Under these circumstances we are forced to terminate all further negotiations. Mr. Toshev's recall is impending tomorrow.[62]

Danev's tone and tactics were too offensive even for Bobchev, and for some time he was uncertain whether he should approach Sazonov.[63] When he saw him on 25 June, he enquired at first if Russia had received the official response and memorandum from Serbia hoping that he would not have to convey to him the contents of Danev's latest telegram. Only when Sazonov replied in the negative, Bobchev followed the instructions from Sofia. Almost in a rage, Sazonov told him that Toshev's recall from Belgrade amounted to a declaration of war:

Your statement does not surprise me. I was informed in advance, a few days ago, about this action of your Government. You have embarked on the course recommended by Austria. Feel free ... the Serbs as a result of their foolishness, you because of your tactlessness toward Russia and Slavdom, are heading toward destruction ... Now, after your declaration, I am making ours: Do not expect anything from us and forget that we are bound by any obligations to the agreement of 1902.[64]

Sazonov's angry outburst must have had a powerful effect on the Bulgarians, because thereafter there was a significant and sudden change in Danev's tone and approach. He denied the accusation that Bulgaria embraced and followed the advice of Austria and informed Sazonov that Toshev's recall had been postponed indefinitely. Half apologetically he explained that the only reason behind the deadline was the desire to avert the outbreak of war. He virtually begged the Russian government to hasten the arbitration procedings in the shortest possible time in order to pacify the generals before he left Sofia for St Petersburg.[65]

Indeed, there was a great deal behind Danev's argument; he was not just bluffing. King Ferdinand and the generals did not forget the date set in the resolution of the conference at Vrana. On 26 June, General Savov reminded the 'esteemed Government' that the deadline was to expire on Sunday, 29 June.' I find it necessary,' continued Savov, 'to ask the Council most urgently to inform me by that date unequivocally and finally of its decision: war or demobilization.'[66]

Sazonov moderated his attitude as well, and for a short time it seemed that a way out of the crisis had been found and Danev and Pašić would finally go to St Petersburg. On 27 June, Sazonov told Bobchev that Russia was still waiting for the memoranda, but he assured him that once they arrived the arbitration could be completed within a week's time, as long as Bulgaria agreed also to submit her dispute with Greece to separate but simultaneous arbitration.[67] The same day Danev replied that he was willing to commence immediate talks with Venizelos,[68] that the Bulgarian memorandum was already prepared, and that he was ready to proceed to St Petersburg.[69] The following day he told Nekliudov that if the Serbian acceptance of the arbitration arrived that afternoon, he planned to depart for Russia the next day, Monday, 30 June.[70]

Initially the Serbs, like the Greeks, accepted Sazonov's call for the encounter of the allied premiers in St Petersburg. They hoped that, by bringing together and discussing jointly the Serbo-Bulgarian and Greco-Bulgarian disputes, the treaty of alliance with Bulgaria would have to be reconsidered and revised. But, when Sazonov gave in to Bulgaria and accepted the principle of simultaneous but separate arbitration for the two disputes, they felt deserted by Russia; Pašić, too, was having some second thoughts.[71] He was no longer eager, or at least no more so than Danev, to travel to the Russian capital. Only after Sazonov exerted tremendous pressure on Belgrade did he promise to appear and announce officially to the Skupština, on 26 June, Serbia's 'unconditional acceptance of Russia's arbitration, the presentation of the memorandum and the trip to St Petersburg.'[72] Even then this decision was postponed twice and at one point, when Danev stated his intention to terminate all further talks and to recall Toshev from Belgrade, Pašić used the occasion to escape both the delivery of the memorandum and the arbitration. He instructed Popović to tell Sazonov that in view of Danev's action they became 'superfluous.'[73] Sazonov's angry outburst and the subsequent retreat of Danev again altered the whole situation. On 27 June, Sazonov demanded the Serbian memorandum and Pašić again promised to have it sent to St Petersburg after he made the announcement to the Skupština.[74] If one can trust Hartwig, this had to be postponed until Monday, 30 June, because there was widespread opposition to the intended declaration.[75]

On the specified day, Pašić appeared before the Skupština and made the announcement in a major foreign policy address which surveyed the evolution of the Serbo-Bulgarian differences and Russia's efforts to find a solution acceptable to both sides. In the debate that followed the opposition censured the government's policy, its vacillation and indecision. It argued that the government should have proclaimed the annexation of all occupied lands a long time ago because there was no reason to hope or believe that Russia's arbitration would provide the best or most acceptable solution for Serbia.[74]

While the debate was gaining momentum, Pašić was informed, and he in turn announced to the assembled deputies, that at two o'clock in the morning the Bulgarian armies launched an attack against the Serbian positions from Štip to Zletovo. The Skupština exploded into an outcry directed at Bulgaria.[77] Pašić and the Skupština were spared the task of making an unwanted decision. King Ferdinand and General Savov decided the issue for them. In Sofia at this particular moment, Danev handed the Bulgarian memorandum to Nekliudov. He was ready to depart for St Petersburg, together with Teodorov, Malinov, and General Dimitriev, aboard a Russian steamship which was anchored in the port of Varna at the request of the Bulgarian government.[78]

III

The seven days' deadline which was dictated by General Savov and approved by King Ferdinand in the meeting at Vrana was expiring on 29 June. A secret telegram signed by General Savov at 8 pm of 28 June ordered the fourth army to attack 'the enemy [Serbia] in a most energetic manner along the entire line' on the night of Sunday, 29 June. Another telegram of the same date ordered the second army to attack simultaneously the Greek positions at Leftera and Chaiazh and to occupy the two ports. These orders were carried out on the night of 29 June and the early morning of 30 June.[79] At 3 pm on 30 June, Savov dispatched Directive No. 24 ordering the fourth army to entrench along the line Kratovo-Kliseli-Veles and the second army to await orders for the attack on Salonica.[80] In a subsequent telegram, dispatched 55 minutes later, Savov explained the objectives behind the attacks. 'Our actions against the Serbs and the Greeks,' wrote Savov, 'were undertaken without a formal declaration of war and for the following considerations': 1) to raise the morale of the Bulgarian armies and to make them look upon their former allies as enemies; 2) to force Russia's diplomacy to hasten the settlement of the problem before the outbreak of war between the allies; 3) to force the allies to make concessions and be more conciliatory; 4) to take the contested zone and other areas, by force of arms, before the European powers intervened. 'Since this intervention could be expected at any moment, you must act fast and energetically.'[81]

The attacks were planned and agreed upon between King Ferdinand and the army high command. Nearly all the sources agree that the government in Sofia did not partake in the decision.[82] In the morning of 30 June, Danev called a special meeting of the cabinet to inform his colleagues that serious armed clashes had taken place and that all available evidence suggested that the Bulgarian troops were responsible. When General Savov was called in, he confirmed that the attacks were launched by the Bulgarian side. However, he maintained that the aim was not to wage a war against the allies, but only to convince them by a single resolute action that Bulgaria was able and prepared to resort to arms if that were required. The government charged him with the highest crime that the commander of the army could commit – commencing a war without the approval or even the knowledge of the legal government, and it relieved him of all his duties. It also decided to order the termination of the hostilities and, finally, to raise the question of its resignation.[83]

After the meeting, Danev called Toshev on the telephone and instructed him to protest the Serbian attacks;[84] Serbia and Greece protested the Bulgarian attacks. Each side rejected the other's protest and blamed the other for causing the outbreaks.[85] Meanwhile, the hostilities went on, quickly escalating into a full-scale war.

On 30 June, the first day of the war, Russia awaited the memoranda and the official Serbian acceptance of the arbitration. All available evidence suggested and pointed to the peaceful settlement of the disputes. Consequently, the Russians took the initial reports of the fighting very lightly. Sazonov thought it was just another incident in the series of recurring clashes that had been taking place since May.[86] He advised Sofia to avoid all complications on the borders because they tended to weaken Pašić's position in Belgrade and therefore made more difficult the delivery of the Serbian memorandum.[87] At the same time he urged Belgrade to respond immediately to the call for arbitration.[88] In a circular to the four allied capitals Pevchevskii Most insisted on the immediate arrival of the premiers in Russia.[89]

It is extremely difficult to reconstruct the sequence of events in the two days following the Bulgarian attacks. It seems certain, however, that the military leaders of all three nations welcomed the war as the best and only acceptable way out of the political stalemate. The government leaders, however, waited for the first results of the fighting before they opted for the war or for the termination of the hostilities. Danev claimed to have ordered the generals to stop all the attacks on 30 June, even before the Serbian protest note was received in Sofia.[90] It is conceivable that he gave oral instructions to this effect to General Savov but they were not carried out. The written orders were sent to the high command only the following morning,[91] by which time it had become obvious that the attacks had failed to produce the desired results and that the entire Bulgarian plan had collapsed. Before the evening was out the orders were executed and the Bulgarian forces were defending their position against Serbian and Greek attacks.[92]

By this time the Russian government realized what was really happening and called for the immediate cessation of the hostilities. As far as it was concerned, it was not necessary or possible and desirable to search for and to establish the guilt for the outbreak of the fighting.[93] Sazonov demanded official public expressions of regret over what had taken place, concrete proofs that orders had been given to stop all hostile actions, and declarations stating that the premiers were ready to arrive in St Petersburg for the conference without delay.[94]

Needless to say, neither Belgrade nor Athens were inclined to listen and obey the directives of Pevchevskii Most. Sazonov's vacillation and indecision during the past few months undermined Russia's influence in the Balkans. She no longer possessed the authority to apply effective pressure over the allies or rather over the former allies.[95] Both the Serbs and the Greeks made if absolutely clear now that they did not intend to return to the method of arbitration. Greece was determined to recapture the lost areas and King Constantine left Athens for Salonica to assume direct command over his armies.[96] In Serbia the situation was already in the hands of the high command. On 1 July, the third day of the fighting, Vojvoda Putnik told Pašić to discard the calls for cessation of the hostilities, 'since all the opportunities' were on their side. There is no doubt that Pašić shared the views of his trusted military chief.[97] The following day he urged him to 'hurry up with the decisive offensive' because he was afraid that as a result of the Bulgarian government's declaration that the attack was launched without its knowledge, and in view of its orders for the cessation of all military hostilities, the great powers might intervene immediately in the conflict.[98]

This did not happen, however, since the powers themselves were divided and did not speak with one voice. The fighting went on and the existing unofficial state of war was formalized by Greece on 5 July and by Serbia and Montenegro on 6 July.[99]

IV

The Bulgarian armies fared very badly against the Serbs and the Greeks. By the end of the first week of July they were retreating on both fronts.[100] More significantly, with the proclamation of the state of war by Serbia and Greece there was the real danger that Rumania would join them and intervene against Bulgaria.

To be sure, following the signing of the Treaty of London, the Rumanian parliament ratified the St. Petersburg Protocol. But it was clear to everyone that the Rumanians remained discontented. They demanded additional territorial concessions if they were to maintain the position of benevolent neutrality toward Bulgaria in the event of another armed conflict in the peninsula.[101] Geshov's attempts to reach an understanding without making further territorial sacrifices came to naught.[102] When Danev took over the reins of government and inquired about the extent of the Rumanian demands, Bucharest always replied that it was ready to consider all 'concrete and specific' Bulgarian proposals.[103] In their talks with the foreign representatives at Bucharest, however, both King Carol and Maiorescu made it known that in case of a war between the allies Rumania would mobilize and occupy the entire area north of the line Tutrakhan-Balchik.[104]

As long as the war of the allies against Turkey lasted, Russia's energetic representations at Bucharest checked the possible intervention of Rumania on the side of Turkey. With the termination of this war, however, events took a turn for the worse for Bulgaria. Russia now used Rumania to counterbalance the aggressive proclivities of Bulgaria in the deepening disputes with Serbia and Greece. On 27 June 1913, Nekliudov warned Danev 'that in the event of an armed conflict of the Bulgarians with the Serbs and the Greeks, we will not raise a finger to hold back Rumania even though the defeat of Bulgaria would bring great grief to us.'[105] Moreover, Pevchevskii Most made it known, and indeed assured Bucharest, that Russia would assume an attitude of complete neutrality toward Rumania if she intervened against the aggressor in a Serbo-Bulgarian war. It reaffirmed this position when the Rumanians enquired specifically whether that was to be Russia's attitude even if Bulgaria proved to be the aggressor.[106]

Such assurances provided Rumania with a free hand in her future dealings with Bulgaria and brought the two neighbouring nations closer to war. On 27 June 1913, Maiorescu instructed Prince Ghika to inform Danev that Rumania intended to mobilize and commence military operations in the event of a Bulgarian war against Serbia.[107] Shortly after the first reports of the armed clashes reached Bucharest, military preparations got under way;[108] and on 3 July, when Belgrade and Athens notified Rumania that they considered themselves in a state of war with Bulgaria,[109] King Carol signed the decree for general mobilization.[110]

The position of the Danev government was very difficult. It failed to bring about the cessation of the hostilities with Greece and Serbia, and was now confronted with an imminent invasion from the north. On 2 July, Danev responded to the pressures from the opposition and submitted the resignation of his cabinet.[111] The crown council, which was held during the following two days, considered the question of the resignation and the entire diastrous situation of the country. But, in spite of the determined and persistent opposition of the liberals, King Ferdinand declined to accept the resignation and in effect approved the government's policy of relying upon Russia for the termination of the war and the warding off of the intervention of Rumania and Turkey.[112]

The leaders of the three liberal parties continued the attacks against the pro-Russian orientation of Bulgaria's foreign relations. They argued that the course established by Geshov and Danev was incompatible with the national interests of Bulgaria. They advocated an immediate break with Russia and complete reliance on Austria-Hungary.[113] On 6 July, V. Radoslavov, N. Genadiev, and D. Tonchev sent to King Ferdinand a letter in which they declared:

We believe that there is no longer any room for errors. We think today as we did yesterday that the road to the Kingdom's salvation lies in close friendship with Austria-Hungary. This policy must be inaugurated promptly, without delays, because every hour is fatal. We call on Your Majesty to undertake today appropriate measures to save Bulgaria from new misfortunes and the dynasty from new burdens.[114]

It is not entirely clear what kind of assistance the liberals expected from Austria-Hungary, for while the Dual Monarchy wished to draw Bulgaria away from Russia, she was not prepared to sacrifice the interests and demands of her long-time ally Rumania. Indeed, Vienna left no doubt that in order to win Austria's friendship and support, Bulgaria would first of all have to appease Rumania by the cession of the area north of the line Tutrakhan-Balchik.[115] The liberals might have gone along with this advice, but at this particular time neither King Ferdinand nor Danev was willing to pay such a high price.[116]

Even though Danev was disillusioned with Sazonov and King Ferdinand with Russia, they continued to believe and hope, mainly because there seemed to be no alternative, that Russia, the liberator and saviour of Bulgaria in the past, 'even now will not deprive the land, drenched with Russian blood, of her powerful support and will prevent the intervention of the Rumanian armies into Bulgaria.'[117] For this reason King Ferdinand authorized Danev to request officially the intercession and mediation of the Russian government.[118]

On 8 July, Danev wrote Bobchev to inform Sazonov:

In view of the danger of Rumanian intervention and the menacing undertakings on the part of Turkey, and in order to put an end to the blood letting, which we regret, Bulgaria is prepared to terminate immediately the military operations and appeals to the Imperial Government to kindly make the necessary representations at Belgrade and Athens.[119]

More significantly, Bulgaria wished to entrust the protection of her interests in all matters pertaining to the restoration of peaceful relations between Bulgaria and Serbia, Greece, and Montenegro, as well as to the claims of Rumania, to the 'friendly intercession and mediation of the Imperial Russian Government.'[120] Sazonov accepted the task on the understanding that Russia would be acting on the initiative of and on behalf of Bulgaria;[121] and that a new basis for the settlement would have to be found since the Serbo-Bulgarian treaty of alliance had lost its force.[122] In accordance with Sazonov's advice, the following day Danev proposed the immediate cessation of all hostilities and the conclusion of an armistice between the belligerents, and a conference of the representatives of the four nations in St Petersburg to decide the terms of peace through the mediation of Russia.[123]

The same day Sazonov communicated this proposal to Belgrade, Athens, and Cetinje and cautioned them that its rejection would amount to no less than the loss of Russia's support.[124] At the same time he issued a stern warning at Bucharest to the effect that there was no longer any justification for military actions against Bulgaria.[125]

These representations were rather late in coming. The Belgrade government replied evasively that its response would depend on the reaction of the Greek government.[126] Venizelos was in no mood to listen to Sazonov. He insisted that Bulgaria must sign the armistice agreement on the battlefield and accept the territorial demands of Greece and Serbia in advance of the peace talks.[127] The Rumanians resolved not to miss what seemed their last great opportunity. They were determined not only to secure their territorial claims, but also to play the decisive role in the final peace settlement in the Balkans.[128] On 10 July, Bucharest recalled Prince Ghika from Sofia and the Rumanian armies crossed the Danube and moved into Bulgaria unresisted.[129] To appease the Bulgarians, at least partially, and the great powers, from the outset the Rumanian government made it known that irrespective of the conquests to be made, Rumania intended to claim only the area north of the line Tutrakhan-Balchik.[130]

Powerless to cope with the circumstances, the Bulgarian government again turned to Russia to act on behalf of Bulgaria to secure a quick armistice agreement.[131] It authorized St Petersburg to decide, if necessary, the nature and extent of the Bulgarian territorial concessions to Serbia, Greece, and Rumania.[132]

Russia's second attempt to terminate the war and bring the belligerents, particularly Serbia and Greece, to the negotiation table proved to be as futile as the first.[133] With the entire situation well under their control, the Greeks and the Serbs refused to commit the final settlement to the discretion of Russia.[134] Pašić would only go so far as to inform Sazonov that he planned to meet Venizelos in Niš and that he was ready to talk to the Bulgarian representatives there.[135] When Danev asked Russia to represent Bulgaria at the meeting, he was rebuked by Sazonov who advised him that Bulgaria should send her own delegates to sign the preliminary peace.[136]

Meanwhile, encouraged by her former enemies, Greece and Serbia, and especially by the complete inaction of the great powers, Turkey decided to take advantage of Bulgaria's hopeless situation to repossess at least some of the lands that she had lost in the previous war.[137] On 7 July, the Porte demanded the immediate evacuation of all Bulgarian troops still found east of the Enos-Media line.[138] Sofia agreed and dispatched a special emissary to Constantinople to work out the procedure.[139] As it turned out, the Turks used this only as a suitable pretext to justify their invasion of Bulgaria in the eyes of the great powers. The Turkish armies, headed by Enver Bey, the popular hero of the defence of Scutari, were already advancing northward.[140] On 16 July, they crossed the Enos-Media line, reoccupied Adrianople, and moved into Old Bulgaria.[141] In a circular to the governments of the great powers, on 19 July, the Porte explained that the Turkish action was necessary because only a borderline extending from Enos northward along the course of the River Maritsa could guarantee the safety of Constantinople and the Straits.[142]

The Bulgarian appeals to the powers to prevent the destruction of the provisions of the Treaty of London which they guaranteed were disregarded.[143] To be sure, Russia protested at Constantinople[144] and proposed a naval demonstration by the great powers.[145] However, Germany rejected the idea outright,[146] Britain and France were not particularly eager to take part, and, left alone, Russia did not wish to risk her prestige.[147] In the end they took the easy way out. On 25 July, they made separate but identical representations which where defied by the Turkish government.[148]

V

Bulgaria's policy of complete reliance on Russia to ward off the national catastrophe collapsed with the invasion of the country by Rumania and Turkey. Danev wrote to Bobchev, on 14 July 1913, expressing

the immense grief, helplessness and despair of the entire nation ... From the 26th of last month [9 July NS] we placed our fate in the hands of Russia. We expected heavy sacrifices ... But the conditions proposed to us surpass by far even the most ominous predictions. In spite of that ... we bowed our head and agreed to such unbearable sacrifices, convinced that our back would be protected at least from Rumania and Turkey. To our great sorrow for a fifth day in a row we watch heart-broken the Rumanians invade our land ... The same scenes are recurring on the Turkish border ... In bewilderment we ask: Has Bulgaria really deserved to be treated so cruelly? Is it possible that the voice of Russia is so feeble that it is not heard at Constantinople and Bucharest? If, on the other hand, Russia has left us at the mercy of fate, let her at least inform us in time, so that we could try to save ourselves with our remaining strength or end in death, but with honour.[149]

On the same day Danev handed in the resignation of his cabinet, which was accepted, the king asking A. Malinov to head the new administration. Only when Malinov's attempt to form a national coalition failed did King Ferdinand finally turn to the liberals.[150]

On 17 July, V. Radoslavov, leader of the Liberal Party, formed a government of 'liberal concentration.' N. Genadiev, head of the National Liberals, became minister of foreign affairs, and D. Tonchev, chief of the Young Liberals, minister of finance.[151] The rise to power of the liberals symbolized the end of Russia's ascendancy in Bulgaria. It marked the beginning of a new course of Bulgarian foreign policy, a course of close and intimate collaboration with the powers of the Triple Alliance.[152]

Austria-Hungary had assured the new Bulgarian leaders of her support and in accordance with her counsel they made immediate overtures to Rumania.[153] Genadiev informed Bucharest through the Italian legation at Sofia that Bulgaria was willing and ready to cede the lands north of the Tutrakhan-Balchik line and requested the withdrawal of the Rumanian forces from the remaining occupied territories. The Rumanians were not prepared to go that far. They ordered their troops to stop advancing, but refused to withdraw them until Bulgaria concluded the armistice and the preliminary peace agreements with the other belligerents.[154]

As was shown earlier, Pašić had invited Bulgaria through Sazonov to send delegates to Niš presumably to negotiate the armistice agreement. They arrived there, accompanied by Colonel Romanovskii, on 20 July.[155] The Rumanian representatives followed shortly thereafter and immediately proposed Bucharest for the preliminary negotiations.[156] Misunderstanding developed at the very outset between Rumania and Bulgaria on the one hand, and Serbia and Greece on the other. It appears that the Greeks and the Serbs had not agreed and consequently had not informed the Bulgarians and the Rumanians about the exact nature of the talks in Niš.[157] Greece wished to combine the armistice and the preliminary peace talks and to conclude them at the theatre of war.[158] Serbia at first vacillated, but in the end sided with her ally.[159] On 24 July, they informed the Rumanian government that they would not agree to an armistice before the preliminary peace was concluded.[160]

The Rumanians suggested a compromise that resolved the deadlocked situation. They proposed the termination of all the military hostilities without a formal armistice agreement and an immediate conference in Bucharest to negotiate the preliminary peace.[161] On the same day, 24 July, Maiorescu invited the Serbian, Greek, Montenegrin, and Bulgarian governments to send their representatives.[162] All parties concerned accepted the proposal. The talks in Niš were dropped and the plenipotentiaries travelled directly to the Rumanian capital.[163] The Turkish government wished to take part in the negotiations as well but its request was turned down by the Rumanian prime minister because, as he put it, the 'talks in question will deal exclusively with the exchange of territories between the allies.'[164]

The summoning of the conference in Bucharest represented a diplomatic defeat for Russia. Sazonov's initial plan for a conference in St Petersburg, as well as his later proposal for an armistice parley in Niš to be followed by a conference in St Petersburg, did not materialize. Barely a month earlier the Balkan states had been competing for the good graces of Russia's diplomacy. Now, they were in fact declaring their lack of confidence in Russia.

The Russian government sought to improve its badly shaken position and declining prestige at the peace conference. But the inroads made by Austria-Hungary and Germany among the former allies, the allies' conflicting aims, and the lack of determined support from England and France made Russia's task extremely difficult.

VI

The first session of the Bucharest peace conference gathered on 30 July 1913, and elected T. Maiorescu its president. After the welcoming speech, the Rumanian premier proposed and the delegates approved unanimously suspension of all hostilities for five days beginning at noon the following day.[165]

As early as the second meeting, which was held on 31 July, the expected confrontation over the territorial delimitations took place. To avoid fruitless debates and thus the unnecessary prolongation of the conference, the delegates decided that the disputing parties should take up the various points at issue in preliminary private discussions.[166]

Rumania and Bulgaria came to terms very early and without encountering too many difficulties. Austria-Hungary and Italy encouraged a separate Bulgaro-Rumanian peace and used their influence to bring about a quick settlement between them.[167] Moreover, the Bulgarians had agreed to the Rumanian demands a week before the opening of the conference.[168] By 3 August, the military experts in the two delegations had traced the new frontier between them on a map.[169] At the sitting of the next day, Maiorescu announced that the two parties had reached a complete accord. At the same time, however, he dispelled any notion that the

The Balkan peninsula after the wars of 1912–13: territorial modifications according to the treaties of London, Bucharest, and Constantinople

Bulgarians might have entertained about a separate peace. He made it clear that the Rumanian government did not regard the arrangement as a separate agreement, but only as an integral part of the labours of the peace conference.[170]

The private talks between Bulgaria and her former allies proved more difficult. Both Serbia and Greece stuck stubbornly to the rather exaggerated territorial claims which were embodied in their secret agreements. The Serbs insisted that the line of the new Serbo-Bulgarian frontier must follow the course of the River Struma from the old Turkish-Bulgarian boundary.[171] The Greeks put forth a line

leaving the Aegean a few miles east of Makri and following a northerly direction until it reached the watershed between the Arda River to the north and the Mesta. The frontier then followed the crest of the mountains in a west-north-westerly direction until it reached a point about two miles south of Napli. There it turned west-south-west until it met the frontier line demanded by Serbia at the confluence of the Struma and the Bistritsa.[172]

The border line proposed by Bulgaria left

the old Bulgarian frontier at a point west of Kiustendil. It ran in a south-south-westerly direction to the confluence of the Bregalnitsa and the Vardar Rivers. After crossing the Vardar, the line continued in the same direction for about fifteen miles when it turned south passing about fifteen miles east of Bitola, and then turning east through Dragomantsi and along the crest of the Pajak Mountains until it again met Vardar west of Ardzan Lake. Here the line turned south again and followed the course of the river for about ten miles. It then ran eastwards until it reached the Gulf of Orfani at a point about six miles west of the mouth of the Struma.[173]

The principal points of contention between Bulgaria and Serbia were the towns of Štip, Kočani, Radomica, and Strumica; and between Bulgaria and Greece the port of Kavalla.[174]

Russia and Austria-Hungary were deeply involved in the negotiations of the disputes. Both wooed Bulgaria: Russia hoping to keep Bulgaria within her own sphere of influence and perhaps to recreate the Serbo-Bulgarian alliance in the future; Austria-Hungary to reconcile Bulgaria with Rumania and to bring Bulgaria into the fold of the Triple Alliance. At Bucharest, Russia faced a much more difficult task than Austria-Hungary. For, while the former wished to conciliate Bulgaria without having to estrange Serbia, which was virtually impossible to do, the latter, having nothing to lose in regard to Serbia, could easily afford to be overly generous and vocal in favour of Bulgaria. Shebeko supported Bulgaria in respect to Kočani, Radomica, and Strumica, but upheld Serbia's right to Štip.[175]

Prince Fürstenberg went much farther – he proposed the River Vardar as the new frontier, leaving the right bank to Serbia, and the left bank together with the valley of the River Bregalnica to Bulgaria.[176]

From the very outset, as Shebeko put it, it became apparent that the question of Kavalla would prove to be the 'stumbling block' of the conference. Both the Bulgarians and the Greeks were uncompromising on this point.[177] Their positions were made even more inflexible by the fact that the representatives of the great powers at Bucharest were divided, that they were far from being in accord on the future of that city. Austria-Hungary and Russia, the two powers that were at loggerheads on most other issues, were naturally united in their backing of Bulgaria in regard to Kavalla.[178] They insisted that Kavalla was indispensable to Bulgaria, after she had lost Seres to Greece, as the only outlet to the sea for the western part of the country.[179]

Venizelos, who was certain of the support of Germany and France,[180] however, was not willing to listen, let alone abide by, the arguments in favour of Bulgaria's economic needs. He was confident that the divided great powers would not be able to agree on a concerted policy or action against Greece during the conference or in the future. Hence, he was ready to, and indeed did, assure everyone that although Greece would not concede Kavalla at the conference, if subsequently the great powers decided otherwise, she would have to submit to their decision.[181]

Although this was obviously an altogether hollow promise, the Rumanians utilized it to prevent the possible collapse of the work of the peace conference. On the last day of July, T. Ionescu proposed to the representatives of the great powers at Bucharest that they secure their government's sanction and declare to the president of the conference that 'whatever the decision come to by the Conference in regard to Kavalla, the Great Powers reserved the right to revise the decision.'[182] Such declarations, wrote Shebeko to Sazonov, were necessary to persuade the Bulgarian delegates to accept the temporary cession of Kavalla to Greece, pending the subsequent and final resolution of the question by the powers.[183]

As was to be expected, the responses from the capitals of the great powers varied. Prince Fürstenberg was the only delegate who was unconditionally authorized to make the declaration and he did so on 4 August. The Russian minister followed suite two days later; he had not yet received the necessary instructions, but, as the most critical sitting of the conference was to take place that afternoon, he assumed the responsibility and his action was subsequently approved.[184]

In the mean time, Maiorescu endeavoured in the background to persuade the allies to tone down their demands. On 4 August, he met privately with the Serbian, Greek, and Montenegrin delegates and urged them to cede Kavalla, Radomica, and Strumica to Bulgaria.[185] They refused[186] and the following day he advised the Bulgarians to give in on all these points. Once again he assured them that Rumania would not oppose the revision of the treaty by the great powers. But at the same time he issued another warning to the Bulgarians to the effect that they should not delay the conference by false hopes and expectations, such as a separate peace with Rumania, because his government was determined to stick it out with the allies till the end.[187]

At the last minute the Serbs made a final concession. They agreed to make a slight alteration in the southern portion of the boundary by ceding Strumica to Bulgaria. In the plenary sitting of 6 August the Bulgarians backed down on all the other contested towns. This brought the actual labour of the conference to an end.[188]

In the plenary session of 8 August, Maiorescu read the Russian and Austro-Hungarian declaration – the first reserving the right of revision of the decision on the question of Kavalla, and the latter the right of revision of the entire treaty. Tonchev responded promptly by announcing that the two declarations induced Bulgaria to accept the conditions of peace.[189]

The Peace Treaty of Bucharest was signed two days later, on 10 August 1913, by Bulgaria on the one hand, and Rumania, Serbia, Greece, and Montenegro on the other.[190] The ratifications were exchanged on 25 August.[191]

The Treaty of Bucharest did not suffer further revision; it became the final peace settlement of the Inter-Allied War. The unanimity of the powers, which, as Venizelos correctly surmised, was necessary for its revision, did not exist and did not develop.

Russia did not, indeed could not, require the revision of the entire treaty for fear of alienating Serbia.[192] But, even on the question of Kavalla, Sazonov's sincerity must be questioned. Before the treaty was signed he indicated to Bobchev that Russia would not be able to act alone.[193] Sazanov complained that Russia's ally, France, insisted on the absolute non-interference of the powers and that she considered the Bucharest settlement as final.[194]

This might have been true once the treaty had been concluded. The fact remains, however, that Sazonov did not really make a serious attempt to win the support of either Paris or London. On 8 August 1913, Pichon, the French foreign minister, revealed to D. Stanchov, Bulgarian minister at Paris, that St Petersburg did not make a single official request to France to fight for Bulgarian Kavalla.[195] This view was corroborated by none other than the Russian ambassador at Paris. In a rejoinder to Sazonov, on 14 August 1913, Izvol'skii wrote:

It is not quite clear to me why, if you attached such a paramount significance to this question, you did not instruct me then to approach Pichon seriously. Until August 5 your telegrams mentioned Kavalla only once, and your arguments in favour of its transfer to Bulgaria were not known to me. Moreover, in your telegram to Hartwig of 3/16 July, you allowed the possibility of Kavalla being conceded to Greece.[196]

Austria-Hungary was undoubtedly more serious and more sincere in her declarations. Tarnowski kept in constant touch with the Sofia government on the issue of revising the treaty.[197] Vienna raised it in St Petersburg on numerous occasions,[198] but by the middle of August Russia lost all interest even in regard to the question of Kavalla and the entire problem of revising the Treaty of Bucharest was dropped altogether.[199]

VII

In the plenary session of 6 August, the representatives of the five Balkan states in Bucharest agreed to enclose in the treaty of peace a declaration calling on the Turkish government to evacuate all areas west of the Enos-Media line which the Turks occupied in contravention of the terms of the Treaty of London.[200] Such an expression of solidarity on their part might have served as a warning to Turkey. At the last minute the declaration was left out completely, because the Greeks changed their mind and refused to endorse it.[201] Without it the problem of Turkey's defiance of the Treaty of London became a strictly Bulgaro-Turkish affair. As in the case of the revision of the Treaty of Bucharest, Russia and Austria-Hungary, the two powers most interested in Bulgaria, were generous in offering advice and support, but in the end the Bulgarians had to face the Turks alone across the conference table.

Defeated and helpless as they were, and with the Turks in actual possession of the disputed lands, the Bulgarians were very anxious to avoid direct talks with the Porte for fear of being forced to sign what they suspected would amount to a dictated peace. For this reason they claimed, as Genadiev wrote to Madzharov: 'The question of Adrianople and Thrace is international. We will do ourselves a great harm if we enter into direct negotiations with the Turks.'[202] In a dispatch to Bobchev, on 25 August 1913, Genadiev reiterated his contention that direct talks with the Turks would constitute 'a dangerous trap for us. If the Porte wants to negotiate let them negotiate with the Great Powers.'[203]

All available evidence suggests that the great powers were not sufficiently interested or united to act against Turkey. Bobchev cautioned his government that the expected assistance from the Concert of Europe would not be forthcoming and that Russia would not act alone.[204] Even Nekliudov advised Genadiev frankly not to rely on Russia's unilateral intervention against Turkey.[205] But, like a sinking ship, the Bulgarian government clung to every rumour and report that affirmed even vaguely the sought-after assistance. Such rumours and misleading reports were plentiful. They were inspired primarily by Russia's or rather Sazonov's constant wavering and vacillation.

Due to military and strategic considerations stemming from her proximity to Constantinople and the Straits, Russia, for a long time, opposed the annexation of Adrianople to Bulgaria. Once it was captured by the Bulgarian armies, Russia grudgingly acquiesced. Now, with the Turks back in Adrianople, the Russian government again faced the same dilemma. 'Although from the material point of view it was in Russia's interest that Adrianople should remain Turkish,' Sazonov explained, 'sentimental reasons obliged Russia to try and help Bulgaria.'[206] Moreover, as Giers pointed out, 'if in the very end Adrianople is left to Turkey, the benefit from that concession, which in itself, in the final analysis, is not particularly perilous to us, will be derived not by us but by our political rivals or friends.'[207]

For these reasons, as well as because Russia believed that there was still a faint hope that Bulgaria might be kept within her fold, Pevchevskii Most took up a pro-Bulgarian stance. But it was a half-hearted effort rather than a definite course of policy; it reflected Sazonov's, and Russia's, inability to decide what to do or what could be done. On 8 August 1913, Sazonov warned Buchanan: 'Whatever the other Powers do, Russia will not change her attitude, and will never allow Turkey to retain Adrianople.'[208] At the same time and, indeed, during the same interview he found it necessary to confess that Russia 'wished to avoid isolated actions or any actions that might lead to the closing of the Straits, which, in view of the approaching harvest would have been a serious blow to Russia's grain exports.'[209]

Russia wished to see Turkey relinquish Adrianople voluntarily or, if it became necessary, to force her to do so through the application of pressure by the Concert of Europe. On 7 August, the ambassadors of the great powers at Constantinople made a collective démarche to the Porte. They threatened to restrict all financial credits unless the Turkish government accepted and acted in accordance with the terms of the Treaty of London.[210] Needless to say, this was a highly hypocritical move 'devoid of any meaning or significance.' Only two days earlier the tobacco régie, which was under French domination, paid Turkey £700,000.[211] Russia's partners in the Triple Entente had great commercial interest in the Ottoman Empire; they were not disposed to forego their economic influence there for the sake of a Bulgarian Adrianople. Yet, as Izvol'skii pointed out, if they restricted their financial aid, Turkey could easily secure the required credits from the powers of the Triple Alliance.[212]

The Turks might have been forced to capitulate only if the great powers were united and agreed on the use of the threat of force if that became necessary.[213] The Russian ambassador at Constantinople urged a naval demonstration and, as in the case of Scutari, a joint occupation of the terminal points of Enos and Media. The effect of such actions would have been considerable and Turkey would undoubtedly have been forced to yield as Montenegro had done a few months earlier.[214] But there was an important difference. Austria-Hungary succeeded in uniting the Concert of Europe for the naval blockade against Montenegro; Russia now failed to win the backing even of her two allies, France and Britain, against Turkey.[215]

Since they were unable to agree on anything else the powers pondered the possibility of yet another collective representation to the Porte. But, on 21 August, the Turks announced that they did not intend to claim the right bank of the River Maritsa and that the Turkish troops already there would be withdrawn. Although this promise fell far short of being an endorsement of the terms of the Treaty of London, the powers accepted it as constituting a major concession and expressed their complete satisfaction.[216] Sazonov, who a little earlier had secured the tsar's consent to protest strongly to Turkey by recalling Giers from Constantinople, deemed such an action no longer opportune or necessary.[217] Indeed, toward the end of August, St Petersburg took the lead in warning Sofia to forget about the Treaty of London and about the Concert of Europe and to settle its affairs directly with Constantinople.[218]

On 29 August 1913, Genadiev informed the grand vizier that Bulgaria accepted the Turkish invitation for direct negotiations on the border question as well as on other political and economic issues of mutual interest.[219] On 5 September, the Bulgarian delegates, General Savov and A. Toshev, and their advisers, arrived in the Ottoman capital to begin the talks.[220] While in Constantinople they were to seek the assistance of and rely upon the advice of the Austro-Hungarian and German ambassadors, particularly the former.[221] Genadiev and the other Bulgarian leaders need not have been overly concerned about secrets of the negotiations being passed to Russia, for, as Nekliudov wrote to Sazonov, neither Savov nor Toshev had any confidence in Russia.[222] The break between Bulgaria and Russia was total.

The peace conference was opened by the grand vizier on 8 September at the Porte. The Turkish delegates were Talaat Bey, Mahmud Pasha, and Khalil Bey.[223] Shortly after the grand vizier left the conference hall, Talaat Bey, who was chosen president, invited the Bulgarians to formulate and present their proposals. Savov replied that since they invited the Bulgarians to Constantinople the Turks should put forth theirs first. Mahmud Pasha obliged in a typically Turkish fashion by declaring: 'Whatever we have seized is ours.' Talaat Bey added: 'You do not give anything from your bag. You will cede to us Adrianople as a token of your good will.'[224] In the end both sides agreed to carry on the talks in private and to meet in formal sessions only after the issues under consideration were adequately discussed and when either side was prepared to make a proposal.[225]

The Turks were willing to bargain over some territorial questions, but from the very beginning, they left no doubt that they had decided to keep Adrianople and Lozengrad (Kirk-Kilisse).[226] Bulgaria was fully aware of and more or less resigned to this fact. As Genadiev wrote to his delegates, they were to resist the Turkish claims to the two cities as long as possible and then, if nothing else worked, to concede them.[227] This took place as early as the second formal session of the conference on 12 September. When Bulgaria advanced a claim to Adrianople and Lozengrad the Turks refused even to listen to it; whereupon the Bulgarian delegates scaled down their demands and proposed to base all further talks on the Turkish circular note of 19 July 1913.[228] They argued that the valley on the right bank of the Maritsa was required for the construction of a railway line to the Bulgarian port of Dedeagach on the Aegean Sea.[229]

The above-mentioned circular aimed to appease the great powers and in that respect it succeeded. However, the Turks did not feel bound by its promises any longer. In private chats with Toshev, Talaat Bey and Djemal Bey, military governor of Constantinople, warned that the Turkish military would not allow the government to relinquish the town of Dimotika because it was considered to be essential for the defense of Adrianople. Bulgaria could only hope to win the other contested towns, Ortakoi, Malko Tūrnovo, and possibly Mustafa Pasha.[230]

On 15 September, at the fourth formal session, Mahmud Pasha presented a detailed boundary line in a 'take it or leave it' fahsion. Besides Adrianople and Lozengrad he claimed for Turkey both Dimotika and Mustafa Pasha. The Bulgarian delegates asked for time to communicate with Sofia and to learn what they already knew very well: there was nothing that Bulgaria could possibly do but submit and accept the terms dictated by Turkey.[231]

On 17 September, the two sides agreed on a borderline which began from the right arm of the mouth of the Maritsa and followed the course of the river to a point on its right bank south of Mondra; from this village it continued to Kurtkoi and through Chermen it reached the Black Sea to the north of Iniada. The following day they concluded a border protocol containing all the appropriate maps.[232]

The remaining outstanding issues between the two countries, such as the question of minorities, the future of Muslim religious and educational institutions in Bulgaria, and all the others, were settled early in the few subsequent sessions.[233] The ceremonial signing of the Peace Treaty of Constantinople took place in the midst of serious talks of a Turkish-Bulgarian alliance,[234] on 29 September 1913, in the great hall Hardjie at the Porte.[235]

The Annexation Crisis inaugurated and the Treaty of Constantinople marked the close of one of the most active stages in the relations among the states of the Balkan peninsula and between them and Russia. During this short period of less than four years the achievement of Balkan unity, as symbolized by the Balkan system of alliances, had given rise to the greatest hopes and expectations. However, the Inter-Allied War, which buried the alliances, dashed these optimistic prospects and produced the most tragic consequences.

8

Conclusion

For Russia as well as for the states of the Balkan peninsula the period from the Annexation Crisis to the end of the Inter-Allied War was perhaps the most eventful and dramatic in the entire history of the Eastern Question. In the course of about five years the Balkan nations joined in a system of alliances, fought a highly successful war against the Ottoman Empire, and in the end destroyed their short-lived unity in a fracticidal war. With the creation of the Balkan system of alliances the Russian Empire attained a position of unprecedented dominance in the Balkans. The Inter-Allied War virtually wiped out its prestige and sway in the affairs of the peninsula.

The moves toward Balkan unity were direct results of, and indeed, reactions to the collapse of the Russian–Austro-Hungarian entente, the aim of which was 'to keep the Balkans on ice.' For in the view of St Petersburg, as well as Belgrade and Cetinje, a united block in the peninsula stretching from the Adriatic to the Black Sea appeared in the aftermath of the Annexation Crisis as the only effective way to stop the continued spread of the Dual Monarchy to the south. Furthermore, the Italian war against the Ottoman Empire and the extremely chaotic situation in its European provinces raised again the threat that the great powers might intervene, as they had done frequently in the past, to impose a European settlement on the Eastern Question. As a result of all these factors the Balkan governments began to contemplate more seriously than ever before the notion of a Balkan solution to the problems and opportunities presented by Turkey's remaining possessions in Europe, for which unity among these governments was an indispensable prerequisite. It was obvious, however, that in spite of their public espousal of the cause of oppressed 'co-nationals' under Turkish rule, they were incited primarily by the prospect of aggrandizement in Albania and, particularly, in Macedonia.

The main weaknesses of the Balkan system of alliances were apparent from the very outset. The allies did not resolve adequately the question that divided them most in the past – namely, the division of the territorial spoils that they expected to derive from a victorious war against the Turks. Although Serbia and Bulgaria agreed, with the aid of Russia, on the partition of Macedonia, Bulgaria and Greece failed to reach an accord and side-tracked the issue. Moreover, the Russians, the protectors of the Serbo-Bulgarian alliance and hence of the entire alliance system, and the allies held divergent points of view. For the former, who failed to take seriously the real intentions of the allies, the system of alliances was meant to be a defensive tool directed against Austria-Hungary. For the latter it constituted primarily an instrument to wage an immediate war against Turkey.

Russia was opposed to such a war. Indeed, before its outbreak St Petersburg cultivated the favour of the Porte and strove to persuade its Balkan protégés to think of Turkey as a potential ally. Once the allies chose to disregard its counsel and warnings, however, St Petersburg had to come to their assistance at least diplomatically, inasmuch as the future of the Balkan system of alliances was at stake. For, no matter what the eventual outcome of the conflict, the allied Balkan states were in need of Russia's aid. If they were defeated, Russia would have to bail them out to prevent them suffering territorial losses and, in case of victory, she would have to safeguard their gains against the opposition of the Dual Monarchy.

Throughout the war the primary objectives of St Petersburg were, first of all, to escape a direct involvement in the conflict and a war with Austria-Hungary, and secondly, to preserve intact the Balkan alliances, particularly the Serbo-Bulgarian alliance. War, for which the empire was not prepared, was avoided by capitulating to Vienna on the questions of the Serbian exit to the Adriatic Sea and Scutari. But by sacrificing some of the objectives of the allies, especially Serbia, Russia endangered her second major aim.

The Belgrade government, deprived of its most notable conquests on the Adriatic coast and in Albania, began to search for recompense elsewhere. The Serbs turned in the only direction open to them, toward Macedonia in the south, and thereby promptly ran into the determined opposition of Bulgaria. The Sofia government's refusal to allow any modification in the territorial provisions of their alliance alienated the two countries from each other. This dispute made the task of Bulgaria in reaching an acceptable solution to her already existing territorial disputes with Greece and Rumania virtually impossible. Above all, as a result of the estrangement with Bulgaria, Serbia found a secret ally in Greece and both began to curry favour with Rumania against Bulgaria.

Although the Russian government was from the very beginning fully aware of the territorial disputes, it did very little about them. Indeed, one may safely suggest that without Russia's – at times implicit and at other times open – encouragement of Rumania, there might not have been a crisis over southern Dobruja; in which case the disputes between the allies, between Bulgaria, Serbia, and Greece, would no doubt have taken a different and less violent turn. Moreover, the disputing parties appealed continually to St Petersburg to help them resolve their quarrels. Since the Russian government was very anxious not to risk alienating any of them, it failed to take a definite and consistent stand on the issues at question. It also failed to carry out the precise arbitration responsibilities toward Serbia and Bulgaria assumed by Tsar Nicholas in accordance with the provisions of the Serbo-Bulgarian treaty of alliance. Sazonov instead promised over and over again to support the territorial pretensions of each party, a task which was virtually impossible since in each case the claims were hopelessly contradictory. In the end, even his last-minute efforts proved too feeble, too inconsistent, and too hesitant to prevent the Inter-Allied War.

The tragic conclusion was not inevitable. It is true that Russia was not sufficiently strong or adequately prepared to resist to the very end the Austro-Hungarian opposition to Serbia's objectives in Albania and on the Adriatic coast. The losses suffered there by Serbia and her subsequent disappointment, however, by no means predetermined the tragedy. It was rather the result of a combination of factors, some of which Russia alone could have influenced, and others controlled or eliminated. But in order to be able to attain such ends, the imperial government would have had to have a less demanding policy, and more consistent, rational, and disciplined decision-making. It needed a foreign policy that had a well-defined direction and purpose.

Russia had been engrossed in the affairs of the Balkan peninsula for over two hundred years, virtually since the reign of Peter the Great. In spite of this long experience, however, successive Russian governments did not grasp the emotional depths of the national rivalries in the peninsula, and thus failed to take to heart one of the principal lessons of Balkan politics. It was obvious that the mutually exclusive territorial pretensions of the Balkan states made it almost impossible for one great power to meet the expectations of all of them and at the same time to establish peacefully its hegemony over the entire peninsula. Hence, out of necessity, Russia as well as any other great power that entertained such ambitions had to choose among the Balkan states.

For strategic, political, and military reasons, Bulgaria and Serbia were Russia's most valuable allies in the Balkans. They were the strongest military powers and their combined territory, which extended virtually from the Adriatic to the Black Sea, was inhabited by peoples who were traditionally pro-Russian. Montenegro and Greece, the two other members of the system of alliances, were not as vital to the foreign policy needs of the Russian Empire. The kingdom of Montenegro was too small to be of great consequence; and in any event, it already depended too much on Russia to risk antagonizing her for very long. Greece was a dubious friend, for in spite of the religion which she shared with Russia, the Greek monarchy looked much more toward Germany and western Europe. Furthermore, the Greek people had developed a pronounced distrust of their neighbours to the north and of the Slavs in general. Consequently, the short- as well as the long-range national interests of the Russian Empire called above all for the preservation of the Serbo-Bulgarian alliance, which in any case constituted the very core of the entire Balkan system of alliances.

However, even after it had won over to Russia's side the three Slavic states and Greece, the St Petersburg government was not fully appeased. It attempted as well to draw Rumania, the fifth Balkan nation, away from Austria-Hungary and into her own orbit. Although Bucharest had declined the overtures from Bulgaria while the alliances were being negotiated, such a course would have been rational and legitimate had Rumania been on good terms with the allies. Yet, as the Russians knew very well, this was not the situation. Since the Congress of Berlin, Rumania and Bulgaria had been at loggerheads. The Rumanians had their eyes set on acquiring southern Dobruja, while the Bulgarians were determined not to give it up. There was really no way in which Russia could have mollified both. Once she began wooing the doubtful friendship of Bucharest, she instantly started alienating Sofia. The resulting conflict between Rumania and Bulgaria incited Greece and Serbia and effected the complete isolation of Bulgaria. Thereupon the lines became rigidly drawn: Bulgaria had to capitulate to her three opponents or there would be war.

Besides the Rumanian complications, St Petersburg's highly inconsistent and indecisive leadership made the territorial disputes very difficult to settle. At no point did the Russian government make its own position clear. It did not act even in regard to the Serbo-Bulgarian dispute for which there were explicit provisions for arbitration. It is true, of course, that Russia could have alienated Serbia by adhering to the letter of their agreement. However, had she defended Bulgaria against the pretensions of Rumania and pronounced in time a decision which attempted to meet at least half-way the exaggerated demands of Serbia and the inflexible position of Bulgaria, it is conceivable that she could have appeased both.

In this as well as in the other disputes, however, Russia wavered and vacillated for too long. She led each disputant to believe that in the end she would support its demands. The upshot of this was that they in turn assumed more belligerent and uncompromising postures which made the Inter-Allied War unavoidable.

The lack of a well-defined direction or purpose in Russian foreign policy was not caused by forces which operated outside the established political system. The influence of pressure groups was not decisive in Russia, and whatever public opinion existed was almost solidly behind Serbia and Bulgaria. It was rather a by-product of the unsystematic and irregular ways in which decisions were reached.

During the imperial period the foreign ministers of Russia were not particularly strong leaders. There were among them some influential individuals – Count K. Nesselrode, Prince A.M. Gorchakov in the immediate post–Crimean War period, and A.P. Izvol'skii later – who enjoyed the confidence of the crown and imposed their mark on Russia's foreign relations. But more often than not they were simply administrators who carried out the will of the tsars.

A figure such as S.D. Sazonov was in this respect the rule rather than the exception. According to most accounts he was a good administrator, but frequently and for prolonged intervals he was absent from the Foreign Ministry due to ill health. More significantly, however, he had not had a long and distinguished diplomatic career; he lacked the proper social and political connections which, in the St Petersburg milieu, were indispensable to a minister of foreign affairs if he were to enjoy a greater say in the decision-making process.

Various other personalities in official St Petersburg were more influential and held a greater sway over the decisions than the head of Pevchevskii Most. They included the grand dukes, many of whom were married to Balkan princesses, high officials of the Ministry of War, and even individual representatives abroad with connections in high places at home. For instance, N. Hartwig, whose views were regarded very highly by his former subordinates in the Asiatic Department, and to a lesser degree E. Demidov and M. Shebeko were able to disregard or modify the instructions from Pevchevskii Most and indeed initiate policy.

Although these individuals claimed to represent the interests of Russia and Slavdom, in actual fact they lacked a general appreciation of Russia's political and strategic needs. They really acted on behalf of one or another Balkan nation to which they felt particularly close by family ties, for sentimental reasons, or, in the case of the envoys, by a prolonged stay there. In dealing with Hartwig, one cannot escape feeling that in addition to his deeply held convictions he was also motivated by a strong desire to repay Pevchevskii Most for his diplomatic exile in Teheran and what was undoubtedly meant to be another exile in provincial Belgrade.

The results of such a disorderly policy were disappointing for Russia. The dominant position that she established in the peninsula by 1912 crumbled like a house of cards in 1913. Bulgaria, the strongest military power in the area, was lost to Russia for a long time to come. With the liberals in power, Sofia embarked on a pro-Austrian and pro–Triple Alliance orientation in foreign policy. Rumania profited most from Russia's assistance. In spite of the debt of gratitude owed to St Petersburg, however, Bucharest chose to remain allied to the powers of the Triple Alliance. Besides, there was the unresolved problem of Bessarabia that divided them. The Greeks made great gains also, but they remained distrustful of the Slavs, and in any event they felt more indebted to Germany and France than to Russia. Only Serbia and Montenegro continued to be bound to Russia, partly due to the debt of gratitude they owed to her, but perhaps more significantly because they had nowhere else to turn for protection against the ever present danger from the north. Although they were important to Russia, their actual value as allies was circumscribed by their geographical location. They were encircled on all sides by Austria-Hungary and her allies and friends, except for Greece to the south.

Finally, at the end of the wars of 1912–13, the situation in the peninsula was even more explosive than before. The perennial Macedonian Question was left unresolved. Bulgaria was determined to overturn the settlement of 1913. Serbia's gains heightened the running feud with Austria-Hungary. On the whole, the Inter-Allied War revived, in much uglier form, the old antagonisms in the Balkans and set the stage for another conflict. When it came in the following year, it proved more devastating than anyone in Europe expected. The Great War caught Russia unprepared, with her most important Balkan flank precariously weak. The resulting military disasters suffered by the Russian armies were in no small measure responsible for the discontent and the upheaval on the home front which destroyed the empire of the tsars.

Notes

ABBREVIATIONS

APS M. Boghitschewitsch (Bogićević) ed *Die auswärtige Politik Serbiens, 1903–1914* 3 vol (Berlin 1928–31)

BD Bulgaria, Ministerstvo na vŭnshnite raboti i na izpovedaniiata *Diplomaticheski dokumenti po namesata na Bŭlgariia v evropeiskata voina* 2 vol (Sofia 1920–1)

British Documents Great Britain, Foreign Office *British Documents on the Origins of the War, 1898–1914* ed G.P. Gooch and H. Temperley, 11 vol (London 1926–38)

DDF France, Ministère des Affaires étrangères, Commission de Publication des Documents relatifs aux Origines de la Guerre de 1914 *Documents diplomatiques français 1871–1914* 41 vol (Paris 1929–59)

DPIK Bulgaria, Narodno sŭbranie *Doklad na parlamentarnata izpitatelna komissia* I (Sofia 1918)

Duma Russia, Gosudarstvennaia duma *Stenograficheskiia otchety* (St Petersburg 1906–17)

FO Foreign Office

FRO Russia, Narodnyi komissariat po inostrannym delam *Materiali po istorii franko-russkikh otnoshenii za 1910–1914 g.g. ...* (Moscow 1922)

GBA Mr Michel de Giers' and Mr Serge Botkin's Archives, Hoover Institution on War, Revolution and Peace, Stanford University, Stanford, California

GP Germany, Auswärtiges Amt *Die Grosse Politik der europäischen Kabinette, 1871–1914* ... ed J. Lepsius, A. Mendelssohn-Bartholdy, and F. Thimme, 40 vol (Berlin 1922–7)

Istorik pregovora M. Milovanović 'Istorik pregovora za zaključenje srpsko-bugarskog ugovora od 29 Februaru 1912' in S. Skoko *Drugi balkanski rat 1913* (Belgrade 1968) 365–99

KA Krasnyi Arkhiv

MO Russia, Komissiia po igdaniiu dokumentov epokhi imperializma *Mezhdunarodnye*

otnosheniia v epokhu imperializma. Dokumenty iz arkhivov tsarskogo i vremennogo pravitel' stv, 1878–1917 ... ed A.P. Bol'shemennikov, A.S. Erusalemskii, A.A. Mogilevich, and F.A. Rothstein, series II 1900–1913, vol XVIII–XX (Moscow 1938–40)

ÖUA Austro-Hungarian Monarchy, Ministerium des k. und k. Hauses und des Äussern *Österreich-Ungarns Aussenpolitik von der Bosnischen Krise 1908 bis zum Kriegsausbruch 1914* ... ed L. Bittner, A.F. Pribram, H. Srbik, and H. Übersberger, 8 vol (Vienna 1930)

Prilozhenie Bulgaria, Narodno sūbranie *Prilozhenie kūm tom pūrvi ot doklada na parlamentarnata izpitatelna komisiia* (Sofia 1918)

RS Russkaiia Starina

Rumanian Documents Rumania, Ministère des Affaires étrangères *Documents diplomatiques. Les événements de la peninsule balkanique. L'action de la Roumanie, septembre 1912–août 1913* (Bucharest 1913)

Siebert B. von Siebert ed *Graf Benckendorffs diplomatischer Schriftwechsel* 3 vol (Berlin and Leipzig 1928)

SSD Russia, Narodnyi komissariat po inostrannym delam *Sbornik sekretnnykh dokumentov byvshago ministerstva inostrannykh del* (Moscow 1917)

Stieve F. Stieve ed *Der diplomatischer Schriftwechsel Iswolskis, 1911–1914. Aus den Geheimakten der Russischen Staatsarchive* 4 vol (Berlin 1925)

INTRODUCTION

1 G.P. Genov *Iztochniiat vūpros* II (Sofia 1925–26) 460
2 *Ibid*
3 B.H. Sumner *Russia and the Balkans 1870–1880* (Oxford 1937); W.N. Medlicott *The Congress of Berlin and After: A Diplomatic History of the Near Eastern Settlement 1878–1880* (London 1938); C. Jelavich *Tsarist Russia and Balkan Nationalism: Russian Influence in the Internal Affairs of Bulgaria and Serbia 1879–1886* (Berkeley, Calif. 1958)
4 A.F. Pribram *The Secret Treaties of Austria-Hungary 1879–1914* I tr A.C. Coolidge (Cambridge, Mass. 1920) 50–63
5 Ibid 79–82
6 See C.E. Black *The Establishment of Constitutional Government in Bulgaria* (Princeton, NJ 1944); W.N. Medlicott 'The Powers and the Unification of the Two Bulgarias 1885' *English Historical Review* LIV (Jan. 1939) 67–82, and LIV (April 1939) 263–84.
7 Genov *Iztochniiat vūpros* II 461
8 Pribram *Secret Treaties* I 37–50. See also E.A. Adamov and I.V. Koz'menko ed *Sbornik dogovorov Rossii s drugimi gosudarstvami 1856–1917* (Moscow 1952) 228–33 no. 31.
9 Pribram *Secret Treaties* I 185–95; Adamov and Koz'menko ed *Sbornik* 303–8 no. 47

10 A.L. Popov ed 'Diplomaticheskaiia podgotovka balkanskoi voiny 1912 g.' *KA* VIII (1925) 3

11 Text in B.D. Kesiiakov ed *Prinos kŭm diplomaticheskata istoria na Bŭlgaria 1878–1925* I (Sofia 1925) 20–1. See also S. Danev 'Konventsiiata mezhdu Russia i Bŭlgaria ot 1902 g.' *Nauchen Pregled* I 3 (1929) 45–8; E.C. Helmreich and C.E. Black 'The Russo-Bulgarian Military Convention of 1902' *Journal of Modern History* IX (Dec. 1937) 471–82.

12 See W.S. Vucinich *Serbia between East and West: The Events of 1903–1908* (Stanford, Calif. 1954).

13 Seat of the Ministry of Foreign Affairs in St Petersburg

14 On the Buchlau Agreement and the Annexation Crisis see B.E. Schmitt *The Annexation of Bosnia 1908–1909* (Cambridge 1937); W.M. Carlgren *Iswolsky und Aehrenthal vor der bosnischen Annexion-krise: russische und österreichisch-ungarische Balkanpolitik, 1906–1908* (Uppsala 1955); A.P. Lavrov *Anneksiia Bosnii i Gertsegoviny i otnoshenie k nei slavianstva* (St Petersburg 1909); K.B. Vinogradov *Bosniiski krizis 1908–1909 g.g.* (Leningrad 1964); M. Ninćić (Nintchitch) *La Crise bosnique (1900–1908) et les puissances européennes* 2 vols (Paris 1937).

15 I.V. Bestuzhev *Bor'ba v Rossii po voprosam vneshnei politiki 1906–1910* (Moscow 1961) 294; P.N. Efremov *Vneshnaiia politika Rossii (1907–1914 g.g.)* (Moscow 1961) 104

16 Miliukov used the term 'diplomatic Tsushima'; P. Miliukov *Balkanskii krizis i politika A.P. Izvol'skogo* (St Petersburg 1910) 133. See also *Russkaia Mysl'* XXX (April 1909) 211.

17 See Miliukov *Balkanskii krizis* 133; *Russkaia Mysl'* XXX (April 1909) 207.

18 S.V. Sigrist *U poroga velikoi voiny* (Petrograd 1924) 10

19 See L.S. Stavrianos *Balkan Federation: A History of the Movement toward Balkan Unity in Modern Times* (Northampton, Mass. 1944).

20 Genov *Iztochniiat vŭpros* 557

21 Berchtold Memoir, October 2, 1912 *ÖUA* IV 528, no. 3928

CHAPTER 1 Toward a Balkan system of alliances

1 Bestuzhev *Bor'ba v Rossii* 294

2 Ibid; Efremov *Vneshnaia politika Rossii* 104

3 Bestuzhev *Bor'ba v Rossii* 295

4 *Russkaia Mysl'* no. 5 (1909) 194

5 Bestuzhev *Bor'ba v Rossii* 297

6 *Duma* Part I, Meeting 31, 12 Dec. 1908, 2657

7 Bestuzhev *Bor'ba v Rossii* 298

8 Miliukov *Balkanskii krizis* 133 ff

9 Bestuzhev *Bor'ba v Rossii* 296

10 *Moskovskii Ezhenedel' nik* 1909 no. 12, 7

11 A.V. Nekliudov *Diplomatic Reminiscences Before and During the World War* tr Alexandra Paget (London 1920) 33

12 *Duma* 2675; *Novoe Vremia* 30 June 1909, 2; *Russkaia Mysl'* xxx (Jan. 1909) 227

13 Bestuzhev *Bor' ba v Rossii* 336–7

14 Ibid 338

15 Ibid 337

16 Pourtalès to Bülow, 18 Sept 1909 *GP* xxvi 2, 856 no. 9569

17 P.N. Miliukov *Vospominaniia (1859–1917)* ii ed M.N. Karpovich and B.I. Elkin (New York 1955) 110 ff

18 *Duma* 2627. See also Louis to Pichon, 17 Mar. 1910 *DDF* 2ᵉ série (1900–1911) xii 711 no. 463; A. Zaionchkovskii *Podgotovka Rossii k mirovoi voine v mezhdunarodnom otnoshenii* (Moscow 1926) 214.

19 Bestuzhev *Bor' ba v Rossii* 301

20 Miliukov *Vospominaniia* ii 105–6; S.D. Sazonov *Fateful Years 1909–1916: The Reminiscences of Serge Sazonov* (New York 1928) 13

21 Berchtold to Aehrenthal (St Petersburg), 4 Apr. 1909 *ÖUA* ii 253–4 no. 1470

22 Nekliudov *Diplomatic Reminiscences* 33

23 Bestuzhev *Bor' ba v Rossii* 303

24 D. Popović 'Diplomati u Petrogradu u vreme balkanskih ratova (trenuti snimci)' *Godišnjica Nikole Čupića* xliii (1934) 88–9. See also S.S. Bobchev *Stranitsi iz moiata diplomaticheska missia v Petrograd (1912–1913)* (Sofia 1940) 32–5.

25 D. Popović 'Diplomati u Petrogradu' 88–9. See also S.S. Bobchev *Stranitsi iz moiata diplomaticheska missia v Petrograd* 32–5.

26 Tschirschky to Bülow, 28 Apr. 1909 *GP* xxvi 2, 782 no. 9531

27 Sazonov *Fateful Years* 21

28 Ibid 26; Miliukov *Vospominaniia* ii 106

29 Nekliudov *Diplomatic Reminiscences* 32–3

30 Nicolson to Hardinge, 9 Oct. 1912 *British Documents* ix 2, 6 no. 10; Buchanan to Grey, 30 Oct. 1912 ibid 65 no. 78

31 Bestuzhev *Bor' ba v Rossii* 65

32 Zaionchkovskii *Podgotovka Rossii* 215–16

33 V. Ćorović *Odnosi između Srbije i Austro-ugarske u XX veku* (Belgrade 1936) 322

34 Ibid; W.L. Langer 'Russia, the Straits Question and the Origins of the Balkan League 1908–1912' *Political Science Quarterly* xliii (1928) 321–63

35 Bestuzhev *Bor' ba v Rossii* 340

36 Zaionchkovskii *Podgotovka Rossii* 220

37 A.A. Savinski *Recollections of a Russian Diplomat* (London 1927) 166–8

38 Bestuzhev *Bor' ba v Rossii* 341; E.C. Helmreich *The Diplomacy of the Balkan Wars 1912–1913* (Cambridge, Mass. 1938) 25

39 Bülow to the Kaiser, 30 May 1909 *GP* XXVII 1, 278 no. 9800. See also B.E. Schmitt *The Annexation of Bosnia 1908–1909* (Cambridge 1937) ch 8.

40 Bethmann Holweg, Memorandum, 15 Nov. 1909 *ÖUA* II 541–2 no. 1811

41 Aehrenthal to Pallavicini, 29 Nov. 1909 *ÖUA* II 563–5 no. 1834

42 Ćorović *Odnosi između Srbije i Austro-ugarske* 324

43 Ibid 323; A. Toshev *Balkanskite voini* I (Sofia 1929) 268 ff; B. Lewis *The Emergence of Modern Turkey* (Oxford 1961) 212–13

44 Lewis *Modern Turkey* 212–13; M. Pandevski 'Političke prilike u Makedoniji pred balkanski rat' in V. Čubrilović ed *Jugoslovenski narodi pred prvi svetski rat* (Belgrade 1967) 678–9

45 Lowther to Grey, 6 Sept. 1910 *British Documents* IX 1, 207 no. 181

46 Zaionchkovskii *Podgotovka Rossii* 214

47 Ćorović *Odnosi između Srbije i Austro-ugarske* 324; Istoriski institut jugoslavenske nardone armije, ed V. Terzić *Prvi balkanski rat 1912–1913* I (Belgrade 1959) 62–3

48 Pašić to FO in Belgrade, St Petersburg, 29 Oct. 1908 *APS* I 44 no. 39. See also E.C. Helmreich *The Diplomacy of the Balkan Wars* 16.

49 See *GP* XXVI 2, 415–88; Schmitt *The Annexation of Bosnia* ch 8.

50 D. Đorđević *Izlazak Srbije na Jadransko more i Konferencija ambasadora u Londonu 1912* (Belgrade 1956) 5; D. Tucović *Srbija i Arbanija* (Belgrade 1945) 100–1, 105, 111

51 D. Đorđević *Izlazak Srbije* 5; D. Tucović *Srbija i Arbanija* 100–1, 105, 111; Lj. Aleksić-Pejković *Odnosi Srbije sa Francuskom i Engleskom 1903–1914* (Belgrade 1965) 483

52 Đorđević *Izlazak Srbije* 8–9; Tucović *Srbija i Arbanija* 100ff; see also J. Cvijić *Balkanski rat i Srbija* (Belgrade 1912) 92, and 'Izlazak Srbije na Jadransko more' *Glasnik srbskog geografskog društva* II 198 no. 2.

53 D. Đorđević 'Pašić i Milovanović u pregovorima za balkanski savez 1912 godine' *Istoriski časopis* IX–X (1959) 468; S. Jovanović 'Milovan Milovanović' *Srpski književni glasnik* LI 6 (1937) 419; Ćorović *Odnosi između Srbije i Austro-ugarske* 327; Aleksić-Pejković *Odnosi Srbije* 489

54 Đorđević 'Pašić i Milovanović u pregovorima' 468

55 Ibid 468–9

56 Ibid; see also P. Stojanov *Makedonija vo vremeto na balkanskite i prvata svetska vojna (1912–1918)* (Skopje 1969) 27 ff.

57 D. Đorđević *Milovan Milovanović* (Belgrade 1962) 131; M. Milovanović *Istorik pregovora* 365–99, 367–8

58 Toshev *Balkanskite voini* I 238

59 Đorđević 'Pašić i Milovanović u pregovorima' 469; Ćorović *Odnosi između Srbije i Austro-urgarske* 318 ff; Jovanović 'Milovan Milovanović' 419

60 Đorđević *Milovan Milovanović* 140

61 See A. Papanchev *Edno prestŭpno tsarstvuvanie*. *Ferdinand I, Tsar na Bŭlgarite* (Sofia 1946) 69–70; T. Vlakhov *Otnosheniiata mezhdu Bŭlgaria i tsentralnite sili po vreme na voinite 1912–1918 g.* (Sofia 1957) 13, 29–30; T. Vlakhov 'Vŭnshnata politika na Ferdinand i Balkanskiia sŭiuz' *Istoricheski pregled* VI 4–5 (1949–50) 427; A.P. Malinov *Stranichki ot nashata nova politicheska istoriia. Spomeni I* (Sofia 1938) 39–40.

62 Sir George Buchanan *My Mission to Russia and Other Diplomatic Memories* I (Boston 1923) 71

63 On the declaration of the independence of Bulgaria see: Malinov *Stranichki ot nashata nova politicheska istoriia*; T. Todorova *Obiaviavane nezavisimosta na Bŭlgariia prez 1908 g. i politikata na imperialisticheskite sili* (Sofia 1960); K. Krachunov *Vŭnshnata politika na Bŭlgariia (Kabinet' t Malinov, 1908–1911)* (Sofia 1931).

64 A.A. Mogilevich and M.E. Airapetian *Na putiakh k mirovoi voine 1914–1918 g.g.* (Moscow 1940) 100; Toshev *Balkanskite voini* I 198–200; V.A. Zhebokritskii *Bolgariia nakanune balkanskikh voin 1912–1913 g.g.* (Kiev 1960) 122

65 Gruić to FO, London, 13 Oct. 1908 *APS* I 15 no. 13

66 Toshev *Balkanskite voini* I 230–1; Krachunov *Vŭnshnata politika* 62 ff; Genov *Iztochniiat vŭpros* II 551

67 Toshev *Balkanskite voini* I 231–4; Krachunov *Vŭnshnata politika* 75–8; Helmreich *The Diplomacy of the Balkan Wars* 21 ff

68 Genov *Iztochniiat vŭpros* II 553

69 A. Girginov *Narodnata katastrofa-voinite 1912–1913 g.* (Sofia 1926) 3; Toshev *Balkanskite voini* I 137

70 Girginov *Narodnata katastrofa* 5–7; Toshev *Balkanskite voini* I 5–9; Ðorđević *Milovan Milovanović* 140; Ministerstvo na narodna otbrana *Mezhdusŭiuznicheskata voina 1913 g.* (Sofia 1963) 8–9

71 Krachunov *Vŭnshnata politika* 115; Girginov *Narodnata katastrofa* 4–5; Ćorović *Odnosi između Srbije i Austro-ugarske* 322–3

72 Toshev *Balkanskite voini* I 5–9; N. Kolarov *Ocherk vŭrkhu diplomaticheskata istoriia na balkanskite voini* (Sofia 1928) 14–15; Zhebokritskii *Bolgariia nakanune* I 17; Papanchev *Edno prestŭpno tsarstvovanie* 85

73 Martsius (A. Girginov) *Borbata protiv lichniia rezhim i negovite krepiteli* (Sofia 1922) 74–5

74 Pašić, memorandum (St Petersburg), 29 Oct. 1908 *APS* I 25–9 no. 24

75 Pašić to FO (St Petersburg), 29 Oct. 1908 *APS* I 44 no. 39

76 Toshev *Balkanskite voini* I 200

77 Paprikov to Toshev, 14 Jan. 1909 ibid 215

78 Ibid 216

79 Ibid 217–18

80 Paprikov to Toshev, 28 Jan. 1909 ibid 219

81 Toshev to Paprikov, 17 Feb. 1909 ibid 220
82 Sementovskii-Kurillo to Charykov, 28 Jan. 1909 *KA* VIII 9
83 Izvol'skii to Sementovskii-Kurillo, 17 Feb. 1909 ibid
84 Same to same, 20 March 1909 ibid 9-10
85 Ćorović *Odnosi između Srbije i Austro-ugarske* 327; Đorđević *Milovan Milovanović* 142
86 Toshev *Balkanskite voini* I 235. See also Buchanan to Grey (Sofia), 16 Apr. 1909 *British Documents* IX 1, 4 no. 4; and Milovanović *Istorik pregovora* 367-9.
87 Toshev *Balkanskite voini* I 236
88 Ibid 237
89 Ibid 236
90 Đorđević *Milovan Milovanović* 142
91 Toshev *Balkanskite voini* I 238
92 Toshev to Paprikov, 13 July 1909 ibid 238-9; see also Milovanović *Istorik pregovora* 369.
93 V. Terzić ed *Prvi balkanski rat* I 62
94 Đorđević *Milovan Milovanović* 142
95 Milovanović, circular, 20 July 1909 *APS* I 129-130 no. 121
96 Đorđević *Milovan Milovanović* 145; Terzić *Prvi balkanski rat* I 64
97 Hamilton to Grey (Belgrade), 27 Sept. 1909 *British Documents* IX 2, 63 no. 58
98 Terzić *Prvi balkanski rat* I
99 Đorđević *Milovan Milovanović* 145. On the question of Macedonian autonomy see A. Hristov 'Princip autonomne Makedonije u programu unutrašnje makedonske revolucionarne organizacije (VMRO)' in V. Čubrilović ed *Jugoslovenski narodi pred prvi svetski rat* (Belgrade 1967) 943-64.
100 Terzić *Prvi balkanski rat* I 64
101 On King Ferdinand's visits to Serbia in October and November 1909 see ibid 65; Toshev *Balkanskite voini* I 244-5; Ćorović *Odnosi između Srbije i Austro-ugarske* 328 ff. See also *British Documents* IX 1, 90 no. 82; *Siebert* I 174 no. 123 and 155-6 no. 108.
102 Đorđević *Milovan Milovanović* 143. See also the Serbian government's confidential memoir to the powers of the Entente of 11 August 1909, *Siebert* I 132-5 no. 93.
103 Izvol'skii to Sergeev, 18 Apr. 1909 *Siebert* I 103 no. 72
104 Izvol'skii to Sementovskii-Kurillo, April 1909 ibid 102-3 no. 71
105 Nekliudov *Diplomatic Reminiscenses* 47-51; Marco (B. Simić) 'Nikola Hartwig-Spoljna politika Srbije pred svetski rat' *Nova Evropa* XVII 8 (1928) 256 ff
106 Marco 'Nikola Hartwig' 257
107 Toshev *Balkanskite voini* I 240
108 Nekliudov *Reminiscences* 47-51
109 Marco 'Nikola Hartwig' 257

110 Nekliudov *Reminiscences* 47–51
111 Toshev *Balkanskite voini* I 240
112 Đorđević *Milovan Milovanović* 143; Marco 'Nikola Hartwig' 276
113 Toshev *Balkanskite voini* I 240
114 Ibid. See also M. Milovanović *Istorik pregovora* 394 ff.
115 Terzić ed *Prvi balkanski rat* I 151–2
116 Paget to Grey, 8 Oct. 1912 *British Documents* IX 2, 8 no. 11
117 Sementovskii-Kurillo to Izvol'skii, 4 May 1909 *Siebert* I 105 no. 74
118 Izvol'skii to Sementovskii-Kurillo, 12 May 1909 ibid 106 no. 75
119 Krachunov *Vŭnshnata politika* 93
120 Zaionchkovskii *Podgotovka Rossii* 214
121 Malinov *Stranichki ot nashata nova politicheska istoriia* 150
122 *Prilozhenie* 285
123 Krachunov *Vŭnshnata politika* 94
124 *SSD* 44–50 no. 2
125 Bestuzhev *Bor'ba v Rossii* 344
126 Zhebokritskii *Bolgariia nakanune* 130; Toshev *Balkanskite voini* I 255; Krachunov *Vŭnshnata politika* 99
127 *Prilozhenie* 284
128 Izvol'skii to Sementovskii, 4 Apr. 1910 *KA* VIII 10
129 Malinov *Stranichki ot nashata nova politicheska istoriia* 150; *Prilozhenie* 285–7
130 Malinov *Stranichki* 152; *Prilozhenie* 287, 292, 295
131 *Prilozhenie* 278
132 Ibid 285–7; Malinov *Stranichki* 151
133 Toshev *Balkanskite voini* I 262
134 Đorđević *Milovan Milovanović* 153; Terzić ed *Prvi balkanski rat* I 66–7
135 Đorđević 'Pašić i Milovanović u pregovorima' 472
136 Ibid 472–3n; M. Milovanović *Istorik pregovora* 368
137 Đorđević *Milovan Milovanović* 153; Milovanović *Istorik pregovora* 368
138 Toshev *Balkanskite voini* I 281
139 Ibid 285 n
140 Terzić ed *Prvi balkanski rat* 75. See also Robertson to Grey, 26 Oct. 1910 *British Documents* IX 1, 229 no. 198.
141 Toshev *Balkanskite voini* I 285–6
142 O'Beirne to Grey, 26 Sept. 1910 *British Documents* IX 1, 212–13 no. 185
143 Ibid; Sazonov to Sementovskii-Kurillo, 29 Sept. 1910 *Siebert* I 362 no. 290
144 Terzić ed *Prvi balkanski rat* 76
145 Toshev *Balkanskite voini* I 289–90
146 Sementovskii-Kurillo to Sazonov, 25 Nov. 1910 *Siebert* I 389–91 no. 306
147 It seems that by this time both St Petersburg and Sofia lost interest in the negotiations.

On the Bulgarian side see: Toshev *Balkanskite voini* I 255; Malinov *Stranichki* 153; *Prilozhenie* 120, 286, 293. On the Russian, see: *MO* XVIII 1, 451–6.

148 Zhebokritskii *Bolgariia nakanune* 131–2
149 Ibid; Toshev *Balkanskite voini* I 298. See also Urusov to Sazonov (Sofia), 28 Mar. 1911 *KA* VIII 13.
150 Toshev to Geshov, 16 Apr. 1911, Toshev *Balkanskite voini* I 298–9
151 Hartwig to Neratov in FO, 29 Apr. 1911 *MO* XVIII 1, 4 n; 23 Apr. 1911 ibid 28–9 no. 31. For a slightly different interpretation of this point see Toshev *Balkanskite voini* I 298–9.
152 On the constitutional reforms see Zhebokritskii *Bolgariia nakanune* 132–40. See also Milovanović *Istorik pregovora* 369.
153 Zhebokritskii *Bolgariia nakanune* 141; Urusov to Neratov, 11 May 1911 *MO* XVIII 1, 4 n; *KA* VIII 13
154 Urusov to Neratov, 26 Apr. 1911 *MO* XVIII 1, 3–4 n; see also Urusov to Neratov, 15 May 1911 ibid 3–6 no. 6; Nekliudov to Neratov, 15 May 1911 ibid 54–5 no. 50.
155 Ibid 4 no. 6
156 Đorđević *Milovan Milovanović* 164
157 Hartwig to Neratov, 27 May 1911 *MO* XVIII 1, 65 n 2; *Siebert* II 102 no. 405
158 Neratov to Hartwig, 30 May 1911 *MO* XVIII 1, 65 no. 65
159 Toshev *Balkanskite voini* I 300; I.E. Geshov *The Balkan League* tr Constantin Mincoff (London 1915) 6–7
160 Geshov *The Balkan League* 3–4 n 1
161 Hartwig to Neratov, 23 May 1911 *MO* XVIII 1, 29 no. 31; Nekliudov to Neratov, 2 June 1911 ibid 75 no. 77
162 Ibid 75 no. 77; Toshev *Balkanskite voini* 300–6
163 Geshov *The Balkan League* 9–10. On the Macedonian organizations in Sofia see Stojanov *Makedonia vo vremeto* ch 3: Helmreich *The Diplomacy of the Balkan Wars* 37 ff; G. Abadzhiev *Balkanskite vojni i Makedonija* (Skopje 1958) 117 ff.

CHAPTER 2   The making of the Balkan system of alliances

1 See V. Ćorović *Odnosi između Srbije i Austro-ugarske u XX veku* (Belgrade 1936) 343–4.
2 Ibid 344. See also M. Pandevski 'Političke prilike u Makedoniji' in V. Čubrilović ed *Jugoslovenski narodi pred prvi svetski rat* 683–92; D. Deakin *The Greek Struggle in Macedonia, 1897–1913* (Thessaloniki 1966); E. Kofos *Nationalism and Communism in Macedonia* (Thessaloniki 1964) ch 2.
3 A. Toshev *Balkanskite voini* I 323

4 See *MO* XIX 1, 169 n. 4. Toshev gives slightly different figures, in *Balkanskite voini* I 323; Pandevski 'Političke prilike' 683.

5 Toshev *Balkanskite voini* I 324

6 I.S. Galkin *Diplomatiia evropeiskikh derzhav v sviazi s osvoboditel' nym dvizheniem narodov evropeiskoi Turtsii 1905–1912 g.g.* (Moscow 1960) 159–65

7 See ibid 164–5; Urusov to Sazonov, 30 March 1912 *MO* XIX 2, 355–6 no. 711; Hartwig to Sazonov 16 May 1912 *MO* XX 1, 10–11 no. 12, and 21 no. 24.

8 Hartwig to Sazonov, 21 May 1913 *MO* XX 1, 39 no. 47.

9 Ćorović *Odnosi između Srbije i Austro-ugarske* 344

10 Quoted in ibid 345

11 On Charykov's activities in Constantinople see *MO* XVII 2 no. 601, 602, 700; XIX no. 124. See also E.C. Thaden *Russia and the Balkan Alliance of 1912* (University Park, Penn. 1965) 38–57; W.L. Langer 'Russia, the Straits Question and the Origins of the Balkan League' *Political Science Quarterly* XLIII (Sept. 1928) 321–6.

12 Thurn to Berchtold, 10 Dec. 1911 *ÖUA* III 663 no. 3084. See also 665 no. 3090.

13 See *MO* XVIII 2 no. 623, 723, 778, 789, 824; *British Documents* IX 1 no. 335, 340; *DDF* XIV no. 441; *ÖUA* III nos. 3008, 3103, 3047.

14 E.A. Adamov ed *Evropeiskie derzhavy i Turtsiia vo vremia voiny Konstantinopol' i Prolivy* (Moscow 1925) 14–16

15 Ćorović *Odnosi između Srbije i Austro-ugarske* 347–9

16 I.E. Geshov *The Balkan League* 10–11

17 Ibid; Nekliudov to Neratov, 2 Oct. 1911 *MO* XVIII 2, 63 no. 511; Hartwig to Neratov, 8 Oct. 1911 ibid 112 no. 563.

18 Nekliudov to Neratov, 2 Oct. 1911 ibid 63 no. 512. On Rizov's discussions in Belgrade see M. Milovanović *Istorik pregovora* 370–4.

19 Hartwig to Neratov, 6 Oct. 1911 *MO* XVIII 2, 91–4 no. 545

20 Same to same, 8 Oct. 1911 ibid 112 no. 563

21 Geshov *The Balkan League* 13; I. Salabashev *Spomeni* (Sofia 1943) 318

22 Geshov did not mention I. Salabashev in his account of the meeting in Vienna.

23 Salabashev *Spomeni* 318–9

24 On the Serbo-Bulgarian treaty of 1904 see Helmreich *The Diplomacy of the Balkan Wars* 3–10; Milovanović *Istorik pregovora* 367.

25 Geshov *The Balkan League* 14

26 Ibid 14–15. See also Hartwig to Neratov, 14 Oct. 1911 *MO* XVIII 2, 162 no. 625; Nekliudov to Neratov, 24 Oct. 1911 ibid 230–1 no. 716; Milovanović *Istorik pregovora* 375–9.

27 Geshov *The Balkan League* 16–17; Milovanović *Istorik pregovora* 379–80

28 Geshov *The Balkan League* 16–17; Milovanović *Istorik pregovora* 379–80

29 Geshov *The Balkan League* 17–19; Hartwig to Neratov, 14 Oct. 1911 *MO* XVIII 2, 162 no. 625; Nekliudov to Neratov, 30 Oct. 1911 ibid 268 no. 757

30 Nekliudov to Neratov, 2 Oct. 1911 *MO* XVIII 2, 63–4 no. 512, 12 Oct. 1911 ibid 140–1 no. 598. On Russia's role in the negotiations see also M. Tanty *Rosja wobec wojen bałkańskich 1912–1913 roku* (Warsaw 1970).
31 *MO* XVIII 2 no. 512 and 598
32 Nekliudov to Neratov, 30 Oct. 1911 ibid 271 no. 758; 31 Oct. 1911 ibid 280 no. 769
33 On the controversy between Hartwig and Nekliudov see Nekliudov to Neratov, 30 Oct. 1911 ibid 268 no. 757; Hartwig to Neratov, 7 Nov. 1911 ibid 327 no. 829; Hartwig to Nekliudov, 17 Nov. 1911 ibid XIX 1, 95 no. 1; Nekliudov to Hartwig, 25 Nov. 1911 ibid 95 no. 98.
34 See Hartwig to Neratov, 14 Nov. 1911 ibid XIX 1, no. 5.
35 Hartwig to Neratov, 6 Oct. 1911 ibid XVIII 91–2 no. 545
36 Ibid; see also 113–14 no. 564.
37 See Nekliudov to Neratov, 6 Nov. 1911 ibid XVIII 315 no. 813.
38 Neratov to Nekliudov, 4 Oct. 1911 ibid 71–2 no. 526
39 Neratov to Nekliudov, 30 Oct. 1911 ibid 266 no. 752
40 See Charykov to Neratov, 28 Oct. 1911 ibid XVIII 2, 261–3 no. 749; Hartwig to Neratov, 2 Nov. 1911 ibid 289 no. 783; Neratov to Hartwig, 4 Nov. 1911, ibid 298 no. 796; Nekliudov to Hartwig, 25 Nov. 1911 ibid XIX 1, 95 no. 98.
41 Hartwig to Neratov, 2 Nov. 1911 ibid XVIII 2, 289 no. 783; 5 Nov. 1911, 309–11 no. 806
42 Neratov to Hartwig and Nekliudov, 4 Nov. 1911 ibid 298 no. 796
43 Nekliudov to Neratov, 30 Oct. 1911 ibid 267 no. 756
44 For the full text see ibid XIX 1, 5–7; for a condensed version see Hartwig to Neratov, 4 Nov. 1911 ibid XVIII 2, 300–1 no. 801.
45 Ibid 301 no. 801
46 Nekliudov to Neratov, 6 Nov. 1912 ibid XVIII 2, 315 no. 813
47 Hartwig to Neratov, 4 Nov. 1912 ibid 301 no. 801
48 Neratov to Hartwig, copy to Sofia, 10 Nov. 1911 ibid 348 no. 850
49 Geshov *The Balkan League* 19–20; Milovanović *Istorik pregovora* 381–4
50 Geshov *The Balkan League* 21–3; Nekliudov to Neratov, 14 Nov. 1911 *MO* XIX 1, 6–7 no. 4; Hartwig to Neratov ibid 7–8 no. 5
51 Geshov *The Balkan League* 23
52 Ibid
53 Milovanović *Istorik pregovora* 384–5
54 Ibid 385–6; Geshov *The Balkan League* 23
55 Ibid 385–6; Geshov *The Balkan League* 23; Hartwig to Neratov, 23 Nov. 1911 *KA* (1925) XI 7 no. 51
56 Rizov and Stanchov gave a lengthy account of the meetings with Milovanović in a confidential letter to Geshov of 20 November 1911. For the full text see Geshov *The Balkan League* 24–32. For Milovanović's account see *Istorik pregovora* 386–7.

57 The formula, which was handed to Milovanović by Stanchov in Paris, stated: 'If after a war waged in common by the two parties – Serbia and Bulgaria – it should be found necessary to end the war with an autonomous government for the provinces inhabited by Serbians and Bulgarians, the two parties will agree to conclude peace guaranteeing autonomy to the said provinces' (Geshov *The Balkan League* 32).

58 Hartwig to Neratov, 29 Dec. 1911 *MO* XIX 1, 257 no. 277; Geshov *The Balkan League* 33; Milovanović *Istorik pregovora* 390–1 and 394–5

59 See Hartwig to Sazonov, 31 Dec. 1911 *MO* XIX 1, 270–1 no. 292; and Neratov to Nekliudov and Hartwig, 1 Jan. 1912 ibid 271 no. 293.

60 Geshov *The Balkan League* 33

61 Nekliudov to Sazonov, 4 Jan. 1912 *MO* XIX 1, 291 no. 313

62 Nekliudov to Sazonov, 6 Jan. 1912 ibid 303 no. 327

63 Nekliudov to Sazonov, 11 Jan. 1912 ibid 312–13 no. 338; Milovanović *Istorik pregovora* 395–6

64 Hartwig to Sazonov, 18 Jan. 1912 *MO* XIX 2, 27 no. 370

65 Ibid 28; see also Milovanović *Istorik pregovora* 396–7.

66 Sazonov to Hartwig, 19 Jan. 1912 *MO* XIX 2, 28 no. 371

67 Ibid

68 Sazonov to Hartwig and Nekliudov, 25 Jan. 1912 *MO* XIX 2, 40–1 no. 388. See also Hartwig to Sazonov, 20 Jan. 1912 no. 374.

69 Nekliudov to Sazonov, 30 Jan. 1912 ibid 65 no. 406, ibid 30–1. See also Hartwig to Sazonov, 29 Jan. 1912 ibid 106 no. 448.

70 See ibid 83 no. 3.

71 On the government crisis in Belgrade see Hartwig to Sazonov, 8 Feb. 1912 ibid 97 no. 439 and n 1; Hartwig to Sazonov, 11 Feb. 1912 ibid 106–7 no. 448.

72 Hartwig to Sazonov, 12 Feb. 1912 ibid 110 no. 452

73 Ibid 111; see also Hartwig to Sazonov, 11 Feb. 1912 ibid 107 no. 448.

74 Nekliudov to Sazonov, 16 Feb. 1912 ibid 147 n 1

75 Hartwig to Sazonov, 21 Feb. 1912 ibid 169 no. 511

76 Ibid

77 Nekliudov to Sazonov, 23 Feb. 1912 ibid 174 no. 520

78 Sazonov to Nekliudov, 24 Feb. 1912 ibid 180 no. 528 and n 7 and 8

79 Sazonov to Hartwig ibid 180 no. 527

80 Nekliudov to Sazonov, 27 Feb. 1912 ibid 198–9 no. 546

81 Ibid

82 See *MO* XIX 2, 199 n 1.

83 Ibid

84 Hartwig to Sazonov, 7 Mar. 1912 ibid 242 no. 599

85 Hartwig to Sazonov, 11 Mar. 1912 *MO* XIX 2, 252 no. 613

86 Nekliudov to Sazonov, 14 Mar. 1912 ibid XIX 2, 279 no. 636; 258 no. 618

87 For the full text of the treaty, the secret annex, and the military convention, see *DPIK* 159–73; B.D. Kesiakov ed *Prinos kŭm diplomaticheskata istoriia na Bŭlgariia* I (Sofia 1925) 36–48; *KA* (1925) IX 23–30; Geshov *The Balkan League* 112–27; *MO* XIX 2, 265–8 for the treaty, and 530–2 for the military convention. The military convention was supplemented on 18 June (1 July) by agreements between the two chiefs of staff in respect to war with Austria-Hungary, with Rumania, and, the following day, with Turkey. Two further agreements in regard to war against Turkey were signed on 23 August (4 September) and 15 (28) September 1912. The texts of these agreements are found in *DPIK* 163–70, and Kesiakov *Prinos kŭm diplomaticheskata istoriia* I 42–8.

88 Article 1 of the treaty bound the two signatories 'absolutely and without reservation to succour each other with their entire forces in the event of one of them being attacked by one or more states'; and article 2 'to come to each other's assistance with all their forces in the event of any Great Power attempting to annex, occupy or temporarily to invade with its armies any part of the Balkan territories which are today under Turkish rule ...' (Geshov *The Balkan League* 112).

89 For the terms of the territorial settlement see article 2 of the secret annex.

90 The question of war was to come into consideration 'in the event of internal troubles arising in Turkey which might endanger the State or the national interests of the contracting parties or of either of them; or in the event of internal or external difficulties of Turkey raising the question of the maintenance of the status quo in the Balkan Peninsula ...' See article 2 of the secret annex, Geshov *The Balkan League* 114.

91 For the provisions making Russia the arbiter of all disputes see articles 1 and 4 of the secret annex.

92 See J.D. Bourchier 'A Balkan Confederation' *Fortnightly Review* LVI (1891) 365 ff; L.S. Stavrianos *Balkan Federation. A History of the Movement toward Balkan Unity in Modern Times* (Northampton, Mass. 1942) 123 ff; N. Kolarov *Ocherk vŭrkhu diplomaticheskata istoriia na balkanskite voini* (Sofia 1938) 21; A. Ad. Kyrou *Oi Valkanikoi geitones mas* (Athens 1962); D. Deakin *The Greek Struggle in Macedonia, 1897–1913*.

93 For the situation in Greece before 1910 see G. Ventiri *I Ellas tou 1910–1920* I (Athens 1931) 18–46; Stavrianos *Balkan Federation* 123 ff; A. Pallis *Greece's Anatolian Venture – and After* (London 1937) 197; A. Ganchev *Balkanskata voina, 1912–1913* g. (Sofia 1939) 42.

94 See N.K. Zorbas *Apomnēmoneymata* (Athens 1925); A. Mazarakis-Ainian *Apomnēmoneymata* (Athens 1948); S.V. Papacosma *The Military in Greek Politics. The 1909 Coup d'Etat* (Kent, Ohio 1977).

95 E.S. Bagger *Eminent Europeans. Studies in Continental Reality* (New York 1922) 59–60; H.A. Gibbons *Venizelos* (London 1911) 102; Stavrianos *Balkan Federation* 164

96 Bagger *Eminent Europeans* 59–60; Ventiri *I Ellas* I 47–55

97 Pallis *Greece's Anatolian Venture* 197

98 On the reform program see especially Ventiri *I Ellas* I 56–85.

99 Pallis *Greece's Anatolian Venture* 198–9; Ganchev *Balkanskata voina* 42; D.I. Drossos *La Fondation de l'alliance balkanique* (Athens 1929) 122; Ventiri *I Ellas* I 89–93

100 Lady Grogan *The Life of J.D. Bourchier* (London 1926) 136

101 *Prilozhenie* 288

102 Ibid

103 See the texts of both proposals in Martsius (A. Girginov) *Borbata protiv lichniia rezhim i negovite krepiteli* (Sofia 1922) 77–9.

104 Ibid; *Prilozhenie* 288

105 Nekliudov to Neratov, 18 April 1911 *MO* XVIII 1, 123 no. 115; Urusov to Sazonov 30 March 1912 ibid XIX 2, 357, no. 711; Grogan *Bourchier* 136. See also Kyrou *Oi Valkanikoi geitones mas* 94.

106 The committee was composed of public figures such as Koromilas, Dragumis, Kalergis, and others. O. Bickel *Russland und die Entstehung des Balkanbundes 1912* (Berlin 1923) 124; see also *DDF* 3ᵉ série II no. 172; IV no. 360.

107 O. Bickel *Russland und die Entstehung des Balkanbundes 1912* (Berlin 1923) 124; see also *DDF* 3ᵉ série II no. 172; IV no. 360. V.A. Zhebokritskii *Bolgariia nakanune balkanskikh voin 1912–1913* (Kiev 1960) 175–6

108 Toshev *Balkanskite voini* I 301; Geshov *The Balkan League* 37

109 Charykov to Neratov, 30 Sept. 1911 *MO* XVIII 2, 48–9 no. 496; Urusov to Sazonov, 30 March 1912 ibid XIV 2, 357 no. 712 (see also no. 534, 844.)

110 Geshov *The Balkan League* 37; Nekliudov to Neratov, 24 Oct. 1911 *MO* XVIII 2, 231 no. 717

111 Ventiri *I Ellas* I 89–93

112 S. Danev *Balkanský svaz a válka s Tureckem, 1912–1913* (Prague 1935) 9

113 Ibid

114 Drossos *La Fondation* 23; Ventiri *I Ellas* I 89–93

115 Geshov *The Balkan League* 37–8. See also Urusov to Neratov, 19 Oct. 1911 *MO* XVIII 2, 188–9 no. 667.

116 Ibid

117 See Urusov to Neratov, 19 Oct. 1911 *MO* XVIII 2, 189 no. 667; Nekliudov to Sazonov, 24 Oct. 1911 ibid 231 no. 717.

118 Ibid no. 667

119 Nekliudov to Neratov, 31 Oct. 1911 *MO* XVIII 2, 280–1 no. 769. See also no. 768.

120 Grogan *Bourchier* 136–7

121 Drossos *La Fondation* 25

122 Urusov to Sazonov, 30 Mar. 1912 *MO* XIX 2, 357 no. 712
123 Ministerstvo na voinata *Voinata mezhdu Būlgariia i Turtsiia, 1912–1913* VII (Sofia 1937) 37, 58, 61
124 Ibid
125 Ventiri *I Ellas* I 93. See also *Zora* (Sofia) 28 Jan. 1931 no. 3468, 5.
126 Geshov *The Balkan League* 38–9; *Prilozhenie* 118
127 Geshov *The Balkan League* 39–40; *Prilozhenie* 118
128 Drossos *La Fondation* 26; Kyrou *Oi Valkanikoi geitones mas* 95
129 Nekliudov to Sazonov, 1 May 1912 *MO* XIX 2, 491 no., 844
130 Nekliudov to Sazonov, 14 May 1912 ibid XX 1, 1 no. 1
131 Geshov *The Balkan League* 40; *Prilozhenie* 118. For the text of the treaty and the military convention see Geshov 127–33; Kesiakov *Prinos kūm diplomaticheskata istoriia* I 48–51; Drossos *La Fondation* 26–32; Ministerstvo na voinata *Voinata* I 57–61; *British Documents* IX 2, 1015–18. The military convention foreseen by the treaty was not concluded until 5 October 1912, five days after the general mobilization had been ordered in each country.
132 Article 3
133 Article 1. It did not apply in case of a war between Greece and Turkey breaking out over the admission of Cretans into the Greek Chamber of Deputies. See the separate declaration appended to the treaty.
134 Article 2. Geshov *The Balkan League* 128–9
135 See article 1.
136 See Helmreich *The Diplomacy of the Balkan Wars* ch 5.
137 See Toshev *Balkanskite voini* I 337–8.
138 See Colonel Romanovskii's dispatches to the quartermaster of the general staff, *MO* XIX 2, 268, 361, 417 no. 626, 716, 772.
139 *MO* XX 1, 341 n 2
140 Ibid 425 n 2
141 Nekliudov to Neratov, 8 Aug. 1912 ibid 428–9 no. 434
142 Toshev *Balkanskite voini* I 355. See also Romanovskii to Danilov, 20 Aug. 1912 *MO* XX 2, 56–7 no. 517; and ibid XX 1, 444–5 n 3.
143 Giers to Sazonov, 26 Apr. 1912 *MO* XX 1, 227 no. 233; 29 Apr. 1912 ibid 236–7 no. 244. On the situation in Albania see also I.G. Senkevich *Osvoboditel' noe dvizhenie albanskogo naroda v 1905–1912 godakh* (Moscow 1959) and 'Natsional' no-osvoboditel'naia bor'ba albanskogo naroda v 1911–1912 g.g.' *Novaia i noveishaia istoriia* 1957 no. 5, 62–5; J. Swire *Albania. The Rise of a Kingdom* (London 1929); and S. Skendi *The Albanian National Awakening, 1878–1912* (Princeton 1967).
144 Giers to Neratov, 19 July 1912 *MO* XX 1, 343 no. 337 and n 1
145 Petraiev to Giers (Bitola), 24 July 1912 ibid 358–60 no. 356, and 352 n 1

146 Giers to Neratov, 8 Aug. 1912 *MO* xx 2, 424 no. 426, and 379 n 2
147 The fourteen points included demands for an amnesty and for military, cultural, administrative, and commercial reforms. See *MO* xx 2, no. 4.
148 See ibid.
149 Ćorović *Odnosi između Srbije i Austro-ugarske* 256–9; Galkin *Diplomatiia evropeiskikh derzhav* 175–6
150 Ćorović *Odnosi između Srbije i Austro-ugarske* 256–9; Galkin *Diplomatiia evropeiskikh derzhav* 175–6; and Neratov to Giers, 28 Aug. 1912 *MO* xx 2, 62 no. 525
151 Neratov to Giers, 21 Aug. 1912 ibid xx 2, 62 no. 525; Neratov to Giers, 6 Aug. 1912 ibid xx 1, 418 no. 419; Giers to Neratov, 8 Aug. 1912 ibid xx 1, 430–1 no. 437.
152 M. Giers to Neratov (Constantinople), 6 July 1912 *MO* xx 1, 264–5 no. 272
153 Ibid and 265–6 n 1
154 Obnorskii to Neratov, 18 July 1912 *MO* xx 1, 335 no. 328, and 20 July 1912, 345 no. 340
155 Neratov to Obnorskii, 3 Aug. 1912 ibid 407 no. 405
156 Obnorskii to Neratov, 3 Aug. 1912 ibid 407 no. 406
157 Ibid 408 n 1
158 A. Giers to Neratov, 5 Aug. 1912 ibid 416 no. 416
159 A. Giers to Neratov, 6 Aug. 1912 ibid 423 no. 424
160 Ibid n 3, and Neratov to M. Giers (Constantinople) and A. Giers (Cetinje), 7 Aug. 1912 ibid 424 no. 427
161 Ibid
162 See Dokladnaia zapiska Sazonova Nikolaiu II, 8 July 1912 *MO* xx 1, 270 no. 277; Dokladnaia zapiska Ministra Inostrannykh Del Nikolaiu II 17 Aug. 1912 ibid xx 2, 31–2 no. 489; M. Giers to Neratov, 12 July 1912 ibid xx 1, 280 no. 287, and 29 July 1912, 389 no. 328.
163 See Neratov to Athens, Belgrade, Sofia, 23 July 1912 *MO* xx 1, 352 no. 352; Nekliudov to Neratov, 10 July 1912 ibid xx 1, 277 no. 283, and 367 no. 364. See also 345, 349, 407, 408, 414 no. 340, 347, 405, 406, 413.
164 Berchtold to Thurn, 8 Aug. 1912 *ÖUA* IV 325–6 no. 3675
165 Ibid 325
166 Circular, 13 Aug. 1912 *ÖUA* IV 339–40 no. 3687. See also *MO* xx 2, 26–7.
167 *ÖUA* IV 340
168 See *MO* xx 2, 112, 120, 129, 131 no. 584, 595, 606, 609.
169 For the response of Russia and the other powers to Count Berchtold's initiative see *MO* xx 2, 37, 38 no. 495, 496; and 46–7 no. 505 (Great Britain); 48 no. 507 (Germany); 66, 74, 113 no. 533, 539, 586 (France).
170 See Nekliudov to Neratov, 24 Aug. 1912 *MO* xx 2, 81 no. 546; Shtrandtman to Neratov, 20 Aug. 1912 ibid 57 no. 518.

171 M. Giers to Neratov, 20 Aug. 1912 ibid 58 no. 520; Sazonov to Nekliudov, 27 Aug. 1912 ibid 95 no. 566. See also *ÖUA* IV no. 3715, 3718, 3729, 3731.

172 Shtrandtman to Neratov (Belgrade), 20 Aug. 1912 *MO* XX 2, 57 no. 518

173 Nekliudov to Neratov, 12 Aug. 1912 ibid XX 1, 445 no. 456; Shtrandtman to Neratov, 13 Aug. 1912 ibid 453 no. 464; Urusov to Neratov, 15 Aug. 1912 ibid 23–4 no. 482

174 Neratov to Sevastopulo (Paris) and Etter (London), 18 Aug. 1912 *MO* XX 2, 37 no. 495. See also Mishev to Geshov (Athens), 6 Aug. 1912 *DPIK* 182 no. 4.

175 See *MO* XX 2, no. 517, 518, 528, 541, 544.

176 A. Giers to Neratov, 21 Aug. 1912 *MO* XX 2, 64 no. 529; Shtrandtman to Neratov, 23 Aug. 1912 ibid 78 no. 542; Nekliudov to Neratov, 26 Aug. 1912 90 no. 558

177 *Prvi balkanski rat* I 154, 160

178 Ibid; and Urusov to Neratov, 24 Aug. 1912 *MO* XX 2, 82 no. 547

179 *Prvi balkanski rat* I 161

180 Ibid

181 Toshev *Balkanskite voini* I 360

182 Ibid 360–1; Geshov *The Balkan League* 42; M. Vojvodić 'Bugarsko-crnogorski pregovori i sporazum 1912 godine' *Zbornik filosofskog fakulteta* (Belgrade) VIII (1964) 746; Z.G. Pavlović *Opsada Skadra, 1912–1913* (Belgrade 1926) 29

183 S. Danev 'Moiata misiia v Krim prez 1912 god' *Rodina* (Sofia) II (1940) 123–33 no. 3; Sazonov to Nekliudov, 23 May 1912 *MO* XX 1, 61 no. 64

184 S. Danev 'Moiata misiia v Krim prez 1912 god' 123–33 no. 3; Sazonov to Nekliudov, 23 May 1912 *MO* XX 1, 61 no. 64

185 Doklad po glavnomu upravleniiu general'nogo shtaba, 2 Oct. 1911 *MO* XVIII 2, 67–8 no. 518

186 Neratov to Obnorskii, 2 Oct. 1911 *MO* XVIII 2, 58 no. 508; Obnorskii to Neratov, 10 Oct. 1912 ibid 72 no. 528

187 Neratov to Obnorskii, 2 Oct. 1911 *MO* XVIII 2, 58 no. 508; Obnorskii to Neratov, 10 Oct. 1912 ibid 72 no. 528; and Obnorskii to Neratov, 14 Oct. 1912 ibid 163 no. 626

188 To win greater freedom of action for himself, King Nikola proposed to exclude article 7 from the agreement, but the Russians turned him down. See Doklad po glavnomu upravleniiu general'nogo shtaba *MO* XVIII 2, 67–8, no. 518; and Dokladnaia zapiska voennogo ministra Nikolaiu II, 3 Feb. 1912 *MO* XIX 2, 78–9 no. 420.

189 *Prvi balkanski rat* I 67–8

190 Arsen'ev to Neratov, 9 Nov. 1911 *MO* XVIII 2, 346–7 no. 847

191 Ibid 346

192 Miller to Sazonov, 15 Feb. 1912 *MO* XIX 2, 129–30 n 3; and 138 n 4, 139 n 1; Sazonov to Miller, 20 Feb. 1912 ibid 161 no. 500

193 Miller to Sazonov, 1 March 1912 ibid 222 no. 574

194 Same to same, 8 March 1912 ibid 222–3 n 1
195 Zàpiska Ministra Inostrannikh Del (Livadia), 10 May 1912 *MO* XIX 2, 520 no. 878.
    See also Sazonov to Nekliudov, 23 May 1912 ibid XX 1, 62.
196 Ibid XIX 2, 520 no. 878 and XX 1, 62
197 Danev 'Moiata misiia v Krim' *Rodina* 125
198 Geshov *The Balkan League* 41; Toshev *Balkanskite voini* I 343
199 Geshov *The Balkan League* 41; Toshev *Balkanskite voini* I 343
200 A. Giers to Sazonov, 20 June 1912 *MO* XX 1, 205–6 no. 212. King Nikola remained in
    Vienna from 8 June to 10 June (205 n 4).
201 Danev *Balkanský svaz a válka s Tureckem, 1912–1913* 11; Toshev *Balkanskite voini* I
    343
202 Toshev *Balkanskite voini* I 343. See also Kolushev to Geshov, 18 July 1912 *DPIK* 197
    no. 1.
203 Toshev *Balkanskite voini* I 343
204 Kolushev to Geshov, 18 July 1912, *DPIK* 197 no. 1
205 Kolushev to Geshov, 30 July 1912 ibid 198 no. 3
206 See Geshov to Kolushev, 14 Aug. 1912 ibid 198 no. 5.
207 Geshov *The Balkan League* 42
208 Geshov to Kolushev, 14 Aug. 1912 *DPIK* 198 no. 5; Kolushev to Geshov ibid 199
    no. 6
209 Geshov to Kolushev, 16 Aug. 1912 ibid 199 no. 7
210 Geshov to Kolushev in Munich, 20 Aug. 1912 ibid 199 no. 8
211 See note 182.
212 Kolushev to Geshov, 23 Sept. 1912 *DPIK* 200 no. 13
213 Summaries of the agreement, which differ in some respects from one another, are
    found in Pavlović *Opsada Skadra* 29–33 (most complete); Stakhovich to the general
    staff, 16 Sept. 1912 *KA* XV (1926) 22 no. 12; Kolushev to Geshov, 30 July 1912
    DPIK 198 no. 3; Ministerstvo na voinata *Voinata mezhdu Bŭlgariia i Turtsiia* I 62.
214 The figure given in Kesiakov ed *Prinos kŭm diplomaticheskata istoriia* is 750,000
    levas a month for the duration of four months (I 45n). The authors of *Voinata mezhdu
    Bŭlgariia i Turtsiia* claim that Montenegro sought a loan of 2,250,000 levas (62).
215 See Geshov *The Balkan League* 50.
216 Toshev *Balkanskite voini* I 362
217 Ibid
218 Ibid 363
219 Dr Milovan Milovanović died on 1 July 1912, at the early age of 49. He was succeeded
    as premier by M. Trifković who presided over a temporary caretaker cabinet. The real
    power was in the hands of N. Pašić, the leader of the Old Radicals and, since 1903, the
    leading political force in Serbia. On 16 July he told Hartwig that in the event of the
    slightest complications in the Balkans a new government would come into power: 'I

will most probably assume the Premiership and the portfolio of Minister of Foreign Affairs.' See Hartwig to Neratov, 16 July 1912 *MO* xx 1, 313–14 no. 308, and 313 n 1.

220 Toshev *Balkanskite voini* I 362
221 Ibid
222 Ibid 363–4
223 Ibid 364–5. On Pašić's views see also *Prvi balkanski rat* I 161 ff.
224 Toshev *Balkanskite voini* I 365
225 For the complete text of the draft see ibid 366.
226 Hartwig to Sazonov, 13 Sept. 1912 *MO* xx 2, 206 no. 678 and 206 n 1
227 Toshev to Geshov, 15 Sept. 1912 *DPIK* 154 no. 7. See also Toshev to Geshov, 13 Sept. 1912 ibid 154 no. 5.
228 Mishev to Geshov, 30 Aug. 1912 ibid 183 no. 5; Geshov to Mishev, 2 Sept. 1912 ibid 183 no. 6; Mishev to Geshov, 5 Sept. 1912 ibid 184 no. 9
229 Geshov to Mishev, 6 Sept. 1912 ibid 185 no. 11
230 Mishev to Geshov, 7 Sept. 1912 ibid 185–6 no. 12, and Geshov to Mishev, 9 Sept. 1912 ibid 186 no. 13
231 Ibid 186 no. 12
232 Mishev to Geshov, 23 Sept. 1912 ibid 186 no. 14. See also A. Souliotes-Nikolaides *Emerologēon tou protou valkanikou polemou* (Thessaloniki 1962) 32–4.
233 Geshov *The Balkan League* 40
234 See Toshev *Balkanskite voini* I 370.
235 See Mishev to Geshov, 27 Sept. 1912 *DPIK* 187 no. 15; Geshov to Mishev, 28 Sept. 1912 ibid 187 no. 16; Mishev to Geshov, 29 Sept. 1912 ibid 188 no. 17; Mishev to Geshov, 30 Sept. 1912 ibid 189 no. 19.
236 Obnorskii to Neratov, 28 July *MO* xx 1, 385 no. 380; Shtrandtman to Neratov, 30 July 1912 ibid 401 no. 395
237 Shtrandtman to Neratov, 8 Aug. 1912 ibid 413 no. 411
238 *Prvi balkanski rat* I 127
239 See *MO* xx 1, 401 n 3, and 413 n 3; Shtrandtman to Neratov, 13 Aug. 1912 ibid 453 no. 464.
240 See *MO* xx 1, 401 n 3, and 413 n 3; Shtrandtman to Neratov, 13 Aug. 1912 ibid 453 no. 464; Shtrandtman to Neratov, 4 Aug. 1912 ibid 413 no. 411.
241 Shtrandtman to Neratov, 30 July 1912 ibid 401 no. 395
242 *Prvi balkanski rat* I 127
243 Ibid; Toshev *Balkanskite voini* I 368
244 Kolushev to Geshov, 19 Sept. 1912 *DPIK* 201 no. 18
245 Z.G. Pavlović *Opsada Skadra* 34; P. Pešić 'Prva konvencija između Srbije i Crne Gore' *Vreme* (Belgrade) VIII (1928) no. 2481; H. Batowski 'Crna Gora i Balkanski savez 1912 godine' *Istoriski zapisi* (1957) no. 1–2, 57

246 Pešić; 'Prva konvencija' I
247 Ibid; *Prvi balkanski rat* I 127
248 Pešić 'Prva konvencija' I
249 Ibid; and *Prvi balkanski rat* I 128. This was the last bilateral agreement concluded by the Balkan states in 1912. Although both Serbia and Montenegro held talks with Greece, for various reasons no treaties were signed. For the talks between Greece and Montenegro see Geshov to Kolushev, 19 Sept. 1912 *DPIK* 201 no. 17; Kolushev to Geshov ibid 201 no. 18; and *MO* xx 2, 196–7 no. 668, 669. For the Serbo-Greek talks see *Prvi balkanski rat* I 131–2; Skoko *Drugi balkanski rat* 95–7.
250 The other major provisions of the political accord bound the signatories to aid each other unconditionally if either was attacked by one or more states; to aid each other in the event that Austria-Hungary attempted to annex, occupy, or even temporarily invade with her armies any part of European Turkey; not to negotiate with the enemy any concessions or to conclude an armistice or peace without the participation of the other; and to regularize their common boundary through a joint commission. The complete texts of the political and military conventions are found in *Prvi balkanski rat* I 128–31.
251 See Nekliudov to Sazonov, 4 Sept. 1912 *MO* xx 2, 144 no. 621; Demidov to Sazonov, 7 Sept. 1912 ibid 157–8 no. 630; Demidov to Sazonov, 7 Sept. 1912 ibid 171–5 no. 644.
252 Romanovskii to Danilov, 4 Sept. 1912 ibid 146 no. 623
253 See Hartwig to Sazonov, 10 Sept. 1912 ibid 183 no. 657.
254 Ibid; Nekliudov to Sazonov, 5 Sept. 1912 ibid 156 no. 629; Hartwig to Neratov, 23 Sept. 1912 ibid 246 no. 740
255 See for example Nekliudov's dispatches in ibid 81, 117–18, 147, 156, 208 no. 546, 591, 623, 629, 683.
256 Geshov to Paprikov, 7 Sept. 1912 *DPIK* 129 no. 2
257 Paprikov to Geshov, 16 Sept. 1912 ibid 133 no. 7
258 Ibid 134–5
259 Ibid. For Sazonov's account of the meeting see Sazonov to Izvol'skii, Krupenskii, Etter, Bronevskii, and Kudashev, 17 Sept. 1912 *MO* xx 2, 211 no. 686.
260 Ibid no. 686
261 See Nekliudov to Sazonov, 6 Sept. 1912 ibid 165 no. 637; Hartwig to Sazonov, 16 Sept. 1912 ibid 210 no. 685.
262 Sazonov to Hartwig, Urusov, Obnorskii, 17 Sept. 1912 ibid 213 no. 690. See also 212 no. 689.
263 Sazonov to Hartwig, Nekliudov, 18 Sept. 1912 ibid 218–19 no. 698
264 Hartwig to Neratov, 23 Sept. 1912 ibid 246–7 no. 740
265 Urusov to Neratov, 19 Sept. 1912 ibid 227 no. 711
266 Hartwig to Neratov, 24 Sept. 1912 ibid 264 no. 759
267 A. Giers to Neratov, 20 Sept. 1912 ibid 235 no. 724

268 Geshov to Madzharov, 21 Sept. 1912 *DPIK* 137 no. 8
269 Sazonov, circular, 17 Sept. 1912 *MO* xx 2, 211 no. 686; also Sazonov to Giers ibid 211 no. 687
270 Ibid no. 686
271 Sazonov to Kudashev, 17 Sept. 1912 ibid 212 no. 688
272 Kudashev to Neratov, 24 Sept. 1912 ibid 261 no. 756, and 243, 244 no. 737, 738
273 Bronevskii to Neratov, 19 Sept. 1912 ibid 225 no. 709
274 Sazonov to Neratov (London), 21 Sept. 1912 ibid 236–7 no. 726
275 Izvol'skii to Neratov, 21 Sept. 1912 ibid 237 no. 727
276 Ibid
277 Izvol'skii to Neratov, 22 Sept. 1912 ibid 239 no. 732
278 For the complete text of the four points see *MO* xx 2, 239–40 no. 733; *DDF* 3rd ser III 549 no. 451; *British Documents* IX 1, 702 no. 734.
279 See *MO* xx 2, 239–40 no. 733; *DDF* 3rd ser III 549 no. 451; *British Documents* IX 1, 702 no. 734; and Izvol'skii to Neratov, 22 Sept. 1912 *MO* xx 2, 246 no. 734.
280 Sazonov to Neratov (London), 25 Sept. 1912 ibid 276 no. 771
281 Izvol'skii to Neratov, 29 Sept. 1912 ibid 241 no. 734
282 Sazonov to Neratov (London), 29 Sept. 1912 ibid 305 no. 811
283 Sazonov, circular, 29 Sept. 1912 ibid 306 no. 813
284 Kolushev to Geshov, 14 Sept. 1912 *DPIK* 200 no. 14
285 Geshov to Kolushev, 17 Sept. 1912 ibid 200 no. 15; Kolushev to Geshov, 19 Sept. 1912 ibid 201 no. 16
286 Geshov to Kolushev, 17 Sept. 1912 ibid 200 no. 15; Kolushev to Geshov, 19 Sept. 1912 ibid 201 no. 16
287 Toshev *Balkanskite voini* I 381
288 Ibid 382
289 Ibid 381; Hartwig to Neratov, 24 Sept. 1912 *MO* xx 2, 265–6 no. 761
290 Hartwig to Neratov, 24 Sept. 1912 ibid xx 2, 264 no. 760, and 264 n 2
291 See Giers to Sazonov, 14 Sept. 1912 ibid 206–7 no. 680; 24 Sept. 1912 ibid 269 no. 764.
292 Toshev *Balkanskite voini* I 383
293 Sarafov to Geshov, 24 Sept. 1912 *DPIK* 138 no. 10. See also Nekliudov to Neratov, 25 Sept. 1912 *MO* xx 2, 282 no. 776.
294 Giers to Neratov, 25 Sept. 1912 *MO* xx 2, 283 no. 780
295 Neratov to Giers, 26 Sept. 1912 ibid 284 no. 782
296 Geshov to Toshev and Mishev, 25 Sept. 1912 *DPIK* 138 no. 11; Geshov to Kolushev, ibid 202 no. 20
297 Geshov to Toshev, 25 Sept. 1912 ibid 140 no. 16
298 Toshev to Geshov, 27 Sept. 1912 ibid 142 no. 22; Hartwig to Neratov, 27 Sept. 1912 *MO* xx 2, 294 no. 794
299 Toshev *Balkanskite voini* I 385, 391

300 Geshov to Toshev, 28 Sept. 1912 *DPIK* 155 no. 13; Toshev to Geshov, 29 Sept. 1912 ibid 156 no. 15

301 Mishev to Geshov, 27 Sept. 1912 ibid 187 no. 18

302 Geshov to Mishev, 28 Sept. 1912 ibid 187 no. 16

303 Mishev to Geshov, 30 Sept. 1912 ibid 189 no. 19

304 On the general mobilizations see *MO* xx 2 no. 827, 829, 840 (Bulgaria); 831, 832, 840 (Serbia); 830, 840 (Greece); 840, 850 (Montenegro); and 852, 853 (Turkey).

305 Geshov to Kolushev, 28 Sept. 1912 *DPIK* 202 no. 22

CHAPTER 3   The war against Turkey

1 Neratov to Sazonov in Balmoral, 27 Sept. 1912 *MO* xx 2, 291 no. 790

2 Szilassy to Berchtold, 1 Oct. 1912 *ÖUA* iv 514 no. 3903

3 Nekliudov to Neratov, 30 Sept. 1912 *MO* xx 2, 318 no. 829

4 Ibid

5 Nekliudov to Neratov, 30 Sept. 1912 ibid xx 2, 317 no. 828

6 A. Giers to Neratov, 3 Oct. 1912 *Stieve* ii 269 no. 466; *MO* xx 2, 329 n 2. See also A. Giers to Neratov, 1 Oct. 1912 *MO* xx 2, 329 no. 850.

7 See Nekliudov to Neratov, 27 Sept. 1912 *MO* xx 2, 293 no. 793.

8 Madzharov to Geshov, 2 Oct. 1912 *DPIK* 1 225 no. 5

9 Toshev *Balkanskite voini* 1 394. See also *MO* xx 2 no. 848.

10 Toshev *Balkanskite voini* 1 394

11 Nekliudov to Neratov, 2 Oct. 1912 *MO* xx 2, 337-8 no. 822

12 Geshov to Stanchov, 1 Oct. 1912 *DPIK* 225 no. 2

13 Spalajković to Belgrade, 4 Oct. 1912 *APS* 1 243-4 no. 197

14 Toshev *Balkanskite voini* 1 400

15 Full text in ibid 1 401. See also A. Giers to Neratov and Sazonov in Paris, 5 Oct. 1912 *MO* xx 2, 362 no. 890; Neratov to Hartwig, 5 Oct. 1912 ibid 363 no. 898.

16 Kolushev to Geshov, 5 Oct. 1912 *DPIK* 1 237 no. 8; Hartwig to Neratov, 6 Oct. 1912 *MO* xx, 2, 364 n

17 Izvol'skii to Neratov, Sazonov in London, 29 Sept. 1912 *MO* xx 2, 306-7 no. 814

18 Neratov to Sazonov in London, 30 Sept. 1912 ibid 314-15 no. 825; also 1 Oct. 1912 ibid 323 no. 839

19 Sazonov to Neratov, 1 Oct. 1912 ibid 326 no. 844

20 N. Giers to Neratov and Sazonov, 1 Oct. 1912 ibid 327 no. 846

21 Sazonov to St Petersburg, Vienna, Constantinople, Rome, Paris, Berlin, (London), 2 Oct. 1912 ibid 334 no. 858

22 See ibid 361 n 2.

23 Sazonov to St Petersburg, Berlin, Vienna, London, Rome, Constantinople, Paris, 4 Oct. 1912 ibid 361 no. 894; also in Russia *FRO* 280 no. 215

24 Sazonov to Neratov (Paris), 4 Oct. 1912 *MO* xx 2, 361 n 2
25 Bronevskii to Neratov, 5 Oct. 1912 ibid 365 no. 902
26 Count Berchtold suggested the term 'European Turkey' instead of 'the Balkans' at the end of the second point. He also proposed to drop the specific mentioning of article 23 and the word 'Christian' from the third point, and, finally, to add 'the sovereignty of His Majesty the Sultan' in addition to the territorial integrity of the Ottoman Empire in the third point. See N. Giers to Sazonov, 5 Oct. 1912 ibid 365–6 no. 903.
27 Benckendorff to Neratov and Sazonov in Paris (London), 6 Oct. 1912 ibid 372–3 no. 913; Sazonov to Neratov and Benckendorff (Paris), 6 Oct. 1912 ibid 374 no. 915
28 Benckendorff to Neratov and Sazonov, 4 Oct. 1912 ibid 360–1 no. 893
29 Ibid 6 Oct. 1912 ibid 371–2 no. 912
30 Ibid 372–3 no. 913
31 See ibid 360 n 3.
32 Benckendorff to Neratov and Sazonov, 6 Oct. 1912 ibid 373 no. 914
33 Text in Sazonov (circular), 6 Oct. 1912 ibid 375 no. 916. See also Sazonov to Neratov (Paris), 7 Oct. 1912 ibid 382 no. 927.
34 Benckendorff to Neratov, 6 Oct. 1912 ibid 372–3 no. 913. On the declaration of the Porte see M. Giers to Neratov and Sazonov, 6 Oct. 1912 ibid 380 no. 922.
35 Benckendorff to Neratov and Sazonov, 6 Oct. 1912 ibid 373–4 no. 914
36 Sazonov to Benckendorff and Neratov (Paris), 6 Oct. 1912 ibid 374 no. 915
37 Sazonov to St Petersburg, Berlin, Vienna, London, Constantinople (Paris), 7 Oct. 1912 ibid 383 no. 944
38 Ibid. See also Sazonov to M. Giers and Neratov (Paris), 8 Oct. 1912 ibid 394 no. 944.
39 Sazonov to Neratov, Nekliudov, Hartwig, Demidov, A. Giers (Paris), 7 Oct. 1912 ibid 383–4 no. 930. See also Stanchov to Geshov, 7 Oct. 1912 *DPIK* 229 no. 11.
40 Neratov to Sazonov, 1 Oct. 1912 *MO* xx 2, 325 no. 842
41 See Neratov to Sazonov, 2 Oct. 1912 ibid 333 no. 857.
42 Nekliudov to Sazonov, 6 Sept. 1912 ibid 163–6 no. 637; 20 Sept. 1912 ibid 233 no. 720; Nekliudov to Neratov, 30 Sept. 1912 ibid 317 no. 828
43 See Nekliudov to Neratov, 1 Oct. 1912 ibid 323 n 4.
44 Neratov to Sazonov in Paris, 1 Oct. 1912 ibid 323 no. 839
45 Ibid 325–6 no. 842
46 See ibid 317 n 7.
47 Sazonov to Neratov, 3 Oct. 1912 ibid 343 no. 871
48 Neratov to Sazonov, 5 Oct. 1912 ibid 362 no. 897
49 M. Giers to Neratov and Sazonov, 4 Oct. 1912 ibid 342 n 3; 8 Oct. 1912 ibid 401–2 no. 953
50 Neratov to Sazonov, 5 Oct. 1912 ibid 363 no. 897
51 Neratov to Sazonov, 6 Oct. 1912 ibid 369 no. 909
52 Hartwig to Neratov and Sazonov in Berlin, 7 Oct. 1912 ibid 385 no. 9. See also Neratov to Hartwig, 6 Oct. 1912 ibid 369 n 2.

53 Ibid 385 no. 932 and n 1
54 Berchtold to Pallavicini, 28 Sept. 1912 *ÖUA* IV 485 no. 3861; Pallavicini to Berchtold, 30 Sept. 1912 ibid 499 no. 3877
55 Zankovich to Danilov, 10 Oct. 1912 *MO* XX 2, 418–9 no. 972. See also 419–20 no. 973, and N. Giers to Neratov, 10 Oct. 1912 ibid 416 no. 971.
56 N. Giers to Sazonov (Vienna), 10 Oct. 1912 *MO* XX 2, 416 no. 971. See also *ÖUA* IV 589–90 no. 4017.
57 Sazonov to Giers, 12 Oct. 1912 *MO* XX 2, 429 no. 990; Szögyény to Berchtold, 10 Oct. 1912 *ÖUA* IV 595 no. 4023
58 Sazonov to Hartwig, 12 Oct. 1912 *MO* XX 2, 433, no. 996. See also Hartwig to Sazonov, 11 Oct. 1912 ibid 425 no. 984, and Sazonov to Izvol'skii, 16 Oct. 1912 ibid 477 no. 1052.
59 See Sazonov to Nekliudov, 11 Oct. 1912 ibid 421 no. 976; Paprikov to Geshov, 11 Oct. 1912, *DPIK* 232 no. 19; Geshov to Paprikov, 11 Oct. 1912 ibid 421 no. 20.
60 Sazonov to Giers, 11 Oct. 1912 *MO* XX 2, 421–2 no. 977
61 See Buchanan to Grey, 10 Oct. 1912 *British Documents* IX 2, 9 no. 10.
62 Nekliudov to Neratov, 8 Oct. 1912 *MO* XX 2, 395 no. 946; Demidov to Neratov, ibid 396 no. 948; Hartwig to Neratov, ibid 396–7 no. 948; A. Giers to Neratov, ibid 400 no. 951. See also *British Documents* IX 2 no. 2, 3, 4, 5.
63 A. Giers to Neratov (Cetinje), 10 Oct. 1912 *MO* XX 2, 421 no. 975
64 Demidov to Neratov, 9 Oct. 1912 ibid 407 no. 962
65 Nekliudov to Neratov, 8 Oct. 1912 ibid 394 no. 945. See also 405 no. 959 and 960.
66 Hartwig to Neratov, 10 Oct. 1912 ibid 420 no. 974
67 Hartwig to Neratov, 8 Oct. 1912 ibid 397 no. 948
68 M. Giers to Neratov, 6 Oct. 1912 *MO* XX 2, 381 no. 924. See also Sarafov to Geshov (Constantinople), 8 Oct. 1912 *DPIK* 230 no. 15.
69 A. Giers to Neratov, 8 Oct. 1912 *MO* XX 2, 400 n 3. See also Kholmsen to Danilov, 8 Oct. 1912 *MO* XX 2, 402 no. 954; Kolushev to Geshov, 8 Oct. 1912 *DPIK* 230 no. 16.
70 A. Giers to Neratov, 9 Oct. 1912 *MO* XX 2, 402 n 2; 407 no. 963; Giers to Sazonov, 9 Oct. GBA 75 no. 199
71 See M. Giers (Constantinople) to Neratov and Sazonov (Berlin), 7 Oct. 1912 *MO* XX 2, 386 no. 937.
72 Neratov to Nekliudov, Hartwig, Demidov, 8 Oct. 1912 ibid 392 no. 942
73 Buchanan to Grey, 9 Oct. 1912 *British Documents* IX 2, 6 no. 2
74 See Toshev *Balkanskite voini* I 409. Bax-Ironside to Grey, 10 Oct. 1912 *British Documents* IX 2, 9 no. 12.
75 The note of the Bulgarian, Greek, and Serbian governments to the Russian and Austro-Hungarian ministers at Sofia, Athens, Belgrade, 13 Oct. 1912 *MO* XX 2, 440–1 no. 1012; Bax-Ironside to Grey, 13 Oct. 1912 *British Documents* IX 2, 16–17 no. 22; Urgon to Berchtold, 13 Oct. 1912 *ÖUA* IV 629 no. 4066 annex 1

76 Toshev *Balkanskite voini* I 410
77 The annex contained nine demands, the most important of which were the following: 1) proportional representation in the imperial Parliament along nationality lines; 2) equality of Ottoman and Christian schools; 3) promise on the part of the Constantinople government not to modify the ethnic character of the provinces by the transplanting of the Muslim population; 4) reorganization of the gendarmerie in the vilayets of European Turkey under the command of Swiss or Belgian officers; 5) Swiss or Belgian *valis* for the Christian vilayets.
78 The note of the Greek, Bulgarian, and Serbian governments to the Turkish government. 13 Oct. 1912 *MO* XX 2, 441–3 no. 1613; Bax-Ironside to Grey, 13 Oct. 1912 *British Documents* IX 2, 17–18 no. 24; Urgon to Berchtold, 13 Oct. 1912 *ÖUA* IV 629–30 no. 4066 annex 2; Descos to Poincaré, 14 Oct. 1912 *DDF* IV 168 no. 162
79 Note of the Turkish government to the ambassadors of Austria-Hungary, France, Great Britain, Germany, and Russia, *MO* XX 2, 453–4 no. 1031; Geshov *The Balkan League* 53–4
80 Nekliudov to Sazonov, 15 Oct. 1912 *MO* XX 2, 469 no. 1041; M. Giers to Sazonov, 15 Oct. ibid 469 no. 1043; Demidov to Sazonov, 16 Oct. ibid 481 no. 1060; Hartwig to Sazonov, 16 Oct. ibid 482 no. 1064
81 Izvol'skii to Sazonov, 11 Oct. 1912 ibid 422–23 no. 979
82 Izvol'skii to Sazonov, 11 Oct. 1912 ibid 423 no. 980; 422–3 no. 979
83 Sazonov to Izvol'skii, 12 Oct. 1912 ibid 432 no. 995. See also Sazonov to M. Giers, 12 Oct. 1912 ibid 420 no. 989.
84 Izvol'skii to Sazonov, 12 Oct. 1912 ibid 435 no. 1001; 435–6 no. 1002
85 Izvol'skii to Sazonov, 13 Oct. 1912 *MO* XX 2, 439 no. 1008; Berchtold to Széczen, 13 Oct. *ÖUA* IV 644 no. 4073; Grey to Bertie, 12 Oct. *British Documents* IX 2, 15 no. 20
86 Sazonov to Izvol'skii, 16 Oct. 1912 *MO* XX 2, 476 no. 1051. See also ibid 456 no. 1033; 448 no. 1022; N. Giers to Sazonov (Vienna), 13 Oct. 1912, ibid 440 no. 1011, and 468–9 no. 1040; Sverbeev to Sazonov (Berlin), 15 Oct. 1912, 468 no. 1039; Grey to Bertie, 12 Oct. 1912 *British Documents* IX 2, 15 no. 20.
87 See *MO* XX 2, 479–80 no. 1056; 481 no. 1059; 487 no. 1073.
88 *MO* XX 2, 477 no. 1053; 422 no. 978. See also Buchanan to Grey, 17 Oct. 1912 *British Documents* IX 2, 33–4 no. 43.
89 On Poincaré's revised proposals see Izvol'skii to Sazonov, 15 Oct. 1912 *MO* XX 2, 467 no. 1037; 467–8 no. 1038; Grey to Bertie, 14 Oct. 1912 *British Documents* IX 2, 31 no. 28; communication from M. Paul Cambon *British Documents* IX 2, 36 no. 46; *DDF* IV 199–200 no. 192.
90 On the termination of the diplomatic relations see *MO* XX 2, 492 no. 1080, and 483 no. 1084; *DPIK* 233 no. 23; Geshov *The Balkan League* 57.
91 On the declarations of war see GBA 70 no. 94; *MO* XX 2, 488 no. 1075; 492 n 2; Toshev *Balkanskite voini* I 419–20.

92 V.A. Zhebokritskii *Bolgariia v period balkanskikh voin 1912–1913 g.g.* (Kiev 1961) 11

93 Toshev *Balkanskite voini* I 392. See also Hartwig to Neratov, 30 Sept. 1912 *MO* XX 2, 319 no. 831.

94 Toshev *Balkanskite voini* I 391

95 L. Trotskii *Balkany i balkanskaia voina. Sochineniia* VI (Moscow and Leningrad 1926) 141

96 Ministerstvo na voinata *Voinata mezhdu Būlgariia i Turtsiia 1912–1913* I (Sofia 1937) 130–1

97 Ibid VI 3–4; A. Ganchev *Balkanskata voina, 1912–1913 g.* (Sofia 1939) 22–4. Ganchev's figures are slightly lower: 180,000, 100,000, and 36,000.

98 Ganchev *Balkanskata voina* 17, 27; Ministerstvo na voinata *Voinata* I 262. See also A. Khristov *Istoriia na osloboditelnata voina 1912–1913 g.* (Sofia 1946) 16, 25.

99 Ganchev *Balkanskata voina* 155; see ch 2.

100 Ibid 155, 173–4; I. Fichev *Balkanskata voina 1912–1913. Prezhivelitsi, belezhki i dokumenti* (Sofia 1940) 38, 83

101 Ganchev *Balkanskata voina* 27–9

102 Ibid 154–5

103 Nekliudov to FO 24 Oct. 1912 GBA 67 no. 205; 28 Oct. no. 213. See also Fichev *Balkanskata voina* 107–20.

104 Ganchev *Balkanskata voina* 66–73, 117

105 Fichev *Balkanskata voina* 120–3; Toshev *Balkanskite voini* II 8–10; Ganchev *Balkanskata voina* 64–6

106 Fichev *Balkanskata voina* 128–58; Toshev *Balkanskite voini* II 14–15; Ganchev *Balkanskata voina* 74–109

107 M. Giers to Sazonov (Constantinople), 27 Nov. 1912 GBA 58 no. 115; Ganchev *Balkanskata voina* 146–52; I. Mishev *Geroizm't na Būlgarskata armiia prez balkanskata voina* (Sofia 1953) 30–40

108 Ganchev *Balkanskata voina* 170–3

109 Ibid

110 Ibid 155–8; Hartwig to Sazonov, 27 Oct. 1912 GBA 80 no. 253; Toshev *Balkanskite voini* II 13

111 Ganchev *Balkanskata voina* 160–1; A. Souliotes-Nikolaides *Emerolegēon tou protou valkanikou polemou* (Thessaloniki 1962)

112 G. Ventiri *I Ellas toy 1910–1920. Istoriki meleti* (Athens 1931) I 108–10; Th. Pagkalou *Ta apomnimoneumata mou, 1897–1947. I tarachodis periodos tis teleutaias penitikontaetias* (Athens 1950) 161–75; Ganchev *Balkanskata voina* 161–3

113 Ventiri *I Ellas* I 111–30; Pagkalou *Ta apomnimoneumata mou* 194–214; V. Dusmanis *Apomnimoneumata. Istorikai selides tas opoias ezisa* (Athens 1964) 46–57

239 Notes to pp 82-4

114 Ventiri *I Ellas* I I I I–30; Pagkalou *Ta apomnimoneumata mou* 194–214; V. Dusmanis
Apomnimoneumata 46–57; Ganchev *Balkanskata voina* 163–7; A. Souliotes-
Nikolaides *Emerolegēon*; A. Zannas *O Makedonikon agōni. Anamnēseis* (Thessaloniki 1960) 65 ff; Stojanov *Makedonija* 47 ff
115 Ganchev *Balkanskata voina* 169–74
116 S.D. Sazonov *Fateful Years* 111
117 See I.I. Fichev 'Obiasneniia i osvetleniia po povod na truda na g. dr. Al. Girginov za
narodnata katastrofa' *Mir* (Sofia) 8 Mar. 1926. King Ferdinand was against it; see
Ferdinand to Geshov, 22 Oct. 1912 *DPIK* 234 no. 29.
118 S.S. Bobchev *Stranitsi iz moiata diplomaticheska missiia v Petrograd (1912–1913)*
(Sofia 1940) 24–5; Toshev *Balkanskite voini* II 4
119 Buchanan to Grey, 22 Oct. 1912 *British Documents* IX 2, 42 no. 53
120 Buchanan to Grey, 18 Oct. 1912 ibid 35 no. 44
121 Grey to Buchanan, 21 Oct. 1912 ibid 41 no. 50; Buchanan to Grey, 22 Oct. 1912 ibid
42 no. 53; Grey to Buchanan, 23 Oct. 1912 ibid 46 no. 58
122 Benckendorff to Sazonov, 21 Oct. 1912 *KA* XVI (1926) 8–9 no. 35; *Siebert* II 452–4
no. 691; 455–9 no. 695
123 Sazonov to Benckendorff, 24 Oct. 1912 *KA* XVI (1926) 9 no. 36; *Siebert* II 462–3 no.
698
124 *KA* XVI (1926) 13 n 1. See also Buchanan to Grey, 24 Oct. 1912 *British Documents* IX
2, 46 no. 59.
125 *KA* XVI (1926) 13–14 n 1; full text in *DDF* IV 283–5 no. 274
126 Buchanan *My Mission to Russia* I 123; A.A. Savinski *Recollections of a Russian
Diplomat* (London 1927) 62
127 Buchanan to Grey, 30 Oct. 1912 *British Documents* IX 2, 63 no. 78
128 Ibid 64
129 Zapis direktora kantselarii ministerstva inostrannykh del, 16 Oct. 1912 *MO* XX 2, 479
no. 1055; Sazonov to Izvol'skii, Benckendorff … also to Constantinople, Athens,
Sofia, Belgrade, 28 Oct. 1912 *KA* XVI (1926) 14 no. 44
130 *MO* XX 2, 479 no. 1055; *KA* XVI (1926) 14 no. 44
131 *MO* XX 2, 479 no. 1055; *KA* XVI (1926) 14 no. 44
132 See Izvol'skii to Sazonov, 27 Oct. 1912 *KA* XVI (1926) 12 no. 42; Sazonov to
Izvol'skii, 28 Oct. 1912 *FRO* 292 no. 2377. This was based to a large degree on the
negative response of London and Paris to Kiderlen-Wächter's initiative of 25 October.
He proposed that England, France, and Germany keep in close touch so that when the
need came to mediate or intervene in the conflict they could act together without delay.
On Kiderlen-Wächter's initiative see Kiderlen to von Schoen, 26 Oct. 1912 *GP* XXXIII
256 no. 12302; Goschen to Grey, 25 Oct. 1912 *British Documents* IX 2, 48–9 no. 61;
Cambon to Poincaré (in Russian), 26 Oct. 1912 *KA* XVI (1926) 10–11 no. 39, 11–12
no. 40.

133 Sazonov *Fateful Years* 71
134 Izvol'skii to Sazonov, 27 Oct. *KA* xvi (1926) 13 no 43
135 Sazonov *Fateful Years* 73; Bobchev to Geshov, 27 Oct. 1912 *DPIK* 237 no. 37
136 Geshov, circular, 1 Nov. 1912 *DPIK* 239 no. 42
137 Hartwig to Sazonov, 9 Nov. 1912 *GBA* 80 no. 276. See also Hartwig to Sazonov, 2
    Nov. 1912 ibid 80 no. 262; Bobchev to Geshov, 2 Nov. 1912, in Bobchev *Stranitsi* 43.
138 See Bobchev to Geshov, 2 Nov. 1912, Bobchev *Stranitsi* 43–4.
139 Buchanan to Grey, 29 Oct. 1912 *British Documents* ix 2, 59 no. 74
140 Buchanan to Grey, 30 Oct. 1912 ibid 65–6 no. 78
141 Sazonov, circular, 31 Oct. 1912 *KA* xvi (1926) 15 no. 45
142 On the relations between Rumania and the allies, and particularly Bulgaria, before and
    during the war see ch 5.
143 Sazonov circular, 16
144 Ibid 17
145 Ibid 17–18. For a summary of the circular in English see *British Documents* ix 2, 61.
146 Sazonov requested Poincaré to take the initiative; Bobchev to Geshov, 2 Nov. 1912 in
    Bobchev *Stranitsi* 44.
147 It called for a conference of the great powers at which the belligerents and Rumania
    were to participate; Izvol'skii to Sazonov, 1 Nov. 1912 *KA* xvi (1926) 19 no. 48.
148 Poincaré to Berlin, Vienna, Rome, 30 Oct. 1912 *DDF* iv 295 no. 284; Izvol'skii to
    Sazonov, 31 Oct. 1912, 'Sbornik diplomaticheskikh dokumentov kasaiushchikhsia
    sobytyii na balkanskom poluostrove (Avgust 1912 – Iul' 1913 g.) *RS* 5 (1915) 252 no.
    37; communication from P. Cambon, 30 Oct. 1912 *British Documents* ix 2, 68 no. 80
149 Izvol'skii to Sazonov, 5 Nov. 1912 *RS* 5 (1915) 252 no. 39. See also *GP* xxxiii no.
    12307, 12311, 12312; *DDF* iv no. 338, 339, 341; *British Documents* ix 2, 73 no. 89 n.
150 Giers to Sazonov, 31 Oct. 1912 *RS* 5 (1915) 252 no. 38; Cartwright to Grey, 1 Nov.
    1912 *British Documents* ix 2, 69 no. 83; report on the visit of the French ambassador of
    31 Oct. 1912 *ÖUA* iv 736 no. 4216; von Tschirschky to Bethmann-Hollweg, 31 Oct.
    1912 *GP* xxxiii 264 no. 12310
151 Grey to Bertie, 3 Nov. 1912 *British Documents* ix 2, 85 no. 106. See also Izvol'skii to
    Sazonov, 2 Nov. 1912 *KA* xvi (1926) 20 no. 50.
152 See ch 1 and 2.
153 Fichev *Balkanskata voina* 86 ff. See also Demidov to Sazonov, 20 Oct. 1912 *KA* xvi
    (1926) 7 no. 33; Neratov to Izvol'skii, 19 Oct. 1912 *FRO* 288 no. 2243.
154 Sazonov, circular, 31 Oct. 1912 *KA* xvi (1926) 18 no. 45
155 Ibid; Sazonov to Nekliudov, 31 Oct. 1912 *KA* xvi (1926) 18 no. 46
156 Bobchev to Geshov, 1 Nov. 1912 *DPIK* 662 no. 17; Bobchev *Stranitsi* 44
157 Sazonov to Nekliudov, 31 Oct. 1912 *KA* xvi (1926) 18 no. 46
158 Izvol'skii to Sazonov, 1 Nov. 1912 *KA* xvi (1926) 20 no. 49. See also *DDF* iv 370–1
    no. 358.

159 Fichev *Balkanskata voina* 201 ff; Efremov *Vneshnaia politika Rossii* 163. See also *ÖUA* IV 778 no. 4282; *GP* XXXIII 274–6, no. 12320. In a marginal note Wilhelm II noted: 'Vielleicht erleben wir Ferdinand den I als Zar von Byzanz? Als Oberhaubt des Balkanbundes?' *GP* XXXIII 253 no. 12297 n.

160 Grey to Buchanan, 2 Nov. 1912 *British Documents* IX 2, 83 no. 102. See also Benckendorff to Sazonov, 2 Nov. 1912 *Siebert* II 474–5 no. 707.

161 Madzharov to Geshov, 31 Oct. 1912 and 3 Nov. 1912, in M.I. Madzharov *Diplomaticheska podgotovka na nashite voini. Spomeni, chastni pisma, shifrovani telegrami i poveritelni dokladi* (Sofia 1932) 74 and 78–80

162 I.E. Geshov *Prestŭpnoto bezumie i anketata po nego. Fakti i dokumenti* (Sofia 1914) 93. See also Fichev *Balkanskata voina* 203 ff; Toshev *Balkanskite voini* II 48.

163 Geshov to Bobchev, 4 Nov. 1912 *DPIK* 663, no. 18; Bobchev *Stranitsi* 44–5

164 Bobchev to Geshov, 6 Nov. 1912 *DPIK* 663 no. 21

165 Bobchev to Geshov, 6 Nov. 1912, in Bobchev *Stranitsi* 45. See also Buchanan to Grey, 4 Nov. 1912 *British Documents* IX 2, 92 no. 119.

166 Sazonov to Nekliudov, 6 Nov. 1912 *RS* 5 (1915) 754 no. 42; Bobchev *Stranitsi* 45; Madzharov *Diplomaticheska podgotovka* 80–1

167 Bertie to Grey, 7 Nov. 1912 *British Documents* IX 2, 117 no. 156

168 Izvol'skii to Sazonov, 6 Nov. 1912 *FRO* 234 no. 340. See also Mogilevich and Airapetian *Na putiakh k mirovoi voiny* 121.

169 Izvol'skii to Sazonov, 6 Nov. 1912 *FRO* 234 no. 340. See also Mogilevich and Airapetian *Na putiakh k mirovoi voiny* 121.

170 Sazonov to Izvol'skii, 6 Nov. 1912 *Stieve* II 552 no. 552. See also Benckendorff to Sazonov, 7 Nov. 1912 *Siebert* II 480–2 no. 712, 713.

171 Buchanan to Grey, 13 Nov. 1912 *British Documents* IX 2, 150 no. 195

172 See Geshov *Prestŭpnoto bezumie* 34–7; Fichev *Balkanskata voina* 201–4; Danev *Balkanský svaz a válka s Tureckem* 22.

173 Bobchev *Stranitsi* 45; Buchanan to Grey, 5 Nov. 1912 *British Documents* IX 2, 99 no. 130

174 Geshov *Prestŭpnoto bezumie* 34–7; Fichev *Balkanskata voina* 201–4

175 Sazonov *Fateful Years* 74. See also Buchanan to Grey, 4 Nov. 1912 *British Documents* IX 2, 92 no. 119.

176 Fichev to Geshov, 16 Nov. 1912 *DPIK* 241 no. 52; Fichev *Balkanskata voina* 174–204; Toshev *Balkanskite voini* II 65 ff

177 Fichev to Geshov, 16 Nov. 1912 *DPIK* 241 no. 52; Fichev *Balkanskata voina* 174–204; Toshev *Balkanskite voini* II 65 ff. See also Buchanan to Grey, 4 Nov. 1912 *British Documents* IX 2, 95 no. 122.

178 Kiamil Pasha to Ferdinand, 13 Nov. 1912 *DPIK* 261–62 no. 3 and 4

179 Geshov *Prestŭpnoto bezumie* 32

180 Ibid 35; *Prilozhenie* 143

181 Geshov to Ferdinand, 14 Nov. 1912 *DPIK* 262–3 no. 5; Girginov *Narodnata katastrofa* 46–7
182 Toshev *Balkanskite voini* II 73; Nekliudov to Sazonov, 28 Nov. 1912 GBA 67 no. 284
183 Ferdinand to Geshov, 18 Nov. 1912 *DPIK* 266 no. 14
184 Danev to Geshov, Nov. 20, 1912 ibid 670 no. 37
185 Toshev *Balkanskite voini* II 73
186 Girginov *Narodnata katastrofa* 44 ff
187 Giers to Nekliudov, 20 Nov. 1912 *DPIK* 267 no. 18
188 Record of the conference with the German chancellor in Buchlau, 7 and 8 Oct. 1912 *ÖUA* IV 415–8 no. 3771
189 Stallberg to Bethmann-Hollweg, 20 Sept. 1912 *GP* XXXIII 111 no. 12154
190 Stallberg to Bethmann-Hollweg, 27 Sept. 1912 *GP* XXXIII 122 no. 12172. See also *ÖUA* IV 478–9 no. 3850 and 490–3 no. 3869.
191 Denkschrift, 2 Oct. 1912 *ÖUA* IV 528–9 no. 3928
192 Protocol of the conference of 16 Oct. 1912 ibid 659–61 no. 4118
193 Protocol of the conference of 19 Oct. 1912 ibid 677 no. 4140
194 Record of the conference held between 25 and 30 Oct. 1912 *ÖUA* IV 698–702 no. 4170
195 Berchtold to Urgon, 27 Oct. 1912 ibid 717 no. 4184
196 Urgon to Berchtold, 2 Nov. 1912 ibid 751–3 no. 4235. See also Ćorović *Odnosi između Srbije i Austro-ugarske* 384; D. Đorđević *Izlazak Srbije na Jadransko more i Konferencija ambasadora u Londonu 1912* (Belgrade 1956) 33.
197 Ćorović *Odnosi između Srbije i Austro-ugarske* 388; Đorđević *Izlazak Srbije* 34
198 Ćorović *Odnosi između Srbije i Austro-ugarske* 388; Đorđević *Izlazak Srbije* 34
199 Ćorović *Odnosi između Srbije i Austro-ugarske* 389. Quoted from the archives of the Belgrade foreign office. For Pašić's account to Hartwig see Hartwig to Sazonov, 27 Oct. 1912 GBA 80 no. 275. See also *ÖUA* IV 841–2 no. 4365.
200 Ćorović *Odnosi između Srbije i Austro-ugarske* 389
201 Ibid
202 See Buchanan to Grey, 10 Nov. 1912 *British Documents* IX 2, 130–1 no. 174. See also *ÖUA* IV no. 4346 and 4347.
203 Pourtalès to Bethmann, 11 Nov. 1912 *GP* XXIII 335 no. 12374. 'Nur nicht wieder eine ähnliche Situation. Ein zweites Mal würde sich Russland nicht demütigen lassen. Das wäre der Krieg!'
204 Poincaré to Izvol'skii, 4 Nov. 1912 *FRO* 297 no. ng
205 Izvol'skii to Sazonov, 7 Nov. 1912 *KA* XVI (1926) 22–3 no. 53; Izvol'skii to Sazonov (letter), no. 7, 1912 *FRO* 295; *Stieve* II 335–7 no. 554
206 Sazonov to Izvol'skii, nd *FRO* 299 no. ng
207 Ibid
208 Izvol'skii to Poincaré, nd *FRO* 297–9 no. ng
209 On the Bogićević affair see Kiderlen to von Tschirschky, 7 Nov. 1912 *GP* XXXIII

292–4 no. 12338; Szögyény to Berchtold, 8 Nov. 1912 *ÖUA* IV 792–3 no. 4305; Goschen to Grey, 7 Nov. 1912 *British Documents* IX 2, 113–14 no. 150, 151; Benckendorff to Sazonov, 12 Nov. 1912 *Siebert* II 486–7 no. 717.

210 Ćorović *Odnosi između Srbije i Austro-ugarske* 390. See also Hartwig to Sazonov, 16 Nov. 1912 GBA 67 no. 312.

211 Ćorović *Odnosi između Srbije i Austro-ugarske* 390; Đorđević *Izlazak Srbije* 56–7

212 Ćorović *Odnosi između Srbije i Austro-ugarske* 395–6; Đorđević *Izlazak Srbije* 61–3; Sazonov *Fateful Years* 74; Marco (B. Simić) 'Nikola Hartvig – Spoljna politika Srbije pred svetski rat' *Nova Evropa* XVII (1928) 256 ff

213 Buchanan to Grey, 10 Nov. 1912 *British Documents* IX 2, 131 no. 174. See also Pourtalès to Berlin, 9 Nov. 1912 GP XXXIII 306 no. 12351; Thurn to Berchtold, 9 Nov. 1912 *ÖUA* 822 no. 4345.

214 Benckendorff to Sazonov, 14 Nov. 1912 *Siebert* II 489–90 no. 720; 490–1 no. 721; Grey to Buchanan, 14 Nov. 1912 *British Documents* IX 2, 154–5 no. 202; P. Cambon to Poincaré *DDF* IV 461 no. 445

215 Buchanan to Grey, 8 Nov. 1912 *British Documents* IX 2, 119 no. 161. See also Benckendorff to Sazonov, 11 Nov. 1912 *Siebert* II 486 no. 716.

216 See Goschen to Grey, 8 Nov. 1912 *British Documents* IX 2, 118 no. 158.

217 Berchtold to Urgon, 8 Nov. 1912 *ÖUA* IV 798–9 no. 4317

218 Benckendorff to Sazonov, 8 Nov. 1912 *Siebert* II 482 no. 714. See also *British Documents* IX 2, 119 and 125, no. 161 and 168.

219 Quoted in Ćorović *Odnosi izumeđu Srbije i Austro-ugarske* 390–1. See also Buchanan to Grey, 9 Nov. 1912 *British Documents* IX 2, 127 no. 171.

220 Sazonov to Hartwig, 9 Nov. 1912 *RS* 5 (1915) 258–9 no. 45; *Stieve* II 339–40 no. 558

221 Đorđević *Izlazak Srbije* 61

222 Bobchev to Geshov, 9 Nov. 1912 *DPIK* I 391 no. 1

223 See Đorđević *Izlazak Srbije* 67 ff; Bobchev *Stranitsi* 48 ff.

224 Geshov to Bobchev, 10 Nov. 1912 *DPIK* 391 no. 2; see also 666 no. 27, and Sazonov to Izvol'skii and Benckendorff, 12 Nov. 1912 *Stieve* II 344 no. 565.

225 Splalajković to Belgrade, 13 Nov. 1912 *APS* I 253 no. 210. See also Toshev *Balkanskite voini* II 56; Buchanan to Grey, 12 Nov. 1912 *British Documents* IX 2, 138 no. 180.

226 Bobchev to Geshov, 11 Nov. 1912 in Bobchev *Stranitsi* 48

227 Buchanan to Grey, 19 Nov. 1912 *British Documents* IX 2, 138 no. 180

228 See GBA 22 no. 2536; *GP* XXXIII no. 12374; *ÖUA* IV no. 4376; *British Documents* IX 2 no. 180.

229 Urgon to Berchtold, 10 Nov. 1912 *ÖUA* IV 829–30 no. 4351; Hartwig to Sazonov, 11 Nov. 1912 GBA 80 no. 289; Paget to Grey, 11 Nov. 1912 *British Documents* IX 2, 133–5 no. 176

230 Urgon to Berchtold, 10 Nov. 1912 *ÖUA* IV 829–30 no. 4351; Hartwig to Sazonov, 11

Nov. 1912 GBA 80 no. 289; Paget to Grey, 11 Nov. 1912 *British Documents* IX 2, 113–15 no. 176. The German and Italian ministers at Belgrade made similar representations on 18 Nov. 1912. Paget to Grey, 18 Nov. 1912 *British Documents* IX 2, 174 no. 232; Hartwig to Sazonov, 18 Nov. 1912 GBA 80 no. 319.

231 Paget to Grey, 18 Nov. 1912 *British Documents* IX 2, 174 no. 232; Hartwig to Sazonov, 18 Nov. 1912 GBA 80 no. 319

232 Giers to Sazonov, 12 Nov. 1912 GBA 75 no. 233

233 Berchtold to Giesl, 17 Nov. 1912 *ÖUA* IV 906–8 no. 4467, 4468. See also Giers to Sazonov, 13 Nov. 1912 GBA 75 no. 223 and 234 and 14 Nov. no. 238, and 17 Nov. no. 251. See also M. Vojvodić 'Jedan neuspeli pokušaj Austro-ugarske da sklopi carinsku uniju sa Crnom Gorom' in V. Čubrilović ed *Jugoslovenski narodi pred prvi svetski rat* 117–24.

234 De Salis to Grey, 18 Nov. 1912 *British Documents* IX 2, 168 no. 223

235 Paget to Grey, 11 Nov. 1912 ibid 133 no. 176 n

236 Đorđević *Izlazak Srbije* 59 and 65

237 Bertie to Grey *British Documents* IX 2, 160 no. 211

238 Grey to Paget, 13 Nov. 1912 ibid 152 no. 197

239 Benckendorff to Sazonov, 13 Nov. 1912 *Siebert* II 487–8 no. 718; Mensdorff to Berchtold, 13 Nov. *ÖUA* IV 864 no. 4404

240 Bertie to Grey, 16 Nov. 1912 *British Documents* IX 2, 161 no. 213. See *DDF* IV 480–2 no. 468, 469.

241 Sazonov to Izvol'skii, 14 Nov. 1912 *Stieve* II 345 no. 566; Grey to Buchanan, 14 Nov. 1912 *British Documents* IX 2, 154 no. 202; P. Cambon to Poincaré, 13 Nov. 1912 *DDF* IV 461 no. 445

242 Sazonov *Fateful Years* 74. See also Buchanan to Grey, 9 Nov. 1912 *British Documents* IX 2, 128 no. 171.

243 Buchanan to Grey, 17 Nov. 1912 *British Documents* IX 2, 165 no. 219; Pourtalès to Bethmann-Hollweg, 20 Nov. 1912 *GP* XXXIII 385 no. 12415

244 Grey to Buchanan, 14 Nov. 1912 *British Documents* IX 2, 154 no. 202; Benckendorff to Sazonov, 14 Nov. 1912 *Siebert* II 489 no. 720, 490–1 no. 721

245 Izvol'skii to Sazonov, 17 Nov. 1912 *FRO* 300 no. 369; *Stieve* II 346 no. 567

246 Buchanan to Grey, 14 Nov. 1912 *British Documents* IX 2, 154 no. 201

247 Sazonov to Benckendorff, 19 Nov. 1912 *Stieve* II 349 no. 572; Buchanan to Grey, 17 Nov. 1912 *British Documents* IX 2, 164 no. 218

248 Sazonov to Izvol'skii and Benckendorff, 17 Nov. 1912 *Stieve* II 347 no. 568. See also *British Documents* IX 2, 162 no. 216; *GP* XXXIII 347 no. 12387; *ÖUA* IV 919–20 no. 4483; *DDF* IV 489 no. 480.

249 Buchanan to Grey, 17 Nov. 1912 *British Documents* IX 2, 162–3 and 164–5 no. 216 and 218

250 See Bertie to Grey, 19 Nov. 1912 ibid 176 no. 234; Grey to Buchanan, 18 Nov. 1912 ibid 169 no. 224.

251 Report on the visit of the German and Italian ambassadors of 20 Nov. 1912 *ÖUA* IV 940 no. 4510; see also no. 4581 and 4612. Buchanan to Grey, 19 Nov. 1912 *British Documents* IX 2, 177 no. 235; Lichnowski to Berlin *GP* XXXIII 398–9 no. 12341; G. Louis to Poincaré *DDF* IV 489 and 492 no. 480, 485

252 Izvol'skii to Sazonov, 22 Nov. 1912 *Stieve* II 354–5 no. 577; Bertie to Grey, 22 Nov. 1912 *British Documents* IX 2, 189–90 no. 255; Széczen to Berchtold, 21 Nov. 1912 *ÖUA* IV 960–1 no. 4543

253 Izvol'skii to Sazonov, 18 Nov. 1912 *FRO* 300 no. 374; 19 Nov. 1912 ibid 301 no. 375; GBA 28 no. 375; *Stieve* II 348 no. 570, 571

254 Izvol'skii to Sazonov, 25 Nov. 1912 *Stieve* II 356 no. 580; Mensdorff to Berchtold, 25 Nov. 1912 *ÖUA* IV 1007–8 no. 4612

255 Izvol'skii to Sazonov, 25 Nov. 1912 *FRO* 304 no. 386. See also Đorđević *Izlazak Srbije* 73.

256 Sazonov to Benckendorff, 21 Nov. 1912 *Stieve* II 353–4; Paget to Grey, 19 Nov. 1912 *British Documents* IX 2, 174 no. 292

257 See Đorđević *Izlazak Srbije* 62 ff.

258 Ibid

259 Ibid. See also Hartwig to Sazonov, 17 Nov 1912 GBA 80 no. 316 and 19 Nov. no. 73.

260 Paget to Grey, 22 Nov. 1912 *British Documents* IX 2, 192 no. 257

261 *Times* (London) 25 Nov. 1912, 8.

262 Ibid 9. See *British Documents* IX 2, 203 n.

263 Đorđević *Izlazak Srbije* 75 ff

264 Hartwig to Sazonov, 13 Dec. 1912 GBA 80 no. 382; Urgon to Berchtold, 15 Nov. 1912 *ÖUA* IV 882–3 no. 4435

265 See Ćorović *Odnosi između Srbije i Austro-urgarske* 400 ff; Đorđević *Izlazak Srbije na Jadransko more* 84 ff; I.S. Galkin *Diplomatiia evropeiskikh derzhav v sviazi s osvoboditel' nym dvizheniem narodov evropeiskoi Turtsii, 1905–1912 g.g.* (Moscow 1960) 184 ff. On the proclamation of Albanian independence see also S. Skendi *The Albanian National Awakening* 438 ff; and J. Swire *Albania. The Rise of a Kingdom* 126 ff.

266 Berchtold to Urgon 17 Nov. 1912 *ÖUA* IV 900–1 no. 4461. On the case of Oscar Prochaska see no. 4316, 4380, 4492, 4493.

267 Giers to Sazonov, 29 Nov. 1912 GBA 22 no 123; Hartwig to Sazonov, 15 Dec. 1912 GBA 80 no. 81. See also Ćorović *Odnosi između Srbije i Austro-ugarske* 401–2; Đorđević *Izlazak Srbije* 97–8.

268 Ćorović *Odnosi između Srbije i Austro-ugarske* 402

269 Cartwright to Grey, 26 Nov. 1912 *British Documents* IX 2, 205 no. 279; Kageneck to Berlin, 25 Nov. 1912 *GP* XXXIII 402–3 no. 12434

270 M. von Auffenberg-Komarow *Aus Österreichs Höhe und Niedergang-Eine lebens-schilderung* (Munich 1927) 218

271 Cartwright to Grey, 27 Nov. 1912 *British Documents* IX 2, 213 no. 289

272 Szögény to Berchtold, 22 Nov. 1912 *ÖUA* IV 971 no. 4559; Sverbeev to Sazonov, 23 Nov. 1912 GBA 16 no. 184
273 Conrad von Hötzendorf *Aus meiner Dienstzeit 1906–1918* (Vienna 1921–5) II 360–72. See also *ÖUA* IV no. 4465, 4650, 4652.
274 Von Tschirschky to Kiderlen, 21 Nov. 1912 *GP* XXXIII 372–3 no. 12404
275 Conrad von Hötzendorf *Aus meiner Dienstzeit* 379. On General Conrad see also Giers to Sazonov, 10 Dec. 1912 GBA 22 no. 129.
276 On the military moves on the eve of the war see Neratov to Sazonov, 30 Sept. 1912 *MO* XX 2, 313 no. 823; Bronevskii to Neratov, 29 Nov. 1912 ibid 307 no. 815; Bronevskii to Neratov, 10 Oct. 1912 ibid 342 no. 870.
277 See Đorđević *Izlazak Srbije* 77.
278 See V.N. Kokovtsov *Out of My Past. The Memoirs of Count Kokovtsov* ed H.H. Fisher (Stanford, Calif. 1935) 342–4; Đorđević *Izlazak Srbije* 77–8.
279 Kokovtsov *Memoirs* 344
280 Ibid
281 Ibid 345
282 Ibid 346
283 Ibid 346–7
284 Đorđević *Izlazak Srbije* 74–5
285 Thurn to Berchtold, 26 Nov. 1912 *ÖUA* IV 1025 no. 4639; Giers to Sazonov (Vienna), 27 Nov. 1912 GBA 22 no. 119. See also Buchanan to Grey, 26 Nov. 1912 *British Documents* IX 2, 206 no. 281.
286 See Ćorović *Odnosi između Srbije i Austro-ugarske* 416; Đorđević *Izlazak Srbije* 99 ff.
287 Cartwright to Grey, 4 Dec. 1912 *British Documents* IX 2, 240 no. 324
288 Đorđević *Izlazak Srbije* 86
289 Ibid 87
290 Sazonov to Izvol'skii, Benckendorff, 10 Dec. 1912 *RS* 6 (1915) 419 no. 55; Buchanan to Grey, 10 Dec. 1912 *British Documents* IX 2, 272 no. 367
291 Thurn to Berchtold, 10 Dec. 1912 *ÖUA* V 88 no. 4859; Sazonov to Giers, 10 Dec. 1912 *RS* II 6 (1915) 420 no. 56
292 Thurn to Berchtold, 13 Dec. 1912 *ÖUA* V 115 no. 4905; Buchanan to Grey, 13 Dec. 1912 *British Documents* IX 2, 284–5 no. 381
293 See Izvol'skii to Sazonov, 8 Dec. 1912 *Stieve* II 379 and 380 no. 610 and 613; Izvol'skii to Sazonov, 10 Dec. 1912 GBA 28 no. 428.
294 Sazonov to Izvol'skii, Benckendorff, 10 Dec. 1912 *RS* 6 (1915) 419–20 no. 55; *Stieve* II 383 no. 617
295 Poincaré to Descos, 11 Dec. 1912 *DDF* V 55 no. 42; Grey to Buchanan, 11 Dec. 1912 *British Documents* IX 2, 275 no. 370 and n 2
296 Quoted in Ćorović *Odnosi između Srbije i Austro-ugarske* 410. See also Hartwig to Sazonov, 27 Nov. 1912 GBA 80 no. 350.

297 See Hartwig to Sazonov, 27 Nov. 1912 GBA 80 no. 350, 2 Dec. 1912 no. 362, 8 Dec. 1912 no. 370. See also Grey to Bertie 4 Dec. 1912 *British Documents* IX 2, 244 no. 328.

298 Ćorović *Odnosi između Srbije i Austro-ugarske* 416. See also Hartwig to Sazonov, 14 Dec. 1912 GBA 80 no. 389.

CHAPTER 4 The peace negotiations

1 Geshov to Toshev, Mishev, Kolushev, 11 Nov. 1912 *DPIK* 263 no. 6

2 Bax-Ironside to Grey, 20 Nov. 1912 *British Documents* IX 2, 180 no. 239

3 See Bertie to Grey, 19 Nov. 1912 ibid 175 no 234. In a minute Nicolson wrote: 'I do not see how S.E. Europe can be remapped and all subsidiary questions settled without a Conference. It is clear that all these great changes will have to be recorded in an instrument to be signed by all the Great Powers. Otherwise there will be confusion and misunderstandings in the future' (ibid 176). See also *DDF* IV 501–2 no. 493.

4 See Grey to Goschen, 27 Nov. 1912 *British Documents* IX 2, 219 no. 293; see also Toshev *Balkanskite voini* II 86.

5 King Ferdinand to Geshov, 18 Nov. 1912 *DPIK* 266 no. 14

6 Geshov to King Ferdinand ibid 264 no. 11; and 19 Nov., 265 no. 12

7 Toshev *Balkanskite voini* II 73; Fichev *Balkanskata voina* 224

8 See Geshov to King Ferdinand, 22 Nov. 1912 *DPIK* 270 no. 24 and n; Geshov to Danev (at military headquarters), 22 Nov. 1912 ibid 271 no. 25; and Toshev *Balkanskite voini* II 73–4.

9 Geshov to King Ferdinand, 19 Nov. 1912 *DPIK* 265–6 no. 12; See also *British Documents* IX 2, 173 no. 230; *DDF* IV 501–2 no. 493; *ÖUA* IV 959 no. 4540.

10 A. Girginov *Narodnata katastrofa – voinite 1912–1913 g.* (Sofia 1926) 53; Toshev *Balkanskite voini* II 75

11 Toshev *Balkanskite voini* II 75; Girginov *Narodnata katastrofa* 53; Fishev *Balkanskata voina* 222–4; Đorđević *Izlazak Srbije* 90; V.A. Zheborkritskii *Bolgariia v period balkanskikh voin 1912–1913 g.g.* (Kiev 1961) 80; D. Popović *Borba za narodno ujedinjenje 1908–1918* (Belgrade 1935) 87

12 Toshev *Balkanskite voini* II 75; Girginov *Narodnata katastrofa* 53; Fichev *Balkanskata voina* 222–4; Đorđević *Izlazak Srbije* 90; V.A. Zheborkritskii *Bolgaria v period balkanskikh voin 1912–1913 g.g.* 80; D. Popović *Borba za narodno ujedinjenje 1908–1918* 87. See also Mogilevich and Airapetian *Na putiakh k mirovoi voine* 136.

13 Danev to Geshov, 4 Dec. 1912 *DPIK* 279 no. 44 and 283–4 no. 54 (gives the complete text of the armistice protocol). See also *British Documents* IX 2, 248–9 no. 332; *GP* XXXIII 447 no. 12476; *DDF* V I no. 1.

14 Izvol'skii to Sazonov, 25 Nov. 1912 *RS* 5 (1915) 260 no. 48; Berchtold, circular, 24

Nov. 1912 *ÖUA* IV 997 no. 4599 and 1007 no. 4611; Grey to Cartwright, 25 Nov. 1912 *British Documents* IX 2, 204 no. 276; *DDF* IV 559 no. 561

15 See ch 3.

16 Kiderlen to Lichnowsky, 18 Nov. 1912 *GP* XXXIV 1, 3 no. 12500; Grey to Goschen, 21 Nov. 1912 *British Documents* IX 2, 182 no. 243; P. Cambon to Poincaré, 18 Nov. 1912 *DDF* IV 491 no. 483

17 Grey to Goschen, 21 Nov. 1912 *British Documents* IX 2, 182 no. 243; Poincaré to P. Cambon, 22 Nov. 1912 *DDF* IV 524 no. 520

18 Grey to Goschen, 21 Nov. 1912 *British Documents* IX 2, 182 no. 243; Lichnowsky to Kiderlen, 20 Nov. 1912 *GP* XXXIV 1, 4–5 no. 12501

19 P. Cambon to Poincaré, 22 Nov. 1912 *DDF* IV 527 no. 524; Grey to Bertie, 22 Nov. 1912 *British Documents* IX 2, 186 no. 294; E. Grey *Twenty-five Years 1892–1916* I 255

20 Buchanan to Grey, 22 Nov. 1912 *British Documents* IX 2, 189 no. 254

21 Buchanan to Grey, 25 Nov. 1912 ibid 200 no. 270. See also Louis to Poincaré, 28 Nov. 1912 *DDF* IV 599–600 no. 586.

22 Grey to Buchanan, 26 Nov. 1912 *British Documents* IX 2, 200–1 ed note

23 Buchanan to Grey, 27 Nov. 1912 ibid 214 no. 290

24 Ibid 215 minute to no. 290

25 P. Cambon to Poincaré, 27 Nov. 1912 *DDF* IV 579–80 no. 582

26 See Grey to Bertie, 27 Nov. 1912 *British Documents* IX 2, 217 no. 292; Poincaré to Louis, 27 Nov. 1912 *DDF* IV 577 no. 580; Benckendorff to Sazonov, 28 Nov. 1912 *Siebert* II 507–8 no. 738; Grey to Buchanan, 28 Nov. 1912 *British Documents* IX 2, 221 and 225 no. 296 and 301.

27 Grey to Goschen, 28 Nov. 1912 *British Documents* IX 2, 222 no. 297; aide-mémoire, 29 Nov. 1912 *GP* XXXIV 1, 9–10 no. 12504. In connection with the second question Grey mentioned Albania, Serbian access to the Adriatic, the Aegean islands, and Constantinople and the Straits as the most obvious points if the allies attempted to claim them.

28 Grey to Cartwright, 29 Nov. 1912 *British Documents* IX 2, 230 no. 307; Mensdorff to Berchtold, 29 Nov. 1912 *ÖUA* IV 1070–1 no. 4707

29 Kiderlen to von Tschirschky, 1 Dec. 1912 *GP* XXXIV 1, 10–11 no. 12505

30 Circular, 1 Dec. 1912 *ÖUA* V 8–10 no. 4735; Berchtold to Mensdorff, 5 Dec. 1912 ibid 38–9 no. 4784

31 Grey to Cartwright, 6 Dec. 1912 *British Documents* IX 2, 256 no. 345; Mensdorff to Berchtold, 6 Dec. 1912 *ÖUA* V 45–6 no. 4797

32 Cartwright to Grey, 7 Dec. 1912 *British Documents* IX 2, 260 no. 351; Berchtold to Mensdorff, 5 Dec. 1912 *ÖUA* V 38–9 no. 4784

33 Grey to Buchanan, 5 Dec. 1912 *British Documents* IX 2, 249 no. 333; Bertie to Grey, 7 Dec. 1912 ibid 259 no. 348; and Buchanan to Grey, 4 Dec. 1912 ibid 241 no. 325

34 Grey to Goschen, 7 Dec. 1912 ibid 259 no. 349; and Grey to Buchanan, 7 Dec. 1912 ibid 259–60 no. 350

35 Sazonov to Benckendorff, Izvol'skii, 9 Dec. 1912 *RS* 5 (1915) 262 no. 54; *Siebert* II 524–7 no. 756

36 Sazonov to Benckendorff, Izvol'skii, 9 Dec. 1912 *RS* 5 (1915) 262 no. 54; *Siebert* II 524–7 no. 756. See also communication from Count Benckendorff, 11 Dec. 1912 *British Documents* IX 2, 278–80 no. 374 and enclosure; Sazonov to Benckendorff, 12 Dec. 1912 *RS* 6 (1915) 420–2 no. 57.

37 Izvol'skii to Sazonov, 17 Dec. 1912 *GBA* 28 no. 453

38 Berchtold to Mensdorff, 15 Dec. 1912 *ÖUA* v 124–9 and 129–31 no. 4924 and 4925

39 Kiderlen to Lichnowsky, 15 Dec. 1912 *GP* XXXIV 1, 44–5 no. 12540; Mérey to Berchtold (Rome), 14 Dec. 1912 *ÖUA* v 140 no. 4935

40 See Helmreich *The Diplomacy of the Balkan Wars 1912–1913* 249.

41 See *British Documents* IX 2, 292 ed note.

42 Grey to Cartwright, 17 Dec. 1912 ibid 292 no. 391; Grey to Bertie, 16 Dec. 1912 ibid 290 no. 387; Grey *Twenty-five Years* I 257

43 For the opening session of the ambassadorial conference see *Siebert* II 538–9 no. 765; 541–2 no. 766; *British Documents* IX 2, 292–3 no. 391; *DDF* v 94–6 no. 78; *GP* XXXIV 1, 53–4 no. 12545.

44 Benckendorff to Sazonov, 17 and 18 Dec. 1912 *Siebert* II no. 765 and 766

45 Benckendorff to Sazonov, 20 Dec. 1912 *GBA* 36 no. 415; *Siebert* II 552–3 no. 778; and Sazonov to Benckendorff, 19 Dec. 1912 *GBA* 36 no. 2930. For the third session see also *British Documents* IX 2, 320–3 no. 403; *ÖUA* v 183–4 no. 4994. After prolonged negotiations Russia and Austria-Hungary reached an agreement in June 1913; for the terms see *ÖUA* VI no. 7535.

46 Grey to Paget, 20 Dec. 1912 *British Documents* IX 2, 304–5 no. 404. See also Hartwig to Sazonov, 19 Dec. 1912 *GBA* 80 no. 401, and Grey to Paget 18 Dec. 1912 *British Documents* IX 2, 293.

47 Đorđević *Izlazak Srbije* 136 ff

48 For an evaluation of the reaction of the press in Russia see Buchanan to Grey, 22 Dec. 1912 *British Documents* IX 2, 311 no. 409, and 23 Dec. 23 1912 ibid 313 no. 412.

49 Hartwig to Sazonov, 19 Dec. 1912 *GBA* 80 no. 401; Đorđević *Izlazak Srbije* 136 ff; *DDF* v 51–2 no. 38

50 Benckendorff to Sazonov, 20 Dec. 1912 *GBA* 36 no. 419; Benckendorff to Sazonov, 20 Dec. 1912 *Siebert* II 555–6 no. 779

51 *GBA* 36 no. 419; *Siebert* II 555–6 no. 779. See also Lichnowsky to Kiderlen, 20 Dec. 1912 *GP* XXXIV 1, 63–4 no. 12557; Mensdorff to Berchtold, 20 Dec. 1912 *ÖUA* v 184 no. 4995.

52 For the second session see *Siebert* II 542–4, no. 768. *British Documents* IX 2, 295–6 no. 394; *GP* XXXIV 1, 56–8 no. 12549; *ÖUA* v 156–7 no. 4957, 4958.

53 Sazonov to Benckendorff, 17 Dec. 1912 GBA 36 no. 2911
54 Benckendorff to Sazonov, 28 Dec. 1912 *Siebert* II 543 no. 768; *British Documents* IX 2, 295–6 no. 394
55 Sazonov to Benckendorff, 21 Dec. 1912 GBA 36 no. 2950. On the question of Mt Athos see also ibid 36 no. 2971, and 70 no. 2926, 171, and 174.
56 See *British Documents* IX 2, 302–3 no. 403; *Siebert* II 555 no. 779; *ÖUA* V 185 no. 4996; *GP* XXXIV 1, 63–4 no. 12557.
57 Giers to Sazonov, 19 Dec. 1912 GBA 75 no. 256; and 20 Dec. 1912, no. 257
58 Giers to Sazonov, 22 Dec. 1912 ibid no. 262
59 Benckendorff to Sazonov, 18 Dec. 1912 *Siebert* II 542–3 no. 768
60 Sazonov to Benckendorff, 20 Dec. 1912 GBA 36 no. 2940; *Siebert* II 551–2 no. 776
61 Sazonov to Benckendorff, 20 Dec. 1912 GBA 36 no. 2940; *Siebert* II 551–2 no. 776
62 Sazonov to Giers, 24 Dec. 1912 GBA 75 no. 2972
63 Hartwig to Sazonov, 4 Jan. 1912 ibid 80 no. 428
64 Hartwig to Sazonov, 22 Dec. 1912 ibid no. 409
65 Hartwig to Sazonov, 30 Dec. 1912 ibid no 422
66 See Sazonov to Benckendorff, 9 Dec. 1912 *Siebert* II 525 no. 756.
67 As Nicolson put it: 'To my mind it is a matter, selfishly speaking, of perfect indifference to us as to who should be the possessor of Scutari, but it is of great importance that we should adopt no line which would in any way weaken or impair our understanding with Russia ...' (Nicolson to Buchanan, 31 Dec. 1912 *British Documents* IX 2, 325 no. 428). See also ibid 310–11 no. 409; and GBA 28 no. 464.
68 Grey to Buchanan, 25 Dec. 1912 *British Documents* IX 2, 315 no. 414; Grey to Rodd, 19 Dec. 1912 ibid 299 no. 399
69 See *British Documents* IX 2, 311, 314, 318 no. 410, 413, 419; *ÖUA* V 237–8 no. 5057 and 5058.
70 Sazonov to Benckendorff, 26 Dec. 1912 *Siebert* II 560 no. 786. See also *ÖUA* V 237–8 no. 5057 and 5058 and 255 no. 5088.
71 Berchtold to Thurn, 27 Dec. 1912 *ÖUA* V 253 no. 5086
72 See Urgon to Berchtold, 4 Jan. 1913 *ÖUA* V 322 no. 5180; Grey to Paget, 8 Jan. 1913 *British Documents* IX 2, 376 no. 472; Grey to Cartwright, 9 Jan. 1913 ibid 379 no. 477.
73 Grey to Buchanan, 2 Jan. 1913 *British Documents* IX 2, 337 no. 438
74 Benckendorff to Sazonov, 3 Jan. 1913 *Siebert* III 9–10 no. 797. See also *British Documents* IX 2, 348–9 no. 443 and 444, and 354, no. 450.
75 See ch 3.
76 Grey to Rodd, 4 Jan. 1913 *British Documents* IX 2, 355, no. 452. See also *ÖUA* V 248 no. 5077, and 349 no. 5216.
77 Mensdorff to Berchtold, 7 Jan. 1913 *ÖUA* V 370–1 no. 5244; Berchtold to Mensdorff, 8 Jan. 1913 ibid 384 no. 5269. See also Grey to Cartwright, 7 Jan. 1913 *British Documents* IX 2, 371 no. 464.

78 Mensdorff to Berchtold, 7 Jan. 1913 *ÖUA* v 370–1 no. 5244; Berchtold to Mensdorff, 8 Jan. 1913 ibid 384 no. 5269. See also Grey to Cartwright, 7 Jan. 1913 *British Documents* IX 2, 371 no. 464.

79 Buchanan to Nicolson, 9 Jan. 1913 *British Documents* IX 2, 383 no. 481

80 See Sazonov to Benckendorff, 4 Jan. 1913 *Siebert* III 12–13 no. 800; Benckendorff to Sazonov, 5 Jan. 1913 ibid 16–17 no. 805; Benckendorff to Sazonov, 14 Jan. 1913 ibid 45, no. 827.

81 Benckendorff to Sazonov, 22 Jan. 1913 *Siebert* III 55–6 no. 835 and 56–8 no. 836. See also *ÖUA* v 515–16 no. 5488 and 5489.

82 Sazonov to Benckendorff, 24 Jan 1913 *RS* 6 (1915) 431 no. 71

83 Benckendorff to Sazonov, 25 Jan. 1913 *Siebert* III 63–6 no. 841. See also *British Documents* IX 2, 447–8 no. 559, and *ÖUA* v 542–3 no. 5535.

84 Lichnowsky to Bethmann-Hollweg, 26 Jan 1913 *GP* XXXIV 1, 270 no. 12748

85 For the composition of the peace delegations see: Nekliudov to Sazonov, 8 Dec. 1912 GBA 67 no. 297 (Bulgarian); Hartwig to Sazonov, 17 Dec. 1912 ibid 80 no. 80 (Serbian); Demidov to Sazonov, 6 Dec. 1912 ibid 70 no. 154 (Greek); Toshev *Balkanskite voini* II 85 (Montenegrin); Giers to Sazonov, 9 Dec. 1912 GBA 58 no. 1157 (Turkish).

86 *British Documents* IX 2, 292 ed note

87 Girginov *Narodnata katastrofa* 61; Toshev *Balkanskite voini* II 148

88 Danev to Geshov, London, 24 Dec. 1912 *DPIK* 287 no. 61

89 Danev to Geshov, 26 Dec. 1912 ibid 287 no. 63

90 Danev to Geshov, 28 Dec. 1912 ibid 288 no. 65

91 Danev to Geshov, 2 Jan. 1913 ibid 291 no. 73, and 4 Jan. 1913 ibid 293 no. 80

92 Ibid 293 no. 80

93 Danev to Geshov, 7 Jan 1913 ibid 296 no. 88

94 Grey to Cartwright, 4 Jan. 1913 *British Documents* IX 2, 354–5 no. 451; Grey to Lowther, 6 Jan. 1913 ibid 358 no. 456. See also *Siebert* III 23–8 no. 809–13.

95 See *British Documents* IX 2 no. 475, 476, 477, 513, 516; *ÖUA* v 394–7 no. 5290–4; GBA 59 no. 27.

96 Giers to Sazonov, Constantinople, 17 Jan. 1913 *RS* 6 (1915), 428 no. 69

97 Giers to Sazonov, 23 Jan. 1913 ibid 429 no. 70; Lowther to Grey, 23 Jan. 1913 *British Documents* IX 2, 438 no. 544

98 Toshev *Balkanskite voini* II 154–5; also Giers to Sazonov 30 Dec. 1912 GBA 58 no. 131

99 See Giers to Sazonov, 23 Jan. 1913 RS 6 (1915) 428 no. 70; Lowther to Grey, 23 Jan. 1913 *British Documents* IX 2 438; Toshev *Balkanskite voini* II 155.

100 Danev to Geshov, 23 Jan. 1913 *DPIK* 301 no. 103; Madzharov to Geshov, 25 Jan. 1913 ibid 302 no. 106. See also ibid 291 and 292 no. 74 and 76; Fichev *Balkanskata voina* 244–7, 278–81; Toshev *Balkanskite voini* II 152–4.

101 See Sazonov to Paris and London, 25 Jan. 1913 *RS* 6 (1915) 430 no. 72, and to Sofia

and Belgrade, 28 Jan. 1913 ibid 431 no. 74; Bobchev to Geshov, 28 Jan. 1913 *DPIK* 305 no. 115.

102 Geshov to Danev, 24 Jan. 1913 *DPIK* 301 no. 104

103 Danev to Geshov 25 Jan. 1913 ibid 303 no. 108, and 26 Jan. 1913 ibid 304 no. 110

104 Danev to Geshov, 26 Jan. 1913 ibid 304 no 111

105 Danev to Geshov, 29 Jan. 1913 ibid 306 no. 117

106 Geshov, circular, 30 Jan. 1913 ibid 249 no. 55, and 306 no. 120

107 Giers to Sazonov, 31 Jan. 1913 *RS* 6 (1915), 431 no. 75; *British Documents* IX 2, 468–70 no. 583

108 Giers to Sazonov, 30 Jan. 1913 *RS* 6 (1915) 432 no. 76

109 Ministerstvo na voinata *Voinata mezhdu Bŭlgariia i Turtsiia* VII 165–73; Ganchev *Balkanskata voina* 178–85

110 Ganchev *Balkanskata voina* 185–96; N. Ivanov *Balkanskata voina, 1912–1913* (Sofia 1924) 193–230; A. Semenov *Blokada i shturm Adrianopolia* (St Petersburg 1914)

111 Sazonov to Nekliudov, 31 Jan. 1913 *RS* 6 (1915) 433 no. 77. See also Sazonov to Nekliudov, 31 Jan. 1913 *FRO* 330 no. 166; Stanchov to Geshov, 1 Feb. 1913 *DPIK* 307 no. 122.

112 Quoted in Mogilevich and Airapetian *Na putiakh k morovoi voine* 145–6; and A. Zaionchkovskii *Podgotovka Rossii k mirovoi voine v mezhdunarodom otnoshenii* (Moscow 1926) 291. See also Bobchev *Stranitsi* 105.

113 Mogilevich and Airapetian *Na putiakh k mirovoi voine* 145–6; and A. Zaionchkovskii *Podgotovka Rossii k mirovoi voine v mezhdunarodom otnoshenii* 291; Bobchev *Stranitsi* 105. See also Izvol'skii to Sazonov, 10 April 1913 *FRO* 362 no. 169; *British Documents* IX 2, 649 no. 800; 655 no. 807; 660 no. 815; *DDF* VI 219–21 no. 181.

114 Ganchev *Balkanskata voina* 179–80. See also M. Vojvodić *Skadarska kriza 1913 godine* (Belgrade 1970).

115 Ganchev *Balkanskata voina* 178–9

116 Ibid 179

117 Grey to de Salis, 28 Jan. 1913 *British Documents* IX 2, 245 no. 565; Vojvodić *Skadarska kriza*

118 Barclay to Grey, 4 Feb. 1913 *British Documents* IX 2, 474 no. 589, and 10 Feb. 487 no. 603; Paget to Grey, 18 Feb. ibid 507 no. 628

119 Buchanan to Grey, 6 Feb. 1913 ibid 478 no. 593

120 Grey to Buchanan, 6 Feb. 1913 ibid 479 no. 594

121 See Ćorović *Odnosi između Srbije i Austro-ugarske* 428–30.

122 Sazonov to Benckendorff, 6 Feb. 1913 *Siebert* III 79–83 no. 856, and *ÖUA* V no. 5675, 5676, 5679, 5697

123 Berchtold to Thurn, 22 Feb. 1913 *ÖUA* V 801–3 no. 5909. See also *British Documents* IX 2, 530 no. 652; 541 no. 661; *GP* XXXIV 2, 456 no. 12934.

124 Ćorović *Odnosi između Srbije i Austro-ugarske* 429
125 Izvol'skii to Sazonov, 10 Feb. 1913 *RS* 6 (1915) 435, no. 79; *FRO* 331 no. 55. See also *British Documents* IX 2, 489 no. 605; 479 no. 594; *ÖUA* V 648 no. 5693.
126 Berchtold, circular, 7 Feb. 1913 *ÖUA* V 667-8 no. 5712; Thurn to Berchtold ibid 671-2 no. 5720
127 Benckendorff to Sazonov, 15 Feb. 1913 *Siebert* III 97-9 no. 875
128 Grey to Buchanan, 20 Feb. 1913 *British Documents* IX 2, 513 no. 634; Berchtold to Mensdorff, 18 Feb. 1913 *ÖUA* V 765-6 no. 5855
129 Paget to Grey, 22 Feb. 1913 *British Documents* IX 2, 527 no. 649
130 Quoted in Ćorović *Odnosi između Srbije i Austro-ugarske* 433
131 Sazonov to Benckendorff, 20 Feb. 1913 *Siebert* III 103-4 no. 882; *RS* 6 (1915) 436 no. 83
132 Sazonov to Benckendorff, 19 Feb. 1913 *Siebert* III 101, and 102 no. 879 and 880
133 Berchtold to Mensdorff, 4 March 1913 *ÖUA* V 867-8 no. 6012 and 876 no. 6024. See also *Siebert* III 129-30 no. 908; *British Documents* IX 2, 555 no. 683, and 556 no. 684.
134 Grey to Buchanan, 10 March 1913 *British Documents* IX 2, 564 no. 692
135 Buchanan to Grey, 12 March 1913 ibid 575 no. 705
136 Berchtold to Mensdorff, 14 March 1913 *ÖUA* V 955-6 no. 6142; Mensdorff to Berchtold, 15 March 1913 ibid 972 no. 6160. See also *British Documents* IX 2, 588 no. 719-20.
137 Grey to Buchanan, 17 March 1913 *British Documents* IX 2, 592-3 no. 724
138 Berchtold to Mensdorff, 20 March 1913 *ÖUA* V 1014 no. 6230; Mensdorff to Berchtold, 21 March 1913 ibid 1022 no. 6244, 6245
139 Grey to Paget, 22 March 1913 *British Documents* IX 2, 612 no. 749. See also *ÖUA* V 1032 no. 6261; *DDF* VI 70-2 no. 49.
140 Sazonov to Benckendorff, 24 Feb. 1913 *RS* 6 (1915) 440 no. 92
141 Buchanan to Grey, 22 March 1913 *British Documents* IX 2, 610 no. 745, and 573 no. 701
142 Communication from Tewfik Pasha, 28 Feb. 1913 ibid 667 no. 668. See also *RS* 6 (1915) 437 no. 86; *DPIK* 310 no. 130.
143 See Sazonov to Paris and London, 6 March 1913 *FRO* 340 no. 498 and *RS* 6 (1915) 438 no. 87; Geshov to Athens, Belgrade, Cetinje, 5 March 1913 *DPIK* 310 no. 132.
144 Puliev to Geshov, Belgrade, 10 March 1913 *DPIK* 314 no. 142 and 313-16 no. 141, 143, 145; *British Documents* IX 2, 583-4 no. 713
145 Elliot to Grey, 23 March 1913 *British Documents* IX 2, 613-14 no. 749 and enclosure; *DPIK* 317 no. 150; *GP* XXXIV 2, 352 no. 13014
146 See *DPIK* 317 no. 149; 333-4 no. 197; and Girginov *Narodnata katastrofa* 81-2.
147 Geshov *Prestŭpnoto bezumie* 77. See also *DPIK* 325 no. 175; 326 no. 178; 329 no. 187.

148 Sazonov to Izvol'skii and Benckendorff, 30 March 1913 *RS* 6 (1915) 448 no. 99
149 Giers to Sazonov, Constantinople, 30 March 1913 ibid 448 no. 100; *British Documents* IX 2, 624 no. 763 and n 3; *DDF* VI 177 no. 141
150 Giers to Sazonov, 1 April 1913 *RS* 6 (1915) 449 no. 101; Lowther to Grey, 1 April 1913 *British Documents* IX 2, 631 no. 775
151 Madzharov *Diplomaticheskata podgotovka* 131; Girginov *Narodnata katastrofa* 89. See also A. Giers to Sazonov, 27 March 1913 *RS* 6 (1915) 447 no. 96.
152 Geshov to Athens, Belgrade, Cetinje, 29 March 1913 *DPIK* 322 no. 164
153 Same to same, 31 March 1913 ibid 324 no. 169
154 Geshov, circular, 2 April 1913 ibid 325 no. 174
155 Geshov to Athens, Belgrade, Cetinje, 5 April 1913 ibid 325 no. 176; Geshov, circular ibid 326 no. 177
156 See Geshov to Athens, Belgrade, Cetinje, 29 March 1913 *DPIK* 322 no. 164; *British Documents* IX 2, 655 no. 808.
157 See Bobchev *Stranitsi* 105 ff.
158 Girginov *Narodnata katastrofa* 91; Toshev *Balkanskite voini* II 214
159 Geshov *Prestŭpnoto bezumie* 79. See also Bobchev to Geshov, 12 April 1913 *DPIK* 330, no. 189.
160 Geshov to Savov, 12 April 1913 *DPIK* 330 no. 188
161 Savov to Geshov, Adrianople, 13 April 1913 ibid 330 no. 190, 331 no. 191, and 18 April ibid 335 no. 200
162 Geshov to Bobchev, 13 April 1913 ibid 332 no. 194
163 Geshov to Athens, Belgrade, Cetinje, 13 April 1913 ibid 332 no. 193. See also ibid 329 no. 185; and *British Documents* IX 2, 686 no. 816 and n.
164 Geshov to Athens, Belgrade, Cetinje, 13 April 1913 ibid 332 no. 193
165 Toshev *Balkanskite voini* II 215; Girginov *Narodnata katastrofa* 93–6. See also *British Documents* IX 2, 705–6 no. 867.
166 Grey to Buchanan, 24 April 1913 *British Documents* IX 2, 717 no. 883
167 Grey to Elliot, 23 April 1913 ibid 710 no. 874
168 See Popović *Borba za narodno ujedinjenje* 118 ff.
169 Ibid. See also Paget to Grey, 1 April 1913 *British Documents* IX 2, 630–1 no. 774; Urgon to Berchtold, 29 March 1913 *ÖUA* V 1092 no. 6357.
170 Sazonov to Giers, 23 March 1913 *RS* 6 (1915) 440 no. 91
171 Popović *Borba za narodno ujedinjenje* 119
172 Ibid 121
173 Giers to Sazonov, 27 March 1913 *RS* 6 (1915) 447 no. 96. On the Scutari crisis see particularly Vojvodić *Skadarska kriza*.
174 A. Lainović 'Pitanje Skadra u prvom balkanskom ratu' *Istoriski zapisi* IV (1949) 70
175 See *Siebert* III 149–51 no. 929, 930, 931; *British Documents* IX 2, 625 no. 766 and 767; *GP* XXXIV 2, 593–4 no. 13058.

176 Benckendorff to Sazonov, 31 March 1913 *RS* 6 (1915) 448 no. 98; Rodd to Grey, 1 April 1913 *British Documents* IX 2, 633 no. 778; Buchanan to Grey, 3 April 1913 ibid 647 no. 798

177 Buchanan to Grey, 2 April 1913 ibid 641 no. 791; Delcassé to Pichon, 2 April 1913 *DDF* V 208–9 no. 169

178 Buchanan to Grey, 3 April 1913 *British Documents* IX 2, 646 no. 796

179 See *British Documents* IX 2, 653 no. 805; *DDF* VI 285–8 no. 194; *ÖUA* VI 31–2 no. 6448–51; *GP* XXXIV 2, 614–16 no. 13082.

180 Popović *Borba za narodno ujedinjenje* 125; Ćorović *Odnosi između Srbije i Austro-ugarske* 442

181 Popović *Borba za narodno ujedinjenje* 125; Ćorović *Odnosi između Srbije i Austro-ugarske* 442. See also Izvol'skii to Sazonov, 12 April 1913 *FRO* 363 no. 172; and *British Documents* IX 2, 669 no. 825; 676 no. 834.

182 De Salis to Grey, 6 April 1913 *British Documents* IX 2, 657 no. 811

183 Same to same, 20 April 1913 ibid 704 no. 865

184 See A. Lainović 'Građa iz borbe oko Skadra 1913 godine' *Istoriski zapisi* V 1–3 (1950) 107–30. See also Vojvodić *Skadarska kriza*.

185 Benckendorff to Sazonov, 23 April 1913 *RS* 7 (1915) 6 no. 110

186 Same to same, 25 April 1913 ibid 7 no. 111; Lainović 'Građa iz borbe' 122 no. 19

187 Grey to Cartwright, 28 April 1913 *British Documents* IX 2, 725 no. 894

188 Sazonov to Izvol'skii and Benckendorff, 26 April 1913 *RS* 7 (1915) 7 no. 112; Buchanan to Grey, 23 April 1913 *British Documents* IX 2, 712–13 no. 878

189 See Ćorović *Odnosi između Srbije i Austro-ugarske* 443.

190 Buchanan to Grey, 23 April 1913 *British Documents* IX 2, 712–13 no. 878; Izvol'skii to Sazonov, 25 April 1913 *FRO* 368 no. 194

191 Grey to Goschen, 1 May 1913 *British Documents* IX 2, 746 no. 922

192 Sazonov, circular, 2 May 1913 *FRO* 373 no. 1126

193 See Ćorović *Odnosi između Srbije i Austro-ugarske* 446.

194 See ibid 447; Popović *Borba za narodno ujedinjenje* 127.

195 De Salis to Grey, 4 May 1913 *British Documents* IX 2, 766 no. 948; also Benckendorff to Sazonov, *RS* 7 (1915) 9 no. 116

196 See *British Documents* IX 2, 730 n 3 and 751 n 7.

197 Madzharov to Geshov, 2 May 1913 *DPIK* 338 no. 209; *British Documents* IX 2, 751 n 8

198 Giers to Sazonov, Constantinople, 3 May 1913 *RS* 7 (1915) 11 no. 120

199 See *GP* XXXIV 2, 807 no. 13279; *DDF* VI 541–2 no. 479; *British Documents* IX 2, 784 no. 967 and n 9.

200 For the text of the notes see *DPIK* 340 no. 217.

201 Geshov to Toshev, 14 May 1913 ibid 349 no. 234

202 See ch 6 and 7.

203 Geshov to Madzharov, 7 May 1913 *DPIK* 340 no. 215; also 339 no. 211; 339–40 no. 213
204 Geshov to Madzharov, 9 May 1913 ibid 344 no. 224
205 Toshev to Geshov, 12 May 1913 ibid 347 no. 229
206 Geshov to Athens, Belgrade, Cetinje, 10 May 1913 ibid 344–5 no. 225
207 Geshov, circular, 12 May 1913 ibid 347 no. 230, and 14 May 349 no. 236
208 Toshev to Geshov, 12 May 1913 ibid 347 no. 229; 343 no. 221; 343–4 no. 223
209 See Nekliudov to Sazonov, 14 May 1913 *RS* 7 (1915) 11 no. 121.
210 Geshov, circular, 14 May 1913 *DPIK* 349 no. 236; Grey to Bax-Ironside, 19 May 1913 *British Documents* IX 2, 798 no. 980 and no. 983
211 Danev to Geshov, London, 21 May 1913 *DPIK* 357 no. 254; 353 no. 244; 350 no. 237; 348 no. 233
212 Madzharov to Geshov, London, 21 May 1913 ibid 358 no. 256; Danev to Geshov ibid 358–9 no. 257; Grey to Elliot, 24 May 1914 *British Documents* IX 2, 811 no. 995
213 Savov to Geshov, Adrianople, 23 May 1913 *DPIK* 357 no. 256
214 Geshov to Savov, 24 May 1913 ibid 363 no. 266
215 Geshov to Bobchev, 21 May 1913 ibid 356 no. 251; Geshov to Madzharov, 20 May 1913 ibid 355 no. 248. See also *British Documents* IX 2, 814 no. 1001.
216 Geshov to Bobchev, 21 May 1913 *DPIK* 356 no. 251; Geshov to London, Paris, St Petersburg, 22 May 1913 ibid 360 no. 259
217 Geshov to Bobchev, 24 May 1913 ibid 365–6 no. 269
218 Grey to Paget, 27 May 1913 *British Documents* IX 2, 817–18 no. 1006, and 816 no. 1003; Danev to Geshov, 27 May 1913 *DPIK* 367 no. 272
219 Madzharov to Geshov, 30 May 1913 *DPIK* 368 no. 276, and Madzharov *Diplomaticheskata podgotovka* 142 ff. For the text of the Peace Treaty of London see *British Documents* IX 2, 1049–51; *DDF* VI 541–2 no. 479; Toshev *Balkanskite voini* II 483–4; Kesiakov *Prinos kŭm diplomaticheskata istoriia* I 51–2; Bobchev *Stranitsi* 141–2.

CHAPTER 5 The Bulgaro-Rumanian dispute

1 A.F. Pribram *Secret Treaties of Austria-Hungary* I 78–84
2 See B.H. Sumner *Russia and the Balkans* 302–39, 463–70, 536–7; General R. Rosetti 'Rumania's Share in the War of 1877' *Slavonic Review* VIII (1929–30) 548–77; R.W. Seton-Watson *A History of the Roumanians from Roman Times to the Completion of Unity* (Cambridge 1934) 337 ff.
3 Sumner *Russia and the Balkans* 537–8, 569–70; Seton-Watson *A History of the Roumanians* 346–7; Sazonov *Fateful Years* 103–5
4 Seton-Watson *A History of the Roumanians* 361

5 Ibid 347
6 Cartwright to Grey, 12 Aug. 1910 *British Documents* IX 1, 196-7 no. 172
7 Fürstenberg to Berchtold (Bucharest), 17 Sept. 1909 *ÖUA* II 468-9 no. 1740
8 Sazonov *Fateful Years* 103
9 Ibid 106
10 Giers to Sazonov, 1 Mar. 1912 GBA 77 no. 9
11 See ibid; Sevastopulo to Sazonov (Paris), 16 Jan. 1913 GBA29 no. ng; Nekliudov to
Sazonov, 7 Jan. 1913 GBA 67 no. 326; Mogilevich and Airapetian *Na putiakh k
mirovoi voine* 141.
12 Ikonomov to Geshov (Bucharest), 24 July 1912 *DPIK* 206 no. 2
13 Geshov to Ikonomov, 2 Aug. 1912 ibid 207 no. 3; G.I. Kalinkov *Romūniia i neinata
politika spremo Bŭlgariia prez 1912 i 1913 g.* (Sofia 1917) 97
14 Ikonomov to Geshov, 7 July 1912 *DPIK* 208 no. 4
15 Kalinkov *Romūniia* 97. The Rumanian leaders were informed of the existence of the
Serbo-Bulgarian treaty of alliance a few weeks after its conclusion by Berlin. See E.
Jäckh *Kiderlen-Wächter, der Staatsmann und Mensch* II (Stuttgart 1925) 186.
16 Geshov to Ikonomov, 24 Aug. 1912 *DPIK* 210-11 no. 5
17 Nekliudov to Sazonov, 4 Sept. 1912 *MO* XX 2, 45 no. 622; I.E. Geshov *Prestŭpnoto
bezumie* 62
18 Lysakovskii to Sazonov (Bucharest), 15 Aug. 1912 *RS* 10 (1915) 17 no. 307
19 Zhebokritskii *Bolgariia nakanune* 231; S. Danev *Balkanský svaz a válka s Tureckem,
1912-1913. Přednašky Slovanského Ústavu v Praze* (Prague 1935) 10
20 Ikonomov to Geshov, 14 Aug. 1912 *DPIK* 208 no. 4. Also Lysakovskii to Sazonov,
26 Aug. 1912 *MO* XX 2, 91-2 no. 560; GBA 77 no. 58
21 Kalinkov to Geshov (Bucharest), 6 Oct. 1912 *DPIK* 657 no. 1; Shebeko to Sazonov, 6
Oct. 1912 *RS* 10 (1915) 18 no. 308
22 Zhebokritskii *Bolgariia nakanune* 232
23 Ibid; Kholmsen to Zhilinskii (Constantinople), 12 Sept. 1912 *MO* XX 2, 203 no. 674
24 S. Danev 'Moiata misiia v Krim prez 1912 god.' *Rodina* (Sofia) II (1940) no. 3, 126
25 Shebeko to Sazonov, 24 Sept. 1912 *MO* XX 2, 263 no. 758
26 Ibid 324 n 2; Shebeko to Sazonov, 24 Sept. 1912 ibid 263 no. 758; Shebeko to
Sazonov, 11 Dec. 1912 GBA 77 no. 146, 12 Dec. 1912 GBA 77 no. 153
27 Kholmsen to Zhilinskii, 12 Sept. 1912 *MO* XX 2, 203 no. 674
28 Neratov to Shebeko, 1 Oct. 1912 ibid XX 2, 324 no. 840
29 Shebeko to Sazonov, 30 Oct. 1912 GBA 77 no. 98
30 Ibid
31 Shebeko to Sazonov, 1 Nov. 1912 GBA77 no. 101; *RS* 10 (1915) 19 no. 310
32 Fürstenberg to Berchtold, 31 Oct. 1912 *ÖUA* IV 732-3 no. 4212
33 Kalinkov to Geshov, 2 Nov. 1912 *DPIK* 661 no. 14; Kalinkov *Romūniia* 116
34 Kalinkov *Romūniia* 116; Geshov *Prestŭpnoto bezumie* 62

35 Kalinkov *Romŭniia* 116; Geshov *Prestŭpnoto bezumie* 62
36 Nekliudov to Sazonov, 4 Nov. 1912 GBA 67 no. 229
37 Berchtold to Fürstenberg, 2 Nov. 1912 *ÖUA* IV 754 no. 4237
38 Kalinkov *Romŭniia* 117
39 Bobchev to Geshov (St Petersburg), 7 Nov. 1912 *DPIK* 665 no. 23; Bobchev *Stranitsi* 46
40 Nekliudov to Sazonov, 8 Nov. 1912 GBA 67 no. 237
41 Toshev *Balkanskite voini* II 52; *Prilozhenie* 29–30
42 Danev to Ferdinand (Budapest), nd *DPIK* 241 no. 51
43 *Prilozhenie* 31. See also S. Danev 'Poseshtenieto mi v Budapeshta prez oktomvri 1912 g.' *Sŭvremennik* (Sofia) II (1923) no. 6, 290 ff. For Count Berchtold's impressions see Berchtold to Fürstenberg, 11 Nov. 1912 *ÖUA* IV 843 no. 4368; 20 Nov. 1912 ibid 944 no. 4515.
44 Shebeko to Sazonov, 9 Nov. 1912 *RS* 10 (1915) 20 no. 311
45 Shebeko to Sazonov, 12 Nov. 1912 GBA 77 no. 110
46 Shebeko to Sazonov, 12 Nov. 1912 ibid 77 no. 112
47 Shebeko to Sazonov, 12 Nov. 1912 ibid 77 no. 113
48 Geshov to Bobchev, 14 Nov. 1912 *DPIK* 392 no. 5
49 Sazonov to Shebeko, 14 Nov. 1912 *RS* 10 (1915) 21 no. 313; Shebeko to Sazonov, 15 Nov. 1912 ibid 21 no. 314
50 Geshov to Ferdinand, 15 Nov. 1912 *DPIK* 666 no. 28
51 Nekliudov to Sazonov, 15 Nov. 1912 *RS* 10 (1915) 21 no. 315
52 Geshov to Ferdinand, 15 Nov. 1912 *DPIK* 666 no. 28; Nekliudov to Sazonov, 15 Nov. 1912 GBA 67 no. 252
53 Nekliudov to Sazonov, 15 Nov. 1912 *RS* 10 (1915) 21 no. 315
54 Geshov to Ferdinand, 15 Nov. 1912 *DPIK* 666 no. 28; Nekliudov to Sazonov, 17 Nov. 1912 *RS* 10 (1915) 22 no. 316
55 Geshov to Kalinkov, 16 Nov. 1912 *DPIK* 668 no. 31; Kalinkov *Romŭniia* 125
56 Kalinkov to Geshov, 13 Nov. 1912 *DPIK* 669 no. 32
57 Kalinkov to Geshov, 17 Nov. 1912 ibid 669 no. 33
58 Sazonov to Nekliudov, 24 Nov. 1912 *RS* 10 (1915) 22–3 no. 318
59 Sazonov to Nekliudov, 24 Nov. 1912 ibid 22 no. 318. See also Sazonov to Nekliudov, 19 Nov. 1912 GBA 67 no. ng.
60 Geshov to Kalinkov, nd *DPIK* 670 no. ng
61 Geshov to Bobchev, 24 Nov. 1912 ibid 672 no. 41; Nekliudov to Sazonov, 8 Dec. 1912 *RS* 10 (1915) 23 no. 320
62 Kalinkov *Romŭniia* 126
63 Shebeko to Sazonov, 11 Dec. 1912 GBA 77 no. 147; *RS* 10 (1915) 24 no. 321
64 Kalinkov to Geshov, 14 Dec. 1912 *DPIK* 672 no. 53
65 Ibid

66 Shebeko to Sazonov, 19 Dec. 1912 GBA 77 no. 159; Kalinkov *Romūniia* 138
67 Kalinkov *Romūniia* 131
68 Ibid 132
69 Shebeko to Sazonov, 24 Dec. 1912 GBA 77 no. 165; *RS* 11 (1915) 186 no. 324
70 Shebeko to Sazonov, 29 Dec. 1912 GBA 77 no. 171
71 Sazonov to Nekliudov, 30 Dec. 1912 *RS* 11 (1915) 186 no. 325; Shebeko to Sazonov, 26 Dec. 1912 GBA 77 no. 186; Kalinkov to Geshov, 25 Dec. 1912 *DPIK* 681 no. 58
72 Geshov to Danev, 24 Dec. 1912 *DPIK* 681 no. 56; 26 Dec. 1912 ibid 682 no. 59
73 Geshov to Danev, 24 Dec. 1912 ibid 681 no. 56
74 *Prilozhenie* 49
75 Benckendorff to Sazonov, 28 Dec. 1912 *RS* 11 (1915) 187 no. 326
76 Geshov to Danev, 29 Dec. 1912 *DPIK* 683 no. 63
77 Bobchev to Geshov, 30 Dec. 1912 ibid 683 no. 64
78 Bobchev to Geshov, 4 Jan. 1913 ibid 691 no. 86
79 Sazonov to Benckendorff, 3 Jan. 1913 *RS* 11 (1915) 188, no. 328; Bobchev to Geshov, 4 Jan. 1913 *DPIK* 686 no. 72; 691–2 no. 86
80 Sazonov to Shebeko, 7 Jan. 1913 *RS* 11 (1915) 189 no. 331
81 Nekliudov to Sazonov, 5 Jan. 1913 GBA 67 no. 321
82 Nekliudov to Sazonov, 5 Jan. 1913 ibid 67 no. 323; *RS* 11 (1915) 191 no. 330; Geshov to Bobchev, 5 Jan. 1913 *DPIK* 686 no. 73
83 Toshev *Balkanskite voini* 11 121–3
84 Danev to Geshov, 3 Jan. 1913 *DPIK* 685 no. 71
85 Danev to Geshov, 6 Jan. 1913 ibid 687 no. 76
86 Ibid; Danev to Geshov, 7 Jan. 1913 ibid 688 no. 79
87 Geshov to Danev, 6 Jan. 1913 ibid 688 no. 76
88 Danev to Geshov, 7 Jan. 1913 ibid 688 no. 79; Kalinkov to Geshov, 8 Jan. 1913 ibid 690 no. 83
89 Shebeko to Sazonov, 8 Jan. 1913 GBA 77 no. 186; Kalinkov to Geshov, 8 Jan. 1913 *DPIK* 689 no. 82
90 Kalinkov to Geshov, 8 Jan. 1913 *DPIK* 689 no. 82
91 Sazonov to Shebeko, 9 Jan. 1913 *RS* 11 (1915) 191 no. 333
92 Geshov to Danev, 8 Jan. 1913 *DPIK* 690 no. 84; Geshov to Kalinkov, 9 Jan. 1913 *DPIK* 692 no. 87; Shebeko to Sazonov, 10 Jan. 1913 GBA 77 no. 188
93 Danev to Geshov, 10 Jan. 1913 *DPIK* 693 no. 89; 694 no. 91
94 Danev to Geshov, 11 Jan. 1913 ibid 697 no. 97
95 Geshov to Danev, Bobchev, 11 Jan. 1913 ibid 697 no. 98
96 Ibid; Geshov to Danev, Bobchev, 11 Jan. 1913 ibid 697–8 no. 99
97 Shebeko to Sazonov, 13 Jan. 1913 GBA 77 no. 190, 193; Teodorov to Geshov (St Petersburg), 15 Jan. 1913 *DPIK* 702 no. 112
98 *DPIK* 702 no. 112

99 Fichev *Balkanskata voina* 280
100 Ibid; Nekliudov to Sazonov, 18 Jan. 1913 GBA 68 no. 4; Geshov *Prestŭpnoto bezumie* 49–50
101 Teodorov to Geshov, 13 Jan. 1913 *DPIK* 699 no. 104
102 Geshov to Teodorov, Danev, 16 Jan. 1913 ibid 704 no. 118
103 Teodorov to Geshov, 17 Jan. 1913 ibid 707 no. 125
104 Kalinkov to Geshov, 16 Jan. 1913 ibid 703 no. 114
105 Sazonov to Shebeko, 16 Jan. 1913 GBA 78 no. 27; Sazonov to Shebeko, 17 Jan. 1913 *RS* 11 (1915) 194–5 no. 339
106 Shebeko to Sazonov, 17 Jan. 1913 GBA 78 no. 3; Shebeko to Sazonov, 18 Jan. 1913 GBA 78 no. 5; Kalinkov to Geshov, 16 Jan. 1913 *DPIK* 703 no. 114
107 Danev to Geshov, 14 Jan. 1913 *DPIK* 703 no. 115
108 Danev to Geshov, 14 Jan. 1913 ibid 703 no. 116
109 Danev to Geshov, 16 Jan. 1913 ibid 705 no. 120
110 Danev to Geshov, 24 Jan. 1913 ibid 709–10 no. 134; Nekliudov to Sazonov, 18 Jan. 1913 *RS* 11 (1915) 195 no. 341, and 197 no. 344
111 Bobchev to Geshov, 20 Jan. 1913 *DPIK* 707 no. 127; Kalinkov to Geshov, 23 Jan. 1913 ibid 709 no. 131
112 Geshov to Danev, 21 Jan. 1913 ibid 708 no. 128; Geshov to Bobchev, 21 Jan. 1913 ibid 708 no. 129
113 A. Marghiloman *Note politice 1897–1924* 1 (Bucharest 1927) 143–5
114 Maiorescu to Mişu, 25 Jan. 1913 *Rumanian Documents* 39 no. 53
115 Danev to Geshov, 25 Jan. 1913 *DPIK* 710 no. 135; Geshov to Danev, 26 Jan. 1913 ibid 710 no. 136
116 Maiorescu to Mişu, 28 Jan. 1913 *Rumanian Documents* 40 no. 56
117 Danev to Geshov, 27 Jan. 1913 *DPIK* 711 no. 139; Shebeko to Sazonov, 28 Jan. 1913 *RS* 11 (1915) 198 no. 346
118 Danev to Geshov, 29 Jan. 1913 *DPIK* 714 no. 146, 147
119 Geshov, circular, 29 Jan. 1913 ibid 714 no. 148; Kalinkov to Geshov, 28 Jan. 1913 ibid 717 no. 154
120 Kalinkov to Geshov, 4 Feb. 1913 ibid 720 no. 158; Geshov to Kalinkov, 5 Feb. 1913 ibid 721 no. 162; Nekliudov to Sazonov, 7 Feb. 1913 *RS* 12 (1915) 381 no. 355
121 Bobchev to Geshov, 2 Feb. 1913 *DPIK* 718 no. 155
122 Danev to Geshov, 3 Feb. 1913 ibid 719 no. 157; Geshov to Bobchev, 3 Feb. 1913 ibid 719 no. 156
123 Sazonov to Shebeko, 29 Jan. 1913 *RS* 11 (1915) 199 no. 348. See also Nano to Maiorescu, 31 Jan. 1913 *Rumanian Documents* 46 no. 63.
124 Shebeko to Sazonov, 31 Jan. 1913 *RS* 11 (1915) 200 no. 349
125 Danev to Geshov, 29 Jan. 1913 *DPIK* 714 no. 146

126 Shebeko to Sazonov, 31 Jan. 1913 *RS* 11 (1915) 200–1 no. 349
127 Bobchev to Geshov, 10 Feb. 1913 *DPIK* 723 no. 167
128 Geshov to Bobchev, 11 Feb. 1913 ibid 723 no. 168
129 Sazonov to Shebeko, 2 Feb. 1913 *RS* 12 (1915) 380 no. 352
130 Sazonov to Shebeko, 10 Feb. 1913 ibid 382–3 no. 357
131 Shebeko to Sazonov, 12 Feb. 1913 ibid 383 no. 358
132 Geshov to Bobchev, 12 Feb. 1913 *DPIK* 724 no. 172
133 Kalinkov to Geshov, 11 Feb. 1913 ibid 723–4 no. 170
134 Geshov to Bobchev, ibid 724 no. 172
135 Bobchev to Geshov, 12 Feb. 1913 ibid 725–6 no. 175
136 Nekliudov to Sazonov, 13 Feb. 1913 *RS* 12 (1915) 385 no. 361
137 Geshov to Bobchev, 13 Feb. 1913 *DPIK* 726 no. 176
138 Bobchev to Geshov, 14 Feb. 1913 ibid 728 no. 179
139 Sazonov to Izvol'skii, Benckendorff, 14 Feb. 1913 *RS* 12 (1915) 385 no. 362
140 Bobchev to Geshov, 15 Feb. 1913 *DPIK* 730 no. 182
141 Nekliudov to Sazonov, 15 Feb. 1913 *RS* 12 (1915) 386 no. 365; Geshov to Kalinkov, Mishev, Toshev, 15 Feb. 1913 *DPIK* 729 no. 180
142 Shebeko to Sazonov, 16 Feb. 1913 *RS* 12 (1915) 387 no. 367; Kalinkov to Geshov, 17 Feb. 1913 *DPIK* 734 no. 193
143 See Geshov, circular, 15 Feb. 1913 *DPIK* 729 no. 180; Shebeko to Sazonov, 16 Feb. 1913 *RS* 12 (1915) 387–8 no. 387; Nekliudov to Sazonov, 17 Feb. 1913 ibid 388 no. 368.
144 Grey to Cartwright, 4 Feb. 1913 *British Documents* IX 2, 497–8 no. 617; Bobchev to Geshov, 17 Feb. 1913 *DPIK* 735 no. 196
145 Sazonov, circular, 16 Feb. 1913 *RS* 12 (1915) 387 no. 366; Stanchov to Geshov (Paris), 17 Feb. 1913 *DPIK* 733 no. 191
146 Geshov, circular, 24 Feb. 1913 *DPIK* 743 no. 216
147 Toshev *Balkanskite voini* II 190
148 Shebeko to Sazonov, 19 Feb. 1913 *RS* 12 (1915) 389 no. 370; Bobchev to Geshov, 20 Feb. 1913 *DPIK* 740 no. 210
149 Sazonov to Shebeko, 19 Feb. 1913 *RS* 12 (1915) 389 no. 371; Bobchev to Geshov, 20 Feb. 1913 *DPIK* 740 no. 210; Kalinkov to Geshov, 20 Feb. 1913 ibid 739 no. 208
150 Shebeko to Sazonov, 22 Feb. 1913 *RS* 12 (1915) 391 no. 376; Kalinkov to Geshov, 22 Feb. 1913 *DPIK* 740 no. 211
151 Kalinkov to Geshov, 5 Mar. 1913 *DPIK* 746 no. 227
152 Sazonov to Shebeko, 22 Feb. 1913 *RS* 12 (1915) 391 no. 375
153 Bobchev to Geshov, 25 Feb. 1913 *DPIK* 744 no. 219; Geshov to Bobchev, 26 Feb. 1913 ibid 744 no. 221; Nekliudov to Sazonov, 25 Feb. 1912 *RS* 12 (1915) 393 no. 379
154 Shebeko to Sazonov, 22 Feb. 1913 *RS* 12 (1915) 391 no. 376

155 Bobchev to Geshov, 12 Mar. 1913 *DPIK* 749 no. 231. See also Bobchev *Stranitsi* 117.
156 See *GP* XXXIV 2, 494–5 no. 12968; and 524–5 no. 12992; *ÖUA* V 986, 1011, 1022–4 no. 6184, 6227, 6246.
157 Bobchev to Geshov, 12 Mar. 1913 *DPIK* 749 no. 231; 15 Mar. 1913 ibid 753 no. 240
158 Sazonov to Nekliudov, 21 Mar. 1913 ibid 754 no. 242
159 Geshov to Bobchev, 4 Apr. 1913 ibid 758 no. 252; 8 Apr. ibid 758 no. 254; Danev to Geshov (St Petersburg), 2 Apr. 1913 ibid 757 no. 250
160 Buchanan *My Mission to Russia* I 133
161 Ibid 161
162 Buchanan to Grey, 31 Mar. 1913 *British Documents* IX 2, 627–8 no. 769
163 Buchanan to Grey, 10 Apr. 1913 ibid IX 2, 670–2 no. 828 and enclosure 1; Thurn to Berchtold, 4 Apr. 1913 *ÖUA* VI 33 no. 6453
164 See *British Documents* IX 2, 670–73, 693–4, and 695–6 no. 828, 853, and 854.
165 Buchanan to Grey, 17 Apr. 1913 ibid 697 no. 856
166 See the text of the St Petersburg Protocol in Bobchev to Geshov, 11 May 1913 *DPIK* 764–5 no. 269; *RS* 12 (1915) 400–1 no. 382 (Russian), 394–6 no. 382 (French); Bobchev *Stranitsi* 118–19; Kalinkov *Romūniia* 196–7; *British Documents* IX 2, 787–8.
167 Geshov to Bobchev, 8 Apr. 1913 *DPIK* 758 no. 254
168 Bobchev to Geshov, 10 May 1913 ibid 762 no. 265; Sazonov to Nekliudov, Shebeko, 10 May 1913 *RS* 12 (1915) 396 no. 383
169 Sazonov *Fateful Years* 88
170 Mogilevich and Airapetian *Na putiakh k mirovoi voine* 156
171 See Geshov *Prestŭpnoto bezumie* 134.
172 Kalinkov to Geshov, 23 May 1913 *DPIK* 766 no. 271
173 Girginov *Narodnata katastrofa* 234
174 Mogilevich and Airapetian *Na putiakh k mirovoi voine* 156

CHAPTER 6 The uncoupling of the Balkan system of alliances

1 'The Serbian problem gave birth to the Greek [problem] or perhaps the other way around. Without the two, the Rumanian [problem] – would not have taken such an acute form.' See P. Todorov *Pogromite na Bŭlgariia* I (Sofia 1930) 227.
2 Geshov *The Balkan League* 40
3 Toshev *Balkanskite voini* II 42–3
4 Ibid; Geshov *The Balkan League* 61; V.A. Zhebokritskii *Bolgariia v period balkanskikh voin 1912–1913 g.g.* (Kiev 1961) 127 ff
5 See ch 2; and I. Panaiotov *Gŭrtsi i Bŭlgari prez vekovete, istoricheski paraleli* (Sofia 1947) 36–7.

6 Mishev to Geshov, 31 Oct. 1912 *DPIK* 561 no. 4
7 Mishev to Geshov, 3 Nov. 1912 ibid 561 no. 5
8 Ibid 571
9 Geshov to Mishev, 5 Nov. 1912 ibid 562 no. 7
10 Mishev to Geshov, 7 Nov. 1912 ibid 563 no. 9
11 Demidov to Sazonov, 16 Nov. 1912 GBA 70 no. 126
12 Demidov to Sazonov, 19 Nov. 1912 ibid no. 133
13 Geshov to Mishev, 9 Nov. 1912 *DPIK* 564 no. 10, and 22 Nov. 1912 ibid 568 no. 17
14 Mishev to Geshov, 18 Nov. 1912 ibid 566–7 no. 15
15 Mishev to Geshov, 16 Nov. 1912 ibid 566 no. 14
16 While the Greeks insisted that Crete and the Aegean islands should not even be taken into account in deciding the division of the spoils, the Bulgarians argued that without their heavy losses Greece would not have been able to conquer them alone. See Geshov to Mishev, 22 Nov. 1912 ibid 568 no. 17; Mishev to Geshov, 24 Nov. 1912 ibid 570 no. 19.
17 Geshov to Mishev, 26 Nov. 1912 ibid 571 no. 22
18 Mishev to Geshov, 28 Nov. 1912 ibid 571 no. 12. For some of the early attempts of the Greek government to divide Bulgaria and Serbia see: Toshev to Geshov, 15 Nov. 1912 ibid 566 no. 13, and Mishev to Geshov, 24 Nov. 1912 ibid 570 no. 19.
19 Geshov to Mishev, 29 Nov. 1913 ibid 573 no. 25, and 573 no. 24
20 Demidov to Sazonov, 16 Nov. 1912 GBA 70 no. 133
21 Nekliudov to Sazonov, 17 Nov. 1912 ibid 67 no. 257
22 Demidov to Sazonov, 20 Nov. 1912 ibid 70 no. ng
23 Sazonov to Demidov, 21 Nov. 1912 ibid 70 no. 2672. See also *RS* 7 (1915) 14–16 no. 126, 128, 129.
24 See for instance A. V. Nekliudov *Diplomatic Reminiscences Before and During the World War* tr. Alexandra Paget (London 1920) 163; Mishev to Geshov, 20 Nov. 1912 *DPIK* 578 no. 16.
25 Mishev to Geshov, 30 Nov. 1912 *DPIK* 575 no. 28
26 Mishev to Geshov, 25 Nov. 1912 ibid 571 no. 21; Mishev to Geshov, 30 Nov. 1912 ibid 575 no. 28
27 Ibid 575 no. 28. See also Girginov *Narodnata katastrofa* 151.
28 Geshov to Mishev, 11 Dec. 1912 *DPIK* 576 no. 29. See also Izvol'skii to Sazonov, 2 Dec. 1912 GBA 28 no. 410; Demidov to Sazonov, 3 Dec. 1912 GBA 70 no. 149.
29 Mishev to Geshov, 1 Dec. 1912 *DPIK* 576 no. 30; Geshov to Mishev, 8 Dec. 1912 ibid 579–80 no. 38; Geshov to Bobchev, 30 Dec. 1912 ibid 577 no. 32; Nekliudov to Sazonov, 2 Dec. 1912 GBA 67 no. 291
30 Geshov to Mishev, 7 Dec. 1912 *DPIK* 579 no. 37; Danev to Geshov, Bucharest, 9 Dec. 1912 ibid 580 no. 39; Geshov to Danev in Vienna, 9 Dec. 1912 ibid 580 no. 40. See also ibid 578–9 no. 36 and no. 37.

31 Geshov to Bobchev 14 Dec. 1912 ibid 581 no. 42. See *GP* xxxiv 1, 38–9 no. 12533, and 43–4 no. 12539.
32 Geshov to Bobchev, 14 Dec. 1912 *DPIK* 581 no. 42. See also *RS* 7 (1915) 16 no. 130, and gba 28 no. 449.
33 Sazonov to Nekliudov, 21 Dec. 1912 *RS* 7 (1915) 18 no. 132
34 Danev to Geshov, London, 26 Dec. 1912 *DPIK* 582 no. 46
35 Danev to Geshov, 31 Dec. 1912 ibid 583 no. 48
36 Danev to Geshov, 3 Jan. 1913 ibid 583 no. 49
37 Toshev *Balkanskite voini* ii 166; Mishev to Geshov, 7 Feb. 1912 *DPIK* 586 no. 53; Nekliudov to Sazonov, 9 Feb. 1912 *RS* 7 (1915) 19 no. 133
38 See D. Đorđević 'Pašić i Milovanović u pregovorima za balkanski savez 1912 godine' *Istoriski časopis* ix–x (1959) 467–86; Toshev *Balkanskite voini* i 349 ff.
39 Toshev *Balkanskite voini* i 350
40 A copy of the secret circular fell into the hands of A. Shopov, the Bulgarian consul general at Salonica. For the text see *DPIK* 142–5.
41 See Toshev *Balkanskite voini* ii 78.
42 Geshov to Madzharov, 25 Dec. 1912 *DPIK* 394 no. 7; Geshov to Danev, 28 Dec. 1912 ibid 396 no. 10. See also Girginov *Narodnata katastrofa* 112–14.
43 See ch 3.
44 Izvol'skii to Sazonov, 11 Dec. 1912 gba 28 no. 438; Toshev *Balkanskite voini* ii 93–4
45 Toshev *Balkanskite voini* ii 95
46 Sazonov to Hartwig, 16 Dec. 1912 gba 80 no. 2901
47 Hartwig to Sazonov, 18 Dec. 1912 ibid no. 82 and 19 Dec. 1912 ibid no. 398
48 Toshev *Balkanskite voini* ii 93, 95–6
49 Teodorov to Geshov, Vienna, 9 Jan. 1913 *DPIK* 396 no. 12; and Geshov to Bobchev, 2 Jan. 1912 ibid 396 no. 11
50 See Girginov *Narodnata katastrofa* 163.
51 See *DPIK* 566.
52 Toshev *Balkanskite voini* ii 101–2, 161; Skoko *Drugi balkanski rat* 139–41; Deakin *The Greek Struggle in Macedonia* 459
53 'This idea of a Balkan alliance with an anti-Bulgarian foundation certainly did not emanate from M. Sazonoff, who was unaware of it at the beginning. It was M. Hartwig who, in his sincere indignation against the Bulgarian proceedings, made himself the initiator and the champion of this new political combination … and as to the Foreign Office – M. Hartwig took charge of that: his ascendancy over the friends he had left there – over those who formerly, in the Asiatic Department, were "the shadow of his shadow" – sufficed to alter completely the course that M. Sazonoff had adopted at the outset of his term of office' (Nekliudov *Diplomatic Reminiscences* 162–3).
54 See Mishev to Geshov, 7 Feb. 1913 *DPIK* 586 no. 53, and 584 no. 52. Toshev *Balkanskite voini* ii 165–6; Skoko *Drugi balkanski rat* 196–7

55 Toshev *Balkanskite voini* II 161
56 Salabashev to Geshov, Vienna, 24 Jan. 1913 *DPIK* 397 no. 15; Salabashev *Spomeni* 432; Toshev to Geshov, 31 Jan. 1913 *DPIK* 398 no. 17
57 Geshov to Bobchev, 26 Jan. 1913 *DPIK* 397–8 no. 16
58 Toshev *Balkanskite voini* II 186
59 Spalajković to Geshov, 13 Feb. 1913 *DPIK* 403 no. 20
60 Geshov to Spalajković, 17 Feb. 1913 ibid 404 no. 21
61 Spalajković to Geshov, 18 Feb. 1913 ibid 404 no. 22; Geshov to Spalajković, 21 Feb. 1913 ibid 404 no. 23
62 Spalajković to Geshov, 29 Feb. 1913 ibid 405–8 no. 24
63 Ibid
64 Ibid
65 Ibid
66 Toshev *Balkanskite voini* II 189
67 Geshov to Toshev, strictly secret, Sofia, nd *DPIK* 409–13 no. 25
68 Ibid
69 Ibid
70 Ibid
71 Toshev *Balkanskite voini* II 195–7
72 Sazonov to Hartwig, 3 Mar. 1913 *RS* 7 (1915) 20 no. 135. See also Bobchev to Geshov, 11 Mar. 1913 *DPIK* 416 no. 33.
73 See *DPIK* 413 n.
74 Toshev to Geshov, 20 March 1913 ibid 418–9 no. 36, and 21 March ibid 420 no. 37
75 Geshov to Toshev, 31 Mar. 1913 ibid 427 no. 44
76 Toshev to Geshov, 2 Apr. 1913 ibid 429 no. 47
77 Toshev *Balkanskite voini* II 198
78 Savov to Geshov, 3 Mar. 1913 *DPIK* 414 no. 28; Kolushev to Geshov, Cetinje, 12 Mar. 1913 ibid 416 no. 32
79 Toshev to Geshov, 31 Mar. 1913 ibid 422 no. 40
80 Khesapchiev to Toshev, Salonica, 9 Mar. 1913 ibid 587 no. 55
81 Geshov *Prestŭpnoto bezumie* 106–8
82 Ibid; and Toshev *Balkanskite voini* II 197–8
83 Geshov to Mishev, 16 Apr. 1913 *DPIK* 596 no. 73
84 Mishev to Geshov, 18 Apr. 1913 ibid 596 no. 74
85 Geshov to Mishev, 23 Apr. 1913 ibid 598–9 no. 80. The line suggested by Demidov on 9 Apr. 1913 was very similar to that proposed by Venizelos to Danev in London. See Mishev to Geshov, 9 Apr. 1913 ibid 592 no. 67, and 18 Apr. 1913 ibid 596 no. 74.
86 Mishev to Geshov, 24 Apr. 1913 ibid 600 no. 83
87 Sazonov to Nekliudov, 10 Mar. 1913 *RS* 7 (1915) 21 no. 136; Nekliudov to Sazonov, 19 Apr. 1913 ibid 23 no. 141; Demidov to Sazonov, 26 Apr. 1913 ibid 32 no. 156

88 Demidov to Sazonov, 5 Apr. 1913 ibid 21 no. 137
89 Khesapchiev to Savov, 28 Apr. 1913 *DPIK* 448 no. 79
90 Demidov to Sazonov, 26 Apr. 1913 *RS* 7 (1915) 32 no. 156
91 See ibid 21–3 no. 136, 138, 140.
92 Geshov to Bobchev, 23 Mar. 1913 *DPIK* 421 no. 39
93 Danev to Geshov, St Petersburg, 30 Mar. 1913 ibid 423 no. 43
94 Geshov to Bobchev, 11 Apr. 1913 ibid 431 no. 51; Geshov *Prestŭpnoto bezumie* 77
95 Danev to Geshov, St Petersburg, nd *DPIK* 591 no. 65
96 See for example Nekliudov *Diplomatic Reminiscences* 162–3.
97 Toshev to Geshov, 15 Apr. 1913 *DPIK* 437 no. 62; Hartwig to Sazonov, 29 Apr. 1913 ibid 442 no. 68
98 Mishev to Geshov, 21 Apr. 1913 *DPIK* 598 no. 78; Demidov to Sazonov, 19 Apr. 1913 *RS* 7 (1915) 24 no. 142
99 Sazonov to Demidov, Hartwig, Nekliudov, 22 Apr. 1913 *RS* 7 (1915) 25 no. 144; Bobchev to Geshov, 23 Apr. 1913 *DPIK* 444 no. 76
100 Nekliudov to Sazonov, 28 Apr. 1913 *RS* 7 (1915) 30 no. 155; see also Geshov to Bobchev, 26 Apr. 1913 *DPIK* 445 no. 77.
101 Nekliudov to Sazonov, 26 Apr. 1913 *RS* 7 (1915) 28 no. 151; Geshov to Bobchev, 26 Apr. 1913 *DPIK* 445 no. 77
102 Geshov to Bobchev, 26 Apr. 1913 *DPIK* 445 no. 77; Nekliudov to Sazonov, 28 Apr. 1913 *RS* 7 (1915) 30 no. 154
103 Bobchev to Geshov, 29 Apr. 1913 *DPIK* 449 no. 80
104 Sazonov to Nekliudov, 30 Apr. 1913 *RS* 7 (1915) 33 no. 158
105 Ibid; see also Bobchev to Geshov, 29 Apr. 1913 *DPIK* 449 no. 80.
106 Nekliudov to Sazonov, 2 May 1913 *RS* 7 (1915) 34 no. 34; Geshov to Bobchev, 2 May 1913 *DPIK* 450 no. 82
107 Geshov to Bobchev, 3 May 1913 *DPIK* 450 no. 83; Geshov *Prestŭpnoto bezumie* 82
108 Bobchev to Geshov, 6 May 1913 ibid 451 no. 85
109 Hartwig to Sazonov, 3 May 1913 *RS* 7 (1915) 36 no. 163
110 Toshev to Geshov, 7 May 1913 *DPIK* 454–5 no. 87
111 Hartwig to Sazonov, 7 May 1913 *RS* 8 (1915) 210 no. 166
112 *The Greek White Book. Diplomatic Documents, 1913–1917* tr T.P. Ion (New York nd) 20–2. See also Stanchov to Geshov, Paris, 9 May 1913 *DPIK* 457 no. 84; Skoko *Drugi balkanski rat* 198–201.
113 See von Jagow to von Tschirschky, 14 March 1913 *GP* XXXIV 2, 491–2 no. 12965.
114 Toshev *Balkanskite voini* II 219
115 Ćorović *Odnosi između Srbije i Austro-ugarske* 457–8. See also Kalinkov to Geshov, Bucharest, 28 May 1913 *DPIK* 769 no. 276.
116 See Toshev *Balkanskite voini* II 219.

117 Kalinkov to Geshov, 23 May 1913 *DPIK* 766 no. 271; Toshev to Geshov, 9 May 1913 ibid 459 no. 99
118 Kalinkov to Geshov, 9 Apr. 1913 ibid 759 no. 255; Geshov to Kalinkov, 16 Apr. 1913 ibid 760 no. 257; Geshov to Bobchev, Madzharov, Stanchov, 19 May 1913 ibid 763 no. 266; Kalinkov to Geshov, 23 May 1913 ibid 766 and 768, no. 271 and 272
119 Salabashev to Geshov, Vienna, 20 May 1913 ibid 770–1 no. 278
120 Salabashev to Geshov, 30 May 1913 ibid 772 no. 281, and 6 June 1913 ibid 773 no. 283
121 Izvol'skii to Sazonov, 6 June 1913 *FRO* 381 no. 269. See also *DPIK* 764 and 769 no. 268 and 273.
122 Geshov to Kalinkov, 29 May 1913 *DPIK* 770 no. 277
123 Danev to Geshov, London, 29 May 1913 ibid 771 no. 279
124 Teodorov to Geshov, Paris, ibid 772 no. 280. See also Girginov *Narodnata katastrofa* 246–7.
125 Nekliudov to Sazonov, 9 May 1913 *RS* 8 (1915) 211 no. 167
126 Sazonov to Nekliudov, 10 May 1913 ibid 211 no. 168
127 Bobchev to Geshov, 17 May 1913 *DPIK* 470 no. 117
128 Ibid 470–1; Sazonov to Nekliudov, 16 May 1913 *RS* 8 (1915) 212–3 no. 169
129 Geshov to Bobchev, 16 May 1913 *DPIK* 464 no. 108; Bobchev to Geshov, 15 May 1913 ibid 467 no. 115
130 Geshov to Danev (London), Teodorov (Paris), 22 May 1913 ibid 472 no. 118. See also Bobchev to Geshov, 20 May 1913 ibid 472–3 no. 119; Sazonov to Nekliudov, 20 May 1913 *FRO* 380 no. 1313; *RS* 8 (1915) 215–16 no. 171.
131 Toshev to Geshov, 15 May 1913 *DPIK* 465 no. 111
132 See Stanchov to Geshov, 18 May 1913 ibid 466 no. 112; Geshov to Bobchev, 31 May 1913 ibid 487 no. 135; Toshev *Balkanskite voini* II 268.
133 Toshev *Balkanskite voini* II 264
134 Geshov to Rizov (Rome), 15 May 1913 *DPIK* 465 no. 110; D. Rizov 'Kak doide katastrofata' *Svobodno mnenie* II 4 (1914) 61
135 Rizov 'Kak doide katastrofata' 61–2
136 Geshov to Bobchev, 27 May 1913 *DPIK* 482 no. 124. It contained Rizov's report of the same day (481n).
137 Toshev *Balkanskite voini* II 277
138 Spalajković to Geshov, 26 May 1913 *DPIK* 474–80 no. 121
139 Ibid
140 Narodna Skupština *Stenografski zapisnici* XLIII (1913) (Belgrade 1913) 514–20. Pašić did not explain the source of the offer. Both Russia and Austria-Hungary denied that they ever made it. There is convincing evidence that Hartwig made such a promise without the authorization of the imperial government. See Geshov to Bobchev, 27

May 1913 *DPIK* 482 no. 124; Toshev *Balkanskite voini* II 284; Rizov 'Kak doide katastrofata' 61.

141 Toshev *Balkanskite voini* II 279
142 Ibid
143 Geshov to Bobchev, Madzharov, Stanchov, 27 May 1913 *DPIK* 483 no. 125; Nekliudov to Sazonov, 26 May 1913 *RS* 8 (1915) 219 no. 177, and 27 May 1913 ibid 219 no. 178
144 Geshov to Mishev, 17 May 1913 *DPIK* 604 no. 93
145 Ibid
146 Mishev to Geshov, 19 May 1913 *DPIK* 606 no. 95
147 Geshov to Mishev, 20 May 1913 ibid 606 no. 96
148 Hartwig to Sazonov, 24 May 1913 *RS* 8 (1915) 217 no. 173; Toshev *Balkanskite voini* II 273
149 Coromilas to Alexandropoulos, 23 May 1913 *Greek White Book* 35 no. 5
150 Ibid 27–9 no. 3; Skoko *Drugi balkanski rat* 202
151 See *Greek White Book* 35–42 no. 5–10; Skoko *Drugi balkanski rat* 203–4.
152 The complete texts of the treaty and the convention are found in *Greek White Book* 23–6 no. 2 and 30–4 no. 4; and in Skoko *Drugi balkanski rat* 405–13.
153 *Greek White Book* 25

CHAPTER 7 The Inter-Allied War

1 See for instance Geshov's testimony in *Prilozhenie* 138.
2 Sazonov to Athens, Belgrade, Cetinje, Sofia, 30 May 1913 *RS* 8 (1915) 224 no. 186
3 Ibid
4 Toshev *Balkanskite voini* II 279, 297
5 Savov to Geshov, 25 May 1913 *DPIK* 483 no. 126; Geshov *Prestŭpnoto bezumie* 86
6 Geshov *Prestŭpnoto bezumie* 59. See also Savov to Geshov, Adrianople, 1 June 1913 *DPIK* 489 no. 138 and Geshov to Savov, 26 May 1913 ibid 607 no. 89.
7 Toshev *Balkanskite voini* II 296
8 Geshov *Prestŭpnoto bezumie* 108–9; *Prilozhenie* 148; B. Vazov ed *Dŭrzhavniiat prevrat, 16 Iuni, 1913 god.* (Sofia 1913) 25
9 Toshev *Balkanskite voini* II 298
10 See *Prilozhenie* 137; Geshov *The Balkan League* 91–2; Geshov *Prestŭpnoto bezumie* 7 and 108–10; Vazov *Dŭrzhavniiat prevrat* 25 ff; Girginov *Narodnata katastrofa* 250 ff.
11 Toshev *Balkanskite voini* II 299
12 Ibid 300
13 Geshov to Bobchev, 2 June 1913 *DPIK* 490 no. 141; Geshov to Savov, 2 June 1913 ibid 489 no. 139; Hartwig to Sazonov, 2 June 1913 *RS* 8 (1915) 229–30 no. 198; Nekliudov to Sazonov, ibid 230 no. 199

14 Toshev *Balkanskite voini* II 301
15 Ibid
16 Neratov to Athens, Belgrade, Cetinje, Sofia, 3 June 1913 *RS* 8 (1915) 231 no. 201
17 Same to same, 7 June 1913 ibid 234 no. 206
18 Geshov *Prestŭpnoto bezumie* 112
19 Vazov *Dŭrzhavniiat prevrat* 29; Bobchev *Stranitsi* 167
20 Bobchev *Stranitsi* 168; Girginov *Narodnata katastrofa* 286–7; Toshev *Balkanskite voini* II 308–9
21 See Teodorov's testimony, *Prilozhenie* 195.
22 See Danev's testimony, ibid 85–7, 93.
23 Geshov, circular, 6 June 1913 *DPIK* 494 no. 147; Sazonov to Demidov and Hartwig, 9 June 1913 *RS* 8 (1915) 236 no. 210
24 See Toshev to Sofia, 9 June 1913 *DPIK* 496 no. 151; Paget to Grey, 10 June 1913 *British Documents* IX 2, 837 no. 1037.
25 Sazonov *Fateful Years* 93
26 Ibid 93–4; Bobchev *Stranitsi* 171
27 Tsar Nicholas II to King Ferdinand and King Peter, 8 June 1913 *RS* 8 (1915) 235–6 no. 209 (French) *RS* 12 (1915) 398–9 (Russian); Toshev *Balkanskite voini* II 316–17; Bobchev *Stranitsi* 171–2
28 See Toshev *Balkanskite voini* II 322–3.
29 Ibid 324–5
30 Sazonov to Demidov, Giers, Hartwig, Nekliudov, 13 June 1913 *FRO* 238–9 no. 1600; *RS* 8 (1915) 238–9 no. 216
31 Ibid; Danev to Bobchev, 16 June 1913 *DPIK* 502 no. 166. The proposed meeting in Salonica was dropped by Sazonov at the request of Pašić. See *RS* 8 (1915) 237–8 no. 212 and 213.
32 Demidov to Sazonov, 14 June 1913 *RS* 9 (1915) 372 no. 219
33 Hartwig to Sazonov, 15 June 1913 ibid 372 no. 221. See also *British Documents* IX 2, 849 no. 1057.
34 Danev to Bobchev, 15 June 1913 *DPIK* 500 no. 162; Nekliudov to Sazonov, *RS* 9 (1915) 372 no. 222
35 Danev to Bobchev, 17 June 1913 *DPIK* 507 no. 171; Nekliudov to Sazonov, 16 June 1913 *RS* 9 (1915) 373 no. 224
36 Sazonov to Nekliudov, 12 June 1913 GBA 68 no. 1588, and 15 June 1913 ibid no. 1609
37 Nekliudov to Sazonov, 16 June 1913 *RS* 9 (1915) 373 no. 223
38 Sazonov to Nekliudov, 16 June 1913 GBA 68 no. 1620; Danev to Bobchev, 17 June 1913 *DPIK* 508 no. 174; Bobchev to Danev, 16 June 1913 ibid 507 no. 170
39 Sazonov to Nekliudov, 17 June 1913 GBA 63 no. 1633. See also *DPIK* 522 and 530–1 no. 182 and 199.
40 Danev to Bobchev, 17 June 1913 *DPIK* 567 no 173
41 Bobchev to Danev, 18 June 1913 ibid 524 no. 186

42 Sazonov to Hartwig, 18 June 1913 GBA 81 no. 1647; *RS* 9 (1915) 378 no. 233
43 Sazonov to Hartwig, 19 June 1913 GBA 81 no. 1664; *RS* 9 (1915) 379 no. 235
44 Hartwig to Sazonov, 21 June 1913 *RS* 9 (1915) 383 no. 241
45 Hartwig to Sazonov, 22 June 1913 GBA 81 no. 666; also 23 June 1913 ibid no. 674
46 Nekliudov to Sazonov, 19 June 1913 ibid 68 no 241; *RS* 9 (1915) 380 no. 236; also Danev to Bobchev, 19 June 1913 *DPIK* 522 no. 183
47 Sazonov to Nekliudov, 20 June 1913 *RS* 9 (1915) 381 no. 238. See also Bobchev to Geshov, 20 June 1913 *DPIK* 525 no. 187 and 21 June 1913 ibid 528 no. 193.
48 Danev to Bobchev, 20 June 1913 *DPIK* 525 no. 188. See also Nekliudov to Sazonov, 21 June 1913 *RS* 9 (1915) 382–3 no. 240.
49 Bobchev to Sazonov, 21 June 1913, in Bobchev *Stranitsi* 187
50 Sazonov to Athens and Sofia, 21 June 1913 *FRO* 385 no. 1695; *RS* 9 (1915) 382 no. 239. See also Bobchev to Danev, 21 June 1913 *DPIK* 529 no. 197.
51 Plachkov's testimony, *Prilozhenie* 351–2; Madzharov *Diplomaticheska podgotovka* 152; Vazov *Dūrzhavniiat prevrat* 30–2
52 Madzharov *Diplomaticheska podgotovka* 152; Vazov *Dūrzhavniiat prevrat* 34
53 Madzharov *Diplomaticheska podgotovka* 152; Vazov *Dūrzhavniiat prevrat* 34; Toshev *Balkanskite voini* II 341
54 See Savov's testimony, *Prilozhenie* 278.
55 Madzharov *Diplomaticheska podgotovka* 152; Toshev *Balkanskite voini* II 341; Teodorov's testimony, *Prilozhenie* 207
56 Girginov *Narodnata katastrofa* 321; Vazov *Dūrzhavniiat prevrat* 34; Toshev *Balkanskite voini* II 342
57 Nekliudov to Sazonov, 22 June 1913 GBA 68 no. 253; *RS* 9 (1915) 384–5 no. 244. See also Nekliudov to Sazonov, 22 June 1913 GBA 68 no. 254, and Danev to Bobchev, 22 June 1913 *DPIK* 530 no. 198.
58 Mishev to Danev, 27 June 1913 *DPIK* 620 no. 128
59 Nekliudov to Sazonov, 24 June 1913 GBA 68 no. 258
60 Sazonov to Nekliudov, 23 June 1913 *RS* 9 (1915) 385 no. 245; Bobchev to Danev, 23 June 1913 *DPIK* 531 no. 200
61 Nekliudov to Sazonov, 24 June 1913 GBA 68 no. 258
62 Danev to Bobchev, 24 June 1913 *DPIK* 532 no. 201. See also Bobchev *Stranitsi* 189.
63 See his personal letter to Teodorov of June 21, 1913, Bobchev *Stranitsi* 184–5.
64 Bobchev to Danev, 25 June 1913 *DPIK* 533 no. 205. See also Sazonov, circular, 25 June 1913 *RS* 9 (1915) 389 no. 253, 389 and 390 no. 254 and 256.
65 Danev to Bobchev, 26 June 1913 *DPIK* 533 no. 206, and 533–4 no. 207 and 210
66 Toshev *Balkanskite voini* II 343. See also Nekliudov to Sazonov 27 June 1913 GBA 68 no. 261.
67 Bobchev to Danev, 27 June 1913 *DPIK* 535 no. 214
68 Nekliudov to Sazonov, 27 June 1913 GBA 68 no. 261; Danev to Bobchev, 28 June 1913 *DPIK* 620 no. 127

69 Nekliudov to Sazonov, 27 June 1913 GBA 68 no. 261 and 264; RS 9 (1915) 392–3 and 393 no. 261 and 262

70 Nekliudov to Sazonov, 29 June 1913 GBA 68 no. 267

71 Hartwig to Sazonov, 23 June 1913 ibid 81 no. 675, and 24 June 1913 ibid 81 no. 682

72 Hartwig to Sazonov, 24 June 1913 ibid no. 681. See also Hartwig to Sazonov, 24 June 1913 RS 9 (1915) 387–8 no. 250; Hartwig to Sazonov, 25 June 1913 GBA 81 no. 688.

73 Sazonov to Hartwig, 27 June 1913 GBA 81 no. 1761

74 Hartwig to Sazonov ibid no. 704

75 Hartwig to Sazonov, 29 June 1913 ibid no. 705. See also RS 9 (1915) 392 and 395 no. 260 and 266.

76 Narodna Skupština Stenografski zapisnici XLIII (1913) 672–7

77 Ibid. See also Hartwig to Sazonov, 30 June 1913 GBA 81 no. 725; Toshev Balkanskite voini II 356.

78 Toshev Balkanskite voini II 357

79 Both telegrams are found in Girginov Narodnata katastrofa 342–3.

80 Ibid 343

81 For the complete text see ibid 343–5, and Toshev Balkanskite voini II 363.

82 For instance see Girginov Narodnata katastrofa 343–5; Toshev Balkanskite voini II 363; Vazov Dŭrzhavniiat prevrat; V.T. Velchev Tselata istina po pogroma i novite opasnosti za Bŭlgariia. Plno osvetlenie vŭrkhu prichinite na bŭlgarskite neuspekhi i vazhni razoblacheniia za roliata na Rusiia (Sofia 1913); T. Vlakhov Otnosheniiata mezhdu Bŭlgariia i tsentralnite sili po vreme na voinite, 1912-1918 g. (Sofia 1957) 63 ff; Skoko Drugi balkanski rat 241; Fichev Balkanskata voina 354 ff; Zhebokritskii Bolgariia v period balkanskikh voin 185–9.

83 Madzharov Diplomaticheskata podgotovka 155. See also Savov's testimony, Prilozhenie 279–80.

84 Toshev Balkanskite voini II 357; Hartwig to Sazonov, 30 June 1913 GBA 81 no. 729

85 See DPIK 537 no. 224; 1154 no. 5; 1153 no. 2 (with Serbia); and 621–2 no. 131, and 1141–2 no. 3 (with Greece).

86 Hartwig to Sazonov, 30 June 1913 GBA 81 no. 729; Nekliudov to Sazonov, 30 June 1913 RS 9 (1915) 397 no. 271; Demidov to Sazonov, 30 June 1913 GBA 71 no. 195

87 Sazonov to Nekliudov, 30 June 1913 GBA 68 no. 1795

88 Sazonov to Hartwig, 30 June 1913 ibid 81 no. 1794

89 Sazonov to Demidov, Giers, Hartwig, Nekliudov, 30 June 1913 ibid 14 no. 1796

90 Nekliudov to Sazonov, 30 June 1913 ibid 68 no. 272; 1 July 1913, ibid no. 275; Danev to Bobchev DPIK 1154 no. 3

91 R. Dimitriev and G.P. Radev to Savov, 1 July 1913 DPIK 538 no. 226

92 Girginov Narodnata katastrofa 368–9; Fichev Balkanskata voina 432 ff

93 Sazonov to Demidov, Giers, Hartwig, Nekliudov, 1 July 1913 GBA 14 no. 1804 and no. 1811

94 Same to same, 2 July 1913 ibid no. 1817

95 Buchanan to Grey, 4 July 1913 *British Documents* IX 2, 884–5 no. 1110
96 Mishev to Danev, 30 June 1913 *DPIK* 621 no. 130, and 2 July 1913 ibid 1144 no. 8
97 Toshev to Danev, 1 July 1913 ibid 1155 no. 8; Nekliudov to Sazonov, 1 July 1913 GBA 68 no. 277
98 Pašić to the high command, 2 July 1913 *APS* I 346 no. 317. See also GBA 8 no. 755, 775, 784.
99 For the official proclamations of war see *DPIK* I 145 no. 11 and 12 (Greece); 1160 no. 24 and 25, 1137 no. 15, and GBA 81 no. 789 (Serbia and Montenegro).
100 See R. Dimitriev to King Ferdinand, 7 July 1913 *DPIK* 1161 and 1162 no. 28 and 29; Danev to King Ferdinand ibid 1162 no. 28.
101 Kalinkov to Geshov, 11 July 1913 ibid 774 no. 286. See also Kalinkov *Romŭniia* 213.
102 Kalinkov to Danev, 25 June 1913 *DPIK* 779 no. 13
103 Shebeko to Sazonov, 27 June 1913 GBA 78 no. 173
104 Danev to Kalinkov, 28 June 1913 *DPIK* 780 no. 304. See also Shebeko to Sazonov, 27 June 1913 GBA 78 no. 173.
105 Nekliudov to Sazonov, 27 June 1913 GBA 68 no. 262
106 Bobchev to Danev, 29 June 1913 *DPIK* 784 no. 316. See also Bobchev *Stranitsi* 195.
107 Danev to Kalinkov, 28 June 1913 *DPIK* 780 no. 304
108 See Shebeko to Sazonov, 1 July 1913 GBA 78 no. 179; Kalinkov to Danev, 2 July 1913 *DPIK* 1785 no. 320.
109 Kalinkov to Danev, 3 July 1913 ibid 787–8 no. 326
110 Ibid; Shebeko to Sazonov, 3 July 1913 GBA 78 no. 183
111 Nekliudov to Sazonov, 2 July 1913 GBA 68 no. 280. See also Toshev *Balkanskite voini* II 373.
112 Danev, circular, 4 July 1913 *DPIK* 1157; Nekliudov to Sazonov, 4 July 1913 GBA 68 no. 293
113 Toshev *Balkanskite voini* II 373; Girginov *Narodnata katastrofa* 393; Teodorov's testimony, *Prilozhenie* 211–212
114 Toshev *Balkanskite voini* II 373; Vazov *Dŭrzhavniiat prevrat* 20–1; A. Girginov *Bŭlgariia pred velikata voina* (Sofia 1932) 5–6; S. Sh. Grinberg 'Vneshnepoliticheskaia orientatsiia Bolgarii nakanune pervoi mirovoi voiny (1912–1914 g.g)' *Slavianskii sbornik* (Moscow 1947) 293
115 Kalinkov to Danev, 5 July 1913 *DPIK* 789–90 no. 333; Shebeko to Sazonov, 6 July 1913 GBA 78 no. 190
116 See for instance Salabashev to Danev, 28 June 1913 *DPIK* 782 no. 309, and Danev to Salabashev, 29 June 1913 ibid 782 no. 310.
117 Danev to Bobchev, 4 July 1913 ibid 788 no. ng. See also Nekliudov to Sazonov, 5 July 1913 GBA 68 no. 296.
118 Danev to King Ferdinand, 8 July 1913 *DPIK* 1162 no. 28; Nekliudov to Sazonov, 8 July 1913 GBA 68 no. 301

119 Danev to Bobchev, 8 July 1913 *DPIK* 798 no. 342
120 Ibid
121 Bobchev to Danev, 9 July 1913 ibid 794 no. 345, and Danev to Bobchev ibid 794 no. 346
122 Bobchev to Danev, 10 July 1913 ibid 1164 no. 36
123 Danev to Bobchev, 9 July 1913 ibid 1164 no. 35, and Bobchev to Danev, ibid 795 no. 348
124 Sazonov to Demidov, Giers, Hartwig, Nekliudov, 9 July 1913 GBA 14 no. 1879. See also Bobchev to Danev, 10 July 1913 *DPIK* 1164 no. 36.
125 Sazonov to Shebeko, 9 July 1913 *RS* 10 (1915) 7 no. 285
126 Toshev *Balkanskite voini* II 390
127 Bobchev to Danev, 12 July 1913 in Bobchev *Stranitsi* 205
128 Shebeko to Sazonov, 9 July 1913 *RS* 10 (1915) 7 no. 286
129 The Rumanian legation to the Ministry of Foreign Affairs, Sofia, 10 July 1913 *DPIK* 796 no. 352; Shebeko to Sazonov, 10 July 1913 *RS* 10 (1915) 8 no. 287. On the Bulgarian reaction see *DPIK* 798 no. 357 and 358.
130 Shebeko to Sazonov, 11 July 1913 *RS* 10 (1915) 8–9 no. 288, 289, and 291; Bobchev to Danev, 14 July 1913 *DPIK* 1165 no. 38
131 Danev to Bobchev, 11 July 1913 *DPIK* 799 no. 359
132 Danev to Bobchev, 13 July 1913 ibid 799 no. 361
133 Bobchev to Danev, 12 July 1913, in Bobchev *Stranitsi* 205; Bobchev to Danev, 14 July 1913 *DPIK* 1165 no. 38
134 See Geshov to Danev, Berlin, 15 July 1913 *DPIK* 1166 no. 40.
135 Bobchev to Danev, 14 July 1913 ibid 1165 no. 38
136 Bobchev to Danev, 16 July 1913 ibid 1166 no. 42, and 15 July 1913 ibid 1166 no. 41
137 See for instance *APS* I 356–7 no. 337 and 339; and GBA 59 no. 114 and 523.
138 Sazonov to Nekliudov, 7 July 1913 GBA 68 no. 1873
139 Nekliudov to Sazonov, 9 July 1913 ibid no. 309
140 Toshev *Balkanskite voini* II 436; Bax-Ironside to Grey, 13 July 1913 *British Documents* IX 2, 907 no. 1139
141 Danev, circular, 16 July 1913 *DPIK* 1125 no. 8; Nekliudov to Sazonov, 23 July 1913 GBA 68 no. 408
142 See *British Documents* IX 2, 923 ed note; *ÖUA* VI 975–6 no. 7894; *GP* XXXV 184–5 no. 13560.
143 Danev, circular, 16 July 1913 *DPIK* 1125 no. 8; Nekliudov to Sazonov, 21 July 1913 GBA 68 no. 396
144 Giers to Sazonov, Constantinople, 25 July 1913 GBA 59 no. 619; Buchanan to Grey, 16 July 1913 *British Documents* IX 2, 916 no. 1152
145 See Buchanan to Grey, 18 July 1913 ibid 920–1 no. 1160.
146 Bronevskii to Sazonov, Berlin, 23 July 1913 GBA 17 no. 184

147 Izvol'skii to Sazonov, 22 July 1913 GBA 29 no. 353. See also *British Documents* IX 2, 933–4 no. 1175; 935 no. 1176.

148 See Toshev *Balkanskite voini* II 439–40.

149 Danev to Bobchev, 14 July 1913 *DPIK* 800 no. 363

150 Girginov *Narodnata katastrofa* 392–8; Toshev *Balkanskite voini* II 399–400; Grinberg *Slavianskii sbornik* 293–4; T. Vlakhov *Otnosheniiata mezhdu Būlgariia i tsentralnite sili po vreme na voinite 1912–1918 g.* 67–70

151 Girginov *Narodnata katastrofa* 392–8; Toshev *Balkanskite voini* II 399–400; Grinberg *Slavianskii sbornik* 293–4; T. Vlakhov *Otnosheniiata mezhdu Būlgariia i tsentralnite sili po vreme na voinite 1912–1918 g.* 67–70.

152 Girginov *Narodnata katastrofa* 392–8; Toshev *Balkanskite voini* II 399–400; Grinberg *Slavianskii sbornik* 293–4; T. Vlakhov *Otnosheniiata mezhdu Būlgariia i tsentralnite sili po vreme na voinite 1912–1918 g.* 67–70. See also V. Radoslavov *Būlgariia i svetovnata kriza* (Sofia 1923) 57; Bobchev *Stranitsi* 209–10.

153 Toshev *Balkanskite voini* II 409. See also *ÖUA* VI no. 7780, 7781, 7814.

154 Shebeko to Sazonov, 20 July 1913 GBA 78 no. 244. See also *RS* 10 (1915) 11–13 no. 295–300.

155 Hartwig to Sazonov, 20 July 1913 GBA 81 no. 966; Shebeko to Sazonov, 20 July 1913 ibid 78 no. 343

156 Shebeko to Sazonov, 22 July 1913 ibid 78 no. 256, and no. 249 and 253

157 Hartwig to Sazonov, 20 July 1913 ibid 81 no. 966, and no. 998; Nekliudov to Sazonov, 23 July 1913 ibid 68 no. 418

158 Barclay to Grey, 21 July 1913 *British Documents* IX 2, 923 no. 1162; Shebeko to Sazonov, 21 July 1913 GBA 81 no. 248; Nekliudov to Sazonov, 22 July 1913 GBA 68 no. 401

159 Hartwig to Sazonov, 23 July 1913 GBA 81 no. 1004; 24 July 1913 ibid no. 1015; Shebeko to Sazonov, 24 July 1913 ibid 78 no. 267

160 Shebeko to Sazonov, 24 July 1913 ibid 78 no. 267

161 Shebeko to Sazonov, 23 July 1913 ibid 78 no. 257

162 Shebeko to Sazonov, 24 July 1913 ibid 78 no. 260

163 Nekliudov to Sazonov, 25 July 1913 ibid 68 no. 426; Hartwig to Sazonov, 26 July 1913 ibid 81 no. 1036; Demidov to Sazonov, 21 July 1913 ibid 71 no. 236, and 22 July 1913 ibid 71 no. 240. The Bulgarian delegation was headed by D. Tonchev, the Greek by E. Venizelos, the Montenegrin by General J. Vukotić, the Serbian by N. Pašić, and the Rumanian by T. Maiorescu. For the composition of the delegations see GBA 68 no. 426 (Bulgarian); GBA 71 no. 236 (Greek); GBA 81 no. 1036 (Serbian and Montenegrin); and GBA 78 no. 272 (Rumanian).

164 See Toshev *Balkanskite voini* II 411.

165 Barclay to Grey, 31 July 1913 *British Documents* IX 2, 944 no. 1188; Shebeko to Sazonov, 30 July 1913 GBA 78 no. 279

166 Shebeko to Sazonov, 1 Aug. 1913 GBA 78 no. 283; Barclay to Grey, 1 Aug. 1913 *British Documents* IX 2, 971 no. 1225

167 Shebeko to Sazonov, 24 July 1913 GBA 78 no. 265; Nekliudov to Sazonov, 30 July 1913 ibid 68 no. 441

168 Shebeko to Sazonov, 24 July 1913 ibid 78 no. 261, and 1 Aug. 1913 ibid 78 no. 286

169 Shebeko to Sazonov, 3 Aug. 1913 ibid 78 no. 291. See also Fichev *Balkanskata voina* 454–5.

170 Ministère des affaires étrangères *Le Traité de paix de Bucarest du 28 juillet (10 août) 1913. Précédé des protocoles de la conference* (Bucharest 1913) 16 no. 5. See also Fichev *Balkanskata voina* 454–8.

171 Shebeko to Sazonov, 1 Aug. 1913 GBA 78 no. 286, and 30 July 1913 ibid no. 276

172 Barclay to Grey, 8 Aug. 1913 *British Documents* IX 2, 972 no. 1225. See also Fichev *Balkanskata voina* 463–4.

173 Barclay to Grey, 8 Aug. 1913 *British Documents* IX 2, 972 no. 1225. See also Shebeko to Sazonov, 3 Aug. 1913 GBA 78 no. 288.

174 Shebeko to Sazonov, 1 Aug. 1913 GBA 78 no. 286, and 3 Aug. 1913 ibid no. 288; Hartwig to Sazonov, 3 Aug. 1913 ibid 81 no. 1078; Nekliudov to Sazonov, 2 Aug. 1913 ibid 68 no. 443

175 Shebeko to Sazonov, 3 Aug. 1913 ibid 78 no. 286; Hartwig to Sazonov, 3 Aug. 1913 ibid 81 no. 1076 and 1078; Fichev *Balkanskata voina* 454

176 Shebeko to Sazonov, 4 Aug. 1913 GBA 78 no. 294, and no. 284; Fichev *Balkanskata voina* 454

177 Shebeko to Sazonov, 1 Aug. 1913 GBA 78 no. 281, and also 30 July 1913 ibid no. 276

178 Fichev *Balkanskata voina* 454

179 See Shebeko to Sazonov, 3 Aug. 1913 GBA 78 no. 289; 30 July 1913 ibid no. 279, and no. 278.

180 See for instance Bronevskii to Sazonov, Berlin, 3 Aug. 1913 ibid 17 no. 195.

181 Shebeko to Sazonov, 3 Aug. 1913 ibid 78 no. 290, and also 30 July 1913 ibid no. 279

182 Barclay to Grey, 8 Aug. 1913 *British Documents* IX 2, 973 no. 1225; Shebeko to Sazonov, 1 Aug. 1913 GBA 78 no. 281

183 Shebeko to Sazonov GBA 78 no. 285

184 Barclay to Grey, 8 Aug. 1913 *British Documents* IX 2, 973 no. 1225. See also GBA 17 no. 193 and 199; GBA 29 no. 373; GBA 23 no. 104; and GBA 78 no. 300.

185 Shebeko to Sazonov, 4 Aug. 1913 GBA 78 no. 295

186 Ibid no. 296

187 Shebeko to Sazonov, 5 Aug. 1913 ibid no. 299

188 Shebeko to Sazonov, 6 Aug. 1913 ibid no. 301. See also GBA 81 no. 1099, and GBA 68 no. 300.

189 Tonchev to Genadiev, 8 Aug. 1913 *BD* 13 no. 7; Shebeko to Sazonov, 9 Aug. 1913 GBA 78 no. 306

190 Shebeko to Sazonov, 10 Aug. 1913 GBA 78 no. 307
191 Arseneev to Sazonov, 25 Aug. 1913 ibid no. 325. For the treaty see *Paix de Bucarest* 67 ff; Kesiakov ed *Prinos küm diplomaticheskata istoriia na Bŭlgaria* I 55–8; Toshev *Balkanskite voini* II 487–90.
192 See Buchanan to Grey, 9 Aug. 1913 *British documents* IX 2, 977 no. 1228.
193 Bobchev to Genadiev, 9 Aug. 1913 *BD* 5 no. 11
194 Ibid 4 no. 10
195 Stanchov to Genadiev, 9 Aug. 1913 ibid 5 no. 12, and Genadiev to Bobchev, 10 Aug. 1913 ibid 6 no. 14
196 Izvol'skii to Sazonov, 14 Aug. 1913 *FRO* 406 no. ng. See also Buchanan to Grey, 19 Aug. 1913 *British Documents* IX 2, 989 no. 1244.
197 See Bax-Ironside to Grey, 8 Aug. 1913 *British Documents* IX 2, 968 no. 1221.
198 Salabashev to Genadiev, 16 Aug. 1913 *BD* 17 no. 33, and 22 Aug. 1913 ibid 29 no. 58. See also *ÖUA* VII 121–3 and 142–3 no. 8356 and 8386.
199 Salabashev to Genadiev, 19 Aug. 1913 *BD* 21 no. 43; Bronevskii to Sazonov, 13 Aug. 1913 GBA 17 no. 206. See also *ÖUA* VII 219–21 no. 8498; *British Documents* IX 2, 982 no. 1235.
200 Shebeko to Sazonov, 6 Aug. 1913 GBA 78 no. 301
201 Shebeko to Sazonov, 10 Aug. 1913 ibid no. 309
202 Genadiev to Madzharov, 18 Aug. 1913, in Madzharov *Diplomaticheskata podgotovka* 166. See also Genadiev to Madzharov 21 Aug. 1913 *BD* 28 no. 53.
203 Genadiev to Bobchev, 25 Aug. 1913 *BD* 36 no. 70
204 Bobchev to Genadiev, 11 Aug. 1913 ibid 7 no. 16
205 Nekliudov to Sazonov, 19 Aug. 1913 GBA 68 no. 22
206 See Buchanan to Grey, 14 Aug. 1913 *British Documents* IX 2, 982 no. 1235.
207 Giers to Sazonov, Constantinople, 8 Aug. 1913 GBA **59** no. 665. See also no. 650, 652, 655.
208 Buchanan to Grey, 8 Aug. 1913 *British Documents* IX 2, 968 no. 1220. See also Radev to Genadiev (Bucharest), 7 Aug. 1913 *BD* 2 no. 4.
209 Buchanan to Grey, 8 Aug. 1913 *British Documents* IX 2, 952 no. 1198
210 Giers to Sazonov, 8 Aug. 1913 GBA 59 no. 678
211 Giers to Sazonov, 7 Aug. 1913 ibid 59 no. 673, and 11 Aug. 1913 ibid no. 707
212 Izvol'skii to Sazonov, 22 Aug. 1913 ibid 30 no. 420 and 421. See also 14 Aug. 1913 *FRO* 404 no. ng.
213 Giers to Sazonov, 11 Aug. 1913 GBA 59 no. 707
214 Giers to Sazonov, 9 Aug. 1913 ibid no. 694. See also *British Documents* IX 2, 988–9 no. 1243.
215 Madzharov to Genadiev, 22 Aug. 1913 *BD* 29 no. 56; Bobchev to Genadiev, 24 Aug. 1913 ibid 36 no. 69
216 See aide-mémoire communicated by Tewfik Pasha, 21 Aug. 1913 *British Documents*

IX 2, 994–5 no. 1250, and 992 no. 1247, no. 1249. See also *ÖUA* VII 174 no. 8439; *GP* XXXVI 37 no. 13790.

217 See Buchanan to Grey, 18 Aug. 1913 *British Documents* IX 2, 987–8 no. 1242, and 20 Aug. 1913 ibid 992 no. 1247.

218 Nachovich to Genadiev, Constantinople, 25 Aug. 1913 *BD* 37 no. 72, and 28 Aug. 1913 ibid 41 no. 79; also 32 no. 63, 38 no. 74 and 75, and 40 no. 77

219 Genadiev to Nachovich, 29 Aug. 1913 ibid 41–2 no. 80; Giers to Sazonov, 30 Aug. 1913 GBA 59 no. 782

220 Genadiev to the grand vizier, 2 Sept. 1913 *BD* 46 no. 88; Nekliudov to Sazonov, 2 Sept. 1913 GBA 68 no. 496

221 Genadiev to Savov, 15 Sept. 1913 *BD* I 52 no. 101; Toshev *Balkanskite voini* II 450

222 Nekliudov to Sazonov, 4 Sept. 1913 GBA 68 no. 28

223 Savov to Genadiev, 9 Sept. 1913 *BD* 46 no. 91; Toshev *Balkanskite voini* II 453

224 Toshev *Balkanskite voini* II 453

225 Giers to Sazonov, 9 Sept. 1913 GBA 60 no. 813

226 Genadiev to Savov, 10 Sept. 1913 *BD* 47–8 no. 94

227 Genadiev to Savov, 11 Sept. 1913 ibid 50 no. 98, and 48–9 no. 95

228 Giers to Sazonov, 12 Sept. 1913 GBA 60 no. 823; Toshev *Balkanskite voini* II 457

229 Genadiev to Savov, 11 Sept. 1913 *BD* 50 no. 98

230 Toshev *Balkanskite voini* II 458

231 Ibid 459

232 Ibid 461; and Giers to Sazonov, 19 Sept. 1913 GBA 60 no. 835

233 See Toshev *Balkanskite voini* II 461–6; Giers to Neratov, 28 Sept. 1913 GBA 60 no. 849.

234 See *BD* 55 no. 108; 56 no. 110; 58 no. 111.

235 Toshev *Balkanskite voini* II 466. The complete text of the treaty and its annexes is found in Kesiakov ed *Prinos kŭm diplomaticheskata istoriia na Bŭlgaria* I 58–69.

Bibliography

I MANUSCRIPTS

Archives of the imperial Russian legation in Darmstadt: Lithographic copies of the confidential correspondence between the foreign office in St Petersburg and the Russian representatives abroad, sent to the minister at Darmstadt for his information (Roll of Mr Michel de Giers' and Mr Serge Botkin's Archives, Hoover Institution on War, Revolution and Peace, Stanford University, Stanford, California):

1 Various and secret instructions of the foreign office given to Russian representatives abroad:

File number	Year
12	1911
13	1912
14	1913

2 Correspondence with Russian representatives accredited with the great powers:

Germany: embassy in Berlin

15	1911
16	1912
17	1913

Austria-Hungary: embassy in Vienna

21	1911
22	1912
23	1913

France: embassy in Paris

25		1911
26	January–June	1912
27	July–October	1912
28	November–December	1912
29	January–July	1913
30	August–December	1913

Great Britain: embassy in London

31	January–June	1911
32	July–December	1911
33	January–March	1912
34	April–May	1912
35	August–October	1912
36	November–December	1912
37	January–July	1913
38	August–November	1913

Italy: embassy in Rome

40		1911
41		1912
42		1913

Turkey: embassy in Constantinople

49	January–March	1911
50	April–June	1911
51	July–September	1911
52	October–November	1911
53	January–March	1912
54	April–June	1912
55	July–August	1912
56	September	1912
57	October	1912
58	November–December	1912
59	January–July	1913
60	August–December	1913

61	Balkan consulates:	
	At Adrianople	1912

At Bitola	1912–1913
At Usküb	1911–1912
At Prizren	1911–1913
At Odrin	1913
At Philippopolis	1911–1912
At Varna-Burgas	1912–1913
At Salonica	1912–1913
At Mt Athos	1912–1913
At Scutari	1912

3 Correspondence with Russian representatives: legations in the Balkan peninsula:

Albania: commissioner at Valona

65 October–November	1913

Bulgaria: legation at Sofia

66	1911
67	1912
68	1913

Greece: legation at Athens

69	1911
70	1912
71	1913

Montenegro: legation at Cetinje

74	1911
75	1912
76	1913

Rumania: legation at Bucharest

77	1911–1912
78	1913

Serbia: legation at Belgrade

79	1911
80	1912
81	1913

282 Bibliography

GOVERNMENT AND OFFICIAL PUBLICATIONS

Austria-Hungary
Bridge, F.R. ed *Austro-Hungarian Documents Relating to the Macedonian Struggle,
1896–1912* Thessaloniki 1976
Ministerium des k. und k. Hauses und des Äussern *Österreich-Ungarns Aussenpolitik von
der Bosnischen Krise 1908 bis zum Kriegsausbruch 1914. Diplomatische Aktenstüke des
Österreichisch-Ungarischen Ministerium des Äussern* ed Ludwig Bittner, Alfred F.
Pribram, Heinrich Srbik, and Hans Übersberger, 8 vol, Vienna 1930
Pribram, A.F. ed *The Secret Treaties of Austria-Hungary 1879–1914* tr A.C. Coolidge,
2 vol, Cambridge, Mass 1920

Bulgaria
Dogovor za mir mezhda Bŭlgaria, Gŭrtsia, Cherna Gora, Romŭnia i Sŭrbia Sofia 1913
Kesiakov, B.D. ed *Prinos kŭm diplomaticheskata istoriia na Bŭlgariia, 1878–1925.
Dogovori, konventsii, spogodbi i drugi sŭglasheniia i diplomaticheski aktove s kratki
obiasnitelni belezhki* 4 vol, Sofia 1925–6
Miletich, L. ed *Dokumenti za protivobŭlgarskite deistviia na srbskite i na grtskite vlasti v
Makedoniia prez 1912–1913 godina* Sofia 1929
Ministerstvo na vŭnshnite raboti i na izpovedaniiata *Diplomaticheski dokumenti po name-
sata na Bŭlgariia v evropeiskata voina* 2 vol, Sofia 1920–1
Ministry of Foreign Affairs *The Bulgarian Question and the Balkan States* Sofia 1919
Narodno sŭbranie *Doklad na parlamentarnata izpitatelna komissiia* 4 vol, Sofia 1918–19
– *Prilozhenie kŭm tom pŭrvi ot doklada na parlamentarnata izpitatelna komisiia* Sofia
1918
*Nashata Duma. Vŭzrazheniia na bivshite ministri I.E. Geshov, Dr. S. Danev, T. Teodorov,
M.I. Madzharov, I. Peev i P. Arbashev sreshtu obvineniiata na dŭrzhavniia sŭd ot 1923
godina* Sofia 1925

France
Ministère des Affaires étrangères, Commission de Publication des Documents relatifs aux
Origines de la Guerre de 1914 *Documents diplomatiques français 1871–1914* 41 vol,
Paris 1929–59

Germany
Auswärtiges Amt *Die Grosse Politik der europäischen Kabinette, 1871–1914. Sammlung
der diplomatischen Akten des Auswärtigen Amtes, im Auftrage des Auswärtigen Amtes* ed
Johannes Lepsius, Albrecht Mendelssohn-Bartholdy, and Friedrich Thimme, 40 vol,
Berlin 1922–7

Great Britain
Foreign Office *British Documents on the Origins of the War 1898–1914* ed G.P. Gooch and Harold Temperley, 11 vol, London 1926–38

Greece
The Greek White Book. Diplomatic Documents, 1913–1917 tr Theodore P. Ion, New York n.d.
The Vindication of Greek Policy, a Report of Speeches Delivered in the Greek Chamber August 23–26, 1917 by E. Venizelos and Others London 1918

Montenegro
'Istorijska Građa ... Balkanski rat' *Zapisi* (Cetinje) 1935 (VIII) vol XIII no. 1–5, vol XVI no. 1–6; 1936 (IX) vol XV no. 1–6, vol XVI no. 1–6; 1937 (X) vol XVIII no. 1
Lainović, A. ed 'Građa iz borbe oko Skadra 1913 godine' *Istoriski Zapisi* (Cetinje) III (1950) vol V no. 1–3 (January–March) 107–30

Rumania
Ministère des Affaires étrangères *Documents diplomatiques. Les événements de la peninsule balkanique. L' action de la Roumaine septembre 1912–août 1913* Bucharest 1913

Russia
Adamov, E.A. and I.V. Koz'menko ed *Sbornik dogovorov Rossii s drugimi gosudarstvami 1856–1917* Moscow 1952
'Doklady b. ministra inostrannykh del S.D. Sazonova Nikolaiu Romanovu, 1912 gg.' *Krasnyi Arkhiv* III (1923) 5–28
Gosudarstvennaia duma *Stenograficheskiia otchety* St Petersburg 1906–17
Khvostov, V.M. and E.M. Gliazer ed 'Tsarskoe pravitel'stvo o probleme prolivov v 1896–1914 g.g.' *Krasnyi Arkhiv* LXI (1933) 135–40
Komissiia po izdaniiu dokumentov epokhi imperializma *Mezhdunarodnye otnosheniia v epokhu imperializma. Dokumenty iz arkhivov tsarskogo i vremennogo pravitel'stv 1878–1917* ed A.P. Bol'shemennikov, A.S. Erusalemskii, A.A. Mogilevich, and F.A. Rothstein, series II 1900–1913 vol XVIII–XX Moscow 1938–40
Marchand, René ed *Un Livre noir. Diplomatie d' avant guerre, d' après les documents des archives russes. Novembre 1910–juillet 1914* 3 vol, Paris 1922–34
Narodnyi komissariiat po inostrannym delam *Evropeiskie derzhavy i Gretsiia v epokhu mirovoi voiny – po sekretnym materialam b. ministerstva inostrannykh del s prilozheniem kopii diplomaticheskikh dokumentov* ed E.A. Adamov, Moscow 1922
– *Evropeiskie derzhavy i Turtsiia vo vremia voiny. Konstantinopol' i Prolivy – po sekretnym dokumentam b. ministerstva inostrannykh del* ed E.A. Adamov, Moscow 1925
– *Materiali po istorii franko-russkikh otnoshenii za 1910–1914 g.g. Sbornik sekretnikh*

dokumentov byvshago imperatorskogo rossiiskogo ministerstva inostrannykh del
Moscow 1922
- *Sbornik sekretnnykh dokumentov byvshago ministerstva inostrannykh del* Moscow 1917
Popov, A. ed 'Diplomaticheskaia podgotovka balkanskoi voiny 1912 g.' *Krasnyi Arkhiv*
VIII (1925) 3–48, and IX (1925) 3–31
- 'Pervaia balkanskaia voina' *Krasnyi Arkhiv* XV (1926) 1–29 and XVI (1926) 1–24
- 'Turetskaia revoliutsiia 1908–1909 gg.' *Krasnyi Arkhiv* XLIII (1930) 3–54, XLIV (1931)
3–39, and XLV (1931) 27–52
'Sbornik diplomaticheskikh dokumentov kasaiushchikhsia sobytii na balkanskom poluo-
strove (Avgust 1912–Iul' 1913 g.)' *Russkaiia Starina* 1915, no. 5, 231–63; no. 6
420–52; no. 7, 5–36; no. 8, 209–40; no. 9, 371–402; no. 10, 5–24; no. 11, 185–202;
no. 12, 379–401
Semennikov, V. 'Epizod iz istorii balkanskoi voiny' *Krasnyi Arkhiv* XXVII (1927) 184–8
- ed *Nikolai II i velikie kniazia. Rodstvennye pis' ma k poslednemu tsar' iu* Moscow and
Leningrad 1925
Siebert, B. von ed *Graf Benckendorffs Diplomatischer Schriftwechsel* 3 vol, Berlin and
Leipzig 1928
Stieve, F. ed *Der Diplomatischer Schriftwechsel Iswolskis 1911–1914. Aus dem
Geheimakten der Russischen Staatsarchive* 4 vol, Berlin 1925
Tsentrarkhiv *Perepiska Vilgel' ma II s Nikolaem II* Moscow 1923
Zakher, Ia. ed 'Konstantinopol' i prolivy' *Krasnyi Arkhiv* VI (1924) 48–76

Serbia
Boghitschewitsch, M. (Bogićević, M.) ed *Die Auswärtige Politik Serbiens, 1903–1914*
3 vol, Berlin 1928–31
Narodna skupština *Stenografski zapisnici* Belgrade 1913
Todorovski, G. ed *Srpski izvori za istorijata na makedonskist narod 1912–1914* Skopje
1979

III MEMOIRS AND BIOGRAPHIES

Auffenberg-Komarow, M. von *Aus Österreichs Höhe und Niedergang – Eine Lebenschil-
derung* Munich 1927
Bethmann-Holweg, Theobald von *Reflections on the World War* tr George Young, London
1920
Bobchev, S.S. 'Audientsiiata mi u Tsar Nikola II' *Rodina* (Sofia) II 4 (1940) 100–8
- *Stranitsi iz moiata diplomaticheska missiia v Petrograd, 1912–1913* Sofia 1940
Bok, M.F. *Vospominaniia o moem ottse P. A. Stolypine* New York 1953
Buchanan, Sir George *My Mission to Russia and Other Diplomatic Memories* 2 vol, Boston
1923

Charykov, V.N. *Glimpses of High Politics: Through War and Peace 1855–1929* London 1931
Danev, Stojan 'Konventsiiata mezhdu Russiia i Bŭlgariia ot 1902 g.' *Nauchen pregled* (Sofia) 13 (1929) 45–8
– 'Moiata misiia v Krim prez 1912 god.' *Rodina* (Sofia) II 3 (1940) 123–33
– 'Moite audientsii u imperatora Nikolai II' *Sila* (Sofia) III 18 (1922) 2–6, 19–20 (1922) 5–11
– 'Poseshtenieto mi v Budapeshta prez oktomvri 1912 g.' *Sŭvremennik* (Sofia) II 6 (1923) 290–306
Đorđević, Dimitrie *Milovan Milovanović* Belgrade 1962
Doysmani, Viktoros *Apomnēmoneymata. Istorikai selides tas opoias ezisa* Athens 1946
Fichev, Ivan I. *Balkanskata voina, 1912–1913. Prezhivelitsi, belezhki i dokumenti* Sofia 1940
Firsova, N.N. *Nikolai II. Opyt lichnoi kharakteristiki preimushchestvenno na osnovanii dnevnika i perepiski* Kazan 1929
Geshov (Gueshoff), I.E. *The Balkan League* tr Constantin Mincoff, London 1915
Gibbons, H.A. *Venizelos* London 1911
Giesl, Wladimir *Zwei Jahrzehnte im Nahem Osten: Aufzeichnungen des Generals der Kavallerie Baron Wladimir Giesl* ed Ritter von Steinitz, Berlin 1927
Grey, E., Viscount of Falladon *Twenty-Five Years 1892–1916* 2 vol, New York 1925
Grogan, Lady *The Life of J.D. Bourchier* London 1926
Gurko, V.I. *Features and Figures of the Past. Government and Opinion in the Reign of Nicholas II* Stanford, Calif. 1939
– *Tsar i Tsaritsa* Paris 1927
Hötzendorf, Conrad von *Aus meiner Dienstzeit 1906–1918* 5 vol, Vienna 1921–5
Ianovici, D. *Take Ionesco* Paris 1919
Ignatiev, A.A. *Piat' desiat let v stroiu* 2 vol, Moscow 1959
Izvol'skii, A.P. *The Memoirs of Alexander Izvolsky* ed and tr C.L. Seeger, London 1920
Jäckh, Ernst *Kiderlen-Wächter: Der Staatsmann und Mensch. Briefwechsel und Nachlass* 2 vol, Stuttgart 1924
Jonescu, T. *Souvenirs* Paris 1919
Kalinkov, G.I. *Romŭniia i neinata politika spremo Bŭlgariia (Prez 1912 i 1913 g.)* Sofia 1917
Kokovtsov, V.N. *Out of My Past. The Memoirs of Count Kokovtsov* ed H.H Fisher, Stanford, Calif. 1935
Lamouche, Léon *Quinze Ans d'histoire balkanique (1904–1918)* Paris 1928
Lichnowsky, Karl M. *Heading for the Abyss. Reminiscences* New York 1928
Louis, Georges *Les Carnets de Georges Louis* Paris 1926
Madol, Hans Roger *Ferdinand – Tsar na Bŭlgarite (Mechtata za vizantiia)* Sofia 1931–2
Madzharov, M.I. *Diplomaticheska podgotovka na nashite voini. Spomeni, chastni pisma, shifrovani telegrami i poveritelni dokladi* Sofia 1932

– 'Kak ce sūzdade albanskata dūrzhava. (Iz moite diplomaticheski spomeni)' *Demokraticheski pregled* XIX 2 (1927) 6–12

Malinov, A.P. *Stranichki ot nashata nova politicheska istoriia. Spomeni I.* Sofia 1938

Mazarakis-Ainian, K.I. *Apomnēmoneymata* Athens 1925

Miliukov, P.N. *Vospominaniia (1859–1917)* ed M.N. Karpovich and B.I. Elkin, 2 vol, New York 1955

Muhdar, Pasha M. *La Turque, l'Allemagne et l'Europe depuis le traité de Berlin jusqu'à la guerre mondiale* Paris 1924

Nekliudov (Nekliudoff), A.V. *Diplomatic Reminiscences Before and During the World War* tr Alexandra Paget, London 1920

Nicolson, Harold *Portrait of a Diplomat* Cambridge, Mass. 1930

Nikola Pašić Belgrade 1937

Pagkalou, Theod. *Ta apomnēmoneymata moy, 1897–1947* I: *1897–1913* Athens 1950

Pašić, N.P. 'Autobiografija Nikole P. Pašića' *Politika* (Belgrade) XXIV (1927) no. 6804–8

Pavlović, A. 'Moje uspomene – prilikom vodenija pregovora između nas i Bugara za rat protiv Turske 1912 g.' *Politika* XXIX (1932) no. 8567 and 8568

Pešić, P. 'Prva vojna konvencija između Srbije i Crne Gore' *Vreme* (Belgrade) VIII (1928) no. 2481

Poincaré, R. *Au Service de la France. Neuf années de souvenirs* 10 vol, Paris 1926–33

Popović, D. 'Diplomati u Petrogradu u vreme balkanskikh ratova (trenuti snimci)' *Godišnjica Nikole Ćupića* XLIII (1934) 57–79

Radoslavov, Vasil *Bŭlgariia i svetovnata kriza* Sofia 1923

Redlich, Josef *Schichksalsjähre Österreichs 1908–1919. Das politische Tagebuch Josef Redlichs* ed Fritz Fellner, 2 vol, Graz 1953–4

Rosen, R.R. *Forty Years of Diplomacy* 2 vol, New York 1922

Salabashev, I. *Spomeni* Sofia 1943

Savinski, Alexander A. *Recollections of a Russian Diplomat* London 1927

Sazonov, S.D. *Fateful Years, 1910–1916. The Reminiscences of Serge Sazonov* New York 1928

Schelking, Eugine de *Recollections of a Russian Diplomat* New York 1918

Sforza, Carlo (Count) *Fifty Years of War and Diplomacy in the Balkans. Pashich and the Union of the Yugoslavs* New York 1940

Shebeko, N. *Souvenirs. Essai historique sur les origines de la guerre de 1914* Paris 1936

Solov'ev, Iv. Ia. *Vospominaniia diplomata 1893–1922* Moscow 1959

Souliotes-Nikolaides, A. *Emerologēon tou protou valkanikou polemou* Thessaloniki 1962

Spalajković, M. 'Gospodin Pašić – Državnik-Diplomat-Filosof' *Spomenica Nikole Pašića, 1845–1925* ed V. Zivotić, Belgrade 1926

– 'Kralj Petar i Bugaraki Kralj Ferdinand 1912. Uspomene na stvaranje Balkanskog saveza' *Politika* XXXVIII (1941) no. 11710 (supplement)

Steed, H.W. *Through Thirty Years, 1892–1922. A Personal Narrative* 2 vol, London 1925

Stolypin, A. *P.A. Stolypin, 1862–1911* Paris 1927

Sukhomlinov, V. *Vospominaniia* Berlin 1924
Toshev, Andrei *Balkanskite voini* 2 vol, Sofia 1929–31
Vitte (Witte), S. Iv. *Vospominaiia* 3 vol, Moscow 1960
Zannas, A. *O Makedonikon agōn. Anamneseis* Thessaloniki 1960
Zivotić, Vukašin ed *Spomenica Nikole Pašića, 1845–1925* Belgrade 1926
Zorbas, N.K. *Apomnēmoneymata* Athens 1925

IV MONOGRAPHS AND GENERAL HISTORICAL WORKS

Abadžiev, G. *Balkanskite vojni i Makedonija* Skopje 1958
Akademiia Nauk SSSR, Institut Slavianovedeniia *Iz Istorii Russko-Bolgarskikh otnoshenii. Sbornik statei* Moscow 1958
– *Mezhdunarodnye otnosheniia v tsentral' noi i vostochnoi evrope* Moscow 1966
Albertini, Luigi *The Origins of the War of 1914* tr and ed Isabella M. Massey, 3 vol, London 1952–7
Aleksić-Pejković, L. *Odnosi Srbije sa Francuskom i Engleskom 1903–1914* Belgrade 1965
Anestopoulos, A.K. *Makedonikos agōn, 1903–1908* Thessaloniki 1965
Arbatskii, F.P. *Tsarstvovanie Nikolaia II* Moscow 1917
Askew, W.C. *Europe and Italy's Acquisition of Lybia, 1911–1912* Durham, NC 1942
Badzhov, P. *Greshkite na g. Dr. Danev* Sofia 1913
Bagger, Eugene S. *Eminent Europeans. Studies in Continental Reality* New York 1922
Balcanicus (Stojan Protić) *Srbi i Bugari u balkanskom ratu* Belgrade 1913
Batowski, Henryk *Potstawy sojuszu bałkańskiego 1912 R. Studium z historii diplomaticznej, 1806–1912* Cracow 1939
Bazhenov, I.P. *Nasha vneshnaia politika na blizhnem vostoke – s natsional' noi tochki zreniia* St Petersburg 1914
Belić, A. *Srbi i Bugari u balkanskom ratu i u meždusobnom ratu* Belgade 1913
Bestuzhev, I.V. *Bor' ba v Rossii po voprosam vneshnei politiki 1906–1910* Moscow 1961
Bezobrazov, P. *Razdel Turtsii* Petrograd 1917
Bickel, Otto *Russland und die Entstehung des Balkanbundes 1912. Ein Beitrag zur Vorgeschichte des Weltkrieges* Königsberg and Berlin 1933
Bitoski, K. *Makedonija i Kneževstvo Bugaria (1893–1903)* Skopje 1977
Black, C.E. *The Establishment of Constitutional Government in Bulgaria* Princeton 1943
Blaisdell, Donald C. *European Financial Control in the Ottoman Empire* New York 1929
Bovykin, V.I. *Iz istorii vozniknoveniia pervoi mirovoi voiny. Otnosheniia Rossii i Frantsii v 1912–1914 gg.* Moscow 1961
– *Ocherki istorii vneshnei politiki Rossii konets XIX veka – 1917 god.* Moscow 1960
Božović, V.B. *Krvavi kamen. Crna Gora v drugom balkanskom ratu sa Bugarskom* Belgrade 1913
Brailsford, H.N. *Macedonia, Its Races and Their Future* London 1908

Bŭlgarska Akademiia na Naukite, Institut za Istoriia *I storiia na Bŭlgariia* ed D. Kosev, Zh. Natan, and A. Burmov, 2nd ed, 3 vol, Sofia 1961–4

Butterfield, Paul R. *The Diplomacy of the Bagdad Railway 1890–1914* Göttingen 1932

Carlgren, W.M. *Iswolski und Aehrenthal vor der Bosnischen Annexionskrise. Russische und Österreich-ungarische Balkanpolitik 1906–1908* Uppsala 1955

Carnegie Endowment for International Peace *Report of the International Commission to Inquire into the Causes and Conduct of the Balkan Wars* Washington, DC 1914

Cassavetti, D.J. *Hellas and the Balkan Wars* London 1914

Ćorović, V. *Borba za nezavisnost Balkana* Belgrade 1937

– *Odnosi između Srbije i Austro-ugarske u XX veku* Belgrade 1936

Čubrilović, V. ed *Jugoslovenski narodi pred prvi svetski rat* Belgrade 1967

– ed *Velike sile i Srbija pred prvi svetski rat* Belgrade 1976

Cvijić, J. *Balkanski rat i Srbija* Belgrade 1912

Danev, Stojan *Balkaský svaz a válka s Tureckem, 1912–1913* Přednašky Slovanského Ústavu v Praze, Svazek VII, Prague 1935

– *Ocherk na diplomaticheskata istoriia na balkanskite dŭrzhavi* 2nd ed, Sofia 1931

Deakin, D. *The Greek Struggle in Macedonia, 1897–1913* Thessaloniki 1966

Dedijer, V. *The Road to Sarajevo* New York 1966

Derzhavin, N.S. *Bolgarsko-Serbskie vzaimnootnosheniia i makedonskii vopros* St Petersburg 1914

Dimevski, Slavko *Makedonskoto nacionalno osloboditelno dviženie i egzarhijata (1893–1912)* Skopje 1963

Dimitrov, S. *Istoriia na balkanskite narodi: 1879–1918* Sofia 1975

Đorđević, D. *Carinski rat Austro-ugarske i Srbije 1906–1911* Belgrade 1962

– *Izlazak Srbije na Jadransko more i Konferencija ambasadora u Londonu 1912* Belgrade 1956

Dramaliev, K. *Teoriia i praktika na velikobŭlgarskiia shovinizm* Sofia 1947

Driault, Eduard and Michel Lhéritier *Histoire diplomatique de la Gréce de 1821 à nos jours* 5 vol, Paris 1925–6

Drossos, D.I. *La Fondation de l'alliance balkanique. Etude d'histoire* Athens 1929

Durham, Mary Edith *The Struggle for Scutari (Turk, Slav and Albanian)* London 1914

– *Twenty Years of Balkan Tangle* London 1920

Dŭrvingov, P. *Istoriia na Makedono-Odrinskoto opolchenie* 2 vol, Sofia 1912–25

Efremov, P.N. *Vneshnaia politika Rossii (1907–1914 g.g.)* Moscow 1961

Evreinov, G.A. *Ideologiia blizhnevostochnogo voprosa* St Petersburg 1911

Fadner, F. *Seventy Years of Pan-Slavism in Russia: Karazin to Danilevskii 1800–1870* Washington, DC 1962

Fay, S.B. *The Origins of the World War* 2nd rev. ed, 2 vol, New York 1935

Fischel, A. *Der Panslavismus bis zum Weltkriege* Berlin 1919

Fortunatov, P. *Voina 1877–1878 g.g. i osvobozhdenie Bolgarii* Moscow 1950

Gabe, P. *Rusiia, Avstriia i Bŭlgariia v bŭlgarskiia pogrom. Kade e spasenieto* Sofia 1914
Galkin, I.S. *Diplomatiia evropeiskikh derzhav v sviazi s osvoboditel' nym dvizheniem narodov evropeiskoi Turtsii 1905–1912 g.g.* Moscow 1960
Ganchev, A. *Balkanskata voina, 1912–1913 g.* Sofia 1939
– *Mezhdusŭiuznicheskata voina 1913 godina* Sofia 1940
Ganev, I. *Prolivite i Bŭlgariia ... istoricheski ocherk na stanovishchata na velikite sili i dogovornite tekstove urezhdashchi rezhima na prolivite od XVII vek do dnes* Sofia 1946
Genov, G.P. *Iztochniiat vŭpros* 2 vol, Sofia 1925–6
Georgiev, G. *Ilindenskoto vŭstanie (1903)* Sofia 1969
Gerko-Kriazhin, V.A. *Blizhnii Vostok i derzhavy* Moscow 1925
Geshov, I.E. *Prestŭpnoto bezumie i anketata po nego. Fakti i dokumenti* Sofia 1914
Giesche, R. *Der serbische Zugang zum Meer und die europäische Krise 1912* Stuttgart 1932
Girginov, A. *Bŭlgariia pred velikata voina* Plovdiv and Sofia 1932
– *Narodnata katastrofa. Voinite 1912–1913 g.* Sofia 1926
Girginov, T. *Istoricheski razvoi na sŭvremenna Bŭlgariia. Ot vŭzrazhdanieto do balkanskata voina 1912 g.* 2 vol, Sofia 1934
Gooch, G.P. *Before the War: Studies in Diplomacy* 2 vol, London 1936–8
Gopćević, S. *Geschichte von Montenegro und Albanien* Gotha 1914
Hanotaux, G. *La Guerre des Balkans et l'Europe 1912–1913. Études diplomatiques* 2nd ed, Paris 1914
Helmreich, E.C. *The Diplomacy of the Balkan Wars 1912–1913* Cambridge, Mass. 1938
Hosking, Geoffrey A. *The Russian Constitutional Experiment. Government and Duma, 1907–1914* Cambridge 1973
Iakushkin, V. *Balkanskie voiny i ikh rezul' taty* Moscow 1914
Ignatiev, A.V. *Russko-Angliiskie otnosheniia nakanune pervoi mirovoi voiny (1908–1914 g.g.)* Moscow 1962
Immanuel *Balkanskata voina 1912–1913* 4 pt in 2 vol, Sofia and Salonica 1913
Iotsov, D. *Rusiia, Bosforot i Dardanelite. Diplomaticheska studiia* Sofia 1944
– *Rusiia i Bŭlgariia (vchera, dnes i utre). Diplomaticheski studii* 2nd ed, Sofia 1945
Istorijski institut jugoslovenske narodne armije *Prvi balkanski rat 1912–1913* I ed V. Terzić, Belgrade 1959
Ivanov, N. *Balkanskata voina 1912–1913* Sofia 1924–5
Jelaćić, A. *Rusija i Balkan. Pregled politićkih i kulturnih veza Rusije i balkanskih zemalja, 866–1940* Belgrade 1940
Jelavich, Barbara *A Century of Russian Foreign Policy 1814–1914* New York 1964
– *St. Petersburg and Moscow: Tsarist and Soviet Foreign Policy 1814–1974* Bloomington 1974
Jelavich, Charles *Tsarist Russia and Balkan Nationalism: Russian Influence in the Internal Affairs of Bulgaria and Serbia 1879–1886* Berkeley, Calif. 1958

Jovanović, J. *Stvaranje crnogorske države i rozvoj crnogorske nacionalnosti* Cetinje 1947
Jovanović, S. *Vlada Aleksandra Obrenovića* 2nd ed, 2 vol, Belgrade 1934–6
Karpov, S. *Bolgariia i poslednie balkanskie voiny* Yaroslavl' 1914
Katardzhiev, T. *Kratka istoriia na balkanskata i sūiuznishkata voina* Sofia 1928
Khristov, A. *Istoricheski pregled na voinata na Bŭlgariia sreschu vsichkite balkanski dŭrzhavi 1913 g.* Sofia 1924
– *Kratka istoriia na osvoboditelnata voina 1912–1913 godina* Sofia 1921
Khristov, Kh. *Agrarnite otnosheniia v Makedoniia prez XIX v. i nachaloto na XX* Sofia 1964
Kofos, E. *Nationalism and Communism in Macedonia* Thessaloniki 1964
Kohn, Hans. *Pan-Slavism: Its History and Ideology* 2nd ed, New York 1960
Kolarov, N. *Ocherk vŭrkhu diplomaticheskata istoriia na balkanskite voini* Sofia 1938
Kolias, G. *Dyo stathmi tis neoteres Ellinikis istorias (1912, 1940)* Athens 1963
Kondis, B. *Greece and Albania 1908–1914* Thessaloniki 1976
Korff, Baron S.A. *Russia's Foreign Relations During the Last Half Century* New York 1922
Kosev, D. *Bŭlgariia prez balkanskata i mezhdusūiuznicheskata voina* Sofia 1948
K'osev, D.G. *Istoriia na makedonskoto natsionalno revoliutsionno dvizhenie* Sofia 1954
Kovalevskii, P.I. *Znachenie natsionalizma v sovremennom dvizhenii balkanskikh slavian* Rostov 1913
Krachunov, K. *Diplomaticheska istoriia na Bŭlgariia (1886–1915)* I Sofia 1928
– *Vŭnshnata politika na Bŭlgariia (Kabinet't Malinov, 1908–1911)* Sofia 1931
Kuiumdzhiev, B.P. *Diplomaticheska i materialna podkrepa ot Rusiia na Bŭlgaria po vreme na balkanskata voina, 1912–1913 g.* Sofia 1968
Kyrou, A.A. *Oi Valkanikoi geitones mas* Athens 1962
Langer, W.C. *The Diplomacy of Imperialism 1890–1902* 2 vol, New York 1935
– *European Alliances and Alignments 1871–1890* New York 1935
Lascaris, M. *To Anatolikon zētima, 1800–1923* 2 vol, Thessaloniki 1948–54
Lavrov, P.A. *Anneksiia Bosnii i Gertsegoviny i otnoshenie k nei slavianstva* St Petersburg 1909
Lazarević, M. *Drugi balkanski rat* Belgrade 1955
Lederer, Ivo. ed *Russian Foreign Policy. Essays in Historical Perspective* New Haven, Conn. 1962
Lewis, B. *The Emergence of Modern Turkey* Oxford 1961
Lisenko, V.K. *Blizhnii vostok kak rinok sbyta russkikh tovarov* St Petersburg 1913
Liszkowski, U. *Zwishen Liberalismus und Imperialismus; die zaristische Aussenpolitik vor dem Ersten Weltkrieg im Urteil Miljukovs und der Kadetten partei 1905–1914* Stuttgart 1974
Maksimović, V. *Srpsko-bugarski spor iz 1912–1913 god. za vardarsku oblast* Belgrade 1928
Malaknos, M.J. *I epanastasis tou 1909* Athens 1965

Martsius (A. Girginov) *Borbata protiv lichniot rezhim i negovite krepiteli*. Chast I: *Upravlenieto na demokraticheskata partiia ot 1908 do 1911 god*. Sofia 1922

Michon, G. *L'Alliance franco-russe 1891–1917* Paris 1927

Miliukov, P. *Balkanskii kirzis i politika A.P. Izvol' skogo* St Petersburg 1910

Miller, A.F. *Turtsiia i problema prolivov* Moscow 1947

Miller, W. *The Ottoman Empire and Its Successors, 1801–1922* Cambridge 1923

Ministerstvo na narodna otbrana *Balkanskata voina 1912–1913* Sofia 1961

– *Mezhdusūiuznicheskata voina 1913 g*. Sofia 1963

Ministerstvo na voinata *Voinata mezhdu Būlgariia i drugite balkanski dūrzhavi prez 1913 g*. Vol I: *Prichinite i podgotovkata na voinata do 21 Juni* Sofia 1941

– *Voinata mezhdu Būlgariia i Turtsiia 1912–1913* 7 vol, Sofia 1937

Mishev, I. *Geroizm' t na būlgarskata armiia prez balkanskata voina* Sofia 1958

Mogilevich, A.A. and M.E. Airapetian *Na putiakh k mirovoi voine 1914–1918 g.g.* Moscow 1940

Naltsos, Ch. *Der San Stefano Vertrag und das Griechtum* Thessaloniki 1956

Nikitin, S.A. *Slavianskie komitety v Rossii* Moscow 1960

Ninćić, M. (M. Nintchitch) *La Crise bosnique (1900–1908) et les puissances européennes* 2 vol, Paris 1937

Ognianova, Militsa *Balkanskata voina* Sofia 1949

Ormandzhiev, I. *Nova i nai-nova istoriia na būlgarskiia narod* Sofia 1943

Pallis, A.A. *Greece's Anatolian Venture – and After. A Survey of the Diplomatic and Political Aspects of the Greek Expedition to Asia Minor (1915–1922)* London 1937

Panaiotov, I. *Gūrtsi i Būlgari prez vekovete. Istoricheski paraleli* Sofia 1947

Pandevski, M.D. *Političkite partii i organizacii vo Makedonija (1908–1912)* Skopje 1965

Papacosma, S.V. *The Military in Greek Politics. The 1909 Coup d'Etat* Kent, Ohio 1977

Papanchev, A. *Edno prestūpno tsarstvuvanie. Ferdinand I, Tsar na Būlgarite* 2nd ed, Sofia 1946

Paulová, M. *Balkanské valky 1912–1913 a Český lid* Prague 1963

Pavlović, Z.G. *Opsada Skadra 1912–1913. (Prolog istoriji prvog balkanskog rata)* Belgrade 1926

Petrov, F.N. ed *Balkanskie strany* Moscow 1946

Petrovich, M.B. *The Emergence of Russian Panslavism, 1856–1870* New York 1956

Pokrovskii, M.N. *Tsarskaia Rossiia i voina* Moscow 1924

– *Vneshnaia politika Rossii v XX veke* Moscow 1926

Poletika, N.P. *Vozniknovenie pervoi mirovoi voiny; iiul' skii krizis 1914 g*. Moscow 1964

Popović, D. *Borba za narodno ujedinjenje, 1908–1918* Belgrade 1935

Popović, V. *Istočno pitanje. Istoriski pregled borbe oko opstanka osmanliske carevine u levantu i na Balkanu* Belgrade 1928

Pržić, I. *Spoljašnja politika Srbije, 1904–1914* Belgrade 1939

Radev, S. *Stroilelite na sūvremenna Būlgariia* 2 vol, Sofia 1910–11

Rankin, R. *The Inner History of the Balkan War* London 1914

Ranković, Z.J. *Grćko-Bugarski rat 1913 godina* Sarajevo 1926

Ratković, B. *Srbija i Crna Gora u balkanskim ratovima 1912–1913* Belgrade 1972

Rothstein, F.A. *Mezhdunarodnye otnosheniia v kontse XIX veka* Moscow and Leningrad 1960

Rozental', E.M. *Diplomaticheskaia istoriia russko-frantsuzskogo soiuza v nachale XX veka* Moscow 1960

Savov, N. *Vinovnitsite za dvete katastrofi na Būlgariia* Vratsa 1918

Schmitt, B.E. *The Annexation of Bosnia 1908–1909* Cambridge 1937

– *The Coming of the War: 1914* 2 vol, New York 1930

Schröder, W. *England, Europa und der Orient. Untersuchung zur englischen Vorkriegpolitik in Vorgeschichte der Balkankriese 1912* Stuttgart 1938

Seligman, V.J. *The Victory of Venizelos. A Study of Greek Politics, 1910–1918* London 1920

Senkevich, I.G. *Osvoboditel' noe dvizhenie albanskogo naroda v 1905–1912 g.g.* Moscow 1959

Seton-Watson, R.W. *A History of the Roumanians from Roman Times to the Completion of Unity* reprint New York 1963

– *The Rise of Nationality in the Balkans* London 1917

Shebukhin, A.N. *Rossiia na blizhnem vostoke* Leningrad 1926

Shopov, A. *Kak ni se nalozhi balkanskata voina* Sofia 1915

Sigrist, S.V. *U poroga velikoi voiny* Petrograd 1924

Silianov, Kh. *Osvoboditelnite borbi na Makedoniia* 2 vol, Sofia 1933

Skendi, S. *The Albanian National Awakening, 1878–1912* Princeton 1967

Skoko, S. *Drugi balkanski rat 1913* Belgrade 1968

Solarov, K. *Balkanskiiat sūiuz i osvoboditelnite voini prez 1912 i 1913 g.* Sofia 1926

– *Būlgariia i Makedonskiiat vūpros. Prichinite na balkanskite voini* Sofia 1925

Sosnosky, T. von *Die Balkanpolitik Österreich-Ungarns seit 1866* 2 vol, Stuttgart 1913

Stanojević, J.V. *Istorja ratova za oslobodenje i ujedinjenje 1912–1918* Belgrade n.d.

Stavrianos, L.S. *Balkan Federation. A History of the Movement toward Balkan Unity in Modern Times* Northampton, Mass. 1942

Stojanov, P. *Makedonija vo vremeto na balkanskite i prvata svetska vojna (1912–1918)* Skopje 1969

Sumner, B.H. *Russia and the Balkans 1870–1880* Oxford 1937

Swire, J. *Albania, the Rise of a Kingdom* London 1929

Tanty, M. *Konflikty bałkańskie w letach 1878–1918* Warsaw 1968

– *Rosja wobec wojen bałkańskich 1912–1913 roku* Warsaw 1970

Tarle, E.V. *Evropa v epokhu imperializma, 1871–1919* Moscow 1928

Thaden, E.C. *Russia and the Balkan Alliance of 1912* University Park, Penn. 1965

Todorov, G. *Vremennoto rusko upravlenie v Būlgariia prez 1877–1879 g.g.* Sofia 1958

Todorov, P. *Pogromite na Būlgariia* 2 vol, Sofia 1930

Todorova, Ts. *Obiaviavane nezavisimosta na Bŭlgariia prez 1908 g. i politikata na imperialisticheskite sili* Sofia 1960

Todorović, M.A. *Solun i balkanskoto pitanje* Belgrade 1913

Trotskii, L. *Balkany i balkanskaia voina. Sochineniia* VI Moscow and Leningrad 1926

Tsanov, N. *Tsarŭt na Bŭlgariia i pogrom't* Sofia 1914

Tucović, D. *Srbija i Arbanija* Belgrade 1945

Tukim, Cemal *Die politischen Beziehungen zwischen Österreich-Ungarn und Bulgarien von 1908 bis zum Bucharester Frieden* Hamburg 1936

Übersberger, Hans *Österreich zwischen Russland und Serbien: Zür südslavischen Frage und der Entstehung des Ersten Weltkrieges* Köln and Graz 1958

Vakas, D. *O El. Venizelos: Polemikos igetis. Istorikai selides apo tin dimourgias tis Megalis Ellados, 1910–1920* Athens 1949

Vazov, B. ed *Dŭrzhavniiat prevrat 16 Iuni 1913 god* Sofia 1913

Velchev, V.T. *Tselata istina po pogroma i novite opasnosti za Bŭlgariia. Pŭlno osvetlenie vŭrkhu prichinite na bŭlgarskite neuspekhi i vazhni razoblacheniia za roliata na Rusiia* Sofia 1913

Ventiri, G. *I Ellas toy 1910–1920* 2 vol, Athens 1931

Vinogradov, K.B. *Bosniiskii krizis 1908–1909 g.g.* Leningrad 1964

Vlakhov, D. *Makedonija. Momenti od istorijata na Makedonskiot narod* Skopje 1950

Vlakhov, T. *Otnosheniiata mezhdu Bŭlgariia i tsentralnite sili po vreme na voinite 1912–1918 g.* Sofia 1957

Vojvodić, M. *Skadarska kriza 1913 godine* Belgrade 1970

Vucinich, W.S. *Serbia between East and West. The Events of 1903–1908* Stanford, Calif. 1954

Wedel, O.H. *Austro-German Diplomatic Relations, 1908–1914* Stanford, Calif. 1932

Zaionchkovskii, A. *Podgotovka Rossii k mirovoi voine v mezhdunarodnom otnoshenii* Moscow 1926

Zhebokritskii, V.A. *Bolgariia nakanune balkanskikh voin 1912–1913* Kiev 1960

– *Bolgariia v period balkanskikh voin 1912–1913 g.g.* Kiev 1961

Zhogov, P.V. *Diplomatiia Germanii i Avstro-Vengrii i pervaia balkanskaia voina 1912–1913 g.g.* Moscow 1969

Živaljević, D.D. *Obnova balkanskog saveza. Fakti i razmišljenja* Niš 1915

Zorin, V.A. ed *Istoriia diplomatii* 3 vol, Moscow 1963

V ARTICLES

Artamanov, Victor V. 'Errinerungen an meine Militärattachézeit in Belgrad' *Berliner Monatschefte* XVI (1938) 583–602

Batowski, Henryk 'Crna Gora i balkanski savez 1912 godine' *Istoriski zapisi* (1957) no. 1–2, 47–60

- 'The Failure of the Balkan Alliance of 1912' *Balkan Studies* VII 1 (1966) 111–22
Bestuzhev, I.V. 'Bor'ba v Rossii po voprosam vneshnei politiki nakanune pervoi mirovoi voiny (1910–1914 gg.)' *Istoricheskie zapiski* LXXXV (1965) 44–85
- 'Otnosheniia Rossii i Avstro-Vengrii pered pervoi mirovoi voinoi' *Evropa v novoe i noveishee vremia. Sbornik statei pamiati akademika N.M. Lukina* Moscow 1966, 556–67
Birman, M.C. 'Serbiia v period balkanskikh voin 1912–1913 g.g.' *Akademiia Nauk SSSR Institut Slavianovedeniia Kratkie soobshcheniia* no. 32 (1961) 27–45
Bourchier, G.H. 'Articles on the Origins of the Balkan League' *Times* (London) 4, 5, 6, 11, and 13 June 1913
Bovykin, V.I. 'Russko-frantsuzskie protivorechiia na balkanakh i blizhnem vostoke nakanune pervoi mirovoi voiny' *Istoricheskie zapiski* LIX (1957) 84–124
Cemović, M.G. 'Srpsko-bugarski ugovor 1912' *Politika* XXII (1925) no. 6202
Charykov, N.V. 'Sazonoff' *Contemporary Review* CXXXIII (1928) 284–8
Christitch, A. 'A Great Balkan Statesman' *The Nineteenth Century and After* XCIX (1926) 687–96
Crampton, R.J. 'Decline of the Concert of Europe in the Balkans 1913–1914' *Slavonic and East European Review* LII (1974) 393–419
Cvijić, J. 'Izlazak Srbije na jadransko more' *Glasnik srpskog geografskog društva* II no. 2
Danev, S. 'Balkanski savez' *Anali* II (1937) 53–61
- 'Balkanskiia sūiuz' *Rodina* II 2 (1939) 50–61
Derenkovskii, G.M. 'Franko-Russkaia morskaia konventsiia 1912g. i anglo-russkie morskie peregovory nakanune pervoi mirovoi voiny' *Istoricheskie zapiski* XXIX (1949) 80–122
Đorđević, D. 'Italiansko-Turski rat 1911–1912 godine i njegov utucaj na Balkan' *Istoriski pregled* 14 (1954) 46–54
- 'Kako su velike sile saznali za sklapanje balkanskego saveza 1912 godine' *Istoriski glasnik* IV (1954) 127–43
- 'Pašić i Milovanović u pregovorima za balkanski savez 1912 godine' *Istoriski časopis* IX–X (1959) 467–86
Drljević, S. 'Crna Gora v balkanskome ratu-posljedna velika inicijativa kralja Nikole' *Godišnjak matice srpske* (1938) 148–53
Durham, M.E. 'King Nikola of Montenegro' *Contemporary Review* CXIX (1921) 471–7
Fichev, I.I. 'Obiasneniia i ostvetleniia' *Mir* 1 March to 19 March 1926 no. 7703–16
Florinsky, M.T. 'Russia and Constantinople: Count Kokovtsov's Evidence' *Foreign Affairs* VIII (1929) 135–41
Galkin, I.S. 'Evropeiskie derzhavy i kritskii vopros v 1908–1912 godakh' *Voprosy istorii* 1956 no. 5, 126–40
- 'Iz istorii natsional'nogo osvoboditel'nogo dvizheniia v Albanii v 1910–1912 godakh' *Voprosy istorii* 1954 no. 11, 35–46

- 'Obrazovanie balkanskogo soiuza 1912 g i politika evropeiskikh derzhav' *Vestnik Moskovskogo Universiteta – Istoriia* 1956 no. 4, 9–41
Grinberg, S. Sh. 'Vneshnepoliticheskaia orientatsiia Bolgarii nakanune pervoi mirovoi voiny (1912–1914 g.g.)' *Slavianskii sbornik* Moscow 1947, 291–335
Helmreich, E.C. 'Montenegro and the Formation of the Balkan League' *Slavonic Review* XV (1937) 426–34
- 'The Serbian-Montenegrin Alliance of September 23/October 6, 1912' *Journal of Central European Affairs* XIX (1960) 411–15
- and C.E. Black 'The Russo-Bulgarian Military Convention of 1902' *Journal of Modern History* IX (1937) 471–82
Iotsov, Ia. 'Balkanskata voina' *Istoricheski pregled* III (1946–7) no. 4–5
- 'Namesata na Būlgariia v pūrvata svetovna voina' *Istoricheski pregled* IV (1947–8) no. 4–5, 417–38
Jelenić, Ć. 'Nikola P. Pašić i srpsko-bugarski spor 1913' *Politika* XXII (1925) no. 6232
Jovanović, J.M. 'Austrija i Rusija na Balkanu (1912–1913)' *Ruski Arhiv* XXX–XXXI (1935) 182–202
- 'Dr. Milovan Milovanović i srpsko-bugarski savez' *Politika* XXIX (1932) no. 8564
- 'Poreklo svetskogo rata' *Godišnjica Nikole Ćupića* XXXIX (1930) 1–42
Jovanović, S. 'Milovan Milovanović' *Srpski književni glasnik* LI (1937) no. 2–6: 2, 106–14; 3, 172–80; 4, 254–61; 5, 337–48; 6, 418–29
- 'Nicholas Pašić: After Ten Years' *The Slavonic and East European Review* XV (1936) 368–76
Kabakchiev, Kh. 'Būlgariia v pūrvata imperialisticheska voina (1915–1918) god' *Istoricheski pregled* V (1947–8) no. 1, 40–56
Kalafatović, D.S. 'Zakljućenje saveza sa Bugarskom pred rat 1912 godine' *Ratnik* XLVIII (1932) 1–20
Khasapchiev, Kh. G. 'Istoricheskata istina po Būlgaro-sūrbskite dogovori ot 1904 i 1905 god' *Mir* 2 and 3 July 1928 no. 8400 and 8401
Kiktev, A. Ia. 'Iz istorii obrazovaniia balkanskogo soiuza 1912 goda' Kiev University *Trudy Istoricheskogo fakulteta* I (1939) 29–40
Kosev, D. 'Revizionisticheski falsifikatsii na būlgarskata istoriia u skopskite istoritsi' *Istoricheski pregled* XV (1959) no. 1, 15–44
Lainović, A. 'Pitanje Skadra u prvom balkanskom ratu' *Istoriski zapisi* IV (1949) 66–76
Langer, W.L. 'Russia, the Straits Question and the European Powers, 1904–1908' *English Historical Review* LIV (1929) 59–85
- 'Russia, the Straits Question and the Origins of the Balkan League, 1908–1912' *Political Science Quarterly* XLIII (1928) 321–63
Marco (Božin Simić) 'Nikola Hartvig-Spoljna politika Srbije pred svetski rat' *Nova Evropa* XVII (1928) no. 8, 256–78

Marković, L. 'Nikola Pašić kao diplomat' *Iz velike epoche 1903–1918* ed M.V. Knežević, Subotica 1929

Martynenko, A.K. 'Pozitsiia Rossii v sviazi s provozglasheniem nezavisimosti Bolgarii v 1908 godu' *Iz istorii russko-bolgarskikh otnoshenii. Sbornik statei* ed V.N. Kondrat'eva, S.A. Nikitin, and L.B. Valev, Moscow 1958

Mishev, D. 'Avtorite na Bŭlgaro-sŭrbskiia dogovor' *Svobodno mnenie* II (1914) no. 3, 2–6
- 'Ideologia na dogovora' ibid no. 4, 53–6
- 'Osnovite na dogovora' ibid no. 5, 69–72
- 'Otgovornite za katastrofata' ibid no. 7, 101–4
- 'Reviziiata na Bukureshchskiia dogovor' ibid no. 18, 277–9
- 'Territorialnite kompensatsii' ibid no. 6, 85–7

Mosely, P.E. 'Russian Policy in 1911–1912' *Journal of Modern History* XII (1940) 69–86

Nikić, F. 'Nikola Pašić' *Letopis matice srpske* CI (1927) 371–7

Nikitin, S.A. 'Russkaia politika na Balkanakh i nachalo vostochnoi voiny' *Voprosy istorii* (1946) no. 4, 3–29

Pavlović, Ž.G. 'Udeo Srbije u balkanskim ratovima 1912–1913 godine' *Godišnjica Nikole Ćupića* XLIV (1935) 92–105

Plamenac, J.S. 'Kako je došlo do balkanskog saveza' *Anali* II (1937) 48–54

Popović, Ć.A. 'Organizacija "Ujedinjene ili smrt" ("Crna Ruka") – Uzroci i način postanka' *Nova Evropa* XV (1927) no. 12, 396–405
- 'Rad organizacije "Ujedinjenje ili smrt". Pripremanje za balkanski rat' *Nova Evropa* XVI (1927) no. 10–11, 308–29
- 'Srpsko-bugarski rat, 1913 godine (Rad organizacije "Ujedinjenje ili smrt")' *Nova Evropa* XVIII (1928) no. 10–11, 309–23

Popović, D. 'Nikola Pašić i Rusija' *Godišnjica Nikole Ćupića* XLVI (1937) 137–56

Prodanović, J.M. 'Nikola P. Pašić' *Srpski književni glasnik* XX (1927) 123–33

Progresist 'Tragediiata na edin dŭrzhavnik' *Svobodno mnenie* II (1914) no. 16, 249–57

Rizov, D. 'Kak doide katastrofata' ibid no. 4, 57–63

Senkevich, I.G. 'Natsional'no-osvoboditel'naia bor'ba albanskogo naroda v 1911–1912 g.g.' *Novaia i noveishaia istoriia* (1957) no. 5, 62–5

Seton-Watson, R.W. 'William II's Balkan Policy' *The Slavonic Review* VII (1928) 1–29

Shopov, A. 'Dopŭlnenie po proekta za rusko-bŭlgarskiia dogovor' *Svobodno mnenie* II (1914) no. 44, 614–16
- 'Proekt za rusko-bŭlgarskiia dogovor' ibid no. 42, 591–4

Sigrist, S. 'Russkaia diplomatiia i balkanskii soiuz 1912–1913 godov' *Russkoe proshloe* III (1923) 52–69

Skendi, S. 'Albanian Political Thought and Revolutionary Activity, 1881–1912' *Südost-Forschungen* XIII (1954) 159–99

Šoć, P. 'Crna Gora u balkanskom ratu' *Balkan* XXII (1938) no. 344

Štedimlija, S.M. 'Rusija i Balkanski savez 1912 g.' *Anali* II (1937) 39–48

Stojanović, K. 'Balkanski savezi' *Bosanska vila* XXIX (1914) no. 1–6, 39–43

Thaden, E.C. 'Charykov and Russian Foreign Policy at Constantinople in 1911' *Journal of Central European Affairs* XVI (1956) 25–44

Velchev, V. 'Būlgari i Rusi v svetlinata na dvizhenieto za slaviansko edinstvo' *Istoricheski pregled* V (1948–9) no. 1, 72–94

Vojvodić, M. 'Bugarsko-crnogorski pregovori i sporazum 1912 godine' Belgrade University *Zbornik filosofskog fakulteta* VIII (1964) 741–51

Vlakhov, T. 'Tursko-būlgarskite otnosheniia prez 1913–1915 g.' *Istoricheski pregled* XI (1955) no. 1, 3–31

– 'Vūnshnata politika na Ferdinand i balkanskiia sūiuz' *Istoricheski pregled* VI (1949–50) no. 4–5, 422–44

Vodovazov, V. 'Balkanskaia voina i Rossiia' *Sovremennik* (1913) no. 11, 264–71

Index

Adrianople 25, 87, 88, 203, 205; siege of 80, 82; captured by Bulgaria 121; reoccupied by Turkey 195
Aegean islands 114
Aehrenthal, Count Alois (Austro-Hungarian minister of foreign affairs 1906–12): and annexation of Bosnia-Herzegovina 5–6
Albania: revolt in (1912) 35, 53; in Austro-Hungarian plans 35; and independence of 102; at ambassadors' conference at London 112–14, 117. *See also* Austria-Hungary, Montenegro, Russia, Scutari, Serbia, war against Turkey.
Alessio (Lješ) 98
Alexander (crown prince of Serbia) 82; encounter with King George and Crown Prince Constantine 163
Alexandropoulos, J. (Greek minister at Belgrade) 163, 177
Ali Riza Bey 108
ambassadors' conference at London 106; plans for 109–11; topics, personnel, and procedure 110–12; and Aegean islands 114; and Albania 112–14, 117, 122–5; and Serbian outlet on the Adriatic 113; and renewal of hostilities 119; and

Scutari 122–5, 128–30; and conditions for the preliminary peace 125–6, 128, 131–3; and the Bulgaro-Rumanian dispute 149
ambassadors' conference at St Petersburg: procedural format of 150; decisions of 151–2
Angista 177
annexation of Bosnia-Herzegovina 5–6; and Balkan unity 7; provokes public debate in Russia 8–11. *See also* Austria-Hungary, Russia, Serbia.
Antivari (Bar) 101
armistice: December 1912 108–9; April 1913 125–8; August 1913 194, 195, 196–7
Assim Bey (Turkish minister at Sofia) 32
Auffenberg, Baron Moritz von (Austro-Hungarian minister of war 1911–12) 103
Austria-Hungary: and annexation of Bosnia-Herzegovina 5–7; and Turkey 15, 90–1; and Albania 35, 54–5, 91–4, 98, 102, 112–14, 122–5; and Sanjak of Novi Pazar 75–6; and Balkan system of alliances 84; and Bulgaria 84, 88, 196, 199, 200, 201; and non-intervention of,